The Return of Malthus

THE RETURN OF MALTHUS

Environmentalism and the
Post-war Population–Resource Crises

Björn-Ola Linnér

The White Horse Press

Set in 10 point Adobe Garamond Pro

British Library Cataloguing in Publication Data
A catalogue record for this book is available from the British Library

ISBN (PB) 978-1-912186-74-7 (eBook) 978-1-912186-73-0

doi: 10.3197/63811987103618.book

To Monica

'Malthus has been buried many times, and Malthusian scarcity with him. But as Garret Hardin remarked, anyone who has been buried so often cannot be entirely dead.'

Herman E. Daly, *Steady State Economics*, 1977

Contents

Foreword – 2002

The past fifty years have been in many ways the most successful half-century in the history of the human species. Introduced by such books as John Kenneth Galbraith's *The Affluent Society*, the period marked an extraordinary increase in the material wealth of virtually all societies. The rich may have gotten richer, but the world's poor did not do so badly either – at least they did well enough to reproduce themselves many times over. Mortality rates fell in every country, and improved health conditions produced an unprecedented increase in world population. The most basic evidence for how well we have been doing as a species was the jump in our numbers from three to six billion. Electricity, air travel, television, and cellular telephones spread to the most remote places. The status of women began to improve dramatically. More countries lived, at least nominally, under democratic systems than ever before. The dream of universal progress seemed closer than ever to realisation.

Why then were so many people so pessimistic during this period? That is the question underlying this important book, *The Return of Malthus*. It traces the astonishing revival of reputation of that gloomy British churchman, the Rev. Thomas Malthus, one of the founders of the dismal science of scarcity economics. While so many opinion leaders of his day were singing the blessings of progress, Malthus dared to write that most people would never enjoy those blessings. They were doomed by the limits of nature to go on living a short, brutish life, always on the edge of starvation and misery. Why did this discouraging man make a comeback in reputation in the middle of the twentieth century? Why, in the midst of such growth in population and affluence, did so many find his pessimism to be so compelling and true? Now that we seem to have returned to a more optimistic sense of the future, we need to ask what lay behind the widespread fears about impending natural resource limits that were pervasive from the 1950s right down to the 1990s. Before we bury Malthus and all his modern disciples, we need to understand what made them so nervous, for it may be that they saw a few realities that we are in danger of forgetting.

Björn-Ola Linnér has written the first comprehensive analysis of the post-war fear of scarcity. He traces that fear back to such American and European thinkers as William Vogt (*Road to Ruin*), Fairfield Osborn (*Our Plundered*

Planet), and Georg Borgström (*World Food Resources*). Fascism had hardly been defeated when they began telling their readers about a global population explosion and warning that the Earth could not support unlimited population and consumption. Linnér breaks new ground by showing that, long before the famous Stockholm conference on the environment in 1972, scientists and diplomats organised world conferences to consider the global resource base of modern life. Steeped in the archives and well versed in critical theory, he traces the development of an international discourse about resources and population that increasingly guided policymakers. They began to look on the Earth as a single, interconnected resource base on which all peoples must draw, wherever they lived, through trade and technology. They came to see that common resource base as limited and vulnerable.

The result of this unanticipated shift in thinking was, in Linnér's words, a new 'conservation ideology', transnational in scope and dark in anxiety. It was also thoroughly anthropocentric. In place of an older tradition that sought to protect the living world of nature in all its beauty and glory, the new conservationists were focused wholly on protecting humans from their own success through a more rational, or 'sustainable', kind of exploitation. They were not nature lovers so much as they were wise users. What distinguished them from more unfettered nature exploiters in business and politics was that they called for all human use of the environment to be carefully controlled and managed by scientific intelligence. They hated waste. They did not trust the cornucopian attitudes of free enterprise. They called for governments to take a stronger hand in protecting the global resource base through population reduction and control over consumption.

One of the most surprising parts of this story is the extent to which neo-Malthusianism could end up serving the project of the United States and other industrialised countries to dominate the modern world. Conservation became part of the programme to 'modernise' the more backward regions, which meant making them more like us in all ways. They too must see the dangers in runaway population growth, the impossibility of growing enough food to satisfy an infinite number of people, the vulnerability inherent in western-style progress. If all that seems morally enlightened, it was in fact mixed with a great deal of self-interest. The United States was fearful that its power might be challenged by a rival communism that fed on discontent and impoverishment. Other affluent nations feared that 'their' resources might be diverted to feed the Third World's hungry masses. Destabilisation of power relations lurked as the spectre behind global resource collapse.

Linnér has framed this history in global terms, as it must be, but he has also given it a human scale and face. He examines the rise of Malthusianism through the career of one of Sweden's most famous environmental thinkers,

Georg Borgström, whose controversial life at home led him to immigrate to the United States. Borgström worried that mass famines might be lurking around the corner. His portrait is both sympathetically and critically drawn. The author is too good a historian to paint Borgström or any of the other conservationists as simple-minded, over-reactive, or misguided, but he sees clearly that their perception of events was not the only one possible nor was it free of bias nor safe from capture by less high-minded individuals.

Cassandras like Borgström questioned whether science and technology could be depended on to save humans from their own excess, yet paradoxically they promoted the authority of scientists and technocrats. They criticised the selfishness of the rich, but their fears of impending scarcity could be turned into a weapon against the poor. If indeed there was not enough food to go around, then why should the haves try to help the have-nots? The vision of an impending age of scarcity could be turned into a reason why the rising expectations of other nations needed to be flattened. And then if the world was truly on the edge of global famine, how could anyone dare question the genetic engineers at agribusinesses like Monsanto, who promised miracles of productivity in the laboratory? Throughout his book Linnér maintains a strong sense of ironic outcomes. He does not take the conservationists merely at their word, and he sees clearly how their humanitarianism could be turned toward non-humanitarian conclusions.

So in the end what are we think about the passing age of neo-Malthusianism? Linnér's great contribution is to help us see that age in a coherent, honest light. But to his great credit he does not ask us to repudiate all its insights and concerns. He would not have us put Pollyanna in place of Cassandra. Borgström and his contemporaries were right to be worried about exploding populations, as we should be worried today – not because any global collapse is threatening but because neither people nor the Earth will be better off with several billion more of us. The resources of the planet remain limited, and we see now that the problem is not one of running out of specific commodities but rather a more ambiguous one of undermining ecological health. Malthus appears, in retrospect, as a bad guide because he had no idea of extinction, pollution, or poisoned food chains. He worried about running out of food when the more serious problem was threats to the integrity of complex ecological systems.

This probing book leaves us with a challenge: What should replace Malthusianism as the core of environmental thought? Should we try to recover that older tradition of nature protection that got buried under the modern conservation ideology? The current emphasis on saving biodiversity seems to be attempting exactly that. Some want to put the preservation of other species and of ecological integrity at the centre of environmental policy. Others, however, want to make 'justice' the dominant principle of environmentalism, by redistributing the Earth's resources more equally. They argue that population growth will eventually come to an end through the law of demographic transition, as fewer children are born per family; when that transition is complete, we will still face the question of equity. Linnér agrees with that latter group, but charting the future of environmental thinking is not his main interest. Instead, he has tried to help us understand the period we have just been through, to penetrate its language and ideas, and to see the complicated conclusions it reached.

Whether always right or not, the scarcity prophets were not irrational to question the gospel of progress. They pointed out the heavy costs and risks in our headlong rush to growth. Linnér tells the story of their great doubt, and it is one of the most important stories of the twentieth century. It is a story filled with pessimists, but those pessimists may have prevented some of our worst extravagances. In the long run they may have given us whatever reason we have to hope.

DONALD WORSTER

Acknowledgements

When writing this book I have been fortunate not to have been, in the poet Wordsworth's phrase, 'voyaging through strange seas of thought alone'. Several people have helped me with this book, sharing both their talent and friendship.

Donald Worster is a rare combination of bright mind, vast knowledge, and passion as well as a warm and generous heart. His insightful suggestions on my manuscript have vastly enhanced the analysis. Most of all I want to thank Don and Bev for being such wonderful friends to my whole family. Elfar Loftsson has encouraged this project from start. He has provided many constructive suggestions and analytical approaches for which I am greatly indebted. Johan Hedrén has generously shared the apples of wisdom from his abundant theoretical orchard. To Mark Cioc, for his warm hospitality in sharing both his friendship and his rich knowledge, I will always be grateful. Ulrik Lohm has throughout been a source of considerable support and greatly encouraged the publication of this study.

Several others have during various stages given valuable help to this book, particularly Thomas Achen, Sten Andersson, Jonas Anselm, John Cantlon, Nils Dahlbeck, Kees Dekker, Ian Dickson, Birger Drake, Thomas Greer, Jonas Hallström, Donna Haraway, Hans Holmén, Karolina Isaksson, Sven Lilja, Carolyn Merchant, John Opie, Henrik Selin, Christer Skoglund, Sverker Sörlin, Håkan Tropp, Julie Wilk and Gunilla Öberg. The Department of Water and Environmental Studies and the History Department at the University of Kansas deserve my gratitude for creative and generous environments. The Food and Culture Seminar at Kansas has given valuable insight to Chapter 9. I am also obliged to all who have graciously given their time to be interviewed, including librarians and archivists who have been tremendously supportive. I am deeply grateful to Andrew and Alison Johnson for doing a wonderful job of editing and for all their efforts in publishing the book.

I want to thank The Swedish Council for Planning and Coordination of Research (FRN) for financing this study as well as The Knut and Alice Wallenberg Foundation, The Swedish Institute and The Swedish Foundation for International Cooperation in Research and Higher Education for supporting my research and studies in the United States.

My warmest thanks to my family and all my friends for bringing me the blessings of such true and encouraging kinship and friendship. Most of all, I extend my gratitude to my wife Monica, who with love, encouragement, and incomprehensible patience stood by me through all good and difficult times, and to my fairy tales Alva, Emil, and Saga. While I was writing this book, you were a perfectly marvellous combination of distraction and inspiration.

BJÖRN-OLA LINNÉR
Linköping, December 2002

While updating the final chapters of *The Return of Malthus*, I was reminded of how much remains the same, even after more than two decades of profound societal and environmental changes. I was also struck by the wealth of research that has been published and how our understanding of the world has advanced, while many insights endure from the scholars that came before us.

For the second edition, I am indebted to the many inspiring scholars that I have been fortunate enough to work with during the last two decades, at various universities and research institutes in different countries, and within different projects. I am grateful to colleagues and students at the Department of Thematic Studies – Environmental Change and the Centre for Climate Science and Policy Research at Linköping University. I am likewise thankful to the research environments that I have been affiliated with or am a fellow of: Stockholm Environment Institute, the Institute for Science, Innovation and Society at Oxford University, Stockholm International Peace Research Institute, the Cooperative Institute for Research in Environmental Sciences at the University of Colorado, and the Royal Swedish Academy of Agriculture and Forestry. The second edition of this book is a deliverable of Mistra Geopolitics, which is funded by MISTRA – the Swedish Foundation for Strategic Environmental Research. The participants in this timely research programme are a true source of inspiration.

In particular, I would like to thank Bwalya Chibwe as well as the editors Andrew Johnson and Sarah Johnson for their invaluable assistance with this revision, and my generous colleagues who have provided insightful comments for the new additions to this book: Inge Gerremo, Marie Fransisco, Alva Linnér, Eva Lövbrand, Tina Neset, Madelene Ostwald, Roger Pielke, Priyatma Singh, Jens Sundström, Victoria Wibeck, Lotten Wiréhn, Stephen Woroniecki, and Jiyai Zhou.

I am blessed by enduring friendships and, most of all, the love and support of my wonderful family: Monica, Alva, Emil, Saga and Love.

BJÖRN-OLA LINNÉR
Linköping, January 2023

1

Crises of Population and Resources

'Doomsday' Debates

Of all the scarcity crises of the twentieth century, the most dramatic and far-reaching have been those to do with food. The long lines of cars at the petrol pumps during the oil crisis of the 1970s stirred up emotions and had profound effects on the world economy. Yet the catastrophic resonance of the food crises was even greater. The magnitude of world population growth and starvation caught the emotions of newspaper readers, political leaders and scientists everywhere. As a consequence, concerns for population growth and resource shortage influenced agricultural, population and security policies after World War II.

After World War II, food production underwent enormous development, through improvements in plant breeding, insecticides, pesticides and storage. The ability of technological development to secure future food supply seemed indisputable. But such optimism was soon to be challenged by disturbing signs. Rapidly declining death rates, particularly as a result of cheaper health measures, resulted in unprecedented population growth in the Southern Hemisphere. Many experts doubted that the decline in birth rates would come fast enough to avoid the scenario where population growth would exceed the supply of natural resources.

Future starvation, even in Europe and in the United States, became a plausible threat in the first decades of the post-war world. Newspaper headlines and policy documents spelled out anxiety about famines spreading across the world, even to the prosperous nations of the Northern Hemisphere. During the twentieth century, the food fears of Europe and North America switched from shortage of food, to the way food is produced, to the quality of food, and to its overconsumption. Yet the fear of starvation lingered in western consciousness for a long time. At least up to the 1970s, many warned that there was an impending danger that world famine would spread even to prosperous nations. This anxiety was expressed not only by dramatising environmentalists, but also by numerous scientists and policymakers. When the world's hungry began to demand their fair slice of the global cake, the rich industrialised countries would no longer be able to import from poorer, increasingly populous countries basic food supplies, or indispensable fertilisers, or fodder produced from resources in those countries.

Thus, natural resource depletion clouded the bright future of peace in the early post-war world. Evident and expected natural resource shortages in Europe and the Third World were placed high on the agenda of international politics, the scientific community and the media. At the centre of this agenda was a concern that overpopulation placed such vast demands on the world's resources that it jeopardised the new world order and perhaps civilisation as a whole. Would resources suffice for present and future generations? In the General Assembly of the United Nations, in the White House, in European parliaments and boardrooms, from lecture pulpits, radio forums, and the front pages of newspapers the warnings of a *population–resource crisis* were declared.[1] And of all shortages, food scarcity was the most vivid in the public imagination.

This book examines the agenda of debates on population growth and resource shortages from the early Cold War years until today. It focuses on the environmental, political, and scientific population–resource debates in the post-war era, often referred to as 'the doomsday debates'.

Malthusianism

During the nineteenth century, technological changes had modernised agriculture. Vast areas of land had been opened up for food production, especially in the United States, Canada, South America, Australia and Asia. The development of these new lands was paired with technological innovations including improved plant varieties, increased use of fertilisers and mechanisation. Europe had experienced its last famine in 1840, when the Irish potato harvest failed.

According to David Grigg's *The World Food Problem* (1993), the calorie intake of people in Europe increased until the beginning of the twentieth century, when it stabilised at around 3000 kilocalories. (Today the recommended basal metabolic rate is 1580 kilocalories for a 56-kilo male). As the intake of calories increased, so did the consumption of animal protein. Beef, pork and chicken products became an increasingly larger part of the diet for consumers in industrialised countries.[2] By the post-war period, the Malthusian dilemma was quite outmoded. In many industrialised countries, policymakers worried more about underpopulation than the opposite.

Despite increased production yields, despite a hundred years without a major famine in the western world, worries about a global food crisis aroused serious concern in the post-war period. This anxiety about a major food collapse lasted at least into the mid-1970s, with two distinct peaks. In the late 1940s and in a long period from the early 1960s to the first half of the 1970s, population–resource concern was especially intense. As we shall see, today the warnings are back in a different guise.

Warnings of an impending resource crisis due to population growth are commonly labelled as neo-Malthusianism, after Thomas Robert Malthus (1766–1834). This British economist and clergyman became the icon of population pessimism when he presented his thesis in *An essay on the principle of population, as it affects the future improvement of society with remarks on the speculations of Mr. Godwin, M. Condorcet, and other writers* (1797). In later editions Malthus added the subtitle *A view of its past and present effects on human happiness: with an inquiry into our prospects respecting the future removal or mitigation of the evils which it occasions.* Malthus's notorious population theory postulated that population would grow faster than the supply of nutrition: '... the power of population is indefinitely greater than the power in the earth to produce subsistence for man'.[3]

Malthus described this impulse as a natural law. Population growth rose geometrically (2, 4, 8, 16, etc.); every 25 years humankind doubled in numbers, if one excluded population-reducing events such as famines, wars, and epidemics.[4] Food production on the other hand only increased arithmetically (1, 2, 3, 4, etc.). Increase in yield did not have a chance to keep up with the constant doubling of unrestrained population growth.

Two types of constraints could be put on population growth: first, unplanned checks like famines, wars and epidemics; second, planned checks, such as when people deliberately restrained the number of births. Malthus proposed the latter. Ethically chosen continence through late marriages and a restrained sex life was the Christian moral code that could avert a catastrophe. Otherwise, humanity would bring a disaster upon itself. Malthus doubted whether poor people would manage to control childbirth. When constraints like starvation or ill health were averted, improved living conditions would only lead to even bigger families. If preventive measures were not taken, the unplanned checks were needed. Thus, Malthus was reluctant to support poor relief. Aid would only be met with more children, more mouths to feed. Poverty was a part of the laws of nature, God's providential design that would spur humankind toward greater efforts and progress.

Of course, Malthus has been heavily criticised, not only for being wrong in his pessimistic principles, but because he defended an unjust social order with speculative scientific laws. Some have argued that this is an unfair description of Malthus. He modified his ideas in later works and also worked for better education and social welfare for England's poor. Regardless, in the twentieth century his name had acquired a bad ring to it, mostly because of his social prejudice and radical proposal to circumscribe the sexual behaviour of the poor. Some of those labelled 'Malthusians' furiously denounce the epithet; nonetheless the neo-Malthusian label sticks, because of the similarity to the Malthusian basic notion: Unless human beings pull off a radical change in reproduction patterns, population will in the foreseeable future outstrip food supply.

I use the term *neo-Malthusianism* with some wariness, since at certain times it has been used as a term of abuse and insult. In this book, Malthusianism is simply defined as a set of ideas that postulate that populations tend to grow faster than the supply of nutrition; thus, in the long run world population growth threatens to outstrip food supply.

The term neo-Malthusianism has its background in the Malthusian League, founded in 1877. Whereas Malthus had stressed the moral threats posed by the poor proliferating, late nineteenth-century Malthusianism developed into a social political movement that emphasised the relationship between baby booms and poverty. The number of births had to be checked, not through late marriages or sexual continence, as Malthus had insisted, but through contraception. With the post-war population surge, Malthus' theory attained a renewed urgency. To prevent mass poverty and famine, the birth rate had to be circumscribed.

During the post-war era, social policy on the population issue was directed toward developing countries with high fertility rates. Family planning, contraceptives, and women's rights, for both social and health reasons, together constituted a central driving force for much international population planning. However, in the post-war era, neo-Malthusianism also became a generic term for ideas about an impending ecological catastrophe.

Points of Departure

This book is about how post-war concern for the population–resource crisis came to affect international politics, science, the food industry and, in particular, conservationism and environmentalism. (I use 'conservationism' and 'environmentalism' as empirical concepts corresponding to the time at which they are used in the debate. Consequently, 'environmentalism' will be the term more frequently used from the 1960s on.)

The book focuses analytically on three sets of issues: (1) the development of post-war neo-Malthusianism, (2) neo-Malthusian conservationists as conveyers of a new conservation ideology, and (3) the process of communication on population–resource issues between scientific communities, conservationists/environmentalists and the political system.

1. The development of post-war neo-Malthusianism.

This study analyses how population–resource crises have been framed and presented over time from the early post-war years until today. It focuses on how post-war population–resource debates affected conservationism – and later, environmentalism – where two radically different strands of neo-Malthusianism appear in the 1960s: *nutritional equity* and *lifeboat ethics*.

Neo-Malthusian concern was certainly not limited to environmentalists. In this study, I also argue that the population–resource debate was to a large extent formed by the transformation of political economy in the West and the geopolitical interests of the United States and its allies. Political and social unrest in poor, resource-scarce countries was a threat to the geopolitical interest of the United States, seeking a new global role in the international arena. At the same time, the development of capitalist accumulation created mass production that reached out for a global mass market and was dependent on a secure supply of raw materials from foreign sources. The expansion of foreign trade entailed globalisation of the supply of natural resources. Today the familiar rhetoric of Malthusianism appears in the multinational food industry's lobbying for genetically modified crops.

Malthusian concern has indeed many faces. One purpose of this study is to sort out the different descriptions of reality, valuations and recommendations for action of neo-Malthusian theories in the post-war era.

2. Protagonists in the population–resource debate as conveyers of a new conservation ideology.

Many influential combatants in the population–resource debate took an active part in the process of reconsidering ecological knowledge. They contributed to a new conservation focus by embracing a new set of ideas on the threat to humankind and its environment. These ideas were so coherent and mutually supportive that I will argue that it is appropriate to designate them as a conservation ideology. Those involved in the population–resource debate often conveyed their ideas vigorously to decision-makers, the scientific community and the public.

The concept *conveyer of ideas* refers to a person's mediating social role between science, politics and society. The concept involves three elements: the conveyer embraces a new set of ideas, takes an active part in the process of re-considering knowledge, and communicates these ideas to decision-makers and to the public. Thus, it is not the aim of this study to measure the importance or degree of influence of certain individuals in the debate: rather, an analysis of neo-Malthusian conservationists' roles as conveyers of ideas can give us a better understanding of the very nature of the population–resource debate itself. In order to analyse them as conveyers, I shall try to discern their main ideas, their sources of inspiration, and reactions to the messages they communicated. What makes them particularly illuminating are their controversial positions, which reflect the lines of conflict in the debate.

What then are the ideas that conservationists concerned with population conveyed? I will argue that a new global view of the relationship between humans and nature emerged in the population–resource debates of the mid–twentieth century. Traditional protection of nature was challenged by a new conservation ideology. In the light of population growth and resource depletion, the survival of humankind became the overshadowing question. On the basis of this new awareness, a new conservation ideology was formed which was embraced by many leading conservationists and, later, environmentalists.

The ecologically ideal state of nature was threatened by prevailing resource utilisation; scientific facts could predict catastrophe, while research reports replaced doomsday prophesies; to protect nature was not only a question of endangered animals or biota – humanity itself was now an endangered species. Therefore, the world must be regarded as a single entity, and the utilisation of its resources must be planned through international cooperation. Global interdependence was not only an ecological and economic fact, but a desired political goal. A political critique was formulated which demanded that the economy should be adjusted to the natural order and the understanding that the world was one household.

3. The process of communication between the scientific community, conservationists, and the political system on population–resource issues.

This analysis sets out to examine the political and scientific agenda concerning natural resources in the early post-war years. It has been commonplace to attribute to scientists the role of discoverers of environmental problems. In this role, they advise politicians who, in the best of worlds, act accordingly. Yet these two power spheres co-evolve in a discursive setting. Research and policy-making develop in symbiosis. The relationship is evident, for example, in the process of the United Nations Scientific Conference on Conservation and Utilisation of Resources as well as in the Green Revolution. The population–resource debate is linked in with political discourses, such as that on planned economy and on international interdependence. This communication process is a crucial part of setting the agenda of the population–resource crisis.

The reactions to post-war proponents of new conservation ideas varied greatly. Many of the protagonists became controversial figures, arousing both praise and resentment, especially in the scientific community. There are numerous stories of environmentalists being marginalised or feeling harassed. The case of Georg Borgström illustrates this point.

The Swedish–American food scientist Georg Borgström vigorously conveyed a kind of conservationism concerned with food–population issues. Before Paul Ehrlich, Borgström was one of the leading neo-Malthusians in the

United States and Europe. In the midst of much commotion and high feeling, Borgström left Sweden for a career in the United States in the 1950s. Powerful Swedish business interests used their influence to get Borgström dismissed from his position as head of a food preservation institute. The controversy blew up into a nation-wide serial story in the newspapers. Later, Swedish environmentalists argued that Borgström was attacked because powerful economic interests found his message too hard to bear. However, as we shall see, the conflicts surrounding Borgström were considerably more complex. In this area of analysis, I shall endeavour to sort out the positions of the main agents and examine their lines of argument. Not only did science play a crucial role in the formation of a natural resources agenda: it was also essential as a legitimating foundation for policy. The scientific controversies reflected the struggle for power in defining the global natural resources situation and in legitimising preferred policies.

Methodology and Sources

The scope of this book demands a complex methodological approach and draws on several theoretical positions. Besides giving a descriptive account of historical events, I have set out to analyse the underlying ideas of the population–resource debate. My aim in this idea analysis has been to present the manifest message, as well as to try to unravel the less outspoken content of statements and to relate these elements of the debate to their wider settings. In addition to the qualitative analysis, computer-scanned material is employed for basic quantitative content analysis of three parts of the study: the natural resources issues presented at the United Nations Scientific Conference on the Conservation and Utilisation of Resources, the ideology of conservation , and the ecological influences on this ideology. This quantitative approach enables a broader analysis of the debate as well as providing a check on the qualitative analysis.

The actors in the debate did indeed become controversial. Why did they create such a stir? If they were displeasing to power interests, how did they ever manage to attain a platform within the discourse? Why did they become of interest to the public debate? To understand what happened, it is necessary to uncover the discursive practices that appear in unrelated population–resource events. As an analytical concept, discourse captures the conforming role of language in power relations. Since the post-war politics of natural resources formed a distinct political field, with its own praxis and institutions, it is appropriate to regard it as a *natural resources discourse*. However, this study is not intended as a discourse analysis, even though it does focus on population–resource debates. *Debate* is understood as embracing a wider communication of ideas, which may, but does not have to, involve the grammatics of a discourse. Nevertheless, the debates on global natural resources took place in a discursive setting, since they involved the act of defining the post-war world. I shall therefore try to distinguish important discursive segments in the debate.

The primary empirical data used in this book comprise publicly communicated material from newspapers, magazines, journals, proceedings, radio programmes and books. To contextualise these sources, I have also employed material collected in archives and through interviews. The genres involved are, on the one hand, those where a message is directly conveyed: letters to the editor, editorials, letters, radio lectures and debates, proceedings, radio interviews, and interviews made for this study; and on the other hand those where the message is indirectly conveyed – news articles and newspaper interviews. Certainly, both the directly and indirectly conveyed statements can involve latent and manifest messages.

In historiography three demands are commonly placed on a source in order for it to be regarded as reliable and useful: *closeness in time, freedom from bias* and *independence*.[5] These demands are useful in an analysis of ideas when establishing the most plausible interpretations of texts. However, these points need to be modified for analysis of historical ideas.[6] This study involves a timespan of several decades. Conceptual changes over time are of central interest here. To understand the role of the population–resource crisis for environmentalism it is important to consider the symbolic value of a historic act in retrospect. The dependency criterion is aimed at avoiding unreliable second-hand sources. Yet, in analysis of historical ideas even those second-hand versions can tell us how people perceived events, how things were talked about. These sources, of course, are of little value as proof to establish 'what really happened', but they address the arguments used in the population– resource debate and what roles accrued to the debaters.

Bias in the sources can also be of great value in a study like this, since it can show how different positions are used in the debate, and lines of conflict can be clarified. No statements in the population–resource debate are regarded as unbiased, since they all occur, consciously or unconsciously, in a discursive struggle.

The Structure of the Book

This book basically follows a chronological account, with a few exceptions. It starts out in Chapter 2, 'A New World Order', with a presentation of the natural resources situation in the post-war world. The chapter provides the background for analysis of the process of communication between scientists and the political sphere. It deals with two major elements of the post-war world order important for post-war conservation: the transformation of the political economy and the geopolitical strategies of the United States. To understand the issue of natural resources in the early post-war era, it is essential to take account of the United States' geopolitical ambitions. Providing for a secure resource situation in the world was regarded as one of the most effective means to hold communism at bay. This situation was tied to the transformation of economic production and its related modes of social and political regulation. In this respect, Fordism and the geopolitics of the West are two sides of the same coin. Mass production required both a global mass market and a secure supply of raw materials from abroad. The expansion of foreign trade entailed a globalisation of the supply of natural resources.

This chapter also describes how the famous former chief forester under the Theodore Roosevelt administration, Governor Gifford Pinchot, proposed an international conservation conference in a letter to President Franklin D. Roosevelt in January 1940. Drawing upon the idea that conservation could be the foundation of enduring peace between nations, he wanted to persuade the president to call for such a conference.

Chapter 3, 'Conservation and Containment', follows how natural resource issues were placed on the agenda of international politics, and conservationists were forced to alter their positions. After World War II, the United States possessed a gigantic industrial capacity fit to respond to worldwide demands. The production mode of a globally expanding economy forced the traditionally conservative protectors of nature to reconsider their focus. In this process, scientists and conservationists in the United States and Europe formulated a radical critique of modern society's utilisation of nature. This reorientation is depicted through the early controversies within the International Union for the Protection of Nature (IUPN), where a line of conflict emerged between the new conservation focus and the ideas held by European colonial powers about nature protection.

Chapter 3 continues the account of plans for an international resources conference. After World War II, Pinchot's idea was revived by President Harry S. Truman, who proposed the arrangement of a *United Nations Scientific Conference on the Conservation and Utilisation of Resources*. The conference, held in 1949, was the first time that the UN gathered together a great number of scientists and experts. This process is related to US aid programmes, both federal and private, such as the work of the Rockefeller Foundation. UNESCO and IUPN co-sponsored a parallel conference, the *International Technical Conference on the Protection of Nature*. Truman anticipated the UN conference to be of great importance to his Point Four Program.

Chapter 4, 'Neo-Malthusianism in Harvest Time', deals with the translation of the international population–resource discussion to Sweden. It focuses on Swedish population–resource debates from the end of the war until the mid 1950s. The Swedish agenda was certainly affected by the international agenda, but also by experiences of rationing and intense arguments over rationalised agriculture, as well as by Social Democratic plans for a planned economy and Sweden's foreign policy ambition of bridge-building between the blocs. This chapter focuses specifically on Sweden's most famous population–resource 'Cassandra', Georg Borgström. We shall follow his 're-education'. As a young scientist, Borgström firmly believed that science would solve the hunger crises of the war-torn world, until he went on a research trip to South America in 1946. Confronted with the ecological degradation of the Pampas, he started to re-evaluate his technology-happy point of view. The United Nations resource conferences in 1949 were the second step in Borgström's re-education. At these meetings Borgström became acquainted with Fairfield Osborn and William Vogt, who had a tremendous influence on the Swedish debate. Vogt visited him in Sweden, and Borgström wrote the introduction to the Swedish translation of Vogt's book *Our Plundered Planet.*

In the late 1940s, Borgström began his career as a public spokesman on population issues, depletion, and food shortage. Just before Christmas 1948, he spoke on radio to the question: 'Will the Food Suffice?' Chapter 4 also outlines the shift towards more negative reactions to Borgström's message, expressed in the debate surrounding his book *Jorden – vårt öde* (*The Earth – Our Destiny*) (1953).[7] His gloomy prognosis and his critique of science and technology aroused particular resentment.

At least in its early phase, Borgström received support for his message of resource depletion from Swedish editorial writers, Liberals as well as Social Democrats, who agreed with his description of the problems facing the world. Borgström's message was used in an ongoing acerbic debate on Swedish agricultural politics as to whether Sweden's agricultural production should be restricted. A central theme in the debate was that shortages of resources jeopardised the survival of humankind. Overpopulation on an overexploited Earth threatened to bring on a catastrophe if society did not alter its course. Traditional protection of nature was replaced by a new conservation ideology. Many scientists and conservationists in the United States and Europe formulated a radical critique of modern society's utilisation of nature.

Chapter 5, 'A New Conservation Ideology', examines the conservationist ideas. I argue that a new conservation ideology emerged in the early post-war years. It implied a new global view of the relationship between humans and nature, which formed an ideological foundation for post-war environmental criticism. Most conservationists used scientific data to support their doomsday scenarios. A new kind of apocalyptic apprehension emerged: *catastrophe empiricism.* When the conservationists warned of a forthcoming disaster, they increased the credibility of their warnings by supporting them with statistical material on population growth and food production. Research reports replaced doomsday prophecies and historical–philosophical theories of decline. The new conservationism tied in closely with the preoccupations of the time, such as the new demands of capitalist production modes and mass consumption (a natural resources discourse as well as a discourse on globalisation) and discussion of the new technological possibilities for mass destruction.

Chapter 6, 'On the Outskirts of Babel', analyses the role of science in the new conservation ideology and in the population–resource debate in general. In the early post-war years, science prescribed the premises for those who emphasised utilisation, as well as for those who advocated conservation. For both sides, science was seen as the normative foundation on which society should be built, although the designs of the construction differed fundamentally.

The scientific conflict between Borgström, together with his supporters, and his critics engendered intense controversy over his work, where both supporters and detractors engaged in disputes over his focus and his conclusions. This was especially true in the great controversy over Borgström's leadership of the Swedish Institute for Food Preservation Research. Following these events, he was later regarded as a martyr in the environmental movement. The Institute was financed reciprocally by the federal government and business interests. Big and powerful food preservation companies were not pleased with Borgström and used their influence to get him dismissed from the position of head of the Institute. His opponents stressed that a good scientist should have acquired, or at least have been able to test, his own conclusions. Borgström, on the other hand, emphasised the need to synthesise and present scientific knowledge to the public. A holistic perspective, 'a universal view', must be established for the future salvation of humanity. The conflict not only concerned Borgström's scientific competence and his employment; it also had consequences for his ambitions to influence the cognitive order of his time. 'The Borgström Case' aroused intense debate in the press as well as in the Swedish parliament. A government commission even investigated the circumstances surrounding Borgström's final resignation before he went into exile in the United States.

The population–resource debates of the 1960s were marked by aspects of the two Green Revolutions: first, a shifting consciousness embodied in emerging environmentalism – in the West as well as in the Third World – and second, the high-yielding technology called the Green Revolution. Chapter 7, 'Green Revolutions', accounts for the development of population–resource concern during the 1960s and 1970s. Two radically different strands of neo-Malthusian environmentalism appeared: lifeboat ethics and nutritional equity. The chapter ends with some explanations as to the decline of neo-Malthusianism from the second half of the 1970s.

In Chapter 8, 'The Return of Neo-Malthusianism', the warnings are back. In the 1990s, neo-Malthusian warnings that world population growth threatens to outstrip food supply in the long run echoed the debates in the late 1960s and early 1970s. This time they were highlighted in official reports of international institutions like the UN, the Food and Agriculture Organization of the United Nations (FAO), the Consultative Group on International Agricultural Research (CGIAR), and the World Bank. With diminishing resources and an additional three billion people all in poorer countries, the food insecurity of poor countries has become the premier rhetorical argument of the big plant-breeding corporations. One obvious goal is to make public opinion in the rich world more positive towards the benefits of genetically modified (GM) crops. This chapter analyses neo-Malthusian rhetoric in debates and policy making about GM crops.

In the final chapter, 'Crisis? What Crisis?' the conclusions of this study are drawn together. I will also try to answer the question of whether the conservationist/environmentalist neo-Malthusians were right or wrong.

2

A New World Order

A new world order emerged in the early post-war years. In spite of some changes, it basically lasted until the fall of the Berlin Wall, when world leaders like President George Bush (the elder) started talking about another new world order. The post-war world involved a regeneration of domains of interest for the superpowers as well as a fundamental transformation of economic production in the world. This chapter presents the political and economic background of the population–resource debate after World War II. Three major strands of post-war world order were particularly important for the natural resource agenda: the worldwide decline in death rates, the transformation of the political economy and the USA's geopolitical strategies.

The Fifth Plate

During the 1930s, shortage of food for a growing world population received some attention. Two nutrition scientists, John Boyd-Orr, future director of FAO, and F. L. McDougall, delivered a plan for the world's food supply to the League of Nations in 1935. The scarcity dilemma was certainly apparent in the interwar period; but it was after World War II that the demands of non-western peoples, their rights of provision of livelihood and self-determination became important topics on the political agenda. The first peak of population–resource concern lasted roughly from the end of World War II until the beginning of the 1950s. This population–resource crisis has been labelled the 'fifth plate', referring to the 20 per cent increase in population that was expected to take its place at the world's dinner table by 1960. As mentioned, it was the result of rapidly declining death rates, particularly through cheaper health measures.[1]

The rapid increase in population growth in the southern hemisphere, rising levels of affluence and increasing globalised trade led to an enormous expansion of agriculture. New lands were cleared, even in marginal areas. Highland regions were ploughed, rainforests were cleared, and arid regions were to be made fruitful. The search for land to plant in fragile areas dramatically increased soil erosion. As historian John R. McNeill points out, the world economic system greatly contributed to such erosion. The demand in richer markets for coffee, citrus fruits, bananas and beef cattle required more fertile tropical lowlands. Subsistence food production had to move onto more marginal land, where often there had been no farming before.[2] Technological changes also placed a heavy toll on soils. Ploughing capacity was greatly increased through the rapid spread of tractors and new heavy machinery after World War II, and it compacted the soils. New irrigation practices, especially through the Green Revolution, brought on new problems of soil salinity. Urbanisation and roads took their share of fertile land. A land area equivalent to the United Kingdom was paved over between 1945 and 1975.[3]

After World War II, the world experienced a decisive boom in economic growth. This economic boost was built on mass production and mass consumption, not only in the United States and Europe but in a global mass market, wherever people had purchasing power.

Mass consumption demanded an enormous input of natural resources. Obviously the supply of resources was of vital concern for corporations, but this new era also marked a turning point in American foreign policy. The United States entirely abandoned its traditional non-intervention policy and decisively entered the international arena.

In this situation, natural resources featured high on the agendas of international politics, the scientific community and the media. Through this process, a new view of the world as well as of the relationship between humans and nature emerged. I will argue in Chapter 5 that this new view formed an ideological foundation for post-war environmental criticism.

The Post-war World

The USA came out of World War II as the most powerful state in the world. Together with its allies, the nation had won a decisive victory over two major powers, Germany and Japan. Its military might was by far the greatest, and on top of it all only the United States had the atomic bomb. Its casualties had been the lowest among the allied states and its territories had been virtually untouched by war. Industrial as well as agricultural production was at an all-time high. The gross national product of the United States had grown from $91 billion in 1939 to $212 billion by 1945. With only six per cent of the world's population, it was producing 60 per cent of the world's entire industrial output.[4]

At the same time, hunger reigned in the countries that had suffered from the war. Farmland had been despoiled and cattle slaughtered. The History of the United Nations Relief and Rehabilitation Administration gives an illuminating account of the war-torn parts of the world. In Poland, almost three out of four horses and two out of three cattle had been killed. In Yugoslavia, retreating armies had devastated means of support by destroying farms, agricultural equipment and livestock and demolishing transportation systems. Its southern and western parts suffered from actual starvation. In the Ukraine over half of the existing tractors were destroyed and a vast portion of the livestock had been killed or seized. The fields lay bare. In China, agricultural production declined, as huge areas of fertile farmland were flooded. Parts of China, as well as the Soviet Union, were also devastated by famine. Undernourished populations were more susceptible to epidemics. Millions of people died from diseases such as cholera, tuberculosis, plague, smallpox and malaria.[5] Food production in Europe had fallen by 1945–6 to two-thirds of its pre-war total. In 1948–9 Asian rice production had still not reached the levels of the mid-1930s.[6]

The Second World War had caused enormous devastation of natural resources, especially metals, oil and fertile soil. After V-day, the struggle to control resources continued to constitute a risk of war. Already before the war was at an end, planning had started for post-war reconstruction of the demolished and ruined areas of the world. Even before the gigantic reconstruction scheme of the Marshall Plan was launched in 1947, the American Relief Administration led by Herbert Hoover, spent more than $4 billion on help to war-stricken countries between 1944 and 1947. The food situation became an issue of priority concern. In 1944 several of the world's leading experts on food supply gathered in Vancouver to plan the food situation in the expected peace to come. After the war the FAO became the first of the permanent new United Nations organisations to be launched. On the very same day that Japan capitulated, the invitations to its first conference were sent to 44 countries. One of the FAO's goals was to make food problems in various parts of the world a common concern for all members.[7]

It was necessary to produce more food either by cultivating additional fertile land or by increasing crop yields in the land already broken. Most agricultural experts at the time agreed that the world was running very low on new available land suitable for agriculture. So, to meet expected needs, either population growth had to be constrained or agricultural output had to increase, or both simultaneously.

Nutrient limits have always been the cap on plant growth. Throughout history agriculture has tried to find ways to deal with this fact, for example through crop rotation and the addition of natural fertilisers or legumes. In the nineteenth century, shipments became so cheap that richer countries could import fertilisers from other continents. Especially, Peruvian and Chilean guano served to restore nutrient depletion in Europe's farmland. The chemical discoveries of extracting superphosphate from rock and attracting nitrogen from the air promised to make possible enormous productivity through industrialised agriculture. One constraint was that these processes were very energy-consuming. By 1940 about four million tons of artificial fertiliser was used in the world, mostly nitrogen and superphosphate.[8]

In the year following the foundation of the FAO, the organisation published its first *World Food Survey* (1946). The survey covered 70 countries, which, at the time represented about 90 per cent of the world population. It described in dramatic terms the poor nutritional state of people in Asia, Africa and Latin America. The FAO concluded that at least half of the world's population did not receive adequate nourishment.[9] This worldwide survey became a forceful confirmation of the impending population–resource crisis.

Cold War Politics of Natural Resources

As superpower rivalry emerged during 1946, the provision of natural resources for the nations of the world became a vital issue. It was of crucial importance for non-communist and communist countries alike, not only for the United States and its allies. Along with the atom bomb, it was the most important piece in the game. President Harry S. Truman held the opinion that it was unlikely that the Soviet Union could win a military arms race against the United States. Even though it was regarded as a superpower, the Soviet Union had no possibility of launching an attack on American land or inflicting any damage to the infrastructure of the American domestic economy. It had no long-range military aircraft, no surface fleet and no atomic bomb.[10] The major threat was the possibility that the superpower rival would take advantage of political unrest and nationalistic tides in poorer countries, thus resulting in an increasing number of these states being overtaken by the communists.

These fears appeared to be well grounded. In Europe the communists were on the rise. In Greece, the Communist Party rose from 10,000 members in 1935 to 70,000 in 1945 and in Italy from 5,000 members in 1943 to 1,700,000 at the end of 1945. In the national elections of 1945, the communists attained 20 per cent in Finland, France and Italy. In Belgium, Denmark, Norway and The Netherlands the vote was almost 10 per cent. In Sweden the Communist Party got 10.3 per cent of the vote in 1944 and this rose to a record high of 11.2 per cent in the local elections of 1946.[11]

Prior to World War II, Eastern Europe had supplied the industrialised Western Europe, and especially Germany, with essential resources like grain, meat, wood, skins, coal, coke and oil. Immediately after the war, the Soviet Union appropriated these valuable resources by signing bilateral trade treaties with its East European neighbours: Bulgaria, Hungary, Poland and Romania.[12] If France or Italy were to elect communists to power, they too could be tied to the Kremlin's sphere by bilateral economic treaties and they might also offer the Soviet Union air transit rights or even base privileges.[13] The political stability of Europe was of the utmost concern to the United States. Providing for a decent standard of living for poor countries was regarded as one of the most effective means to hold communism at bay.[14]

This line of reasoning, which linked the international resource situation to national security policies, I will call the *resource–security theory*. Simplified, it forecast the following causal chain of events: Resource exhaustion caused by overpopulation and waste could cause destitution and hunger. Out of the despair that would follow, social unrest could lead to political instability, which would make the country vulnerable to extremist insurrection and have a negative impact on American geopolitical and economic interests. In the end, these events might shift the balance over to the Soviet Union.

A stable Europe was crucial, but American striving for security also impelled the superpower to worldwide concern. For instance, the US State Department had substantial anxieties that the Mexican regime might turn towards socialism or that the military might attempt a fascist coup. In trying to avoid a totalitarian state at its southern border, it was important for the Franklin D. Roosevelt administration to eradicate the root cause, i.e. social unrest spurred by destitute living conditions.[15] When the Vice President-elect Henry A. Wallace visited Mexico in 1940, the US ambassador gave an account of the plight of poor rural Mexicans, which had made a strong impression on him. Returning to the United States, he held talks with Nelson Rockefeller and other representatives of the Rockefeller Foundation. These contacts were the commencement of the Foundation's long engagement in trying to develop high-yielding agricultural practices. In 1941, the Rockefeller Foundation employed experts on development programmes for agricultural production in Mexico.[16]

As we shall see, resource–security theory came to have a profound impact, not only on conservationists concerned about population, but on the very ideology of conservationism. Before we go further into this chain of events, the second development of great importance for the debate will be discussed: the transition to a global economy.

The Transformation of the World Economy

In the twentieth century, the United States replaced Great Britain as the hegemonic economic power of the world. 'Hegemony' could be defined as to the capability of a state to exercise leadership over a system of independent nations. In so doing, the hegemonic nation is perceived to pursue a general interest,[17] or else it gives other nations hardly any choice but to follow its economic path. Four factors specifically contributed to the development of the United States into a hegemonic power. The vast natural resources of the United States were made accessible by improvements in transportation by the 1890s. This natural resource base paired with an enormous domestic market made possible its economic and technical dominance in the twentieth century. On top of these processes, America's isolated position became less a commercial disadvantage as interlinked transportation and communications improved. Political scientists

Joshua S. Goldstein and David P. Rapkin point out that as the Pacific Ocean became a rival economic zone to the Atlantic Ocean, the geographical position of the United States became central. In this way it came to hold a privileged position in the spatial formation of the capitalist world economy. It was 'a continent-sized island' with complete access to both of the world's major oceans. Thus it held an enormous domestic market and subsequently a favourable trading situation. The world wars and their aftermath brought about a redistribution of financial assets from Britain to the United States which hastened the transition in economic leadership.[18] Industries based on technologies that had matured during the interwar years and were rationalised in World War II production boomed in the post-war world. Construction, the automobile industry, shipbuilding, steel, petrochemicals and consumer electrical goods were the impelling motors of economic growth.[19]

In *The Long Twentieth Century: Money, Power and the Origins of Our Times* (1994), sociologist Giovanni Arrighi identifies four great cycles of capital accumulation, 'four long centuries' starting with the Genoese in the fifteenth century, which was followed by the Dutch, the British and finally the US systemic cycle of accumulation. Every cycle passes through three phases, which Arrighi develops from Karl Marx's formula MCM'. Money (M) is transformed into Capital (C) which in turn generates a surplus of Money (M') to be invested in a continuing accumulation dialectic. M implies liquidity and flexibility, whereas C denotes investment in a concrete, fixed input–output combination for expected profit. M' means an increased liquidity and flexibility. In the first phase, a trade economy, a quantity of money originates in one way or another. In the second phase this money is turned into capital through investment in agricultural or commodity production. Money is 'territorialised'. At a certain point it is no longer profitable to reinvest the profit into the same production as that which generated the profit. At this point an accumulation regime enters its third phase, which is dominated by financial capital. According to French historian Fernand Braudel, this phase of financial expansion is always 'a sign of autumn' for the cycle of accumulation.[20]

According to Arrighi's analysis, the 1950s and 1960s constituted an (MC) phase of material expansion of the capitalist world economy. During this period surplus capital was reinvested into commodity trade and production. This was done on such a massive scale that it was possible to create conditions of renewed cooperation and division of labour within and among various governmental and business organisations of the capitalist world economy. 'To be sure, the speed, scale, and scope of the conversion of surplus capital into commodities were greater in the US cycle than in any previous cycle.'[21] Consequently the world experienced an unseen pressure on its limited resources, not only because of enormous population growth but even more so owing to the consumption demand arising from welfare.

The British geographer David Harvey points out that this expansion of demand rested on two pillars. One was consumption by the privileged work-force in the core productive regions of the world. The other was state-sponsored reconstruction of war-torn economies, for example through urban renewal, suburbanisation and infrastructural development. These economic centralities withdrew huge quantities of raw materials from the rest of the non-communist world. Their products gave rise to an increasingly homogeneous mass world market.[22]

The logic of capitalist accumulation brought about a radical change in economic production and its related modes of social and political regulation at the beginning of the twentieth century. This transformation of the political economy is often referred to as 'Fordism'. The organisational and technological innovations introduced by Henry Ford in his industrial enterprises exemplify such economic reasoning. However, it is important to note that the term Fordism does not designate merely the conscious strategy of a single individual. It should be understood as a general social process for which the strategies of Henry Ford stand as a symbol.

The rise of managerial corporations goes back to the building of the great national railroads in the American Midwest by a set of powerful corporations. Alfred Chandler traces the development of the managerial ethos in American capitalism from the 1870s onward.[23] Henry Ford's company is thus only one later example of managerial or corporate capitalism. However, the concept of Fordism not only covers the managerial ethos, but also illuminates how this was combined with the rise of a consumer and welfare-based society.

Fordism is characterised by the 'recognition that mass production meant mass consumption, a new system of the reproduction of labour power, a new politics of labour control and management, new aesthetics and psychology, in short, a new kind of rationalised modernist, and populist democratic society'.[24] Fordist mass production was based on systems of specialised machines, run by large, bureaucratic, corporations. As it developed, the Fordist system was formed by responses to the crisis tendencies of capitalism, especially during the Great Depression of the 1930s. The wartime mobilisation that followed required large-scale planning and comprehensive rationalisation of the labour process.[25]

Economic growth depended on the state taking on new Keynesian roles. Economists like John Maynard Keynes argued that it was necessary to have scientific managerial strategies as well as state powers that could stabilise capi-talism. Keynes's economic thesis forms one part of a specific phase of capitalist development – the Fordist-Keynesian regime of accumulation. According to

Arrighi, this regime is characterised by investments in fixed capital that create the potential for regular increases in productivity and mass consumption. For this potential to be realised, adequate governmental policies and actions, social institutions, norms and habits of behaviour ('the mode of regulation') were required. 'Keynesianism' may be defined as the mode of regulation that enabled the emergent Fordist regime fully to realise its potential.[26]

Braudel distinguishes between market economy and capitalism. Where many people regard them as more or less the same thing, both concepts conveying opposition to state regulation, Braudel sees capitalism as completely dependent on governmental power, both for its emergence and for its expansion. It is rather the antithesis to market economy.[27].

The state became intimately linked to Fordism. The nation state had a crucial role in the system of social regulation. If people became frustrated with the society which resulted from mass industrialisation, it ran the risk of being exposed to growing discontent. The legitimisation of state power (as well as of Fordism itself) depended on the ability to spread the benefits of industrialisation to the vast majority of the population. The growth of both mass production and mass consumption was to ensure relatively full employment. They were, supposedly, important means for holding off unrest and securing a contented workforce. Fordism paired with properly deployed state power proved to be an effective regime of accumulation, well serving the interests of corporate enterprise. Standards of living rose and capitalism's crisis tendencies were restrained. 'The Golden Age of Capitalism' was on the rise The post-war boom lasted almost intact until the oil crisis of 1973. Historian Thomas J. McCormick identifies the 23-year period, between the beginning of the Korean War and the end of the Vietnam War with the Paris Peace Accords in early 1973, as 'the most sustained and profitable period of economic growth in the history of world capitalism'.[28]

Yet events in this new world order were not that orderly. It was not the case that all agents cooperated smoothly without conflict. In fact, there was a great deal of conflict. Within capitalist countries, there was at times ferocious confrontation between labour and capital as well as cut-throat competition between corporations. There were also bitter conflicts between federal governments and business corporations, for example between the Franklin D. Roosevelt administration and the Ford Motor Company. The administration often struggled against businesses that resisted expansion of government regulation. There was certainly no general 'Fordist' conspiracy between corporations and the state. Nevertheless, in spite of the differences of interest, there appears to have been at least a partly shared vision between political power and the business community. The spread of an American-style consumer society, domestically as well as internationally, was beneficial for both parties. To many economists and business leaders it appeared necessary to limit the social costs of aggressive, market-driven, profit-driven capital, in order to achieve a stable capitalism.

So called 'commonwealth liberals' in the Roosevelt administration, such as Harold L. Ickes and Henry A. Wallace, imposed limits on market economy. An unrestrained market threatened a sound and fair distribution of natural resources. Long-range national planning and political management would safeguard natural resources for the common good.[29] One of the great projects of New Deal conservationists during the 1930s was to elevate the southern United States from rural poverty. Tennessee Valley Authority brought comprehensive planning to the river basin that involved building hydroelectric dams, reforesting eroded hillsides and improving agriculture. In other words, conservation became a part of the economic development of an underdeveloped region. In many ways it anticipated the post-war international development programmes of Point Four and the World Bank. It was bitterly attacked as 'socialistic'. Regardless if the motives were altruistic or not, it served to soften the edges of brutal capitalism. It used the power of government to lift people from a degraded environment, which otherwise would be neglected by or even exploited by capitalism.

Mass industrialisation was made possible by the social system's co-evolution with the fossil fuel economy. Lifestyle and consumer habits adapted to the expanding number of hydrocarbon-dependent technologies. Institutions were adapted to correct the negative effects of a fossil fuel economy. It had freed societies from immediate constraints, but the constraints of the resources themselves aroused concern (and later, so did the effect of carbon dioxide in the atmosphere). Harvey argues that post-war Fordism has to be seen not just as a system of mass production but as a total way of life. Mass production brought about a standardisation of products and mass consumption, which resulted in a commodification of culture.[30] This dependency gave natural resources a vital position in international politics.

Post-war Fordism was certainly international in its scope. Fordism was slow to develop outside the United States in the interwar period, but due to the war effort it was firmly established in Europe and Japan in the 1940s. Indeed, the post-war boom depended upon an enormous expansion of international trade and investment flows. It was spread either directly, through policies imposed by the occupation authorities, or indirectly, through policies like the Marshall Plan and the Technical Assistance Program. After the War, the United States launched investment programmes which attempted to surmount restraints on international demand and to expand market outlets for American products.[31]

The productive capacity and liquidity of the United States made it the centre of the world economy. While surplus capital mounted up in the United States, economic distress in Europe and Asia spurred social and political unrest.

In spite of economic centralisation, industry in the United States did not on its own have the power to create the conditions for its self-expansion in a chaotic world, according to Arrighi. No tax subsidy, insurance scheme, or exchange guarantee was sufficient to overcome the fundamental asymmetry between the cohesiveness and wealth of the USA's domestic market and the fragmentation and poverty of foreign markets. What cost-benefit calculations could not and did not achieve, fear did.[32]

So policymakers in the United States had to worry not only about the direct effects of natural resource constraints for domestic industry, but about the necessity of economic and social stability in the context of the global resource situation. The opening of foreign markets, primarily in Europe, permitted the surplus productive capacity of American business to be disposed elsewhere. As international mass markets were formed, they resulted in the engagement of the mass of the world's population, outside the communist world, into the global dynamics of a new phase of capitalism. Economist Angus Maddison's index for volume of world trade illustrates the enormous growth of international commodity exchange.

Table 1. Volume of world exports, Index 1870–1970

1870	25.00
1913	100.00
1950	151.50
1970	588.10

(Year 1913=100) Source: Maddison, p. 254[33]

The expansion of foreign trade further enhanced a globalisation of trade in natural resources. Global Fordism was created by capitalism's demand for new markets and by the geopolitical ambitions of western nations, predominately the United States and Great Britain. It was secured by the USA's economic power and its military alliances. When the economic system of the post-war world was planned in July 1944, with the Bretton Woods agreement, the dollar became the reserve currency of the world. The construction of an international payment system granted an instrument that promoted free trade. At the end of the 1940s, the General Agreement on Tariffs and Trade (GATT), achieved in 1947, and the Organisation for European Economic Cooperation (OEEC), established in 1948, reduced tariffs and quantitative restrictions in international trade.[34] This tendency towards worldwide economic planning was essential for the natural resource agenda. Besides its geopolitical concern for stable political regimes, the capitalist economy depended on political planning and administration of resources.

A rudimentary standard of living for all subjects of a state became one of the key objectives for the members of the post-war interstate system. Arrighi argues that 'the ideology of US hegemony had elevated the welfare of all the subjects ("high mass consumption") above the absolute rights of property and the absolute rights of government'. [35]

The International Monetary Fund and the World Bank, founded at Bretton Woods, were born out of the idea that economic and material distress fomented political radicalism. In the same way as the legitimisation of state power depended on the ability to spread the benefits of Fordism, the adoption of the western world order could rely on its ability to make the prospect of at least basic consumer benefits available to a wider segment of the world population.

The transition in the world economy brought conservation into focus in two respects. The heavy pressure on known global natural resources, caused by the enormous demand of the expanding economy paired with the devastation of war and a growing population, naturally made conservation measures essential. Also the emphasis on economic planning of resources to secure consumption and political stability made conservation management of great interest. At least at the beginning of the post-war era, conservation was seen by many policy-makers as an important instrument to ensure international as well as domestic stability in the new world order.

As an opposing reform movement, conservation could serve to check the manic international economy and prevent its destabilising effects. My point is not that conservation tradition in United States, or elsewhere, was in any simple way a tool of capitalism or a mere subordinate part of it. As a reform movement it tried to change the mode of ruthless capitalist exploitation. Nevertheless, this opposing force *could* also tie in with the welfare state's reformation of capitalism.

Conservation and Peace

For the Truman administration, the United Nations consequently became an important medium through which to deal with the natural resource situation. In September 1946, the president urged John G. Winant, the US representative in the United Nations Economic and Social Council (ECOSOC), to work towards a UN-organised international scientific conference on the utilisation and conservation of natural resources. In a letter to Winant, the President stated his arguments as to why such a conference was necessary.

> It is my belief that the need for such an exchange was never greater. Warfare has taken a heavy toll of many natural resources; the rebuilding of the nations and the industrialisation of under-developed areas will require an additional large depletion of them. Waste, destruction and uneconomic use of resources anywhere damage mankind's common estate. The real or exaggerated fear of resource shortages and declining standards of living has in the past involved nations in warfare … Conservation can become a major basis of peace.[36]

Planning for the conference had already begun as war was raging in Europe. In January 1940, Governor Gifford Pinchot, famous former Chief Forester under the Theodore Roosevelt administration, proposed the project in a letter to Franklin D. Roosevelt. Drawing on the idea that conservation could be the foundation of enduring peace between nations, he wanted to persuade the President to call for an international conservation conference. He outlined his idea in a memorandum entitled 'A Plan for Permanent Peace through International Cooperation in the Conservation and Distribution of Natural Resources'. [37]

Conservation is a broad term in the American tradition. From the late nineteenth century it was used by a broad spectrum of agents, with the common theme of concern for the prevailing use of nature's resources. Two strands are commonly identified, of which one can be categorised as management: prior to World War II this style of conservation focused on long-term efficient use of physical resources. The other, given much attention, is the tradition passed on from John Muir and other so-called 'preservationists'.

The concept of conservation as efficient utilisation of natural resources was congenial and basic to the practice of civil engineering. In the American conservation movement, the engineers and scientific experts had played an important role in its focus and actions. Prior to World War II these conservationists concentrated on efficient use of physical resources. At the end of the nineteenth century, awareness grew that the American frontier was not a bottomless cornucopia. For the first time, restraint really entered into the USA's resource policies. At the same time the mapping of the nation's resources became more and more sophisticated. The perceived ability to master the situation increased. The issue was placed higher on the national agenda by the Theodore Roosevelt administration. Symbolising and leading this course was Gifford Pinchot.[38]

As Theodore Roosevelt's chief forester, he recognised that the nation's prosperity was endangered by a wasteful frontier approach. So Pinchot pushed for a long-range programme that through careful sustained-yield management would develop the country's resources in a rational and efficient way for the greatest good of the nation. Through science, humans could improve nature and make its produce more abundant. The goal of resource management would not be private gain and further concentration of wealth, but the greatest economic benefit to all citizens. Reckless exhaustion might threaten the nation's security. In the words of environmental historian Donald Worster: 'Protecting the nation's economy, not nature's, was the central theme of his conservation philosophy.'[39]

The different resource areas of forest, water, soil and grazing were categorised in an overall concept: natural resources. As Samuel P. Hays recognised, State departments of natural resources emerged in the interwar period and some university departments of forestry were transformed to departments of natural resources.[40]

The dominant theme in early conservationism was the emphasis on efficient management in natural resource development. But conservation was not merely an enterprise for careful management: ever since the Civil War, state and national parks were established to set aside areas – nature reserves, national parks and natural monuments – which should be protected from cultivation, or at least from unrestricted use.[41]

Alongside the Pinchot style of utilitarian-commercial conservation, there was another style of conservation: the tradition descending from John Muir and other 'preservationists', directed towards an aesthetic-ethical protection of nature. Inspired by romanticists and transcendentalists like Ralph Waldo Emerson and Henry David Thoreau they strove to protect nature chiefly for its own sake.[42]

Initially, in the United States, land was seen as a resource for commercial enterprise: farming, ranching, and mining typified the nation's relationship to the land. Accordingly, these commercial interests opposed establishing parks that would limit their access to the resources they had traditionally benefited from. Once the parks were established, however, the capital derived from tourism was a major argument for their continued existence. The political and economic status of the parks changed little: the land was still commodified, but within new discursive frames.[43]

The post-war conservation debate was part of a well-established tradition from the Progressive era. In the interwar period soil erosion struck the Midwest through the dust bowl catastrophe. In 1933 the Soil Erosion Service was set up within the Department of the Interior. Two years later the Soil Conservation Service was established under the Department of Agriculture. A soil conservation programme was established that aimed at efficient use and management of the nation's soil resources in order to implement a sustainable agriculture.[44] During the New Deal era, national plans were made for several of the natural resource categories. The Secretary of the Interior, Ickes, was a strong advocate of national planning. In the area of natural resources this concern resulted, for example, in the massive volume *National Plan for American Forestry* (1933). Recommendations were given in it for forming a 'Wilderness Planning Board'.[45]

Conservation at the beginning of the century did not evolve as a radical or direct critique of political power. Rather it was directed towards limiting the effects of crude exploitation. Of course, there was criticism of the prevailing order, but this criticism was usually provided with a platform by the political system. Conservation, it was reasoned, could be an engineering tool for safe-guarding a stable economy and security for the nation.

Pinchot's Proposal

Pinchot again raised the issue of an international conservation conference during a visit to the White House in late June 1944. With the devastating war coming to a close, Roosevelt became interested and encouraged Pinchot to prepare a plan. Two months later the Governor submitted a 'Proposal for an International Conference on Conservation', in the form of a draft letter from the President to the member states of the United Nations. The worthiest of tasks for the world would be to make future wars impracticable. That could only be done by reducing the incentive to war, i.e. the geopolitical contest for natural resources. They were the material foundations of human security and progress, and thus the key to peace and stability, or war and despair. Conservation, stated Pinchot, meant a planned and orderly use of all the products of the earth, for the greatest good of the greatest number for the longest time. The struggle for permanent peace was impossible to win until general plenty for all was assured through a concerted effort to both safeguard the world's natural resources and ensure that they would equitably be available to all countries.

The first step was to ascertain the status of natural resources world wide. Therefore the proposed conference should try to accomplish an inventory of the natural resources of the world and to establish a set of principles for their conservation and fair access in the interests of peace. It should be arranged as a United Nations conference, hosted by the United States. This was a matter of worldwide concern, according to the former chief forester. 'Conservation as a policy', he declared, 'is universally accepted as sound'. Pinchot concluded the draft: 'Without worldwide conservation, lasting peace is impossible.' [46]

Roosevelt concurred with the proposal. Even though the President was tied up in his 1944 campaign, he wrote to Cordell Hull, Secretary of State, to foster the idea. In his meetings with other nations, the President revealed, he had a feeling that too little attention was being paid to the subject of the conservation and use of natural resources. He repeatedly propounded the Pinchot slogan 'Conservation is a basis of permanent peace'. Subsequently he moved the emphasis to the utilisation of the resources. 'Many different kinds of natural resources are being wasted; other kinds are being ignored; still other kinds can be put to more practical use for humanity if more is known about them.'

Roosevelt proposed that the conference should be held prior to the planned comprehensive meeting to establish the United Nations. It would be valuable to arrange the conference in the United States with all united and associated nations, for a first step toward a worldwide study of conservation and use of natural resources. Faced with a world torn by war, the President concluded: 'I think the time is ripe.'[47]

Not all members of the administration were as convinced. Acting Secretary of State, Edward R. Stettenius, responded negatively to the proposal. In an attached memorandum he stressed the commodifying aspect of international resources. He doubted whether it was possible to reach a substantial international agreement on multilateral conservation programmes without taking into account the prospect of systematic development and marketing of natural resources. Conservation is but one part, however important, of the 'total problem of international cooperation in the wisest use of the world's productive resources'. Besides this objection, Stettenius indicated that the draft constitution of the FAO stated that the organisation should deal with these issues. Thus it was unnecessary to hold a separate conference.[48]

Roosevelt was irritated by this answer from Stettenius. 'Whoever wrote the memorandum for you has just failed to grasp the real need of finding out more about the world's resources and what we can do to improve them.' Yet, in his arguments for the conference, the President himself added the commodity argument. Persia served as an example. Its once forested northern parts were now bare and populated by destitute people. There was an acute water shortage. Something drastic had to be done, but it would take several hundred years to accomplish it and Persia had no resources to buy US products. With the proposed conference as a starting point, Roosevelt concluded, 'in a short period of time we could begin a programme to build up non-buying nations into good customers'.[49]

The President's words illustrate the underlying argument in the White House for conservation. Along the rationale of Fordism, the Roosevelt administration's prime interest in international conservation was as a means to promote its economic expansion to new markets. Stettenius retreated swiftly, stating that the department had misunderstood his proposal.[50] With the Yalta Conference at hand, the President asked Pinchot to prepare a preliminary statement on the conservation conference. According to Pinchot, Roosevelt wanted to present the idea to Winston Churchill and Joseph Stalin. In the meantime Pinchot was to prepare a more detailed plan. As the important San Francisco Conference, where the United Nations was to be set up, drew nearer, the preparations for the conservation conference had to be held over for a while.[51]

Roosevelt rejected Churchill's attempt to divide the post-war world into spheres of influence. Speaking at a joint session of Congress on March

1, 1945, Roosevelt stated that the recently concluded Yalta Accord implied the end of the old ways of performing world politics; balances of power and spheres of influence were abolished from the new peaceful world order. In their place would come a new way centred on a world organisation for peace – the United Nations. This public rhetoric expressed universal principles of self-determination and free elections for the people of the world and an adherence to the Atlantic Charter and the wartime alliance.[52] For the first time in modern history the idea of world government involving the nations of the entire globe was institutionalised in the United Nations Organisation. The sovereignty of independent nations was also restricted by post-war organisations like the International Monetary Fund (IMF) and GATT.[53]

According to Daniel Yergin, Roosevelt was torn between several objectives. With the Soviets he talked power politics and proposed the 'four policemen' – the United States, the Soviet Union, Great Britain and China – to guarantee the peace. Roosevelt assured Stalin that he understood the need for the Soviet Union to secure its borders. Domestically 'he continued to obscure this basic programme in the idealistic Wilsonian language, which by then had become the lingua franca of post-war thinking.'[54] However, Roosevelt's correspondence with the State Department seems to indicate a sincere desire to bring the conference about. Since plans for it were not yet publicly announced it was not merely intended as public rhetoric at that point in time.

In his last letter to Roosevelt, two days before the President died, Pinchot expressed hopes that some action on the conference would be taken at the San Francisco meeting.[55] Yet the State Department continued to work against the conference, arguing that it would conflict with international commodity agreements. The State Department argued that the US programme for the conference recognised that it was vital to consider conservation in future international commodity agreements. However, many of the general challenges to conservation would naturally be covered by a forthcoming trade and employment conference. Thus, conservation would not need a conference of its own, in the State Department's view. It would be covered by 'the general topics of commercial policy, commodity arrangements, cartels, international aspects of domestic full-employment programmes and international organisations related to these matters'.[56]

Roosevelt died on April 12. Nearly a month later the war ended in Europe and the unifying ecumenical rhetoric of the allies began to be challenged. Still, Truman seemed determined to continue Roosevelt's general policy of prolonged cooperation between the allies – a line which he basically continued over the San Francisco Conference and the peace in the Pacific, all throughout the year of 1945.[57]

After Roosevelt's death, Pinchot tried to interest a number of influential people in the conference, such as Harry Hopkins, Roosevelt's confidant and occasional envoy, the President's secretary William D. Hassett, William L. Clayton, Assistant Secretary of Economic Affairs, and not least Truman himself.[58] At the end of May Ickes, the Secretary of the Interior, wrote to Truman pushing for the conference. Ickes, who had discussed the question with Roosevelt prior to the Yalta conference, urged it strongly. His prime argument was the heavy toll the war had taken on the natural wealth of the world. Substantial supplies of raw materials widely distributed throughout the world were necessary to provide economic well-being, without which world peace could not for long be preserved.

> It is essential, therefore, not only that we fulfill the Atlantic Charter declaration of providing access, on equal terms, by all nations to the raw materials of the world, but that we undertake an all-out attack, far more comprehensive than anything visualised in the past, against unnecessary depletion of the world's resources.[59]

Truman responded favourably. The President set aside fifteen minutes on May 23 to let Pinchot personally brief him on the issue.[60] He repeatedly discussed the issue with both Ickes and Pinchot and was 'deeply interested'. However, considering all the other conferences in train, he wanted the conservation conference to take place after the Fall.[61]

After a report on trade expansion, the Executive Committee on Economic Foreign Policy decided in October 1945 to establish a committee to consider the problem of conservation of natural resources in relation to international trade. The committee included representatives from the Departments of Commerce, State, Labour, War and the Navy as well as the United States Tariff Commission, the Forest Service and the Bureau of Mines.[62] Conservation as an issue of economic foreign policy was established within the Truman administration.

Pinchot's proposal for a world conservation conference was not new. Nature protection had been on the international agenda since the turn of the century. In the years immediately prior to World War I, conservation societies developed an international system for wildlife protection in the northern European countries and their colonies. Ever since the beginning of the century the importance of international agreements for the protection of nature had been emphasised. After the success of promoting conservation at the White House Conference in 1908, President Theodore Roosevelt and his Chief Forester Pinchot called for a North American Conservation Conference in February 1909. The delegates agreed to work for a world conference to be held the following September in The Netherlands. Fifty-eight countries received invitations from the Theodore Roosevelt administration. However, Roosevelt's successor as president, William Howard Taft, abandoned the undertaking. The world had to wait another four years for its first world conference to promote international collaboration on nature protection.

A Commission for the International Protection of Nature was formed in order to organise international conferences. The International Congress on the Protection of Nature was held in Paris in 1909. The Swiss government called for the Internationalen Konferenz für Naturschutz in Bern in 1913. Delegates from 16 countries participated; not, however, the United States. One of the goals for the conference was to accomplish international regulation for nature protection. These agreements were directed toward issues concerning the preservation of threatened species like the musk ox in Greenland and reindeer on Spitzbergen. The delegates also resolved to establish an information agency for nature protection everywhere in the world.[63] Nine months later the outbreak of war interrupted the plans and international nature protection went into hibernation. The war not only impeded international cooperation, it turned the focus towards more immediate goals, such as the supply of natural resources to the beleaguered populace and the war machine. After the war, reconstruction preoccupied the interest and effort of governments.

During the interwar period, international protection of nature was acknowledged primarily through the interest shown by the colonial powers in threatened species in their territories. A number of committees and special conferences on the protection of international flora and fauna were initiated. Some smaller international agreements were reached on pollution from shipping, as well as on protection of whales and African wildlife.[64]

In 1925 and 1926, the Dutch conservationist P. G. Van Tienhoven organised committees for the international protection of nature in France, The Netherlands and Belgium. Backed by the International Union of Biological Sciences, van Tienhoven established an International Office for the Protection of Nature in Brussels. In 1931 Conseil International de la Chasse focused on bird protection outside national borders. In the same year the second International Congress for the Protection of Nature was held, organised by van Tienhoven. The very same year the American Committee for International Wildlife Protection was constituted. In October 1933 the House of Lords hosted the London meeting of the Convention for the Protection of African Flora and Fauna, a meeting which historian Roderick Nash labels as the 'high point of institutionalised global nature protection before the Second World War'.[65] However, it was merely directed towards the promotion of national parks and regulations on some game merchandising, such as trade in animal trophies. The resolutions never became national law, only advocacy.[66] In October 1940, while a new great war was raging in Europe, conservationists from various countries on the

American continent met in Washington under the auspices of the Pan-American Union. The meeting was directed towards wildlife issues. It not only reaffirmed the London convention of 1933 but also called for parks where recreational practices would be banned. It also advocated reserves where preservation and resource exploitation would go hand in hand. The United States ratified the conference document six months before it engaged in the war.[67]

The spread of consumer society, the affluent way of life, put a devastating demand on the world's resources. In that respect the growth of capitalist as well as socialist economy was an environmentally destabilising force. The enormous consumption of resources was certainly one of the reasons behind the population–resource crisis. At least in the early post-war years, conservation was seen by many in power as one way to stabilise the disturbing effects. As we shall see in the next two chapters, the development of the new world order came to have a profound effect on the position of some scientists on conservation issues.

3

Conservation and Containment

The United Nations Scientific Conference on the Conservation and Utilisation of Resources was the first UN conference to involve a large number of scientists and experts. Truman anticipated this UN conference to be of great importance to his Point Four Program. Parallel to it, conservationists held an alternative meeting: the International Technical Conference on the Protection of Nature. This chapter deals with the planning and the agenda of these conferences. These events are also related to American aid initiatives, such as that of the Rockefeller Foundation. As the issue of natural resources was placed on the agenda of international politics, conservationists were forced to alter their positions. This reorientation is depicted through the foundation of the International Union for the Protection of Nature.

The Agenda Takes Shape

In the USA, the planning of the conservation conference continued during the fall of 1945. Truman requested an outline for the conference by December 15.[1] At the same time, in the late part of 1945 and in early 1946, the Truman administration became increasingly worried about the intentions of the Soviet Union. The London Foreign Ministers' Conference had highlighted the differences between the superpowers. In Greece, a successful communist insurrection threatened to put a leftist regime in power. In Iran the Soviet Union was delaying its agreed troop withdrawal, sharpening the conflict with Great Britain over Iranian oil. In January, Albania was proclaimed a People's Republic. Domestically, the Republican Party openly challenged the Democrats on foreign affairs and accused the Truman administration of being soft on communism.[2]

The White House response brought about a decisive change in the relationship between the former allied superpowers, in February and March of 1946. The American Chargé d'Affaires in Moscow, George F. Kennan, wrote his famous 'long telegram' on February 22, warning the White House that the Kremlin sought world domination.

Guided by their traditional insecurity and Marxist–Leninist dogma, the Soviet leaders would seek to expand everywhere, taking advantage of any weakness on the part of the West. Kennan argued that, since the Kremlin was not susceptible to reason, manifestation of force was the language it would understand. On March 5, Winston Churchill gave his Fulton address where he coined the 'iron curtain' metaphor, urging for containment of the Soviet Union before it was too late. Later in March the President declared the Truman Doctrine. Military help was specifically offered to Greece and Turkey, but what is more important, the United States offered to help all democratic countries whose freedom and independence were threatened by foreign countries or movements. With the threat of an armed conflict, the Soviet Union backed down over Iran in late March. The politics of Soviet containment was established as the lodestar of American foreign policy.[3] Besides military strategies, this course also involved economic programmes, like the Marshall Plan. In June 1947, Secretary of State George C. Marshall presented the plan, designed to rebuild the European economy. An insolvent European market could not buy American products and there was a risk of a post-war depression. Destitute living conditions could stir unrest and promote communist agitation and subversive activities. The European Recovery Program was established to assist with some 13 billion dollars between 1948 and 1952, to set the European economy straight.

The new Central Intelligence Agency was instrumental in applying Marshall Plan methods to Egypt and Iran, following resource–security theory. The assumption was that developing nations aspired to emulate western societies' industrial and economic development models. With the adequate support for planning capacity and technology transfer, these countries would be less vulnerable to communist agendas.[4] Such attempts were forerunners of the culmination of the resource–security theory – Truman's Point Four Program.

Early in September 1946, the proposed resource conference was the subject of prolonged discussions between representatives of the Departments of State, Agriculture, Commerce and Interior. The Department of State was in general agreement with the proposed programme and the draft of the Winant letter. Henry Wallace, who took an active role in the preparations, wrote to the President strongly favouring the planned conference.[5] Finally, in late September, the Department of Interior had finished a preliminary programme and sent a letter of proposal to the American representative of ECOSOC. The US proposal gained support when presented to the council, though the Soviet Union was sceptical towards the American initiative.[6]

In December the Secretary General of the UN, Trygve Lie, presented the proposal to the 51 member countries and concerned member organisations. Since the UN was recently constituted, this was a way to institutionalise the organisation and at the same time set the tone for its future work. 19 countries, together with the FAO and the World Bank, supported the conference, with a few reservations. There were two main objections. Firstly, the field the conference encompassed was too wide. A delegate of the South African Legation complained that it covered every aspect of science, technology, sociology and economics.[7] The state of natural resources was a controversial subject that required careful preparation if it was going to be treated in an international context.[8] Secondly, there was heavy pressure from several countries, especially South Africa, Guatemala and the Philippines, that the Conference should not lead to any resolutions or undertakings for national governments.[9] According to the proceedings, the size and complexity of the planned programmes were much restrained in the early preparatory work. Nils Dahlbeck, a Swedish representative at the conference, argued that it was a precondition for the realisation of the conference that it should not deal with birth control as a check on overpopulation.[10]

There were other objections as well. The Netherlands suggested that the meeting should be moved to another year, since 1947 was already occupied by other international conferences. It would, for example, collide with the ongoing World Power Conference, an international congregation with 30 countries, which dealt with the energy resource situation of the post-war world.[11]

In March 1947, ECOSOC agreed on a resolution stating that a conference should be arranged with the following motivation:

> Recognising the importance of the world's natural resources, particularly due to the drain of the war on such resources, and their importance to the reconstruction of devastated areas, and recognising further the need for continuous development and widespread application of the techniques of resource conservation and utilisation.[12]

ECOSOC decided at an early stage that the conference should be devoted solely to an exchange of ideas and experience among engineers, resource technicians, economists and other experts in related fields. In February 1948, the council requested that the Secretary General continue the preparations for a conference 'keeping in mind that the task of the conference is to be limited to an exchange of experience in the techniques of the conservation and utilisation of resources'.[13] In a letter to the participating countries, Lie assured that the 'Conference is to be scientific and not policy-making. It will have no power to bind governments and it will not formulate recommendations to them.'[14] As we shall see this position attracted disappointment and criticism from conservationists.

Of course, population issues were controversial for both religious and political reasons. Ever since the days of Thomas Malthus, they had stirred up emotions in public debate. Demography appeared as a respected field of academic study in America in the 1930s and 1940s. By connecting population growth and food production with national security, experts in universities and philanthropic organisations were successful in capturing the attention of political leaders in the United States. In the late 1940s, demography was integrated into American national security planning.

An early demographer, Warrens S. Thompson, saw population growth as a strategic political problem. In 1929 he published *Danger Spots in World Population*, in which he argued that high population densities together with limited resources were a key factor in causing war. He continued this line of thought in 1946, in *Population and Peace in the Pacific*. He warned that the large populations of China and Japan threatened the post-war possibilities for peace in East Asia. If peace were to be secured, the United States had to recognise and deal with the pressure on the natural resource base of these increasing populations. John H. Perkins, biologist and historian, points out that there were at least two tendencies of neo-Malthusianism: one political, of which Thompson is a representative, linking population densities to national and international economics, and one ecological, linking population densities to resource degradation.[15]

During the war, innovations in transport, communication, and destructive capacity had outmoded geographical isolation and threatened the security of even the geographically privileged and militarily strong United States. The world shrank mentally as well as technically. Friendly and professional governments were seen as sureties for social and political stability. Just as the New Deal brought social and political security to the United States, so it was hoped that Franklin D. Roosevelt's vision of one world would bring this security to the world arena.[16]

The rationale of the New Deal was the idea that societal stability and security could be achieved by liberal spending of public finance by big government. This notion transferred to the post-war world implied that post-war security would require liberal expenditure by the United States to overcome the social turmoil that followed the War's destruction. Aid to less-developed nations could have the same effects as the welfare programmes of the New Deal. Besides overcoming the threat of revolutionary chaos, these countries would also be drawn into the world market system. Historian Franz Schurmann points out that the implicit idea was that these countries would become responsible if they were brought into the general system. If help were brought to Western Europe economic aid would impel economic growth. This way transatlantic trade would be stimulated and in the long run this would benefit the American economy. At the cost of huge deficits the United States had spent enormous sums in order to sustain the war effort. These investments had resulted in astounding economic growth. Likewise, post-war spending on precarious regions could produce similar effects on a worldwide scale.[17]

The United Nations became of key importance for the United States. Its General Assembly brought together all nations on a supposedly equal footing. Arrighi even calls the global 'decolonisation' and the formation of the organisation 'the most significant correlates of US hegemony'.[18]

Schurmann argues that it was crucial for the post-war ambitions of Franklin D. Roosevelt, and later Truman, that security for the world was based on US power exercised through international systems. 'But for such a scheme to have a broad ideological appeal to the suffering peoples of the world, it had to emanate from an institution less esoteric than an international monetary system and less crude than a set of military alliances or bases.'[19]

Conservation at a Crossroads

As natural resource issues were placed on the agenda of international politics, conservationists were forced to alter their positions. The early conservationists generally accepted the existing economic–political order and social structure. Even though some wanted a return to a more soil-bound way of life, away from ever expanding industrialised society, the dominant message among traditional conservationists was a moderate questioning of industrial modernisation[20]. Their aim was often quite conservative, to protect threatened land areas within the traditional social order.[21]

Liberal utilisation practice put traditionally conservative nature protection under severe pressure. The gigantic industrial capacity that emerged after the war placed huge demands on the world's resources. In this process, scientists and conservationists in the United States and Europe formulated a radical critique of modern society's utilisation of nature. A central theme in the debate was that shortage of resources jeopardised the survival of humankind. Overpopulation on an overexploited earth threatened to bring about a catastrophe if society did not alter its course. These ecological neo-Malthusians reached out to a public audience through accessible scientific publications.

In the early post-war years several influential actors in the debate expressed a politicised conservationism.[22] Two of the most distinguished were William Vogt and Fairfield Osborn. Vogt was one of the founders of the Conservation Society and former editor of the *Audubon Society Magazine*. Between 1939 and 1942, Vogt worked for the Guano commission in Lima, Peru. As with Borgström, Vogt's South American experience made him concerned about overpopulation and the misuse of natural resources. From 1943 until 1949 Vogt was the head of the conservation section of the Pan-American Union, an organisation made up of 21 American countries aiming at economic and social cooperation between the American nations. In his book of 1948, *Road to Survival*, he profoundly endorsed a planned economy on natural resource issues. In neo-Malthusian manner, Vogt pointed out the grave consequences that would follow through the devastation of the earth's natural resources and the ever-increasing world population. Humankind must change from a profit-based economy to an all-embracing Pinchot-style approach based on maximum sustained yield. The free market economy was to blame for the impending catastrophe. To Vogt, the only road to survival was an adjustment of the economic system to the laws of nature. A revolution in the sense of a profound change of fundamental ideas was required.

> Conservation is not going to save the world. Nor is control of populations. Economic, political, educational, and other measures also are indispensable; but unless population control and conservation are included, other means are certain to fail.[23]

Vogt put his hopes in a 'rational, national standard', through scientific planning of population and natural resources. Scientists should provide research and education to bring society into balance with nature, and should advise international bodies on the necessary roads to survival. The plans for an international scientific natural resources conference were thus right at the heart of the matter for Vogt. Most of all, it was crucial to limit population growth if a global sustained-yield economy was to be achieved. Without population control, 'we might as well give up the struggle'.[24]

In spite of his radical political message in *Road to Survival*, Vogt persuaded the millionaire statesman, Bernard Baruch to write the introduction. This way the book attained some discursive legitimisation that could help prevent critics from putting a communist tag on him. Vogt would need all the help he could get from the Establishment. Besides attacking free-market economy, Vogt attacked the foundation of the American dream, accusing the American pioneers of being 'one of the most destructive groups of human beings that ever raped the earth'.[25]

Road to Survival was a great success. It was translated into seven languages. *Reader's Digest* even made a condensed version of it, which was translated into eleven languages. The book was estimated to have reached between 20 and 30 million readers. According to historian Christopher Lewis, most of the reviews of *Road to Survival* responded favourably to the book. 'But most reviewers failed to notice or comment on Vogt's argument that there was a basic contradiction between industrial capitalism and the health of the global environment. Instead, they tended to repeat his apocalyptic message.'[26]

Less hostile to free enterprise, Fairfield Osborn perceived industrialism's continually increasing withdrawal of non-renewable resources to be the key problem. Osborn was something of a 'Mr Conservation' at this time. The former New York banker was chairman and one of the founders of the Conservation

Foundation, chairman of the New York Zoological Society and active in the
International Union for the Protection of Nature. He was also appointed to the
preparatory committee of the UN resource conference. Osborn was a Republican, and as a former investment banker he was acquainted with the business
elite in New York such as Laurence Rockefeller.[27] During the preparatory stages
of the conference, he published his book *Our Plundered Planet* (1948). In it,
Osborn confronted global resource problems such as overpopulation, starvation,
erosion and desertification. His conclusion was that if civilisation was to avoid
extinction, humankind must find global solutions and become reconciled with
the rules of nature. Osborn urged for more centralised planning to cope with
the depletion of resources.[28]

It was an illusion that 'America can feed the world'. Instead Osborn
argued that it was necessary for international bodies to recognise the need for
conservation of the constituent nations' land and control of their population
growth. In *Our Plundered Planet*, Osborn made a crack at the Truman Doctrine.
'As far as the "investment for democracy" in Greece is concerned, nature holds
the trump card.'[29] The USA's efforts would be fruitless unless Greece could
control its burgeoning population growth and soil erosion.[30]

It is analytically useful to make a distinction between aesthetic–moral,
health-based and economic–demographic environmental degradation, when
dealing with the trajectory of environmentalism.[31] All three types had been
acknowledged and disputed prior to World War II, but the first seems to have
dominated; or at least, concerns about the aesthetic–moral implications of
environmental degradation have been more noticed by environmental historians. During the twentieth century, economic–demographic opportunities and
constraints, as well as impacts on human health, aroused increasing concern.
This process characterises conservation's change of focus. In the post-war conservation debate on natural resources, the two latter constituted the centre of
the argumentation. They became the new trump cards in the hand of nature
protection.

Immediately after the war, internationally-inclined conservationists
worked towards closer cooperation between countries on nature protection.
The post-war leaning towards international institutions favoured the idea of
resuming interwar collaboration. Closer international engagement was a burning
issue in several areas of nature protection. The International Birdlife Committee
held its first meeting in 1947, where several of the leaders in wildlife conservation met, for example, William Vogt. In June 1947, the Swiss League for the
Protection of Nature sponsored a conference, which gathered conservationists
in Brunnen, Switzerland. Prominent conservationists from around the world,
among them Julian Huxley and P. G. Van Tienhoven, met to confer on how
international nature protection could be organised. The American notion of

nature protection had, ever since its beginning and to a larger extent than its European counterpart, included an economising of natural resources. The main thrust of European nature protection was aimed at preserving species in smaller or larger reserve areas. At this preliminary meeting of the International Union for the Protection of Nature (IUPN)[32] in 1947, the participants discussed whether international nature preservation should be directed towards global ecological problems, especially shrinking resources and overpopulation. Nils Dahlbeck, secretary of the Swedish Society for Nature Conservation and a Swedish representative at the meeting, asserts that it was quite a struggle to settle these issues. As Nash puts it: 'Once again a coterie of nature importers took steps to protect their interests in foreign countries.'[33]

According to Dahlbeck, it was also the colonial powers, Great Britain, France and the Benelux countries, that opposed a shift of direction from the traditional domain of nature protection. However, already by the following summer when the IUPN was formally constituted at Fontainebleau, France, attitudes had shifted and the participants agreed that IUPN should direct itself towards the new perspective on nature protection.[34]

Founded by scientists and experts, IUPN became an intergovernmental expert organisation mediating between the scientific world and political institutions, promoting the exchange of scientific information and policy advice between governments and international organisations. According to Russell J. Dalton these 'administrative functions limited its ability to mobilise public opinion and financial support on behalf of conservation causes.'[35] But the IUPN put a lot of emphasis on the importance of making scientific ecological knowledge accessible to public. As we shall see, this was one of the key issues at the first IUPN-sponsored international scientific conference: International Technical Conference on the Protection of Nature.

The preamble of the Union stated that human civilisation's dependency upon renewable resources demanded the preservation of the entire world's biotic environment. The new direction was explicitly expressed in the statutes of IUPN. There were social, educational and cultural reasons, as well as economic, for protecting nature.[36] One of the leading persons in the Union, Jean-Paul Harroy, emphasised that it was an adventure for the board of the IUPN when it deliberately broke with the traditional practice of nature protection: to focus on 'perfecting conservation legislation and managing reserve areas'.[37] Conservation had come to a crossroads.

The background to present day environmentalism is sometimes sought in two waves of environmental mobilisation. The first wave dates from the turn of the century, starting in the United States at the time of the Civil War and in Europe in the 1880s, and terminating around the outbreak of World War I. The second wave, in the 1960s, led to the formation of an environmental discourse.

In extremely simplified terms, the earlier concern for protection of nature is sometimes portrayed as the focus of an educated elite and administrative bodies on the national and scientific importance of protecting spectacular nature as part of the cultural heritage and as research objects, whereas the latter peak of concern is seen as more attentive to the problems of mass consumption and advanced industrial society.[38] However, this is a gross simplification. Rather, the two kinds of conservation ran alongside each other, often in conflict. Certainly, there are many examples of people who have expressed what can be regarded as environmental views previously in history, such as George Perkins Marsh. The human-centred resource conservation side has mostly been the dominant one, whereas nature protection has usually been a weaker force.

Yet, when dealing with a conservationist *mobilisation* against the modern economy's depletion of natural resources, the periodisation is fairly well maintained. Population–resource conservationism in the early post-war period was situated in an unprecedented international economic and demographic transition.

Conservation or Utilisation?

Early in the planning of the proposed resource conference, Roosevelt added an emphasis on *utilisation* to Pinchot's *conservation*.[39] Consequently, the meeting was named the United Nations Scientific Conference on the Conservation and Utilisation of Resources. In charge of the preparations was a group of experts nominated by member organisations of the UN: FAO; United Nations Educational, Scientific, and Cultural Organisation (UNESCO); and the World Health Organisation's provisional committee.

During the preparatory work, a line of conflict evolved in the expert group between adherents of the two different approaches: conservation and utilisation. The conflict did not run between East and West or rich and poor countries. These tensions had been forestalled by the appointment of scientists only from the West, predominantly from the United States. Truman and Lie also pushed for a technical committee of American experts to assist in the preparations.[40] The schism appeared between those who stressed conservation and those who emphasised utilisation.

As president of the Conservation Foundation, Osborn served on the Conservation Advisory Council reporting to Secretary of Interior Julius Krug. This position also gave him an opportunity to participate in the preparatory committee of the resources conference. In the expert group, Osborn argued strongly that the conference should be directed towards the conservation rather than the utilisation of natural resources. He stressed that it was of vital importance that the conference also dealt with the problem of overpopulation and the necessity of broad public education on the protection of nature.[41]

When his book *Our Plundered Planet* was published during the preparatory stages of the conference, it aroused a great deal of discussion. *Time* magazine called Osborn's message 'his familiar Malthusian bogey of ever-shrinking resources, ever-increasing population'.[42] Vannevar Bush, wartime head of the Office of Scientific Research and Development, launched a hard attack on Osborn's conclusions. Contrary to what Osborn predicted in *Our Plundered Planet*, the world's population and scientific innovations grew simultaneously, but Bush emphasised, 'science gets there first'. Pesticides were one example of how the dispersion of American technology would make a more effective use of the world's resources possible. According to Bush, they would bring about an increased standard of living for the people of the world.[43]

This was also the belief of the advocates of utilisation in the preparatory group of the UN conference. The economist Morris E. Garnsey pointed out that the conference should concentrate on the economic aspects of both conservation and utilisation of resources. Its foremost important task was the exchange of experience and knowledge for improved extraction of natural resources.[44]

In spite of the tension within the group of experts between the conservation side and the utilisation side, there appears to have been relative unity on the framing of the problem. They agreed that a crisis was at hand if nothing was done. The conflict revolved around the question of whether scientific progress could solve the problems. There was a struggle over the recommendations for action. They were going in separate directions: from sustaining natural resources through global economic planning, to continued investment in technology to make a more effective exploitation of natural resources possible.

The preparatory work and the following conferences can here be seen as parts of a diffraction of the natural resource discourse. Two types of enunciation, two concepts – conservation and utilisation – appear in the same discursive formation. Foucault characterises the alternatives within a discourse, in one instance, as *points of equivalence*. These alternatives are formed in the same way and on the basis of the same rules. Foucault argues that

> the conditions of their appearance are identical; they are situated at the same level; and instead of constituting a mere defect in coherence, they form an alternative: even if they do not have the same importance and even if they are not equally represented in statements, they appear in the form of 'either... or'[45]

In the natural resource discourse, utilisation and conservation form such points of equivalence. They do not appear as incompatible elements, since participants could use both words. Nevertheless, they came to symbolise two radically different approaches; and utilisation was gradually getting the upper hand in the natural resource discourse.

Truman's Point Four Program

Truman saw the issue of natural resources as vitally important to his national security policy. This was perhaps expressed most clearly in the aid programme – Point Four – that he presented in his inauguration speech in January 1949. The address was dominated by foreign policy and the programme was named after its fourth article: aid to the 'underdeveloped areas'.[46] American science and technological development should be made accessible to these less successful countries. The American dream was to be exported and would be made possible even for the poor of this world. More than half of the world's population lived on the brink of misery. Their poverty was a hazard not only to themselves but also to more successful countries.

For the first time in human history, Truman declared, the knowledge and skill were at hand to prevent this misery. The United States was 'pre-eminent among nations in the development of industrial and scientific techniques'. It should use this position in a 'worldwide effort for the achievement of peace, plenty, and freedom' by sharing its knowledge, rather than its financial assets.[47] 'The material resources which we can afford to use for assistance are limited. But our imponderable resources in technical knowledge are constantly growing and are inexhaustible.' US aid was available to 'peace loving peoples'. The underlying Cold War rhetoric was clear. 'Democracy alone can supply the vitalising force to stir the peoples of the world into triumphant action, not only against their human oppressors but also against their ancient enemies – hunger, misery and despair.'[48]

To understand the rationale behind Point Four, it is necessary to see it in its context. Truman's Inauguration Speech was mostly directed towards the containment of communism, which posed a threat to recovery and peace in the post-war world. By resorting to universal principles, he justified specific policies. In Point Three of the speech, Truman called for a joint defence arrangement in the North Atlantic area, a proposal that was eventually manifested in the North Atlantic Treaty Organisation.[49]

The speech was a great success. The *Washington Post* declared in its headline: 'Truman Proposes "Fair Deal" Plan for the World.' According to the editorial of the *New York Times*, Franklin Roosevelt, Woodrow Wilson, Theodore Roosevelt and Abraham Lincoln would have approved and joined in the applause.[50] He received a positive response from the scientific world too. John A. Hannah, President of the Association of Land Grant Colleges and Universities, wrote to Truman immediately after his inauguration speech and offered him the aid of the state universities. Truman welcomed the support. Since the economy of underdeveloped countries was predominantly dependent on agriculture, land grant universities gained a key role in his aid strategy.[51]

Truman linked Point Four with the planned resource conference. In April 1949, he wrote to Secretary of State Dean Acheson on the issue. Truman called it the 'UN scientific conference... concerning utilization of resources'. The conservation side of the conference seems to have diminished in the President's mind.

> Shouldn't [the conference] be tied in to the Point Four Program? Point Four centres around technical knowledge to develop economic resources so the conference ought to be a good way of getting the factual information which it needs as a background. The Conference would also be another good link between the Point Four Program and the UN.[52]

The planned conference served US foreign policy well. Yet, to explain the political interest in the state of the world's natural resources solely in Cold War terms is probably misleading. There was a manifest concern that the global resources situation could be a threat to future living conditions. The food situation in the world was an urgent and serious matter for western governments. Colonel Laurens van der Post gives one example that illustrates how the British perceived the problem. In his popular book *Venture to the Interior* (1952) he describes his journey as a British envoy to investigate the little known territory of Nyasaland in central Africa in 1949.

> The matter was urgent. Production of food in the world and particularly in the Empire and Britain was beginning to fail, in a sort of geometric retrogression, to keep up with increases of population. Moreover, as our troubles with the Argentine so clearly showed, anything that could help to make Britain independent of alien sources of food should be done, and done as quickly as possible. There was a chance that these areas might help.[53]

Many of the people that were involved in the United States' Foreign Aid Programs had got their working experience from the domestic development programmes that were launched during the Franklin D. Roosevelt era, such as the Farmers' Security Administration, Farmers' Credit Administration and Rural Electricity Agency. The relative success of these programmes had suggested that it was possible to improve living conditions and had probably created a confidence that much could also be done against global misery. The positive experiences arising from the New Deal could now be brought to the international arena. According to the Truman biographer David McCoullough, Truman's inauguration speech in 1949 became so celebrated because it extended 'the promise of America, beyond America'.[54]

The fourth point of Truman's inauguration speech was institutionalised through the Economic Cooperation Administration. The Point Four Program was modest at the start, but within three years aid agreements were signed with 34 countries, amounting to an annual cost of $155.6 million. $30 million were spent in South Korea before the outbreak of the Korean War and $110 million after it ended, $100 million in Southeast Asia, and another $180 million in Taiwan.[55]

Contemporary American views on the programme varied greatly: from a gift to the two-thirds of the earth's people who were hungry, ill-clothed and inadequately sheltered, to altruism combined with stockpiling of strategic materials and stimulation of markets for the products of industrial countries. The State Department's official chronicler of the Marshall Plan, Joseph Marion Jones, wrote that the Point Four Program suggested 'not the limits but the infinite possibilities of influencing the policies, attitudes, and actions of other countries by statesmanship in Washington'.[56] Some argued that assistance should be available to all that needed and accepted it, others that it should be restricted to those whose political and economic views did not conflict with those of the United States. The famous Harvard economist John Kenneth Galbraith stated: 'Above and far beyond Point Four, *We must put ourselves on the side of truly popular government with whatever pressure we can properly employ.*'[57]

In an essay 'Let's examine our Santa Claus Complex' in the *Saturday Evening Post* in 1949, Vogt criticised the Point Four plans. His continued critique of the programme in the 1950s and insistence that US foreign aid should only be given to countries with birth control programmes, made him a target for accusations of being a fascist as well as a racist.[58]

Historian Walter A. McDougall sees in Point Four and even in the Marshall Plan the beginning of a tradition in American foreign policy which he labels 'Global Meliorism'. It was characterised by idealistic crusades, driven by a 'do-gooder impulse' and by the belief that only the United States had the power, technology, wealth and altruism necessary to reform nations. McDougall tries to separate the global melioristic tradition (which he scorns) from the tradition of containment (of which he approves).[59] However, the conclusion of this study is the opposite of McDougall's politically motivated simplifications. These two 'traditions' spring from the same root, both originating from the resource–security discourse. Social unrest spurred by resource shortage was of great concern to American security interests. Economic and political stability was a crucial means to curb communist, as well as fascist, revolts.

Even though some conservationists criticised the Truman administration's aid plans, the geopolitical concerns of the United States in fact created a platform even for critical scientists like Vogt. One such forum that was particularly important for post-war conservationists was the planned natural resource conference at Lake Success.

The United Nations Summons Resource Experts

'Today the United Nations is embarking on a new phase of its programme to build the foundations for permanent peace.'[60] The words are Secretary General Lie's in his introductory speech at the United Nations Scientific Conference on the Conservation and Utilization of Resources (UNSCCUR) August 17, 1949. Three years after President Truman's proposal, 550 participants from 48 countries gathered at Lake Success, New York, for the Conference. Their respective governments appointed the participants and, in addition to them, representatives from non-governmental organisations and so-called independent experts were invited by the conference secretariat.[61]

One year before the conference, Andrei Gromyko, then USSR's representative to the UN and Deputy Minister of Foreign Affairs, gave his assurance that the USSR had no objections to make to the preliminary programme.[62] But with the growing tensions between the superpowers, the Soviet Union finally backed out in the spring of 1949. Except for Czechoslovakia and Yugoslavia, none of the East European countries took part in the conference. The Guomindang regime in China was positive to the conference idea, but the country did not attend since, at that time, it was in the midst of a civil war.[63] News media from all over the world covered the event. CBS, for example, broadcast a series of radio programmes in connection with the conference with the title *You and Survival*. Even though western journalists dominated, the information bureau was very satisfied that media from all continents covered the conference.[64]

In his introductory speech Lie declared that the United Nations was calling on science to 'mobilise technical knowledge in support of one of the high purposes of the Charter – to raise the standards of living'. Lie related the conference to the resource–security theory. Lie reminded the congregated scientists and policymakers that an increased standard of living was indeed one of the keys to peace. 'For behind most wars stand the spectres of hunger and want – effective warmongers of the past.' Solutions to these problems might not be as spectacular as those in the political field, but they were of vital importance to world peace.[65]

Lie set the tone for the conference, stressing the motive as it had evolved in the preparatory work.

> Together you hold the technical keys which can unlock new wealth from the earth for the benefit of mankind. You know that underlying all economic shortages is the basic problem of how to develop and, in developing, how to conserve the earth's resources.[66]

The scientists should point at scientific and technical solutions, but not address their political implications. The outcome of the conference was to be a source of scientific and technical information, emphatically not resolutions that governments would be compelled to follow.

Julius A. Krug, United States Secretary of the Interior, expressed high confidence in the ability of the scientists gathered there to take care of resource shortages. Scientific progress would serve world peace by providing for an efficient use of resources. The work of the scientists at the conference would begin to show politicians what could and should happen in the world. Krug hoped that scientific progress and service in the peaceful and constructive fields represented at the conference would wipe out the destruction of the last war from human memory. Krug's vision was in somewhat Messianic vein.

> When the historian of the year 2000 looks back over the twentieth century, he may find that the soil and plant and forest scientists, the fuel, power and mineral experts, and the resource economists made up a team that helped save the world's resource base when it was in great danger. And he may say that these groups crowded two hundred and fifty years of industrial progress into fifty years and raised the living standards of the whole under-developed world beyond anything known in history. He may say that the United Nations gained confidence, unity and power in the process.[67]

According to Fairfield Osborn, in his key address at UNSCCUR, the accomplishing of the conference was a sign that a new and penetrating awareness had reached the nations. They now perceived their welfare to be intimately linked with conditions in countries on the other side of the globe.[68]

How was the natural resources situation presented at the conference? There were two major themes on the nature of population–resource issues. Several speakers started from the assumption that *scarcity problems* were fundamental to the natural resource situation. Many likewise expressed the *global character* of natural resource problems.

This conclusion is supported by a content analysis of the proceedings from the Plenary Meeting at UNSCCUR in 1949. It indicates that two thirds of the contributions expressed in some form the notion that natural resource issues involved a scarcity problem. Almost as many presented resource problems to be of global concern. Of course, for some it may also have been an unspoken presupposition, so that they started from an assumption of scarcity without putting it in words. Nevertheless, at the Land Resources session, which addressed more nation specific issues, only a minority explicitly represented these views. Roughly one third expressed the scarcity notion and not even one fifth the global. One might perhaps have expected more participants to speak in global terms at an international conference. However, most of the participants had been chosen by their own countries and were giving national experience papers, discussing

Table 2. Perceived natural resource problems at UNSCCUR,
number of articles (%)

	Number of articles	Scarcity problem	Global problem
Plenary session	88	56 (63.6%)	53 (62.5%)
Land resources session	143	55 (37.1%)	26 (18.2%)
Total	241	111 (46.1%)	80 (33.7%)

Number of articles containing word-indicators referring to natural resources as a scarcity problem and a global problem respectively, in Proceedings, Vol. 1 and 6. The texts were scanned and searched by computer. The following words were used to indicate a perceived natural resources shortage: 'limit' (either discussed as a natural resources constraint per se or as caused by social, educational, technical or economic factors) OR 'shortage' OR 'scarce'. For natural resources discussed in global perspective the following indicator words were used: 'global' OR 'universal' OR 'world' AND 'resources' OR (including various kinds of resources, e.g. fish, oil, timber) OR 'unity' OR 'whole' OR 'one' OR 'over' OR 'population' OR 'need' OR 'demand' OR 'problems' OR 'future' OR 'comparison' OR 'scale'. The words were then read in their context and all irrelevant passages were discarded.

how each country was dealing with a specific resource area. This background was especially reflected at a more specialised session like 'Land Resources'.

That resources were viewed in terms of a constraint problem did not mean that most speakers emphasised the need for conservation. The solutions were to be found in scientific development. The famous soil scientist Charles E. Kellogg was typical of this approach.

> Every natural soil has certain limits to its potentialities, and through modern science these limits may be expanded in terms of kinds of crops and yields. No very close relationship exists between the natural fertility of soils and their actual productivity in society. The important factor is their response to management.[69]

The UN conference had turned out to be restricted in its mandate. It was not to result in any resolutions or deal with the issues of birth control and family planning. Carmelia Bryce Pinchot, the widow of Gifford Pinchot, was upset by the restrictions on formulating recommendations to governments. She was requested to give a brief statement during the concluding addresses, where she took the opportunity of attacking the remit of the conference.

> What upside-down, Humpty Dumpty nonsense is this? I should like to ask Mr. Lie since when have scientists become so dangerous that they are not to be trusted even with the little power implied in the making of a recommendation? What lack of faith in the creative mechanisms of democracy is responsible for this implied prohibition to function in the field of policy-making?[70]

The primary purpose of the restricted conference was to accomplish an inventory of the earth's natural resources. The agenda was divided into eight categories of resources: minerals, fuel, energy, water, forests, land, wildlife and fish. The reports that were presented dealt mainly with which resources were limited, what future needs could restrain industrial expansion, and how the present and the predicted shortages of natural resources could be overcome by applications of advanced science and technology. The disagreements revolved around what nature could endure. Colin Clark, economic advisor to the government of Queensland, Australia, repudiated the notion that high fertility rates should be artificially reduced as 'groundless economically'. There was no problem in population growth since technology would increase food supplies. The FAO's vice director Herbert Broadly argued that the world agricultural area needed to be increased by one third in order to meet the needs of the growing population. For the most part, this need could be supplied by cultivation of the Tropics.[71] Broadly's proposal met great opposition from many participants. They dismissed it as unrealistic and argued that it would lead to the devastation of the natural resources of the Tropics, in particular because the soil would be stripped of nutrients

The conference revealed growing concern from poorer countries about the depletion of their natural resources. Most delegates from the South confined themselves to urging Western industries not to draw as unrestrictedly as in the past on their countries' raw materials. A few of them, like the geological adviser to the Indian Department of Scientific Research, went further, criticising Western resource imperialism: 'A growing trend towards conservation of mineral resources in hitherto backward countries and their utilisation (or barter) for national benefit will be the most significant development of the coming decade.' He expected the result to be that Western industries would not be able to continue such exploitation of raw materials, unless it was on 'the basis of reciprocity and on more liberal terms of exchange with manufactured goods which these backward countries need in building up a more healthy national economy and standard of living'.[72]

Most speeches were essentially directed towards technical perfection of resource management. The rare calls for equitable distribution contrasted with the majority of the reports at UNSCCUR and its appeals for technical keys to unlock new wealth from the earth's resources.

Although in a minority, several speakers at the conference emphasised the need for a new conservation-inspired approach, and for a moral basis for science. India's Ambassador to the United States claimed in her concluding address that the common man 'feels the time has come, when, in the interest of his own survival – in the interests of civilisation and of humanity, science must have a moral basis'.[73]

The chairman of the National Research Council in the United States made the case for Lewis Mumford's 'biotechnic civilisation': He argued that it was appropriate, both directly and by analogy, that the United Nations, which was devoted to the elimination of conflict between humans, should sponsor this Conference. Because conservation and wise utilisation of resources required the elimination of another equally serious conflict – that between man and nature. Both these crusades depended upon a reaffirmation of human values. Stimulated by the rapid growth of physical science, people had thought too much about humanity's supposed conquest of nature, and too little of their place in the pattern of nature. Human welfare and survival demands appreciation of biological needs, as well as a better understanding of the means whereby humanity can be adapted more effectively to the environment of which it is a part. He warned that if nations continued to seek satisfaction and survival by pillaging nature and sister nations, then a catastrophe for all the human race lay ahead. In contrast nations could, through science, peacefully gain those material benefits which they had sought in vain to acquire through armed conflict. For this to be achieved, there must be a more intimate partnership between scientists and policymakers.[74]

A representative of the Fisheries Laboratory in England also connected to Lewis Mumford's diagnosis 'that society, to survive, must work to the pattern of nature, not against it'. Graham saw a direct parallel between present western culture and the declining Roman Empire as described by Edward Gibbon in *Decline and Fall of the Roman Empire* (1776–88). The exhaustion of natural resources, political quarrelling and rigidity incapable of coping with attacks from barbarians or the impact of natural catastrophes had marked the fall of the empire. 'The connection is easy to see: greed and grab naturally lead straight to quarrelling.'[75]

Osborn concluded that the natural resource situation was not a problem only for scientists. 'Conservation becomes a political and administrative problem, an educational, even a social, cultural, and ethical problem. Therefore, it is not one with which the scientists or technologists can deal single-handed.' [76]

After describing the stupendous speed of industrialisation, Osborn concluded that the rapid exhaustion of the world's resources called for a new economic order in the world. Conservation 'in the sense that it implies the wise use and equitable distribution of the Earth's resources, offers a point of synthesis for international cooperation for which the world is waiting'. [77] He was not the only one to express this view. The notion of a 'world household', which stressed global interdependence on natural resources, was expressed by 32 out of 88 speakers at the Plenary Session.[78] Yet, the more radical conservationists were certainly in a minority. Osborn's political suggestions of equitable distribution contrasted with the majority of the reports, which were more in the line of Lie's appeal for technical keys which could unlock new wealth from the earth's resources.

The conservationists' focus troubled some of the participants. James Thorn, president of ECOSOC, felt compelled to define the sort of conservation that was in question in his concluding address. 'Conservation, therefore, does not mean the hoarding of resources. It means the application of practices of wise utilisation which you have been discussing here. It is now a wall set up for static defence against distant and doubtful dangers.'[79] With this definition the title of the conference became a tautology, a natural consequence when utilisation practice defined conservation for its own purposes.

Conservation could serve as an instrument, part of the machinery of the economy. But in its character as a reform movement it was not as easily manageable by political power. It was hardly bland or non-controversial. Conservationists were invited to policy discussions after the war, and were given a media platform. However, they were never wholeheartedly embraced, and all became increasingly controversial as critics of the present order.

The Conservation Alternative

But the conservationists, who had had to relinquish their key issues in the preparation committee, had in the meantime been working for an alternative conference at Lake Success. UNESCO's General Assembly decided in Beirut, in 1948, to work towards a conference arranged by UNESCO together with the IUPN, which would deal with a worldwide programme for the conservation of food resources. The International Technical Conference on the Protection of Nature (ITCPN) gathered 250 participants from 58 countries and was held at Lake Success at same time as UNSCCUR. This parallel meeting was scheduled so that it was possible to take part in sessions at both of the conferences, an opportunity of which many took advantage, including Borgström and Osborn.[80]

ITCPN concentrated on five main topics, of which two completely dominated the programme: ecology and education. Ecology took up most of the programme. Everything is connected together, all things are dependent on one another – that was the central line of thought that was repeated time and time again in the addresses to the conference.[81] At UNSCCUR, too, many of the speakers emphasised that the complex problems of natural resources had to be solved through this insight; but it was those participants who were also taking part in the alternative conference who particularly advocated this view.[82]

The general secretary of the parallel conference, Jean-Paul Harroy, regarded the handling of these issues as 'a new orientation to the idea of Nature Protection', in essence a deepened understanding of ecological interplay.[83] Several of the participants in the conference expressed the opinion that the education of the public had a decisively important role for the success of nature protection. If it did not leave its scientific Helicon and become rooted among the public it ran the risk of always having to yield to economic interests.[84] Harroy summarised the ideas of moral edification from nature's intrinsic value and the pedagogical task of explaining humans' dependence on their environment.

> Unless a population is aware of its moral obligation and the material advantages that are to be had by respecting the living communities which form its environment and from which sustenance is derived, no laws, no matter how severe, can save these natural communities from disintegration and even destruction when some kind of economic profit is at stake.[85]

ITCPN's first resolution was to exhort UN councils to promote the study of human ecology. The importance of interdisciplinary studies was also emphasised. Since ecological issues trespassed the boundaries of academic subjects, they required the abandonment of separate disciplines and scientific specialisation.

Harroy emphasised that they were promoting a new conceptualisation of natural protection. The time had passed when conservation could be directed merely towards constructing regulations and setting apart pieces of land for nature reserve areas to safeguard biota for aesthetic scientific reasons. The precarious situation of the world demanded that conservation direct itself towards the political management of the global issues of natural resources.[86]

Both the conferences at Lake Success gave the participants new influence and contributed to increased international connections. It gave the newly founded IUPN a great impetus. As we shall see in the next chapter, it also effected a new take on domestic conservation.

The Third World Emerges

UNSCCUR had the socially symbolic function of displaying an ultimate global collective unity. Fredric Jameson speaks of *socially symbolic acts* that, consciously or unconsciously, are aimed at solving or neutralising society's contradictions, both explicitly and symbolically.[87] In this respect, UNSCCUR can be seen as an attempt to solve contradictions in the post-war world order: to neutralise the different political and social interests in natural resources of different people and classes the world over, by pointing to the globality of resource problems. UNSCCUR also declared that the population–resource crisis should be regarded first as a scientific rather than a political problem. It could be described as a political problem only to the extent that science failed, through either lack of support or lack of co-ordination. In contrast, the examination of the planning of the conference and Truman's Point Four Program reveals it was indeed a political issue.

Both David Harvey and geographer Robert D. Sack have claimed that spatial practices are not neutral in social affairs. The way in which spatial categories are conceptualised forms, among other things, policy making. It is therefore important to note that the globalisation agenda arose from a Euro-American definition of the common destiny of the world. Globalisation as a concept involves a mental intensification of the awareness of the world as a unity, as well as a physical compression of the world through international institutions, worldwide transportation, information technology, and transnational flow of capital and information.[88]

To understand what United States President Harry S. Truman implied when he introduced the concept of 'underdeveloped areas', it is necessary to relate his statement to the system of statements that was used by the political powers of the time in speaking about world relations. Truman's statement as well as the UN conference itself was a part of the globalisation discourse. The term 'discourse', as employed by French philosopher Foucault , is an ongoing historic process of creating meaning by systematising statements, revealing power regulations in language and rhetorical techniques. Discourse is a comprehensive term for what is said, written, symbolised or manifested about a certain area, e.g., natural resource policies. The order of a discourse is maintained through public statements as well as through unspoken and unconscious procedures. Discourse is thus expressed in a manner of talking about its particular object as well as through related practices and institutions. Symbols must be understood in relation to their specific use within a discourse, and the rules that guide this use – their *grammatics,* as Michel Foucault calls it.

In this definition, discourse is seen as sustained by social and political power and in turn it legitimises a given order. Institutions give it authority, for example, the university system, the juridical system, legislative bodies etc. A discourse is understood to make generalising claims: the world is defined in universalising terms. It relies upon rules of exclusion that approve certain cognitions, but exclude others through its ordering procedures. These selective mechanisms involve claims of truth and rules about what it is possible and not possible to say, and who is allowed to speak – in short, what is accepted as the normal and rational way to see and deal with things. As Foucault points out, science is used as an exclusion mechanism for that which is regarded as irrational or abnormal to the discourse.[89] Following this line of reasoning, it is not surprising that the first major UN conference, a conference that was intended to outline strategies for the conservation and utilisation of the world's resources, was a scientific one.

Development philosopher Wolfgang Sachs has emphasised that Truman's definition of the poorer countries as 'underdeveloped areas' in his inaugural address was an expression of the President's worldview. All nations of the world were perceived to be moving along the same track, sharing the same goal and intended destiny. The West was leading this march, the others were following at different paces.[90]

Sociologist Ernest Gellner states that one of the essential concomitants of industrial society is the kind of cultural homogeneity demanded by nationalism.[91] However, cultural homogeneity is not tied only to nationalism. It is only one of industrial society's important characteristics and globalism is certainly another. The nation state provided the shared common culture that was necessary for industrialism's demand for a flexible social order. The development of Fordism demanded not only greater markets but greater cultural unity. Globalisation of the economy can be seen as the inevitable development of the logic of capitalism. After the industrial nation state had fulfilled its function, globalism took over. Of course, we have not yet seen the complete fulfilment of this phase in late capitalism.

Unrest in many of the so-called less developed countries grew in the late 1940s. In spite of the Truman administration's efforts, the appeal of communism attracted many nationalist leaders. In countries like Vietnam, Indonesia, Iran, Tunisia, Morocco and Egypt there were concerted efforts to free the countries from their colonial past and to gain domestic control of their own resources. Movements towards national liberation in the colonies often focused on discontent over the adoption of Fordism. Resources were exploited, local cultures were destroyed, and an indigenous elite benefited. These movements could appear threatening to the world order, especially if they had socialist tendencies. As Harvey states:

> The USA's geopolitical hegemony was threatened, and having begun the post-war era by using anticommunism and militarism as a vehicle for geopolitical and economic stabilisation, the United States soon found itself facing the problem of 'guns or butter' in its own fiscal economic policy.[92]

The Truman administration opposed European colonialism, and not only because it interfered with American trade policies. In the words of historian Melvyn P. Leffler: 'Because economic relationships and standards of living shaped geopolitical relationships and correlations of power, American policymakers wanted to co-opt nationalist movements in what became known as the Third World.'[93] The Truman administration opposed European colonialism, denounced British policy, and was especially concerned with the status of the Philippines. It is important to note that an enormously extensive and powerful apparatus of western military force accompanied the immense project of decolonisation.

Primarily through the UN, the ex-colonial countries took on a more independent role. At the Bandung conference in Java in 1955, 29 Asian and African countries, among them Burma, the People's Republic of China, Ceylon, the Indian Union and Indonesia, renounced both old and new capitalism and proclaimed themselves to be a third force, beside the Eastern and Western blocs. During the period from 1955 to 1971 UN membership grew rapidly, as former colonies became independent nations. The organisation had started with 51 members in 1945. By 1959 total membership had reached 83. By 1972 there were 132 members.[94] With these new nations, a growing majority of the member-states had an interest in strengthening the role of ECOSOC on behalf of the Security Council. However, until the late 1950s the UN was still of great importance to US interests; but gradually the world organisation became less the instrument of its foreign policy. As the Cold War evolved, Roosevelt's emphasis on 'one world' was replaced by the 'free world' of the Truman doctrine.[95]

After 1945, multilateral aid was directed towards regions damaged by the world war. Gradually, as the number of member states from Asia, Africa and South America increased, development issues in these areas attained increased attention in the UN. In 1949 the General Assembly decided on a new and finally extended development programme: Expanded Programme of Technical Assistance. It was financed outside the regular budget of the UN through voluntary contributions from member states. The aid consisted primarily of sending out experts and awarding grants. Another example of a multilateral aid initiative was the Colombo Plan. It aimed at strengthening the ties between the countries in the Commonwealth by co-ordinating development and aid initiatives between them. Bilateral aid dominated, of which Point Four stands out as the prime example. However, other countries followed at around the same time. Sweden, which contributed to the UN programmes, started its bilateral aid in 1952 with technical aid, and in 1962 for the first time financial bilateral aid was granted by the government.[96]

The globalisation discourse was expressed in various aspects of society, such as film-making. In contrast to the depiction of nature in the poorer continents seen in blockbuster movies of the 1930s like *King Kong* (1933), a more sensitive approach to making films about wildlife began after World War II. Films like *Savage Splendour* (1949) or Disney's *True Life Adventure* series had an educational and conservationist slant. In the early 1950s, nature films made their appearance on television, and transmitted a view of the nature and peoples of the 'dark' continents with intensified impact. According to environmental historians William Beinart and Peter Coates, these new trends in wildlife films 'popularised new scientific approaches that internationalised conservation thinking in a way which could incorporate American predilections for extravagant scenery'.[97]

In these post-war processes, the inhabitants of the poorer continents emerged as agents, and as such they were potential consumers. When this mass of individuals – world population – became apparent, the resources the world supplied appeared in a new light. The population–resource crisis was seen as imminent.

Through metaphors, language can be renewed and can thereby provide new conditions for understanding the world. Philosopher Paul Ricœur has two starting points in his theory of metaphors. First, when a word meets a receiver, appears in a context, it becomes an event. Second, words are polysemous. That is, a metaphor can only exist in a context, a word in itself can not be a metaphor. The metaphor is thus a statement, a short parable. The metaphor tells something about something. It has a predicate function by providing a statement about the subject in the clause. Thus, the metaphor is not just a figurative synonym, it also provides an opportunity to go beyond lexical language.[98]

There is a collision between the signified and signifier in *living* metaphors. A literal understanding becomes absurd; it has to be reinterpreted to make sense. The meaning cannot be found in dictionary definitions. By abandoning the current lexical codifying rules, living metaphors can express new thoughts. Old words attain a new meaning by being placed in a new context. Metaphors are the principal means in the struggle of indefinitely extending the battlefront of the expressed at the expense of the unexpressed.[99]

The receiver's association to old frames of reference and to the new context provides new information, creates a new understanding. Something new can be said of our existence. New meanings appear, which previously could not be expressed through language.[100] Through metaphors we can get a glimpse of the moments of epistemological change that open new doors in our understanding.

The shift in cognitive perception that saw the inhabitants of poorer countries as agents within a world population is expressed by the development of new metaphors, such as 'under-developed' and 'the Third World'. By the end of the 1940s 'under-developed' appears as a label for countries and regions inhabited by these masses, describing them as economically and socially incompletely developed.[101] The term 'the Third World' was coined in 1952 by the French demographer Alfred Sauvy in an article in *L'Observateur*. He ends his essay 'Three worlds, one planet' with an allusion to the French Revolution. 'For at last this forgotten, impoverished, despised Third World, just like the Third Estate, shall also become something.'[102] This process was important for the development of the notion of a 'world household' – a key theme in the new conservation ideology.

Population and Power Politics

Before the war, the USA was not involved in any military alliances; it had no troops stationed in foreign countries and a relatively small military budget. At the end of 1950, it had provided economic aid to western Europe through the Marshall Plan; it had established a military alliance, NATO, and it was deeply engaged in building up a new security order in Europe. In an attempt to halt the spread of communism throughout Asia, the United States engaged in a war in Korea.

At the turn of the new decade, international developments enforced the older fears of a communist takeover. In 1949, the communists seized power in mainland China and proclaimed aspirations for leadership in South East Asia. In late 1950, the People's Republic of China intervened in the Korean conflict. Two of the largest and most populous nations on earth, the Soviet Union and China, had become communist allies. In 1949, the Soviet Union claimed to have mastered the atomic bomb in addition to its already superior conventional capacity in Europe. Advances in military aviation meant that American territory was no longer safe from a Soviet attack. The industrial infrastructure of the United States, the source of its superior power, could be destroyed. And the United States could no longer count on being able to mobilise after an armed conflict had begun. Therefore, it might be compelled to avoid using its atomic arsenal against the Soviet Union. According to Leffler 'These scenarios struck fear in US policymakers and made them even more dubious about their ability to take risks to counter mounting revolutionary nationalism on the periphery.'[103] Truman gave the go-ahead to develop the hydrogen bomb. Paul Nitze, who called for an immediate build-up of American forces to keep the military technological advantage with the United States, replaced the more moderate Kennan as Secretary of State. [104]

The growing concern that communist agitation would take advantage of unstable conditions, caused by overpopulation and subsequent resource shortages, strengthened the idea of agricultural science as an important means to create stable political conditions. When the Rockefeller Foundation initiated an agricultural programme in Mexico, no concerns were voiced about population growth. From 1946 onwards, the Foundation became increasingly concerned with the concept of 'population explosion'. In December 1947, trustee John D. Rockefeller III, became personally involved and advocated a greater stress by the Foundation on the population issue. In 1948 the International Health Division of the Foundation began drafting a plan on population research. For this purpose they employed an ecologist to work with one of its physicians.

Having read Vogt's book, the new president of the Rockefeller Foundation, Chester I. Barnard, became concerned by its implications. He linked the message to the Mexican programme. In 1949 the population experts finished a report, in which they articulated a conceptual framework for *human ecology*.[105] Even though the Foundation never reached a consensus that could lead to a programme on population control, the subject was implanted in the Foundation's enterprises. This approach was well in line with studies that saw finite limits to agricultural means of support, and high population growth as a cause of poverty. Following the resource–security reasoning, it also acknowledged a political danger in areas where population reached the limit of food subsistence.[106]

In 1950, the Rockefeller Foundation expanded its Mexican programme to Columbia. In 1951 the foundation published a report, 'The World Food Problem, Agriculture, and the Rockefeller Foundation', which linked concerns about overpopulation to geopolitics. Overpopulation and inadequate or unequally divided resources were the root cause of global political tensions. Agriculture thus had an important political role to play in the Superpower struggle. After Mao Zedong's forces had prevailed in 1949, India was seen as the next likely country to go communist. Following a recommendation by one of the trustees, the President of Massachusetts Institute of Technology, the Foundation's new agricultural programme was directed towards India. This new strategy linked scientific research on high crop yields and the issues of overpopulation. 'I suspect that India may be fertile ground for activity in this field. The overpopulation, the low living standards and the threat of Communism are of course well-known.'[107] This conviction was to become one of the key factors behind the Green Revolution, for which the Foundation got credit when its scientist, Norman E. Borlaug, received the Nobel Peace Prize in 1970. Nelson Rockefeller was in 1950 appointed to chair the International Development Advisory Board. The Board linked national security issues with population and resource supply. The Board urged for strong efforts by the government to cooperate with underdeveloped countries 'in a vigorous food production drive which would break the back of famine and hunger'.[108]

The *Second World Food Survey* was published by the FAO in 1952. The methodologies for estimating the level of food supplies in the world had improved. Still, it presented a gloomy picture. It even raised certain figures. The report estimated that two thirds of the world population were undernourished.

Natural resources continued to be essential for the USA's Cold War strategy during the 1950s. In 1952, for instance, the Material Policy Commission appointed by the Eisenhower administration reported that it was of vital importance to make national plans to overcome shortages of raw material if the United States was going to fight the Cold War successfully.[109] Eisenhower became convinced about the necessity of his predecessor's aid programme, in the light of the emergence of the non-aligned movement in 1955 and the Suez crisis of 1956. He endorsed the resource–security theory stating that 'the freedom of nations can be menaced not only by guns but by the poverty that communism can exploit'.[110]

The USA's geopolitical ambitions are essential for understanding the issue of natural resources in the early post-war era. The situation must be tied to the transformation of economic production and its related modes of social and political regulation. Fordism and the geopolitics of the West are like two halves of the same walnut. The development of capitalist accumulation created a mass production that reached out for a global mass market, which depended on a secure supply of raw materials from foreign markets.

The debate on natural resources reflects the development of the world economy. Emerging environmental concern was to a large extent a feature of the new mass middle class that arose after World War II. Environmental historian Samuel P. Hays interprets the emergence of environmentalism as a major influence in shaping a new, consumer-oriented economy after 1945. Environmental impulses served as a major influence on the modernisation of the economy, according to Hays. New demand factors were brought to the fore that eventually generated new modes of production. Modern technology was promoted, which supposedly made production more resource-efficient and less polluting.[111] In this respect, the message of the conservationists served the discourse of modernisation well: although the wider implications of that message were not as pleasant for the political powers, especially since consumption continued to rise dramatically and new components were constantly being introduced.

In 1953, the Population Council was created, headed by John D. Rockefeller III. The organisation was to predict population increases, survey resources and study the potentialities of science. *The New York Times* applauded the creation of the organisation, since the task of feeding a world had to be faced 'as resolutely as we face the task of fighting a ruthless enemy in world war'. In its editorial the newspaper attributed the awareness of a population–resource crisis to Osborn and Vogt

> In the last ten years we have witnessed a revival of the Malthusian doctrine that the world's population is increasing more rapidly than its supply of food, minerals and other commodities considered necessary for the

maintenance of a high standard of living. We owe this revival largely to Fairfield Osborn ('Our Plundered Planet') and to William Vogt ('Road to Survival') who have been followed by economists, public health officials and governments with predictions of misery.[112]

And others would follow, such as Karl Sax who estimated that population growth by the year 2600 would have resulted in a population density that would only give each human being one square meter. Hence the title of his book: *Standing Room Only: The Challenge of Overpopulation* (1955).[113]

In the science fiction genre, Frederik Pohl and C. M. Kornbluth's satire, *The Space Merchants* (1953) reflected environmentalist apprehension. They pictured a future, not very distant, that was marked by the growth of consumer capitalism and corporate America in an overpopulated and polluted world, where privacy had to be bought by the minute. The main character is in charge of the biggest sales job of his career: convincing people to sign up to become pioneer settlers of the sterile planet Venus. To be associated with the 'consies', the subversive conservation movement, is high treason in this overpopulated world of consumerism. Finally they succeed in taking over the entire expedition to Venus, where they will start human civilisation anew. The main character's wife, an undercover conservationist, confesses on the way to Venus: 'Sure, we Consies wanted space travel. The human race needs Venus. It needs an unspoiled, unwracked, unexploited, unlooted, ...unpirated, undevastated... There aren't too many planets around that the race can expand into.'[114]

In the 1950s the new conservationism developed with the mood of the times, such as new demands for capitalist production modes and mass consumption, globalisation discourse and new technological possibilities of mass destruction. The focus on natural resources had created a public arena for conservationists in the United States. The priority given to the issue on the political agenda legitimised their framing of the problem. According to Russell J. Dalton, the situation was much the same throughout western Europe. In Britain, the destruction of resources during the war made conservation a legitimate concern; in particular, the wartime need for agricultural products had transformed rural Britain. Conservationists saw an opportunity in the post-war planning for reconstruction of the country. British legislation established the Nature Conservancy as a government agency in 1949. The destruction wrought by the war gave the same impetus to conservation ideas and resource planning in Belgium, France and The Netherlands.[115]

With the escalation of the Cold War, the utilisation of natural resources became an increasingly important factor for the aspirations of the superpowers. From an initial emphasis on both conservation and utilisation, the focus came to be directed solely towards improved utilisation. In a world marked by escalating competition for world hegemony, the critics of prevalent political–economical utilisation practices became voices crying in the wilderness.

US domestic resource shortage was no longer a major concern by the 1950s, as it had been in the immediate post-war years. It was completely overshadowed by an enormous confidence in the ability of science and technology to produce endless abundance. Kenneth Galbraith described it as 'the affluent society'. There seemed to be no limit to what could be produced and consumed.[116]

It is sometimes argued that Malthus has not had much credibility in North America, because of its abundance of space, land, and resources. Nevertheless, as this chapter has shown, during the first years after the war, there was at least some concern that resource shortage might affect even the North American continent. Malthusian concerns were prominent in policy making and debate after World War II. In fact, as the next chapter will make evident, American conservationists inspired Malthusianism internationally.

4

Neo-Malthusianism in Harvest Time

While most of Europe was recovering from the war, the Swedish economy was thriving and the welfare state could distribute a rich harvest to its citizens. The period between 1945 and 1951 has accordingly been designated in Sweden as the 'first harvest time'. The government tried to accomplish full employment, social reforms, efficient production and increased opportunity for workers' participation. Yet in spite of the political prospects of a bright future for the Swedish people, this was also the time when neo-Malthusian warnings exploded in the Swedish media.

The topic of this chapter is how the population–resource crisis was presented in Sweden after World War II. With the increasing post-war exploitation of natural resources, Swedish nature protection fell more and more into line with the direction conservation was taking internationally. Following a nationally broadcast debate on the radio around Christmas time 1948, resource shortage became a topic of frequent discussion in the Swedish mass media. The UN conference on the resources of the world in August 1949 reinforced the Swedish public debate on natural resources.

This chapter will also focus on the work of the influential Swedish-American food scientist Georg Borgström (1912–1990) as a case study.[1] The rise of neo-Malthusianism in this part of Europe is depicted not only through his work as a food scientist, but through his work and his network of contacts as a protagonist in the debate as well. In his time he was an internationally famous advocate in the food-and-people dilemma. Borgström became an influential intermediary, bringing the American debate to the European scene. Like most prominent neo-Malthusians, he was extremely controversial and aroused both resentment and praise; in fact he still does, to this very day.

A Glamour Boy of Modern Food

'He is the "glamour boy" of modern food' a Swedish magazine enthused in 1955. Borgström was 'the man who holds a magic wand in his hand, while he stands on the podium. His talent is undisputed, his rhetoric stunning, his receptivity enormous, his ruthlessness unbounded and his charm devastating.' The writer concluded rhetorically: 'What may become of this man?'[2]

One of the many answers to this question was given 13 years later by the Norwegian philosopher Hartvig Sætra. 'All politics has changed since Borgström', Sætra proclaimed at a Norwegian Student Union meeting in 1968. Perhaps some eyebrows were raised in surprise among the audience, when the socialist Sætra gave such credit to a Swedish food scientist and old-style Liberal like Borgström. Later Sætra explained that he was not arguing that Borgström was a great political thinker. His epoch-making achievement was that he had clearly shown that the resources of the Earth were limited, and that he had emphasised that this understanding must guide all political decision making.[3] Sætra certainly was not alone in this opinion among Scandinavian environmentalists. Borgström is generally regarded as one of the precursors of the Scandinavian environmental debate. Among Swedish environmentalists, he has been celebrated as a pioneer, the man who 'created the modern environmental debate in Sweden'.[4] One of the early leading environmentalists in the 1960s, Rolf Edberg, called him 'The Swedish Cassandra Voice'.[5] Even the Swedish king, Carl XVI Gustaf, celebrates Borgström for his role as the first 'alarm clock' for environmental issues in Sweden.[6]

Borgström was acquainted with leading American conservationists such as Fairfield Osborn and William Vogt. Inspired by American conservationists, he stirred up the debate in Scandinavia by warning of coming disasters due to overpopulation and resource shortages. Borgström also became well known in the debate in the United States. Through interviews and articles he received nationwide coverage. Several of his books became bestsellers and he was frequently quoted in works on population–resource issues.[7]

Borgström had a doctoral degree in plant physiology. In the 1940s, he set up a research institute sponsored by the food industry. However, he was a pro-technologist who grew sceptical of science's ability to solve human problems. In 1948, Borgström began his mission, to 'point with alarm' at what he believed to be the non-sustainable trajectories of modern technological utilisation. Because of his controversial role, influential representatives of the food industry compelled him to resign as head of the Swedish Institute of Food Preservation Research in 1956. He was then offered a position as Professor of Food Technology at Michigan State University. From this platform, Borgström continued to participate in international debates on overpopulation and natural resources. As this study will show, his career was illustrative of the transformation of conservation issues.

Harvest Time

During World War II, Sweden was ruled by a coalition caretaker government, including all the parties of the parliament with the exception of the communists. Swedish industry and trade were severely regulated. Monopolies and Government control agencies were formed to promote production and distribute scarce resources. There was no major opposition against the planned wartime economy. The difficult situation caused by the war contributed to a common conviction that a government-controlled economy was necessary.[8]

The Social Democratic policy succeeded quite well and Sweden was even able to raise its production during the war years. In his memoirs, Tage Erlander, Swedish Prime Minister from 1946, stated that this success was a result of the determination to use scarce resources in a planned manner. 'The importance of planned economy was the lesson from the war years.'[9]

When the world war drew to an end, there was a marked pessimism among leading Swedish Social Democrats concerning economic development. Sweden's internationally renowned economist Gunnar Myrdal had an important position as chairman of the Government Commission for Economic Post-war Planning and as Minister of Trade during the first years after the war. The post-war programme expressed concern about a peacetime depression.[10] In 1944, Myrdal wrote in *Varning för Fredsoptimism (Warning against Peacetime Optimism)* that everything seemed to indicate that the United States after the war would pull the world into very troublesome economic development, which would soon fall apart into depression and unemployment.[11]

The coalition government, led by the Social Democrats, intended to avert the expected world depression from having serious effects on the Swedish economy. In order to prevent mass unemployment, which would be the result of a post-war recession, consumer demand had to be stimulated. The Government would plan and organise nationally important industries, trade and resources. Myrdal expected the whole market for raw materials to be supranationally regulated within ten years. This reasoning was well in line with the tendency of the new world order towards worldwide economic planning of natural resources.[12]

Peacetime euphoria broke out in Sweden after peace was concluded on the European front in the spring of 1945. A world of peace and rational cooperation lay ahead. This optimism was reinforced by the economic boom, which Sweden's intact industry was ready to supply. The apprehensions of recession expressed during the war soon petered out. Already in 1945 an inflationary boom was at hand.[13]

In the summer of 1945, a Social Democratic one-party government replaced the caretaker coalition. Myrdal predicted 'the harvest time' of the Social Democrats.[14] Accordingly, in Swedish history books the period between 1945 and 1951 has been called 'the first harvest time'. Until the election in 1948, social democratic policies in this period were to a large extent based on the post-war programme of the labour movement from 1944. With the support of the Communists, the Social Democrats tried to accomplish full employment, social reforms, efficient production and worker participation. The welfare state should distribute a rich harvest to its citizens. In the Harvest Time a number of these intentions were realised.

Economic growth during the remainder of the 1940s was remarkable. Between 1946 and 1950 the gross domestic product rose by five per cent a year on average. Demand resulted in Swedish imports becoming considerably larger than expected, especially during 1946 and 1947. The deficit in balance of payments grew, and one consequence was that the foreign exchange reserve of the Bank of Sweden almost ran out completely.[15] In 1946 the state retirement pension was raised and Parliament passed a resolution in principle on public health insurance. In 1947 a general child allowance was introduced. In 1948 new Occupational Safety and Health Acts were passed.

Among leading Social Democrats, there was an awareness that Sweden was facing a new age. It was a golden opportunity to plan and construct the future of the nation. Some figures from the changing Sweden are indicative. From 1921 to 1950 Sweden's population increased from some 6.1 million to slightly more than 7 million citizens.[16] The percentage of people working with agriculture or forestry decreased from 43.5 per cent to 21.5 per cent between 1920 and 1950.[17] Construction projects increased and total gravel consumption was estimated at 9.9 million cubic meters in 1951 and 21.4 million in 1960.

The Social Democrats were committed to full employment and embraced economic growth to achieve their goal. In the booming Swedish post-war economy this seemed to be the right track to the 'people's home' of the Swedish Social Democrats. The consensus politics of inter- and post-war Social Democracy depended on a growing economy for levelling out economic differences, distribution of wealth and welfare reforms. Technical and economic development were to be the foundation stones of the Swedish welfare state. In spite of the impending threat of a superpower confrontation, the belief in a new and better world that would rise out of the ruins of Europe was sustained.

Despite the promising abundance of this harvest time, dark clouds lingered on Sweden's sunny post-war sky. At the end of the war, it was expected that rations and regulations imposed on consumers and industry would be abolished. Nevertheless the Government was prepared to keep at least some part of such restrictions, especially since a recession was expected. During

1946 the restrictions eased to a large extent, but in March 1947 regulations were reintroduced. Coffee rationing, price regulations, and a temporary halt to construction were imposed. In April the following year petrol rationing was introduced. Thus rationing was not only a war-time phenomenon for the Swedish public. The threat of resource shortage remained. The political debate on rationing was quite heated. The non-socialist opposition coined the word 'Trouble Sweden', accusing the Social Democrats of making life difficult for the Swedes by enthusiasm for regulations and a desire to entangle the Swedes in a system of centrally- directed control.[18]

The rationing of food during and after the war induced a greater sensitivity to scarcity. Rationing certainly raised awareness of resource shortage to which neo-Malthusian warnings could be related. Scarcities would strike not only poor countries on distant continents, but even Sweden itself.[19] Ironically, the period metaphorically called the harvest time became an era of widespread concern for the harvest of crops, internationally as well as domestically.

Planned Economy

In their manifesto of 1944, the Social Democrats expressed their vision for a post-war planned economy. With the election debates followed by the release of the post war programme, the Swedish political scene from 1944 until the election of 1948 was marked by controversy over the Social Democrats' project for a planned economy.

A planned economy that was aimed at a complete and efficient use of the productive resources of society could provide the entire population of working age with secure employment. In this way, citizens would be secured a standard of living in keeping with the aggregated proceeds from such work. To realise such an economy, their Programme argued that it was necessary to coordinate different forms of economic enterprise under the management of society. Key areas, such as natural resources, industrial enterprises, credit institutes, means of transportation and communication systems should be transferred to ownership of the State.[20] The planned economy was recommended not only as a domestic policy. The natural resources of the entire world needed to be governed by political planning. In the epilogue to the Social Democratic post-war programme, 'We and the World after the War', the need for international planning and cooperation was emphasised. In Social Democratic newspapers, Myrdal made the connection between the Swedish planned economy and international post-war planning.[21]

The Social Democrats also tackled the question of greater progressiveness in the fiscal system. The non-socialist opposition attacked these proposals violently. This controversy led to an intense and fierce debate on planned economy.[22] In the first full-dress debate in parliament after the dissolution of the coalition, socialism and the issue of a centrally directed economy were at the heart of the disagreement between the Social Democrats and the non-socialist parties.

The non-socialist critique followed two lines: freedom and efficiency. The freedom critique focused on a fear of increasing the sphere of state power. The efficiency critique centred on scepticism towards the ability of the state to improve conditions for production.[23] The Social Democrats declared that socialism was of no key importance, only some parts of trade and industry were in question. The important issue was the rational utilisation of the nation's production resources.[24]

Political scientist Leif Lewin, who has analysed the Swedish debates on planned economy from the 1920s until 1966, argues that the Social Democratic Party, through their policy of planned economy in the 1930s, found a solution to the discrepancy between vision and everyday politics. An ideology of the planned economy replaced the policy of socialism. Keynes's theories on expansive economy were applied to the socialistic goals of the Social Democrats. It was a vital task to render production more efficient, to meet the anticipated times of unemployment and recession.

The Swedish Minister of Finance, Ernst Wigforss, redefined central concepts of social democratic thought. Socialism came to mean nationalisation, whereas planned economy was general government control of the economy. For leading Social Democrats, such as Wigforss, both private and state-controlled enterprises could exist side by side in a planned economy. A free market with a free formation of prices should not be abolished. It was primarily nationally important natural resources and banking that should be subject to government control. With rationalisation as its guiding star, the proponents argued that a more efficient economy would benefit both private enterprise and the individual household. With this in mind, there were some hopes of reaching an agreement with the non-socialist parties on this issue, hopes that were shattered when the non-socialists launched a strong opposition. In spite of this, some nationalisation was implemented during the 1930s. The state acquired rights to shares in new ore deposits and, in 1939, the nationalisation of the railway system was virtually completed.[25]

The government supported state control of businesses where private enterprise would bring about mismanagement of resources. The aim was to nationalise vital natural resources as well as to accumulate more capital.[26] In the autumn of 1945, the Social Democrats proposed nationalisation of the oil trade and the aggregate industry. The oil monopoly was not motivated by the need to conserve resources, but to save Swedish capital. The oil companies were suspected of forming cartels and of tax evasion. The distribution system appeared over-intricate, with every company having its own sales organisation and its own stockrooms, causing Swedish consumers to pay unnecessarily high prices, according to the government.[27]

From the summer of 1945 until the spring of 1947, the debate in the media was intense. Whereas the Social Democratic press defended the proposal to nationalise the oil industry, the non-socialist press strongly opposed it. It was regarded as a first step towards a completely socialist state.

The Social Democratic government argued that a planned economy did not necessarily have to be in conflict with free international trade. In fact it advocated both policies, and maintained that they did not contradict each other. Planned economy was merely the tool for making the domestic economy more efficient in certain sectors where it was needed. But opposition was fierce among the non-socialist parties. A lobby group was formed to oppose the proposal. The Opposition against Economic Planning (PHM), as it was called by the Social Democrats, was sponsored by a private enterprise organisation. It lobbied quite effectively and ran big advertising campaigns against extended governmental economic planning.

The proposals in the post-war programme for efficiency and democracy in trade and industry were in fact never implemented. No substantial nationalisation or state control of the planning of private enterprise was ever carried out. In the local elections in 1946 the Social Democrats lost support, from 46.7 per cent to 44.4 per cent, whereas the Communist Party had their best election ever with 11.2 per cent. The economic boom led to an inflationary crisis in 1947. In March several radical measures were taken to curb the drain of foreign currency and the devaluation of the Swedish Kronor. The Social Democrats were forced to cooperate with the non-socialist opposition. Faced by intense criticism of their economic policy, which had focused on a wrong prediction for a post-war recession, the Social Democrats had to retreat from the more radical parts of their economic policy, in particular the nationalisation of the oil industry.[28]

At the end of the 1940s the Social Democratic Party converged towards the non-socialist parties. Two reasons for this seem to be likely. The profits of industry resulted in higher wages and the ideological climate after the Prague Coup in February 1948 had strengthened the non-socialist parties. The Social Democrats tried to distance themselves from the Communists. One month before the Prague Coup, the Minister of Finance, Wigforss, proposed the 'the third way' between communism and capitalism.[29] The Social Democrats began talks with the Farmers' Party about a coalition, which was eventually formed three years later.

There are several interpretations of why the nationalisation of the oil industry failed. Lewin explains the failure of the policy of economic planning, and primarily the nationalisation of oil, by three important factors: currency crisis, strong opposition within industry in addition to political opposition, and the economic boom. By 1947 the Swedish economy was booming; industry was thriving and the country experienced full employment, for the first time since World War I. Industry and trade went through substantial rationalisations without government interference. The argument for government-controlled rationalisation was severely weakened.[30]

Another explanation is that the policy of planned economy was on a collision course with the American project of a new economic world order based on free trade. The United States State Department was not at all keen on Swedish plans for an oil monopoly. When the financial crisis made Sweden dependent on the United States for dollar loans, the government was forced to back down on its plans on oil monopoly. The different reasons for the failure of plans to nationalise oil have been disputed in Swedish historiography.[31] Regardless, there was substantial domestic criticism of the planned economy. The issue aroused sentiments that, as we shall see, inadvertently came to cast its shadow on the message of conservationists.

In a Spiritual Prison

Borgström started his academic career as a student in plant physiology at the Department of Botany in Lund. Plant physiology emerged as a discipline in the mid-nineteenth century, primarily in Germany. Based on plant physiology the so-called 'new' botany, which focused on the structure and function of vegetation and its relation to the environment, created a methodology based on experimental laboratory studies. Plant ecology developed at the turn of the century. Methodologically and theoretically it was influenced by 'new' botany as well as by descendants from natural history, such as traditional botany, floristics and plant geography. Contrary to the hopes of some early plant physiologists, agricultural scientists and ecologists did not join forces.[32]

The Department of Botany in Lund conducted biochemical research on a laboratory basis and had a tradition of 'systematical, cytological and embryological dissertations'. According to science historian Thomas Söderqvist, Borgström's supervisor Professor Harald Kylin 'taught cryptograms and embryology, and studied algal pigments, largely without noticing that physiology had been revolutionised since the start of his career. Hence, ecologising in Kylin's department was difficult.'[33]

The University of Lund was, at that time, a small community where most of the active students knew one another.[34] Borgström became a well-known figure at the university, especially since he served as president of the Lund University Student Union between 1937 and 1938. In this position Borgström made several acquaintances among the political and administrative elite, since many of the leading persons in society had their student background either at Lund or Uppsala University.

But he also made enemies. When the Government in 1939 proposed that ten Jewish physicians should get political asylum and employment in Sweden, there were fierce protests at Swedish universities. The University of Uppsala student union voted against the proposal. In Lund the issue was also raised in a great debate that gathered about a thousand students, remarkably almost half of the entire student body. The debate was intense. Of 15 debaters, eight supported the motion that Sweden should receive the physicians, among them Borgström. But those who opposed Jewish immigration won by 724 to 342 votes. Among Borgström's outspoken opponents in the debate was the son of Sweden's leading plant heredity scientist and his supervisor's predecessor at the Chair of Botany, Herman Nilsson-Ehle.[35] This kind of conflict created a delicate situation in a small community such as the university, where it mattered who became your friend or enemy.

When Borgström defended his dissertation for the doctoral degree in 1940, his own supervisor was very critical, arguing in the grading committee that Borgström's experiments were too few and unsatisfactory. Following his supervisor's lead, the committee only gave the dissertation the third grade on a five-grade scale. The ordeal of his dissertation examination seems to have reinforced his criticism of the traditional university as rigid and ignorant. Borgström had previously criticised the undergraduate examination system and called it a 'test without value', a reference to the postal term for free samples of toothpaste, etc.[37] According to him, many dissertations were just a trial of strength to get the qualification, and did not accomplish anything useful. As an undergraduate, Borgström was already displaying his desire to make science accessible. He wrote articles in newspapers and non-scientific journals.[36] In articles and debates he advocated the need for university students and graduates to be engaged in society.[38] As we shall see, this view remained a cornerstone in Borgström's critique of traditional university education and research. Scholarly knowledge was valuable, but not sufficient. Scientists must leave their academic studies and be more practically oriented. Research must address problems in society. In a letter a decade later, after a visit to the University of Lund, he congratulated himself on being lucky to have escaped 'this spiritual prison'.[39]

Sweden remained neutral throughout World War II, but the country was on a state of alert and many Swedes were called up for military service. Borgström served as a chemist at a mobile gas protection laboratory until the summer of 1940, when he was employed as an assistant at the Chemical Institution of the Armed Forces. During the war, Borgström attained some recognition in many of the Swedish newspapers for his ideas on an 'agricultural elixir'. He tried to gain support for research on indolyl acetic acid, which he believed would im-

mensely increase Swedish food production.[40] Even though he was critical of the
traditional university, he still had great confidence in what scientific research
could accomplish in producing new inventions to solve problems facing society.
At this time, in the early 1940s, Borgström was not a conservationist. Rather
he appeared as a genuine representative for the utilisation side's confidence in
science and technology, a reliance that he would later designate as 'scientific
superstition'.[41] In an article in 1940 he wrote an enthusiastic presentation of 'the
present front lines of biology, where an exciting conquest of the territory of life
is in progress, and where refractory nature is subdued with modern weapons'.[42]
He was a technology optimist, stressing the economic benefits that could be
achieved through more scientific research. As such, he was a reformer, in his
desire to find ways of improving conditions for humankind.

In May 1941, the Johnson Shipping Line, one of Sweden's major shipping
companies, employed Borgström. His mission was to plan and organise their
affiliated Institute for Plant Research and Cold Storage (IVK)[43] in Nynäshamn.
The research done at IVK was primarily directed towards fruit storage and
cultivation of potatoes.

Borgström was excited about his new position. 'With great enthusiasm,
I am taking up a mission in life, where I will perhaps be able to create in a time
of destruction.' Borgström described the possibilities of making something
practical as 'like a fairy tale'.

> Never again do I have to waste even a second on futile academic twaddle. Now,
> when I have the advantage of observing the universities from the outside, I have
> lost the last remainder of belief in them. Progress has passed them by. Their
> sterile self-conceit prevents the progressive work that forms society.[44]

To form society was indeed at the heart of Borgström's commitment. Of course
the reverse is certainly true – society formed Borgström and his message.

Borgström's Re-education

The Harvest Time was the time for what Borgström called his 're-education',
from a science-solves-it optimist to a worried conservationist. As a young scientist
he firmly believed that science would solve the hunger crises of the war-torn
world, until he went on a research trip to South America in 1946. Confronted
with the ecological degradation of the Pampas, this belief began to crumble.

In 1946 Borgström had gone on a six-month tour of South America. As
head of IVK, his mission was to investigate how cold storage transport from the
South American continent to Sweden could be improved. He spent four months
in Argentina and Chile. By his own account, on this trip he reconsidered his

optimistic confidence in inventions and scientific discoveries as the salvation for the dilemmas of the world. The Pampas especially made a profound impression on him, as he witnessed the soil destruction and the disturbances of its biological system. Later in life Borgström recalled that this experience was his 'awakening' to global ecological concerns. It was his first step in his 're-education', from an academic specialist to a globally-directed scientist aware of complexity.[45]

Obviously, he did not change his technological optimism right away. When a newspaper asked him to summarise his impressions from the trip, he stated that he was impressed by the way every scientific means was to be used in the struggle against plant diseases and vermin.[46] On the other hand, he complained in another interview over the excessive depletion in South American forests.[47]

Borgström had previously expressed opinions close to contemporary views on aesthetic, social and scientific nature protection. As president of a Local Cultural Heritage Society in the small town where he lived in the 1940s, he sometimes expressed anti-urban and anti-modern views. The German Heimatschutz movement inspired the Local Cultural Heritage Movement in Sweden.[48] This influence is also apparent in some of Borgström's speeches as president. In his speech at the local society's midsummer festivity in 1943 he blamed urbanisation for being one of the causes of the present war.

> Do you believe that the people of Europe would have gone to war and let loose the forces of destruction if they had been fostered in love for the soil of home so that they had learned to value the nature of their native land and its cultural treasures, and had assimilated the wisdom of the past and acquired motivation for the task of building society? It is Europe's rootless big city populations, without either a spiritual or a physical place of abode, that constitute the spiritual substrate for rash action.[49]

Also, technological development was to blame for the destruction of culture and beauty in nature. 'Human technology has in its grasp the power to put itself above all the laws of life and nature, and the Swedish local cultural heritage movement has not been strong enough to stop it rampaging.'[50] Inspired by reading books like Lewis Mumford's *The Condition of Men*, his technological optimism slowly started to crumble.

Despite his initial enthusiasm at IVK, Borgström did not feel comfortable working for industry. The famous ship owner Axel Johnson had a reputation for demanding loyalty and Borgström did not always agree with him. In 1948, Borgström was recruited to organise and administer the Swedish Institute for Food Preservation Research (SIK) in Gothenburg. When the opportunity was given, he left without hesitation. At the same time, his career as a public spokesman on global food issues commenced.

The Crisis Hits the Headlines

Just before Christmas 1948, the issue of natural resources made its appearance in the Swedish public debate. Under the title 'Will There Be Enough Food?' Borgström gave a radio lecture about the connection between population issues, depletion and food shortage. Since preservation of food could be an important element of conserving food resources, it is not surprising that Borgström became involved in the wider implications of the issue. In October 1948 he had attended an FAO conference in Copenhagen that dealt with the world food situation.

The title aimed at associating the programme with the ongoing political debate on rationing, albeit with the purpose of giving it an 'infinitely much wider perspective'.[51] Borgström confronted the radio audience with appalling figures. Present food production could supply a balanced diet for 1.6 billion people, whereas the total world population was 2.2 billion. World population had already surpassed the world's food production, meaning that 20 million people died of starvation each year, more than the direct and indirect combat casualties in the entire Second World War.

No easy solutions where at hand. There were no new continents to conquer. Science could offer a small contribution to improving yield by more effective measures against soil erosion and by improved fertilisers. More efficient distribution, improved preservation methods, more extensive use of pesticides, new chemically produced foods and fisheries could also contribute. Yet, Borgström concluded, all this would not suffice if the nations of the world would not cooperate.[52] Three days earlier he had published an article with the same message in one of Sweden's influential newspapers, *Göteborgs Handels- och Sjöfartstidning*.[53]

Borgström's speech was followed the next day by a debate between him and three prominent scientists. The debate reveals the different standpoints in the early post-war population–resource problematic. There were the science optimists: a plant breeder, Professor Åke Åkerman, claimed that if science got the right government support there were great possibilities for increasing the world production of food; the president of the Royal Academy of Engineering, Professor Edy Velander promoted chemically produced food substitutes, such as margarine. In 1948, the idea of changing from animal to vegetable consumption had been proposed in the press by several people, among them Velander. A newspaper asked rhetorically if it was the vegetarians and the plant breeders who would save the world from hunger.[54]

Then there were the neo-Malthusians, who among themselves had rather different points of view: the traditional Malthusian and the conservationist. A population expert from the Farmers' Party, Professor Sten Wahlund, gave voice to crude Malthusian rhetoric. He proposed birth control in regions where there was an overpopulation problem. However, every country had its own situation, so thinly populated Sweden could increase its population. Even more, the population expert argued against sending food to poor and overpopulated countries, such as China, since it would interfere with the natural checks on population growth; that is, if their soils cannot support them, the best thing would be not to interfere, but to let them perish!

The conservationist arguments, presented by Borgström, represented another, more moderate side of neo-Malthusianism. In the debate, he expounded his two key solutions: an interdisciplinary cooperation among experts as well as an international cooperation among the countries of the world. 'We must regard the whole world as one single farm.'[55] Even if Borgström put his hope in scientific cooperation, at this point of time he still regarded the population–resource dilemma as foremost a political responsibility. In a follow-up article he explicitly stated that the world's future food supply was a political task.[56] Borgström focused on food shortage and destruction of soil. However, he did not at this time explicitly align with nature protection. In neither of the radio broadcasts did he even mention the word 'nature'.

The impact of the programmes was tremendous. At this time, Swedish radio was state-owned and had only one channel, which gave the broadcasts a huge impact. Not only did many people listen to the radio, but the programmes were also commented on extensively in the newspapers the following day. The state-owned radio channel was of great importance in its national integrating and normative role. The head of Swedish Radio stressed the educational role of the radio, and debate programmes where different opinions would be discussed were encouraged.[57]

These two particular broadcasts received a great response and got wide coverage in a majority of the Swedish newspapers. They aroused comment in more than 50 articles altogether; in editorials, radio review columns, news articles and letters to the editor in more than 30 Swedish newspapers and magazines. One of the editors at *Göteborgs Handels- och Sjöfartstidning* noted that when the newspaper had published Borgström's article three days earlier there had been no reaction whatsoever, whereas after the radio programme the editorial office had been showered with telephone calls from upset people. In a conversation with one of its readers, they agreed that it must have been 'his energetic and expressive intonation through the loudspeaker which roused some anxiety complex in the subconscious'.[58]

Generally the response to the warning of a global food crisis was very positive in the newspapers. The prevalent picture was that he had raised an extremely important issue with great clarity. Many reporters shared the view of the conservative *Svenska Dagbladets* radio columnist, who claimed that Borgström 'put his finger on humanity's great, all-overshadowing problem'.[59]

Aside from the general acceptance of his picture, political interpretations of the implications of Borgström's radio address varied greatly.

Just months before the radio debate, domestic food shortage had become apparent for Swedes as they celebrated Christmas. Especially in the non-socialist press, there had been a lot of complaints about how much Christmas-time trouble rationing caused for the nation. Hardship was symbolised in the difficulty Swedish housewives faced in getting hold of the traditional ham for the Christmas table. Social Democratic newspapers accused the non-socialist press of using these stories to try to illustrate Social Democratic misrule of the country. In an editorial following Borgström's radio appearance, a Social Democratic newspaper hoped that the bourgeois journalists and people who complained over Swedish rationing had listened to the programme. 'The Swedish Christmas ham problems are small indeed, when faced with the tremendous problems that the world population's food supply pose. It looks as if in future very harsh food rationing will need to be instituted among all people.'[60]

Some social democratic and liberal newspapers focused on birth control,[61] whereas conservative and Farmers' Party newspapers used the radio address to attack the agricultural committee's proposals on rationalisation and a downsized agricultural sector.[62] One conservative editorial declared that Borgström's statistics pointed at a need among the poorer countries, which a civilised country ought to compensate, not only for economic but also for moral reasons.[63] Newspapers of various political colours argued that it made a strong case for the FAO, of which Sweden was still not a member, in spite of its international involvement.[64]

The rationalisation policies initiated by the Swedish government in the 1940s had succeeded in one area: agriculture. There was a general agreement that Swedish farmers needed state support to increase productivity, and protection from too many imports of agricultural produce to Sweden. This was in order to secure a decent income. Swedish farming had been in crisis ever since the First World War and there had been a large migration of people from rural areas into the towns.

The Social Democrats wanted to lower prices for the poorer consumer groups without causing a loss of income for the poorer farmers and farm workers. This was to be accomplished through an extensive rationalisation policy, a transformation from farming to urban industries, and subsidised consumption for some groups. In 1947 the parliament decided guidelines for future agriculture policies. A key purpose was to maintain a production of 92 per cent of the self-sufficiency capacity for reasons of preparedness. Another important task was to even out the differences in income between farm workers and other workers. This was accomplished by subsidies for agricultural produce, primarily through import duties. The rationalisation was to be carried out not only by migration but also by intensified technical rationalisation and by merging farmland into larger units.[65] Considering the Swedish agricultural debate, criticising large-scale land use also meant promoting small-scale farming. Consequently, Borgström found some of his most outspoken supporters among the advocates of small farms, such as the Liberal Member of Parliament Waldemar Svensson.

Almost all political parties used the warnings of resource shortage. Liberals and Conservatives pointed at domestic problems, whereas the ruling Social Democrats called attention to the international scene. Only the communist papers were sceptical of the neo-Malthusian message per se.

The radio programmes at Christmas time 1948, and not least the tremendous newspaper response, established the population–resource dilemma on the news agenda for many years. It also gave Borgström a prominent position in the awakened Swedish population–resource debate. Events the following year would draw him even closer to conservationist ideas. He was about to take the last step in his 're-education'. At the same time, the Cold War politics of resources markedly affected political reaction to his ideas.

The first step in Borgström's 're-education' was his South American journey in 1946. In his articles, from December 1948 until the Lake Success conferences in August the following year, he uses the word 'nature' only once, when he criticised the fact that humankind has been 'a bad keeper of the wealth of nature'.[66] After the two parallel conservation conferences in 1949 his message connected more explicitly to the protection of nature.

International Conservation Influence

Sweden sent a relatively large national group to the United Nations Scientific Conference on the Utilisation and Conservation of Resources, headed by the president of the Royal Academy of Engineering. To his disappointment, Borgström had not been appointed as a member of the official delegation. He had then written to the head of the FAO's Fisheries Division, at the beginning of May 1949. His comments about his Swedish colleagues were rather frank.

> I still nourish a hope to participate in the conference on natural resources this autumn. Do you think I could get a private invitation? Those official delegates who have been discussed as usual know almost nothing about international problems – with the exception of Velander. Decision is not yet made, but rumours say it will be one ignorant politician and possibly a seed-testing scientist with very little knowledge in these fields. Of course they need education but I do not think either FAO or UNESCO considers giving tuition when summoning conferences.[67]

Borgström's contact within the FAO acted on his behalf, and presented him to the chief organiser of the conference as 'one of the best qualified food specialists in Scandinavia'.[68] So finally Borgström received his invitation.

Most speeches at the conference were essentially directed towards the technical perfecting of resource management, and so too was Borgström's. Against the background of Swedish problems in food preservation, Borgström discussed how improved utilisation of perishable food might be achieved. He presented a survey of the extent of storage and marketing losses and the role played by home preservation. He discussed juice and juice concentrate production as a means of saving large amounts of fruit and vegetables. Methods for dehydration of wild rose hips and the freezing of cabbage demonstrated the value of technology in utilisation. Borgström also stressed the importance for improved utilisation of modernising the canning industry, together with developing freezing operations, such as an increase in ice production and in refrigerated warehouse space.[69] In spite the criticisms he had made at home of relying on technical solutions, it was to be another four years yet until Borgström as a conservationist would deliver his population–resource warnings from an international conference podium.

The Lake Success conferences had a decisive impact on Borgström. He became acquainted with both Osborn and Vogt, to whom he attributed great influence on his own work. Osborn's *Our Plundered Planet* had already been translated into Swedish with an introduction by Borgström. Vogt's *Road to Survival* was followed by a Swedish edition the year after. Vogt did not deliver a speech at either conference, but he served on the General Committee of the parallel ITCPN. Borgström states that the conferences were the last step in his 're-education' into a scientist aware of the complexity and global character of the issues vital to humanity. A political–ecological dimension was now established as one of the key concepts in his worldview. If a catastrophe were to be avoided, it was essential for society to conform to an ecological viewpoint.[70]

Speakers at both conferences pointed at the dangers of scientific specialisation and of the need for synthesis.[71] Such statements fit very well with Borgström's ideas and quite possibly inspired him to elaborate a critique of the scientific community, which after Lake Success becomes an increasingly important topic in his social critique. Vogt introduced George Perkins Marsh's writings to Borgström, who stated that his *Man and Nature: Physical Geography as Modified by Human Action* (1864) was maybe the single most important book in widening his perspective. Marsh, an American diplomat in Italy, argued that human actions had a profound and mostly destructive effect upon the environment. Humanity's present usage threatened the resources on which it depended. What struck Borgström was Marsh's point that it was humans who transformed the earth, rather than the common idea that it was the other way round. He was not the only one among his contemporaries, but perhaps the most notable, to attribute the disturbance of the balance of nature to human activities.[72] Borgström and Vogt continued to correspond and meet each other through the 1950s and 1960s. There is, however, no correspondence between Osborn and Borgström. When Vogt writes to Osborn trying to work out a travel grant for Borgström to go to the United States, it appears as if Osborn did not know about him.[73] But there is no doubt that Borgström was inspired by the famous conservationist.

A New Swedish Conservationism

In American expositions of environmental history the roots of green ideas are often traced back to Transcendentalists and romanticism. In the Swedish tradition, however, the environmental mindset is rather the legacy of scientific experts. Concern about the unwanted effects of cultivation was primarily a crusade for members of the Royal Swedish Academy of Sciences, particularly geologists and biologists.[74]

Sweden had some neo-romantic authors, like Nobel Prize winner Selma Lagerlöf, but they were not nearly as programmatic as the American authors Ralph Waldo Emerson or Henry David Thoreau were. In the early 1940s the Thoreau-inspired feminist and pacifist Elin Wägner acquired some attention with her critique of civilisation. She herself was disappointed by the small impact her message made.[75] However, Borgström read and was inspired by her work.

During the 1930s the Swedish Society for Nature Conservation (literally 'Nature Protection Society') moved towards socially directed conservation. Two of the leading persons in the Conservation Society, Lars-Gunnar Romell, and Nils Dahlbeck proposed that the central issue in nature protection must be 'planned economising' with values rooted in nature. It was an attempt to attach their work to the American concept of *conservation*.

This new form of conservation should appeal not only to a few scientific experts; nature protection should be everyone's concern. These conservationists favoured compromises. It was justifiable to deplete natural resources, when it could be shown that exploitation was advantageous to the national economy. Some leading conservationists hoped in this way to achieve trade-offs. However, unplanned exploitation, e.g., of gravel ridges and waterpower, should be banned by society.[76]

This approach succeeded in becoming the guideline for the Swedish Conservation Society in the 1940s and 1950s. The cultural and social emphasis was reflected in the official governmental report on nature protection in 1946 and in the following law on nature protection that was passed in 1952. But in the instructions to the report commission, the Government stated that as a rule economic as well as social and economic policy viewpoints would have priority when compared with conservation viewpoints.[77] According to the Swedish political scientist Lennart J. Lundqvist, the Government was not inclined to make any concessions to conservation, nor did it acknowledge the significance of conservation for long-term rational utilisation of resources.[78]

With the increasing exploitation of natural resources during the 1950s, Swedish nature protection became more and more preoccupied with rational conservation and use of natural resources.[79] In the 1949 yearbook of the Conservation Society, Dahlbeck reported from the IUPN's Fontainebleau conference. In a review of the yearbook the Swedish author and former chairman of the conservation society, Sten Selander, focused on the report from the IUPN meeting. Selander concluded that 'in recent years' it had become clear that nature protection was 'a practical issue...even the most important of all practical issues'. For if humans did not learn how to exploit the earth in a reasonable manner, humanity would in some hundred years live in a permanent famine and eventually mostly starve to death.[80]

In 1949, resource shortage was a frequent topic in Swedish newspapers. When Fairfield Osborn's *Our Plundered Planet*[81] was translated in the spring of 1949 it aroused a significant response. For example, *Samtid och Framtid (Present and Future)*, an influential liberal magazine on political ideas and culture, made a major feature of the dilemma of natural resources, inviting Borgström and five other well-known spokespeople to comment on Osborn's book.[82] The magazine introduced its natural resources feature by explaining its vital importance for world affairs.

> Food shortage, world hunger, sharpened by population growth, and soil devastation caused by erosion through water and wind, mismanagement and predatory cultivation are realities which do not, other than during catastrophic events, make it to the major stories of the daily news, but beyond a doubt they add up to some of the most important reasons behind unrest in the world.[83]

Erosion of fertile soil attracted attention in Swedish news coverage. Features on the dust bowl darkening the skies of the American Midwest and sandstorms in Skåne, the southern province of Sweden, which wiped away the top soil, became iconic visualisations of the threats to humanity's means of support.[84] A Conservative Member of Parliament argued for increased stock raising since farming without livestock decreased the content of organic matter in soil, thus making it more vulnerable to erosion.[85] Borgström had advocated the opposite, since protein shortage should force us to cut down on stock raising and cultivate crops instead.

After the post-war debate on a planned economy had started, Borgström avoided using the specific term 'planned economy'. Yet, with his emphasis on the need for a thorough political planning process to accomplish the necessary economising of resources, what he implied pointed in that direction. Borgström was surely evoking the intense arguments of 1946 and 1947 when he made use of well-known concepts of the planned economy, for example 'a planned food supply' where a policy for improved production was coupled with population policy.[86]

The UN conference on the resources of the world in August 1949 gave issues of natural resources an even greater significance in the Swedish public debate. Many of the Swedish newspapers had a broad coverage of the conference, on the news pages as well as in editorials. In relation to UNSCCUR 1949, some Social Democratic newspapers connected it to the debate on planned economy. One newspaper, when raising, once again, the issue of planned economy, referred in its editorial to Borgström's proposal in the Swedish media for a complementary economic conference. 'Planned economy is a term that has jarred badly in many places, but with the provision perspective humanity is facing, total planning is evidently inevitable.'[87]

Borgström was a born liberal. Furthermore, he had been involved since his youth in the Temperance Movement, which had strong ties with the Liberal Party. In 1946, he was elected to the county council for the Liberal Party, a seat he held until he moved in 1948.

How is it that a liberal like Borgström could associate himself with 'planned economy'? First of all, there had been quite a political consensus on wartime planning. And the concept was not as controversial among so-called social liberals as among other non-socialists. The Liberal Party leader Bertil Ohlin certainly opposed state expansion and nationalisation. Nevertheless, at the same time he underscored the government's responsibilities to predict economic development and to plan accordingly in order to make the nation's economy as efficient as possible.[88] He even regretted that the Social Democrats had appropriated the concept for their nationalisation policy, since he had wanted to use it for his own social liberal policies of decentralised planning.

Borgström, as a liberal, never advocated nationalisation of industry. On the contrary, he spoke of 'socialist incompetence'.[89] He found it very gratifying to see that the farm workers' magazine had brought up the world's food problem for debate in 1949. 'Otherwise the Social Democrats have to the very last buried their heads in the sand.'[90] His judgment of Social Democracy was harsh. In a letter to his friend Gunnar Dahmén he wrote:

> We can see, to be sure, how in England and in Sweden we are rushing toward the same conditions as in Hitler's Germany, where the rights of individuals were eliminated more and more and the class or the guild was put first – for this everything has to yield – even the right.

And he concluded: '...this modern Swedish socialism, which thus is very close to National Socialism.'[91] Borgström's liberal views induced this harsh criticism of domestic social democratic policies. On international policies the matter was different. There his views were more in line with the official Swedish bridge-building policy.

Although he was very critical of the Soviet Union and communism, it was not primarily an ideological change towards liberalism he pursued, but a change in conceptualisation of the problem and in cooperation. The important part was to adhere to the principle of a world household, to the need for universal cooperation and acknowledgment of deteriorating resources. 'All planning – it may be Soviet, Socialistic or Capitalist – is meaningless if it winks at these realities.'[92]

For Borgström it was important to emphasise that even though he forcefully advocated universal solidarity and cooperation, it was crucial not to ignore the fundamental values of western civilisation. In his advocacy for a moral world order, Borgström was a good representative of official Swedish foreign policy.

Bridge Building

The intensifying conflicts between the western and the eastern blocs clouded optimism about a peacefully coexisting world. Sweden maintained its policy of non-alignment. Swedish foreign policy came to be directed by an 'internationalist neutrality policy'. A global emphasis was an important part of the Swedish so-called bridge-building policy. Foreign minister Östen Undén argued that it was in the interest of the whole of humanity to prevent a split between East and West. Already before the war ended, Gunnar Myrdal argued that since Sweden was a small country dependent on international peace, security and free trade, it was especially chosen to be 'the advocate of the world's interest'.[93]

Conservationist proposals for international cooperation thus fell on fertile ground, or rather, were part of a broad movement working for peaceful international cooperation. After the war, a radical peace movement flourished in Europe. In Sweden peace groups were formed in the mood of the Atlantic Charter, with its proclaimed anti-colonial and democratic outlook, groups such as The Information Bureau for Interpopulation Cooperation,[94] World Rallying for Peace[95] and Cooperation Committee for Democratic Construction.[96] They arranged public lectures and study groups, published booklets and were involved in humanitarian aid.[97]

Borgström's views on international cooperation tied in closely with official Swedish policy. As we shall see, the bridge-building approach came to characterise his internationalistic programme, especially in the key role given to international organisations. For Sweden the UN became a key factor for maintaining the confident cooperation that was necessary in building a secure and peaceful world.

The notion of international anarchy as the root cause of international conflicts was prevalent. Once Sweden had joined the UN, the Foreign Office embraced the peace order that was to be administered by the organisation quite enthusiastically. To the Foreign Office, the source of conflict was more an 'anarchical state system' than the political character of particular governments. Peace was a question of coordination and planning. A system marked by disorganisation, power struggle and the self-interest of the nations should be replaced by a system where supranational planning and harmonisation of interests between states should be the guiding principle. The Swedish Foreign Minister Undén adhered to the belief that collective security could be achieved through appropriate international organisation.[98] This approach had a substantial influence on the Swedish debate on the international natural resources situation.

The rebuilding of Europe was an important issue for Swedish foreign policy. Sweden put effort into the formation of Economic Cooperation for Europe (ECE), a UN commission for the recovery of Europe. Myrdal was chosen as its chairman. It was important for Sweden that the organisation should not contribute to bloc building. Thus it could serve the purpose of a neutral country well. If an international organisation like the UN was to lead in the construction of the new world order, Sweden could take a full part in the work, without the risk of openly siding with the United States and its allies.[99] Scandinavian bridge-building policy in the early post-war years therefore raised the issue of whether the European recovery programme within the Marshall Plan should be administered by the ECE. The Scandinavian countries argued that the chances of getting the Soviet Union and the East European countries to partake would improve, because they were participating in the commission. Both the Norwegian and the Swedish governments emphasised the importance of a social democratic model in foreign and security policy. General Secretary Lie and Swedish Foreign Minister Undén tried to counteract the bipolarisation of the UN by trying to form a social democratic 'third force' in the UN, in between the eastern and western blocs. This effort did not, however, gain the support of the most important social democratic government in Europe: the British. Overshadowed by the Marshall plan and torn by internal conflicts, the ECE never had much chance of succeeding.

The UN had tremendous bipartisan support in Sweden, both as a negotiator between blocs and as a force for western democracy, as happened later in the Korean War.[100] The UN was so important that the Swedish government even took sides in the Korean conflict when they supplied a field hospital at the request of the General Secretary.[101] When a new General Secretary was

appointed in 1953, Dag Hammarskjöld from non-aligned Sweden was chosen.
Sweden's proclaimed neutral position gave the country substantial influence in
the UN. As a neutral country, Sweden could become in a way the voice of the
Third World in the First World.

The universality of the UN was of the utmost importance for Sweden.
Undén emphasised that according to the UN charter it was possible for all nations who met the requirements of that charter to apply for membership. One
of the great disadvantages with the League of Nations in the interwar period
was that neither the Soviet Union nor the United States had been members. All
nations must be under the same organisational structure or the world would be
divided up into alliances.[102] In the interest of universality, the internal conditions
of nations should not be considered. The organisation must thus be open to
both democracies and dictatorships. Governments did not need to adhere to
the same principles, other than that they agreed to cooperate.

After 1948 there was little hope of reforming the UN to be a universal
security organisation. It was necessary to adjust to the new balance of power.
Sweden played down its bridge-building policy to a more traditional policy of
neutrality.[103] However, this differed from previous neutrality in one important
aspect: in the post-war world, a moral dimension was added to the traditional
Swedish policy. During the 1930s, in the shadow of the fascist regimes on the
continent, the Social Democrats' policy of neutrality had had an isolationist
character.[104] But in the climate of the Cold War, neutrality was presented as a
way to attain peace and understanding between rival powers. For a small country
like Sweden, a 'moral' world order could be vital for its safety as an alternative
to making alliances. It was in the nation's own interest to promote a world order
based on a regulatory system rather than on military might. The Swedish line
in the UN was based on the premise that it was possible for a small country to
work for trust in the international arena.[105]

As it turned out, several events between the end of the war and 1949
established Sweden's status in the West; for example, Sweden's participation in the
Marshall plan and the recovery plan, membership of OEEC, and participation in
the embargo policy towards the USSR.[106] A group of left-wing Swedish authors
and artists argued that Swedish criticisms should be equally directed towards
capitalism as well as Stalinism. They argued that Sweden should not take sides
with either of the superpowers, but stick to a *third position*. One author claimed
that the young generation was 'seeking a navigable way, a third possible position
between the mendaciousness of the utopia and the apocalypse'.[107]

At the beginning of the 1950s, controversy emerged over the so-called
third position. The climate of the Cold War caused strong anti-communist
sentiment in most of the nation's editorial boards. Those who argued for the
third way were heavily attacked, especially in some liberal newspapers, which

criticised the Government's policy of non-alignment. The Swedish professor of political science and liberal chief editor Herbert Tingsten headed an intensive campaign in favour of Sweden joining the Atlantic Pact.[108] He criticised the Social Democratic government for being soft on Stalinist terror. In spite of this campaign in the liberal press, the Liberal Party supported the policy of neutrality, but emphasised that Sweden culturally and politically belonged to the West.

Borgström's arguments about the necessity of international institutions to solve global resource issues tied in perfectly with the ambitions of Swedish foreign policy. As a country that held neutrality as its official position, Sweden gave work for global security high priority and focused on the construction of international organisations. Nevertheless, criticism of Borgström was on the rise.

The Tempest

The threat of food shortage continued to create headlines in Swedish newspapers during the first years of the 1950s. In the summer of 1953, the debate was given new fuel by a series of radio lectures by Borgström on population growth, resource depletion and the hazards of technology.[109] He made a stir in both the media and the auditorium. During the summer and fall of 1953 his warnings were something of a serial story in the newspapers. It is important to note that he was far from the only one in Sweden involved in these issues. On the contrary, there were numerous voices warning that overpopulation was depleting nature. By being the most articulate, Borgström became one of the most controversial and high-profile in the media debate. After the radio broadcasts, a newspaper placard announced: 'The dark voice from Gothenburg'. In many newspapers he was also known as 'the Gothenburg alarm clock'.[110]

In his book, *Jorden – vårt öde (The Earth – Our Destiny)*, published in the fall the same year, he elaborated his critique. His warnings about the state of the world were repeated in newspapers, radio, and university lectures. To judge by the extent of the debate in the press, the alarm clock of the global resource dilemma rang loudly in the ears of the Swedish public that year.

The book covered food production in all continents. In the preface, Borgström wrote: 'This book has a mission. It is to make it as clear as possible to reflective people that providing for the world requires exceptional measures, if a catastrophe is to be avoided.'[111] In spite of the neo-neo-Malthusian tone, Borgström strongly defended himself against being associated with Malthus. In a postscript to the preface he notes that he has deliberately left out all references to Malthus, since they only give the wrong impression and so cause the facts to be dismissed. 'Malthusianism' was practically an insult, used as a label for someone whom one wanted to exclude from the debate. Borgström was therefore eager to dissociate himself from Malthus's 'many reactionary ideas'.[112] To Borgström, the population issue was not a matter only for the poorer countries. He pointed out that Europe was more densely populated than Asia. The wealth of Europe was an illusion, made possible because we lived in a historical era that had enabled Europeans to exchange industrial products for agricultural produce on a world market. A cardinal issue was protein deficit caused by wasteful food production in the rich countries, for example, through livestock rearing.

Since the continents that supplied the rich world eventually would, and should, demand their resources for themselves, Sweden ought to be self-sufficient in agricultural produce and decrease its population. He also advocated rationing. As long as the world's food production and international distribution were inefficient, rationing and price control were necessary to guarantee a proper diet. As world trade grew, the pressure on Swedish food production was going to increase.[113]

In a way, this line of reasoning reveals Borgström as very optimistic. His argument about an impending starvation crisis in Europe was based on the assumption that the rich world in solidarity with underdeveloped countries would allow them access to the 'fleshpots'. To Borgström this was not only a moral standpoint, it was a likely scenario. The underdeveloped nations had started to industrialise and would not in the future exchange their resources for industrial goods. The present utilisation of soil led to the depletion of inorganic nutrients. Through modern agriculture and forestry irreplaceable amounts had been wasted and could only be replaced to a limited degree by compost and natural fertilisers. Erosion wasted a substantial amount of nutrients, but Borgström also laid a large part of the responsibility on the world trade in food. To Europe's 'deficit areas', millions of tons of nutrients had been imported by transoceanic transports of bone meal and grain. This was a crucial explanation as to why Europe could boast some of the world's highest yields per hectare.[114]

The Earth's population was around 2,460 million and increased annually by 25 million. To give every human being a sufficient diet, all the hectares of the Earth were needed. But the Earth's productive area was only 1600 million hectares. Half of it, at the most, was under cereals and vegetables, the other half was used for stockbreeding. So, in conclusion, only half a hectare was available for each human. Thus it was only in a few rich countries, like Scandinavia, the United States, Canada, Switzerland, Austria, New Zealand, that people could get enough food at the present time. And the situation was very likely to get even worse.

The Earth's most valuable resource, besides soil, was water. Lack of water was the reason why half of humanity had been crowded onto one fifteenth of the surface of the Earth and why the other fourteen fifteenths yielded insufficient food supplies. In relation to this, Borgström pointed out that sewage treatment was a very important issue. On average, 150 litres of waste water per person per day ran out of Europe's modern cities, containing nutrients, mineral salts, fat and protein. Borgström had been one of the driving forces behind a publication of the Royal Swedish Academy of Engineering Sciences which pointed at the water problems facing Sweden, such as pollution hazards and waste of nutrients in sewage treatment.[115]

The intense debate over the Social Democrats' intended 'planned economy' in effect politically contaminated the phrase. To use it would be to step into a minefield. Borgström advocated that 'economising and planning' had to be the number one priority. He also proposed 'central planning' and wrote favourably of 'general plans' in order to prevent a starvation crisis in India and to take care of the irrigation problems of the Rio Grande Valley.[115] Even though he avoided the controversial term, it was first and foremost an international planned economy in the social democratic style, combined with small-scale agriculture, that could avert resource collapse and worldwide catastrophe.

What other solutions were at hand for Swedish neo-Malthusians? Borgström was ambivalent towards technology. He stressed that technology had given us both banes and blessing. But in its present application, driven to extreme specialisation, it threatened the existence of humanity.[117]

Borgström blamed rationalised farming and over-confidence in industrialisation for the population–resource crisis, but he concentrated most of all on criticism of scientific specialists. 'The specialisation of our time has become a misfortune that is threatening to undermine our whole existence.'[118] He concluded that four primary measures were needed:[119]

- The abandonment of short-sighted specialisation. A 'universal view' of problems could be acquired through a new type of university and scientific cooperation.
- A peace plan for the world, 'a general command of peace'.
- A new ethic where the 'golden rule' – do as you would be done by – was the guiding moral norm. A new societal order was needed, where the Earth's resources were regarded as everybody's property and should be used for the benefit of all humanity. 'For the first time in the history of mankind the golden rule of Christianity: *Always treat others as you would like them to treat you*, is the only realistic programme for action in the long run and our only chance to secure a future for mankind'.[120]
- Public education in 'the fundamental law of biological necessity'.

At the beginning of the book a table of population growth in shape of a flooded Ararat-like mountain illustrated the dramatic predicament of humankind. Borgström's concluding words formed a striking counterpart to his table. Like

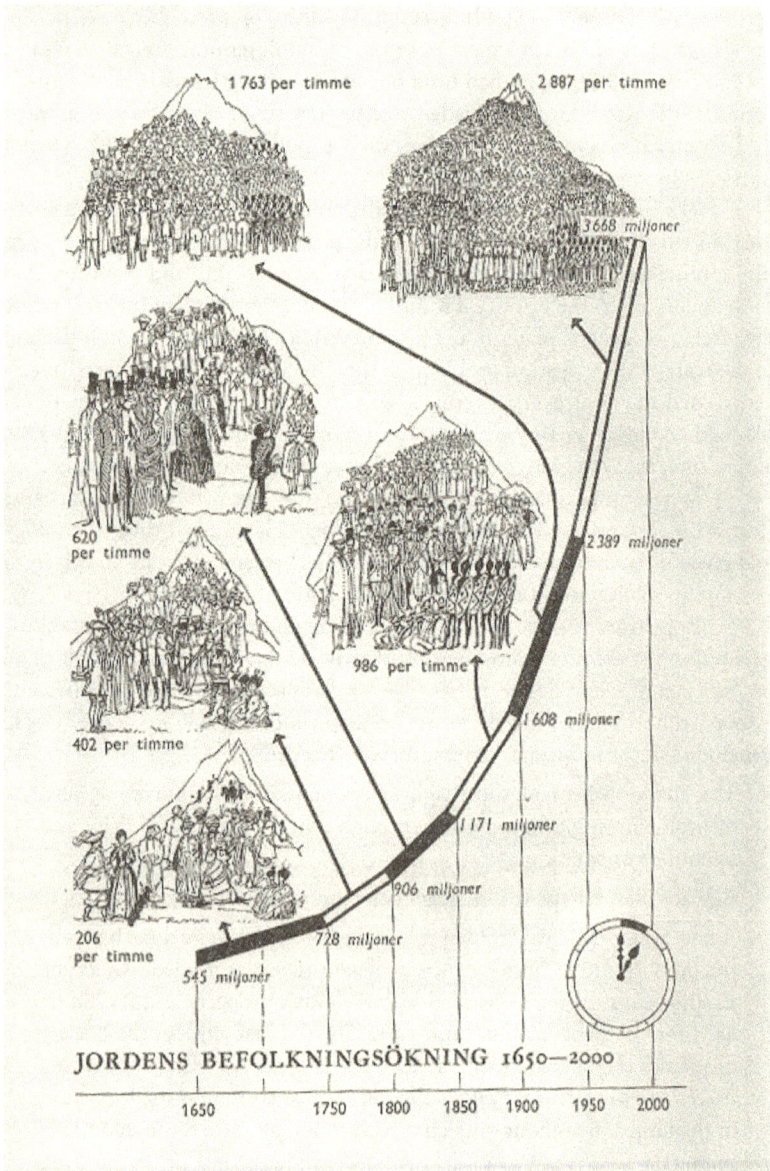

Figure 1 World population growth 1650–2000

Figure from Borgström 1953. The illustrations showing population increase per hour.

a modern Noah, Borgström proclaimed:

> If informed opinion can be communicated over a broad front, there is still hope that humanity can be saved from the Flood that will otherwise pour down over our children's generation. It is not the next million years that instil anxiety, it is the next fifty.[121]

Metaphors played an important role in the population–resource debate. Borgström was skilful in his use of them. He often took a system of signification from another area to illustrate his message. To describe population growth, he used apocalyptic concepts like 'the Flood' and 'signs of the times'; when writing about the unequal distribution of the world's resources, he borrowed economic terms, as in 'the calorie swindle' and 'the biological budget of mankind'.[122]

The 400-page book was printed only once, in 3000 copies. Even though *The Earth – Our Destiny* never became a bestseller, it was a very expensive book for its time, something which some pro-Borgström reviewers regretted. Nevertheless, its message was widely spread through the media debate that followed its release.

Five years after the radio debate in 1948, media reactions to Borgström's message were far more hostile. After one of the radio programmes in the summer of 1953, a newspaper editorial declared: 'Regardless of whether you think he is right or wrong, his doomsday prophecies have stirred up people's minds.'[123] The impending scenario was generally accepted by commentators – a serious situation was at hand if nothing was done. None of the reviewers or commentators dismissed the complexity of the problems; on the contrary, it is clear that many saw it as one of the most urgent issues humanity was facing, and to some it was even more compelling than the threats of the atom and hydrogen bombs.[124]

Many who considered the book to be of the greatest importance were nevertheless sceptical of Borgström's data. Halvdan Åstrand, head of the Research Institute for Agriculture, pointed out that it was an important problem, but it did not benefit from Borgström's statements.[124] Åstrand summed up his criticism: 'a scientist's duty in society is not to be a reformer but to seek the truth'.[126] Borgström's scepticism towards the capacity of science and technology to solve the problems and his 'gloomy' prognostications for the future aroused resentment. Borgström, in an allusion to Shakespeare, characterised the massive criticism that his message aroused when his book was published as 'The Tempest'.[127]

Several scientific reviewers accused Borgström of being negligent with his data.[128] Borgström fought back. He argued that he had based his figures on official data; it was his opponents who refused to see the facts. The list of references had not been included since it would have made the book too expensive, according to the publisher. For that reason, Borgström duplicated the list and it could be ordered as a stencil by writing to him. However, there were no footnotes and very few references in the text, so it was difficult for readers to work out where Borgström had found specific figures. In his preface Borgström made the point that in order to contribute to creating public awareness, as many facts as possible had been mobilised.[129]

The list of references contains 920 entries, with various books and reports on nutrition, natural resource surveys and population growth. For his estimates on population growth he used works like the United Nations *Demographic Yearbook* from 1948 and the Milbank Memorial Fund's *Demographic Studies of Selected Areas of Rapid Growth* from 1944. Borgström stressed that his figures were based on official reports, open for examination.

Even some of Borgström's strong supporters, such as Åke Gullander and Sten Selander, admitted that there were errors, even though Borgström built his arguments on official statistics. A closer examination of the book makes it plain that Borgström gave some contradictory data in the book. On the first page the world population in year 2000 was estimated at 3,668 million people, whereas if one turned over the page the figure was 3,000 million. The population of India varied in the book. On page 145 the United States' reserve of uncultivated land was said to be 32 million hectares and the Soviet Union's 12 million, in the diagram on the next page the respective numbers were 6 and 56 million. Corn was said to be cultivated at 80° north in the Soviet Union, which would be in the Arctic Ocean.[130]

Vogt also commented that Borgström sometimes got his facts wrong. In spite this, Vogt had a high opinion of Borgström's English synopsis of *The Earth – Our Destiny* and tried to persuade his publisher Houghton Mifflin to publish it.[131] Selander blamed the inconsistencies on hasty proofreading and claimed they did not blur his arguments and impressive overview of the world's food resource situation.[132]

How does Borgström's 1953 estimate of world population growth stand when compared with later estimates of population growth? In a comparison with seven other works on the subject, Borgström seems to be well in line, and he has not exaggerated the population size in his own time (See table 3). In Chapter Seven his prognoses for the future will be compared with recent UN estimates.

The debate was captured by *Stockholms-Tidningen* who invited both proponents and opponents of Borgström's views to a big debate. The theme was 'Starvation on Earth' and was introduced with a presentation of how the issue was framed by 'the irreconcilable experts'.[133] Borgström's pessimism was criticised, but surprisingly not his very radical critique of the present economic order. One social democratic newspaper concluded that Borgström belonged to the bourgeoisie in domestic party politics, but in international matters he

Table 3 Estimates on Past Human Population Sizes, in millions.

	1650	1750	1800	1850	1900	1950
Borgström 1953	545	728	906	1,171	1,608	2,389
Deevey 1960	545	728	906	–	1,610	2,400
McEvedy and Jones 1978	545	720	900	1,200	1,625	2,500
Biraben 1979	–	771	954	1,241	1,634	2,530
Blaxter 1986	–	770	954	1,241	1,633	2,513
United Nations 1992	–	–	–	–	–	2,516
Kremer 1993	545	720	900	1,200	1,625	2,516

Sources: Borgström, 1953; Joel E. Cohen, 1995; United Nations, 1992

represented some advanced form of communism;[133] whereas a communist newspaper, *Arbetartidningen,* accused Borgström and others like him of serving, consciously or unconsciously, the warmongers. The Soviet Union had found the political solution to the problem, and had with 'brilliant results transformed nature and taken natural laws into the service of humankind'.[135] Two other communist newspapers accused him of neglecting the class issue and refusing to see that socialism would solve the problem.[136]

Even though a social democratic newspaper noticed that Borgström was rather a communist in international issues, most newspapers did not comment on his proposals for economic redistribution. This also happened with American reviewers of *Road to Survival,* who failed to recognise Vogt's economic critique. In the discourse on natural resources, scarcity figured as an accepted problem, and pessimism and optimism warred over the ability of science and technology to solve it. Redistribution as a means to nutritional equity, however, seems to have been a non-issue.

Borgström explained the hostility towards his message as the reaction of people who saw their traditional worldview threatened. The editor of *Göteborgs Handels- och Sjöfartstidning,* one of Sweden's leading newspapers at the time, completely discounted the book when it was released.[137] Later in life, Borgström attributed this animosity to the convictions of the believers in post-war progress. The end of every big war, Borgström argued, inspired faith that now the world was to be created again and everything would be arranged for the best. This was the dominant conviction after World War II, according to Borgström. With some 'know-how' and aid, the believers in progress argued, the recently acknowledged threat of world famine could be eliminated. In Sweden, as in the other western countries, it was widely assumed that the western world should teach underdeveloped countries the right way to proceed. Borgström felt that those who opposed this optimism frustrated many people.[138] Selander wrote apropos the radio reviewers: 'It was as if Borgström had said something indecent, when he indicated that material progress during the last century was an isolated case.'[139] In contrast, Selander called *The Earth – Our Destiny* the most important non-fiction book written by a Swede in the last few years. 'Everybody who is involved in the management of our country, government, parliament and national and local public officials, and everybody who manages Swedish soil and Swedish natural resources should be required to read it thoroughly.'[140]

A Pro-technology Backslider

When Borgström first presented his warnings in 1948, the population–resource crisis was a novelty in media reports. People were moved by this serious issue. The idea of scarcity was probably reinforced by rationing experiences during and after the war. And there were people starving even in Europe. Five years later Borgström's message certainly clashed with the optimistic future envisaged in the 1950s. Many of his opponents called him a doomsday prophet, a description he strenuously rejected. There were also more specific reasons that can explain why he met with criticism.

Perhaps most importantly, in 1948 Borgström did not concentrate on a critique of scientific specialisation. In the 1950s, on the other hand, this came to be a main theme in his message. He had probably been inspired by Vogt's attack on specialised technicians and his proposals for a broader conservation education[141] as well as by ITCPN's recommendations on interdisciplinary studies and his own university experiences. This time the reaction from the scientific world was stunning. His data attracted criticism from mainstream scientists reviewing the book. Some of the objections to his scientific approach can be seen as attempts to exclude him from the discourse by the process of rarefication. Procedures of rarefication of agents determine the conditions under which the discourse may be employed, imposing a certain number of rules upon those individuals who are qualified to employ it. As Foucault points out 'none may enter into the discourse on a specific subject unless he has satisfied certain conditions, or if he is not, from the outset, qualified to do so.'[141] Since he did not represent 'proper' science, his message was dismissed as unreliable.

We shall return to his scientific role in Chapter Six. For now we can observe that, in his emphasis on synthesis and practically-oriented interdisciplinary research, Borgström heralded a new type of scientist.

Since 1948, population growth and resource depletion had been a much-discussed topic. Borgström's argument that population growth put pressure on resources had generally been accepted, as had his point that humans might be wasting resources. It was also primarily these two points that the commentators had focused on in 1948 and 1949. But international books had appeared on the subject and had been translated into Swedish, works that offered different solutions. In 1953 two books, besides *The Earth – Our Destiny* became much discussed in Swedish newspapers: *The Geography of Hunger* by the UN's expert on nutrition, Jousé de Castro, and *The Next Million Years*, by Charles Galton Darwin, a technology optimist, and grandson of the famous evolutionist.

Borgström's proposed 'central planning' evoked the old debate on planned economy, which had gone completely out of fashion, as had even Ohlin's liberal decentralised planning. The time for proposing a planned economy as the solution for the population–resource crisis was yet to come: in the late 1960s, Hans Palmstierna, an influential Swedish social democratic environmentalist, argued along the lines of the early William Vogt that it was market liberalism that deteriorated the Earth. If the world was to be saved, a new economic system was required – a real internationalism with a harsh, *planned economising of the Earth's resources*.[142]

Contrary to the warnings of harsher times, economic growth had not been not curbed. In the 1950s, the Korean War created an international economic boom which had a significant effect in Sweden. After a short recession in 1951, the economy was stable during 1953 and 1954. The predicted rationing seemed far away. Environmental historian Jeffrey C. Ellis argues that the Cold War atmosphere and the McCarthy era made conservationists like Vogt and Osborn less keen on criticising free market economy. Instead they focused more on overpopulation as the root cause of resource depletion.[143]

Borgström, on the contrary, continued and even refined his economic critique. And apparently, among some Social Democrats, his appeal for international equity aroused the old communist ghost. The debate on resource depletion did not make any deeper imprint on the parliamentary affairs. When two Conservative Members of Parliament proposed a bill on measures to increase the Swedish population, they merely mentioned that they would not discuss the effect of high birth rates on the world's 'housekeeping' and provisioning.[144]

At this time, Borgström was not as controversial abroad, since he had not yet entered the international public debate on population–resource policies. Internationally he barely addressed anything other than food technology issues and, to some extent, their relation to world food problems. These articles and papers were only published in scientific journals and at conferences.[145] One exception was his speech on 'European aspects of overpopulation: Balance between resources and population' at the Fourth International Conference on Planned Parenthood in Stockholm 1953.[146] Until 1958, Borgström had only published one article outside Sweden, in an Italian magazine, that specifically addressed the political implications of population–resource problems.[147]

In 'the Tempest', Borgström was supported by conservationist and farming interests, especially by small farmers. By 1953 agricultural production had increased to 100 per cent self-sufficiency, and there were no quantitative limits on import. The Social Democrats attempted to decrease subsidised agricultural production. A new law was passed in the fall of 1955 with a fixed import fee. As Selander's review shows, Borgström's message also fitted the new approach of the Swedish Society for Nature Conservation and was well in line with international conservationism. Borgström was one of the conveyers of a new conservation ideology.

The concept *conveyer of ideas* embraces three specific roles. The conveyer takes on board a new set of ideas, plays an active part in the process of reconsidering knowledge and communicates these new ideas to decision-makers and to the public. Thus, the social role of conveyer of ideas is one of mediation between politics and society. It can include *intellectuals*, but it is a wider concept including all kinds of involvement in a mediating process of ideas. Since the *conveyer of ideas* is seen as an agent, the concept does not support an actor perspective, where a single intellectual actively creates, invents and reinvents cultural forms. It can also refer to *ideological representatives* of social movements, even if it does not have to.[148] In the case of Borgström, he attained this role in the 1960s, when he was characterised both as a symbol and as an epistemic informant: he could make use of this role, but environmentalists were also making use of him.

When a conveyer of ideas speaks to power, he has to get past the discursive process of rarefication. Doing so does not mean he is always acceptable to political and scientific spheres and included in the discourse. Yet he has to find at least one discursive position where he can express his message. This is certainly true of Borgström. His message was far from fully embraced, but he found himself a niche as a food scientist, speaking about a politically prioritised subject. In this role he, like many other conservationists, was given a platform. From this position he could also deliver statements that ran contrary to the discourse. Because he was addressing a politically important problem as a scientist, he was given space in the media, which he used to deliver a radical critique of the way society handled the population–resource crisis.

5

A New Conservation Ideology

The debate on natural resources after the war indicates an altered view of the plight of humanity and the relationship between humankind and nature. The inhabitants of the poorer continents emerged as agents. Faced with a world population of potential consumers, global resource supply appeared in a new light. Resource scarcities were no longer mere local, transparent problems, but acute and complex threats to the world order. The survival of humankind became the great imponderable. Protecting nature was not only a matter of endangered animals or biotas; humanity itself was now an endangered species. Not only nuclear armaments, but also material welfare became a threat to civilisation. In this process a new, global view of humankind's relationship to nature emerged, which formed the ideological foundation for post-war environmental criticism. In this chapter I shall argue that the ideas of the new conservationism form an ideology because they support and depend on one another and are connected with norms for society.

Ideology has been a continuously debated and redefined term since it was introduced to philosophical analysis at the end of the eighteenth century. A wide range of definitions of ideology has been used, from *social determination of thought* to *allocation of false ideas in the interest of a ruling class*. I will therefore briefly expound the definition used in this book.

On Ideology

The term ideology often functions as a convenient way of categorising a variety of ideas under a single heading. Rather than some permanent essence of an ideology, there is a web of interwoven features associated with it. Different ideas are connected by their *family resemblance*.[1] But to make the concept analytically useful it needs a more precise formulation. It is necessary to identify the main features of integral and comprehensive worldviews, i.e., a core in a network of signs, meanings and values.

The concept of ideology used here consists of three analytical parts: *descriptions of reality*, *valuations* and *recommendations of action*. When these parts support and depend on one another and are connected with norms for society, they constitute an ideology.[2] Descriptions of reality clarify the perceived reasons behind the state of the world. Valuations declare how it ought to be. Recommendations of action propose how this should be realised. Ideology is primarily a question of gathering a jointly shared, right understanding of the world. With the right knowledge, it is possible to make a true interpretation of the world and advocate actions accordingly. To communicate this knowledge, ideology connects itself to a suitable institutionalised practice.

The concept of ideology is sometimes seen as adhering solely to a dominant political power. I think it is more appropriate to regard it as a set of ideas whereby people posit, motivate and rationalise aims and means of social action, specifically political action. Thus, a set of ideas can be regarded as an ideology whether it seeks to preserve or to overhaul the existing social order.[3]

In the face of conflicting interests, social formations promote beliefs and values favourable to them. In a discursive struggle, where there is a conflict over issues fundamental to the reproduction of social power, an ideology can be used to legitimate the cause of social groups. In an ideological setting the promoted values are naturalised and universalised, so as to render them self-evident and inevitable; and ideas that might challenge the ideology are disparaged, in an attempt to counteract conflicting forms of thought.[4] Ideology refers, according to Terry Eagleton, to 'the processes whereby interests of a certain kind become masked, rationalised, naturalised, universalised, legitimated in the name of certain forms of political power'.[5]

These concepts may denote ideology as a distortive strategy, but do not necessarily have to do so. I want to emphasise that ideology, as defined in this chapter, is not by definition an expression for a false consciousness or distortion. Ideology is no unfounded fantasy, but evolves from real material conditions. It must have at least enough cognitive meaning to help organise people's lives. As Paul Ricoeur shows in *Lectures in Ideology and Utopia,* ideology (as well as utopia) has 'a constructive and a destructive role, a constitutive and a pathological dimension'.[6] In other words, an ideology functions as a symbolic structure for social life, that can help us understand why we live, act and think the way we do. As such it can have a dissimulating as well as an authenticating function. [7]

The concept of ideology can also help to disclose the relations of utterances and symbolic acts to their social context. The communicated views have to be related to their material conditions of possibility, through the discursive struggles which are central to the reproduction of social life. However, in this chapter I will primarily focus on the first part of the ideological analysis: identifying the core. The aim is not primarily to evaluate the cognitive statements being made in the ideological struggle. It is rather to analyse the affective side of ideological interaction, the ideas that are being communicated. Ideology is regarded as a materially anchored and sustained social manifestation. It is also a discursive and semiotic phenomenon. Since an ideology should be under-stood in a discursive setting, the cognitive statements being made are probably more practical than theoretical. This may entail the assumption that ideology is particularly action-oriented in character.[8]

This approach, which is not focused on evaluation and critique, seeks to identify the central ideas of a social group. It analyses these ideas, how they are used to support societal pursuits, and finds factors in the social situations that determine the ideas. A truly non-evaluative approach is not possible. Contextualisation implies relativisation. Certain aspects are always emphasised in contrast to others, in a process of selection and accentuation, which thus entails value judgments.[9]

The Conservation Ideology

In accordance with the definition elaborated above, a conservation ideology can be distinguished in the early post-war debates on natural resources. The descriptions, valuations and recommendations for action that formed the new ideology can be outlined in five main themes: *the order of nature, catastrophe empiricism, endangered humanity, the world household* and *political change*. These categories are analytical. Since, as elements of an ideology, they involve each other, the categories will overlap. In the following, I shall describe these five ideological cornerstones.

The Order of Nature

There is an ecologically ideal state of nature – this assertion was fundamental to conservation ideology. Since the root cause of the world's dilemma was that humanity had been neglecting the order of nature, this understanding should govern all human activity. Humans had not realised that they were a link in nature's great chain. The unity of the world implied both human and ecological interdependencies. Many of the participating scientists in the debate on natural resources had their training in biological sciences related to ecology, particularly plant physiology and zoology. At the International Technical Conference on the Protection of Nature, the parallel conference to UNSCCUR arranged jointly by UNESCO and IUPN, presentations of ecological issues predominated. Most of them were reports from different parts of the world in the field of ecology, dealing with such matters as DDT and large-scale agricultural enterprises as threats to the balance of nature. The resolutions from the conference promoted the study of human ecology and urged that the insight of human dependency on the environment should be communicated to the public.[10] Many of the participants at UNSCCUR also concluded that the issue of natural resources had to be tackled from the ecological position that everything on earth is interrelated and interdependent.[11]

In Swedish debates too, this notion is often expressed; the cause of the world's present dilemma is neglect of the order of nature. Humankind had not realised that it is a link in the natural chain. Famines were impending as a result of humankind's 'disturbance of the balance'. Future disasters could only be avoided by an 'interplay' with nature.[12] The metaphors used in the Swedish debates are dominated by normative concepts such as balance, equilibrium, frames and harmony, words that indicate an aspiration towards an ecologically ideal state of nature. This approach seems also to dominate the works of Vogt and Osborn. In *Our Plundered Planet* the 'order of nature' is expressed through metaphors like 'organic circle', 'earth symphony', but also 'the machinery of nature'.[13]

Root metaphors are metaphors that are used time and time again, but are still perceived as living. Some metaphors are so strong that they survive and generate more metaphors to make a concept comprehensible. 'Root metaphors' take their name from their ability to evoke a network of new metaphors to describe a concept. Ricoeur takes the root metaphors of God as an example. In Hebrew tradition God is likened to a king, father, lord, shepherd, judge, rock, castle etc.[14] Root metaphors together assemble images to make such an abstract concept as God understandable. They can thus lead to a deeper insight. Other phenomena, too, may be so complex and difficult to grasp that they require the emergence of root metaphors, and one such phenomenon is human interaction with nature. In the new conservation ideology this relationship was expressed in metaphors like balance, harmony, equilibrium, metaphors that are central in today's environmental discourse.[15]

The order of nature theme was not at all new; its metaphors had been central in natural history since the beginning of Western civilisation. In *Traces on the Rhodian Shore* (1966), his extensive book on nature and culture in Western thought from antiquity to the end of the eighteenth century, historian Clarence Glacken starts out by declaring: 'What is most striking in conceptions of nature, even mythological ones, is the yearning for purpose and order.'[16] The idea of a 'balance of nature' has been supposed implicit in natural history at least since antiquity. Yet, as a root metaphor, the metaphoric power of this concept is still vivid. It has been a presupposition, rather than a theory of natural history. Biologist Frank N. Egerton argues that attempts to define the concept in science have been very rare. During the twentieth century some ecologists began to question the concept[17]; but it still continued to be employed by both ecologists and conservationists. For some it may have functioned as a heuristic device, rather than as a theory of nature. Nevertheless, the metaphor still conveyed a fundamental assumption of nature's order.[18] Even though the concept of balance of nature was challenged by some, the basic assumption that nature has an intrinsic order, in ecological equilibrium or not, that might collapse if manipulated, was at heart of the arguments.

Catastrophe Empiricism

'Prophets of Doom' was a common way to label the radical post-war conservationists. Certainly, many of their contributions to the debate were studies in modern eschatology. One apocalyptic motif was repeated throughout their arguments: If society did not change its present course, civilisation was heading toward a catastrophe. According to several Swedish newspapers, that was also the message to be derived from the Lake Success conferences.[19] Osborn expressed this conception in his adverted plenary speech.

> It is certainly no exaggeration to say that the future of mankind will depend upon the degree to which natural resources can continue to be available. Despite the growing evidence of cooperation between nations, it is unlikely that this world meeting would be taking place, even now, were it not for conditions of obvious and increasing seriousness.[20]

Do these apocalyptic accounts represent something new in the Western conception of humankind's relationship to nature? I believe so. The concept of catastrophe is old, and a well known figure of thought in the Jewish–Christian tradition. Nevertheless, a new kind of apocalyptic reasoning emerged in the debate that differed in its character from Jewish-Christian eschatology and the cultural pessimism of the interwar period. To support their catastrophe scenarios, the proponents referred to scientific data. In a book on catastrophe apprehensions in Germany, Heinz Theisen used the term 'katastrophempiri' to distinguish the new element in ecological extinction anxiety from earlier apocalyptic currents.[21] At the dawn of the Cold War there was no need for godsent prophets who preached esoteric knowledge or revelations of the apocalypse. Everyone who studied scientific facts could foresee it. Research reports replaced doomsday prophecies and historical–philosophical theories of decline. When the conservationists warned of a forthcoming catastrophe they increased the credibility of their warnings by supporting them with statistical material on population growth and food production. A report in a Swedish newspaper from one of Borgström's many public lectures can illustrate this. 'Associate Professor Borgström demonstrated with a multitude of drastic examples how mankind's interference with the order of nature has disturbed the equilibrium to a precarious extent.'[22] Following the radio debate of 1948, a newspaper reported that the idea of an acute food shortage by the year 1972 was proposed with 'great scientific authority'.[23]

Catastrophe Empiricism

Nature is presented to us through *symbolic acts.* They include any kind of mediators between human individuals and the external world. Besides written alphabetical and spoken language, they can include, e.g., signs, technologies, graphs and maps. Science is such a mediator, not only through written and spoken communication, but also through the symbolic function of scientific activity, for example, the legitimacy that accrues to a field of study. In that way, ecology is not just a study of 'what is out there', it is a set of signs whereby we, using certain points of reference, can interpret the human predicament.

Symbolic acts are activities and artefacts that serve to provide a representation of existing objects or states of being. As symbols they bring order to human existence. Symbolic acts can be aesthetic, a novel or a work of art, and they can be *expressive acts,* such as a public debate, a diagram or a newspaper photograph as when Borgström posed for a press picture with a balance containing babies in one pan and wheat in the other, surrounded by charts and diagrams.

When an ideology's descriptions of reality are wedded to its normative statements, this is done through ideological *institutions.* These institutions that mediate the ideology may include organisations, media or artistic genres. To be persuasive, the institutions should attach themselves to discursive practices, and in conservation ideology science was the most important institution.

In earlier apocalyptic thinking, contemporary events had provided signs that the time of an impending catastrophe was nigh. However, as indicated by the expression *empiricism,* this is now a matter for science-based arguments. According to the virtues of positivistic science, it should be possible for anyone with scientific training to test such evidence of an impending catastrophe. There are previous examples of what can be regarded as catastrophe empiricism, for instance in the Malthusian tradition, but not to the same extent and with the same empirical arsenal. Historian Christopher Lewis identifies a shared apocalyptic rhetoric and ecological worldview among critical ecologists from Vogt, Osborn and Aldo Leopold to later influential environmentalists such as Rachel Carson, Barry Commoner and Paul Ehrlich. Using the science of ecology, they forecast the end of the modern world and the extinction of humanity.[24]

With the new conservationism, apocalypticism goes modern. Rationality is one of the key features of the capitalistic formation of Western society, which had profound consequences for the interpretation of reality. Not least, it discredited belief systems which sought to provide untestable interpretations for human life. It eroded the metaphysical rationales of religions, ideologies and historical exegesis. In Weberian vocabulary, the world became disenchanted. Catastrophe empiricism, with its rationalisation of apocalyptic angst, is an important part of this process. It contributed to a continued market for theories of decline in the modern world.

Political scientist Michael Butkin in his study of apocalyptic notions in the 1960s draws the same conclusion. He concludes that although there is a presence of religious motifs in the rhetoric of secular protagonists, their apocalypticism is secular rather than religious, indebted to science and to social criticism rather than to theology.[25]

In a dissertation on 'ecological apocalypticism', Lewis claims that postwar ecologists participate in a Christian apocalyptic tradition predicting an end to human civilisation.[26] The word *apocalypse* does in fact come from the Greek name for the last book in the Bible, Revelation, St John's vision of the end of the world and the Last Judgement. In a way what Lewis says is obviously true, since this is a part of Christian culture. Of course, catastrophe empiricism attached itself to the apocalyptic tradition of the conservationists' own cultures. Leopold referred to St John's four horsemen, Vogt to the Day of Judgement, Osborn to the Day of Atonement and Borgström to the Flood, whereas Osvald refers to 'Ragnarök' the doomsday of the Norse Aesir tradition.[27] I think it is misleading to see it as a direct ancestral line from Biblical eschatology. Western apocalypse has at least five faces.

Predestined apocalypse. Predestination implies that an actor has determined history in advance. Everything that happens has been foreseen and is a part of a master plan. A predestined history requires some kind of transcendental being to have made the plans. Thus in the Jewish–Christian view of history, apocalypse is a one-time phenomenon. God has predestined that humanity will be in Satan's power and therefore the Earth must perish.

Determined apocalypse. Everything happens by necessity and is causally conditioned. Events are regulated by law and are the inevitable result of previous events. Thus, in the determined apocalypse the end is unavoidable, even though it can be a cyclic phenomenon. The determined apocalypse does not need a god as a guarantor for the end result, but the outcome is just as inescapable since the causality cannot be altered.

The apocalypse of the disheartened. Bad times can make people temporarily resign themselves, give up hope and predict that everything is going to hell. Rather than a statement of a historical theory, it is an expression of despair in a specific situation. This apocalypse of pessimism is not predestined or determined, but a likely way for humanity. This notion also implies that an ending can be the causal result of present actions. But if the actions are altered, the end result, being subject to the laws of cause and effect, might be different.

Apocalypse as re-creation. Apocalyptic thinking often contains a notion of catastrophe as the impetus to re-creation. There is a millennial aspect to this version of apocalypse: Paradise will be regained. This form of apocalypse obviously corresponds to the Jewish–Christian tradition, but it is also present among secular thinkers. This present civilisation may have little or no hope, except that out of catastrophe something new may sprout. Historian of literature Klaus Vondung argues in *Die Apocalypse in Deutschland* (1988) that one of the constant features of visions of doom is their transformation to utopia. The old culture is so ruined and false that it must perish, but the catastrophe carries the seed towards a new creation.[28] A secular example is Oswald Sprengler's *Der Untergang des Abendlandes* (1918–22), where a new culture will grow out of the ruins of the old.

Rhetorical apocalypse. Some of the apocalyptic statements made in the course of the debate might not necessarily reflect a view on history, but rather serve a rhetorical purpose: to make people *aware* of a perceived problem or a danger. When the catastrophe idea is primarily a device to criticise contemporary society, I regard it as *rhetorical apocalypse* to separate it from perceptions of the future that regard an apocalypse as either determined or predestined. Apocalyptic anxiety can serve a purpose. It can make people aware of a problem or a threat. This does not mean that the threat is not regarded as real, but the prediction is

primarily used to accomplish another purpose than the expression of a historical view. 'It is not too late, but it is urgent' has been a slogan in contemporary
environmental discourse. It implies that the disaster can be avoided if the
appropriate measures are taken right away. As Borgström expressed it in his
previously quoted Noah reference: 'If an insightful opinion can be spread on a
broad front, then there is still hope.'[29] That this type of argument has been used
time and time again over many years shows its significance. The main purpose
of *rhetorical apocalypse* is to become a driving force. Vogt's response when asked
about the despair in his book is also illustrative: 'If I didn't think there was a
very good chance of solving our problems, I never would have written *Road
to Survival.*'[30] Even if the intention was rhetorical, that did not imply that the
threats were not regarded as real or impending. Rather it might be the rhetoric
of the disheartened.

It is not the task of this study to evaluate the validity of the arguments
used by the various agents; and little would be gained by judging whether or
not feelings or moods make any sense. Fear about, as well as faith in the future
has always taken hold through the signs of the time. Historical events come and
go. Thus these signs must change, and optimism as well as pessimism must find
new arguments for their cause. As the historian Frank Kermode notes: 'since
anxiety attaches itself with the eschatological means available, it is associated
with changing images.'[31] The advent of heavenly horsemen in medieval times
was as probable for believers then as overpopulation was in the 1950s and as
human-induced climate change is today.

The sociologist Johan Asplund identified the idea of catastrophe (as
well as the idea of progress) as a figure of thought in modern discourses on the
future.[32] *Figures of thought* form the underlying structure of discourse. They
are constituted by unreflected and unarticulated regulative concepts. Foucault
identifies, for example, a certain 'idea of man' as a scientific object as a figure of
thought in modern human sciences. Cultural theorist Johan Hedrén recognises
the 'eco-machine' as a figure of thought in Swedish environmental discourse.
In the population–resource crisis the idea of catastrophe is fundamental in
discourse about the future. Philosopher Hannah Arendt claimed that the natural way always heads towards decline and that a society that blindly follows
its resolved laws will always perish. Prophets will therefore by necessity be
prophets of doom, since decay can always be foretold. Therefore, it is always
the salvation, not the catastrophe, that is the miracle, since it is the salvation,
not the decline that is dependent on human freedom and capacity to change
the world and alter its direction.[33]

Perhaps the catastrophe notions of many neo-Malthusians were apoc-
alypses of disheartened scientists or conservationists. Even more, criticism of
contemporary society was a compelling rhetorical device to call attention to

the crisis *before* it was too late. Even though Vogt and Borgström employ met-aphors from Biblical eschatology, they take them into a modern setting. In its catastrophe empiricism, the apocalypse of the post-war conservationists hinges upon contemporary science.

Borgström would probably not have agreed with my analysis of his apocalypticism. In 1986, he declared that: 'I have never declared any doomsday, nor proclaimed any apocalyptic vision!!! Instead I have as a scientist presented the truth I have seen, and that I see, on the grounds of comprehensive and systematic research and studies.'[34]

Endangered Humanity

So what kind of catastrophe was impending? What sort of decline would be the result of the present course? What was at stake? The catastrophe rhetoric in the population–resource debate was often unclear in this respect. It could be contemporary material standards, culture, civilisation, or the human species. However, the last category – humanity at risk – was one of the most telling characteristics of the new ideology.

How would the earth's shrinking natural resources suffice for a growing world population? The provision dilemma became a key issue for conservationists. Manipulation of nature threatened to ruin not only resources for industry, but also scientific, national and historical treasures. The human species was now facing the possibility of its own extinction, 'the complete catastrophe' as one Swedish protagonist put it.[35]

Stories about global catastrophes caused by modern civilisation and science became popular in the 1930s. Apocalyptic films and fiction became profitable genres.[36] As historian Warren Wagar shows in *Terminal Visions: The Literature of Last Things* (1982), since 1914, humans themselves have become the most common cause of world-ending disasters in apocalyptic novels. Before World War I, natural catastrophes were the chief cause. In more than 300 books studied by Wagar, roughly two-thirds of those written after the outbreak of the First World War featured manmade disasters. This proportion is more or less constant throughout the the the twentieth century until the 1980s. The most common way humans bring catastrophe on the world in this fiction is through advanced weapon systems. However, after the Second World War there is some increase in stories about an ecological doomsday resulting from waste and pollution, or science fiction plots based on environmental catastrophes.[37]

The idea of a crisis for human civilisation arising out of population growth was widespread in the early post-war years, as in *Population Roads to Peace and War* by Guy Irving Burch and Elmer Pendell, published in 1945, and *The World's Hunger* by Frank Pearson and Floyd Harper. In an editorial in 1952, applauding the creation of the Population Council, *The New York Times* expressed the prevailing sense of seriousness about the issue. 'There is no question that the world must prepare itself to face crisis in another fifty years. How far science can go in satisfying the world's needs is largely a question of romantic speculation.' [38] The dramatic appeal of this alarming pronouncement put it in the headlines of many of the world's newspapers.

The atomic bomb spread a dark cloud over the optimism of the 1950s. Scientists who later became frontrunners of the environmental movement, such as Rachel Carson, Barry Commoner and Paul Ehrlich, were deeply troubled by a society which had developed such a horribly self-destructive device. Much post-war pessimism about the human species and the fate of the planet undoubtedly stemmed from anxiety about a nuclear holocaust. The mushroom clouds over Hiroshima and Bikini Atoll were potent symbols of the threat to humanity. They confirmed with unwanted starkness that humanity was capable of exterminating itself. The apocalyptic vision of the population–resource crisis was often linked to nuclear fear. As Borgström argued in *The Earth – Our Destiny*: 'It is thus not only the atom bomb, that forces humanity to make a resolute front against desolation. Technology, even as it is manifested in present agriculture, can not escape its responsibility for a new formation of the future.'[39]

The publisher of *The Saturday Review of Literature* captured this extinction angst in his 1948 article 'What Shall We Do to Be Saved?'

> Three years after the Second World War the course of political and economic events has persuaded vast numbers of people that the doom of mankind is sealed... To the warnings of the fatal result of an atomic and biological war there are added the death knells rung by prophets of man's starvation, resulting from the increase in the population of the globe from man's continuing destruction of nature's resources.[40]

In *Road to Survival*, Vogt warned that an atomic war might exterminate at least three-quarters of the world's inhabitants, if humankind did not end its war against nature and come to understand their mutual inter-dependence. [41] Aldo Leopold expressed the new conservation focus:

> There remains a doubt whether war, famine, and pestilence are the only horsemen to be feared. A new one, unnamed in holy writ, is now much in the headlines: a condition of unstable equilibrium between soils and waters, and their dependent plants and animals.[42]

The fate of humankind and providing for it came into focus. This catastrophe idea was not merely peripheral among scientists. After the publication of *Road to Survival* and *Our Plundered Planet*, the American Association for the Advancement of Science devoted its 1948 meeting to a discussion of the future of humanity. Osborn spoke on the subject 'What Hope for Man?' A reporter from *The New York Times* described the atmosphere at the meeting: 'Scientists...

envisioned a dark outlook for the human race in the next century. They linked this outlook to over-population and the dwindling of natural resources both of which are the direct consequences of progress in science and technology.'[43] The debate within the IUPN in 1947–8 about the direction of its work illustrates this shift of perspective; whether nature protection should stick solely to endangered species and biotas or reorient towards population issues and broader natural resource issues. Vogt's work illustrates the shifting focus. In the early 1930s he became engaged in the protection of endangered birds. Later in that decade he became concerned with the conservation of natural resources, and by the mid 1940s he was concentrating on the ecological threat to humanity.[44] Although mainstream conservation had always had human welfare as its incentive, it now became anthropocentric in the literal meaning of the word. Humankind's fate was seen in a new light. *Homo incestus* emerged on the stage of history: humanity as both threatened and threatening.

In the journal of the Swedish Conservation society, Borgström stressed the need to 'mobilise nature protection and to recreate it into caring for nature in a way that guarantees that wild nature survives the ravages of the human masses – in reality, the fundamental prerequisite for the continued existence of the human race'.[45]

The domination of this apocalyptic notion in post-war conservation debate can be illustrated by a quotation from an article in the *Nation* reporting from UNSCCUR. The reporter complained that 'the emotional tension over this issue has become so great in some scientific circles that anybody who denies that the world is in danger of coming to an early end through exhaustion of its resources is immediately accused of being against conservation.'[46]

The World Household

The world must be regarded as a unity and wise use of its resources must be planned through international cooperation. This idea, summarised here in the metaphor *the world household*, became central in the debate on natural resources.

'Other people demand their rightful share of the world cake', Borgström declared on the radio on Christmas day 1949.[47] The distress in the world became an important argument for conservationists, through which they could appeal for a sustainable maintenance of natural resources. Osborn expressed this idea in his introductory address at UNSCCUR. As a symbolic act, the conference held enormous importance. To Osborn, it was an astonishing feat for the UN to have succeeded in gathering scientists from all around the world to confront the state of global resources. It was a sign that nations now realised 'with a new and piercing clarity' that their prosperity was intimately linked to conditions in countries on the other side of the globe.[48]

The metaphor 'world household' epitomises some essential aspects of the critical debate on natural resources. The term carries global, economic and conservation connotations. Household is a reference to domestic economy; according to this metaphor the world should be managed like a house. The Greek word for house, 'oikos', is the root of both 'economy' and 'ecology', so the latter might also have been included. This was not stressed, however, when the metaphor was introduced. In an article with the headline 'The Dilemma of the World Household' in one of Sweden's influential newspapers, Borgström accounted for some of the conclusions that he argued could be derived from UNSCCUR. The natural resources of the world ought to be regarded as a unity. The prime task for politicians and experts was to organise the most efficient conservation and distribution of resources, in order to provide decent living conditions for all the people of the world. To accomplish this, two things were necessary. Political leaders and experts had to achieve international joint planning for resource use, while the inhabitants of the western world had to accept economic sacrifices which would lower their standard of living. In the climax of the article, Borgström referred to the world household metaphor: 'more careful housekeeping is probably an unavoidable choice for the well-being of the whole of humanity'.[49]

When Boyd-Orr received the Nobel Peace Prize in 1949, Borgström wrote an article on the occasion. He quoted from a lecture given by the prize-winner, which he had attended the previous year. 'The world has now become so small that our only hope for survival is to cooperate to abolish poverty – to raise the people in the undeveloped countries. We must do it, if nothing else, to save ourselves.' And Borgström continued in his own words: 'It is but another expression of the increasingly conspicuous truth that the world has become *one* and indivisible. No part remains unaffected by what happens in other countries and continents.'[50]

Swedish exponents of the argument constantly emphasised that the world had shrunk in recent years. What had previously been observed on a small scale in Sweden was now being described from a 'planetary viewpoint'.[51] A new view of Sweden's position as an integral part of the world had emerged. This can be illustrated by a quotation from the local newspaper of Borgström's hometown at that time. 'The world has become so small, we are all dependent on one another, and we have failed with the most important issue – in spite of all progress a great part of the world's population is starving.'[52]

Reports from World War II and the liberation of the colonies certainly contributed to the shrinkage of the world and the widening of horizons. Borgström's South American journey is one example of this process. His lectures about the journey gathered big audiences and local newspapers gave animated reports from these meetings.[53] All the more, the world household idea was connected to contemporary internationalisation and improved communications. By the middle of the century, modern airplanes, ships and missiles had rendered geographical isolationism obsolete, thus forcing national interests towards a global perspective. Most of all, the globally-expanding economy of post-war Fordism brought about a transformation in economic production and its related modes of social and political regulation. As a metaphor for international relations 'global' appeared in economics in the 1920s.[54]

This process could be observed in other fields. Historian of science Donna Haraway states that 'population' replaced 'race' as the key object of knowledge for the science of biology after the Second World War. To break the bio-scientific nexus of race, blood and culture, 96 internationally distinguished scientists signed the 1951 UNESCO statement on race. It refuted the tie between race and culture and advocated a populationist evolutionary biology. Typological taxonomies became bad science. 'This was a scientific humanism that emphasised flexibility, progress, cooperation, and universalism.' Plasticity and educability, not racial differences, now characterised humanity. According to Haraway, a new universal man was born.[55] In *Our Plundered Planet*, Osborn noted that '[t]he saying "We are all brothers under the skin" has a basis in scientific fact'.[56]

Today globalisation attracts both praise and execration. Either it is the sister- and brotherhood of humanity come true, or a disguised attempt, conscious or unconscious, to impose once again the values of the Western world on all other cultures of the world, a manifestation of the imperialism of high modernity. As argued in Chapter Three, the globalisation discourse defined a Euro-American concept of a common world destiny. All nations of the world were perceived to be moving along the same track, sharing the same goal and intended destiny. So, while globalisation's emphasis on planetary unity was a reaction against absurd racism, it also involved ideas necessary to the global expansion of Fordism.

The notion that all members of the world's population shared the same historic striving was prevalent among the new conservationists as well. This common track might not be development, but the concept of a commonly defined historical goal for all people was at the heart of the new global vision. A discourse of globalisation was established which to a large extent still prevails. Peter J. Taylor and Frederick H. Buttel's analysis of later attempts to define global environmental problems could be taken from the globalisation agenda of the early post-war years:

> In technocratic formulations, objective, scientific and (typically) quantitative analyses are employed to identify the policies that society ... needs in order to restore order or ensure its sustainability or survival – policies to which individuals, citizens, and countries would then submit.... The solutions appeal to

common, undifferentiated interests as a corrective to corrupt, self-serving, naive
or scientifically ignorant governance.[57]

The idea of a world household was thus in some ways congruent with the globalisation discourse. This circumstance allowed it access to public platforms.
Conservationists emphasised the common interest of the world's population in
making restorative efforts for nature. In this regard, they rarely addressed the
fact that different groups, people and nations could have diverse interests in how
natural resources were managed. In the post-war debates, many protagonists
acted as if there was a common cause. A unitary and undifferentiated global *we*
was defined for humankind.[58] According to political scientists Frank Fischer and
Maarten A. Hajer, global environmental discourse has 'suggested much more
unity and shared understanding between the countries and the cultures of the
world than can be legitimately assumed'.[59] In a universalising globalisation,
environmental issues can function as a symbolic umbrella that stretches over
all in a common society open to common risk. We all have a common cause,
with common values and common interests.

However, this critique of the conservationists might be unfair, if it does
not take into account that it might have been necessary to go from the particular
to the general, to relate a specific situation to a general structure, in order to be
able to comprehend it. The credibility of conservation ideology also benefited
from its global aspiration. If a group is successful in universalising its aims, it
avoids appearing as a sectional interest. As philosopher Georg Lukács points
out, a certain group (class) in *praxis* needs to inscribe its own condition within
a wider context if it is to change that condition. In doing so it may challenge
the ideology of those who have an interest in blocking emancipatory knowledge. Many reformers, including those whose project has been to end slavery,
racism, etc., have done this.[60]

Another kind of globalisation emerges in the 1960s, a *reflexive globalisation*. This involves awareness that we live in a global society where perceptions
of discrete spaces have become fictive. However, aspects of the present variety of
globalisation can be criticised, such as cultural homogeneity or the hegemony of
the capitalism of the North. All humans do not share the same understanding
of the environment, merely because we all share the globe as a common planet
of settlement.[61] To understand the process of globalisation of environmental
issues, it is necessary to acknowledge this struggle between universalising and
reflexive globalisation.[62]

Again, I am not arguing that conservation was invented by the rich,
powerful nations to help impose their will on the world. Conservationism as
represented by people like Leopold, Vogt, Osborn, Borgström and others in
the same tradition, certainly was not *invented* as a disguised neo-imperialism.

On the contrary it could be a very critical and subversive ideology that challenged the ruling order. Nevertheless, it was part of a globalisation discourse, a common way of talking about an interlinked world. Discourse can combine people with opposing goals in a common way to talk about the issues. The western take on global environmental problems has been criticised by people in the global South, as yet another viewpoint imposed by the North on other peoples in the world. The conservationists' message of an interdependent world *could* tie in with economic interest. As will be evident in Chapters 8 and 9, conservationist-style neo-Malthusianism has been picked up by other interest groups at least partly for this purpose.

The Ecological Society

Environmental issues moved politically from mainly local questions toward regarding society itself as the problem. If society was violating the order of nature, it was inevitable that it was going to collapse. Therefore it was necessary to attain by political means a change in the direction of society, so that it was adjusted to the capacities of nature. Using the authority of science to argue that human survival was threatened, post-war conservationists developed a political critique of industrial society. This theme is here called *the ecological society,* since it involved norms drawn from ecological studies. However, it is an analytical concept. Conservationists expressing this theme do not necessarily have to use the word 'ecology'.

Criticism against the contemporary political order was mostly reformatory in scope. Going back to agrarian society was simply not an option for Borgström. Trained as a food scientist, he could well foresee starvation among millions more people, if Western society were to be transformed back to the production modes of agrarian society. The critique of civilisation did not imply that the modern project had failed. It was unfinished and needed to be corrected. Society must alter its direction and be organised according to the laws of nature. His suggested changes can be summarised in four ideas: Through *public education on ecological issues, international political cooperation, a greater endeavour in scientific research,* and *a fairer world order,* humanity could get back on the right track again and thus avoid an ecological catastrophe.

In various contributions to the debate, the authors demanded that the question of humankind's relationship to nature had to be dealt with within an overall plan. If the problems were to be solved, they could not be divided into separate compartments.[63] After the sessions on ecology at IUPN, Harroy arrived at this conclusion: since the lesson derived from the meetings was that everything was interwoven, it was necessary to end specialisation in science as well as in politics.[64]

How was this alteration of society's course to come about? According to the resolutions at the UNESCO conference, it required new ethics and increased interdisciplinary education. At ITCPN one of the main preoccupations was how to convey the insights of researchers and experts to the public. Without the support of the public, ecological thinking would always be in the shadow of short-term economic profits. The new society was to be realised through education; it demanded enlightenment of the people.[65] Several writers in Sweden shared the view of Gunnar Beskow, that by far the most pressing political necessity for the moment was to make the rulers aware of biological laws. 'Our only hope is if public awareness becomes so penetrated by how matters actually stand that even politicians and economists have to show respect.'[66]

The effects the authors set out to achieve might differ from text to text. The intentions depend on context and in what circumstances the article is written. At a conference like UNSCCUR, the object seems to be to convince politicians and fellow scientists. ITCPN, which gathered together like-minded scientist and conservationists, appears to be directed towards strategies for action. Over all, though, the new conservation ideologists seem to be primarily focused on public education as a way to influence political power. Most of the publications are intended for a broader audience, for whom their scientific arguments are made accessible. The most important political chore was to get the legislators to understand biological laws.[67]

Moreover there also appeared demands for radical changes in economic politics. The threats towards nature were not an aberration of the socio-economic order, but a direct consequence of it. In the early post-war years several influential writers expressed this politicised conservationism.[68]

As mentioned in Chapter Three, Vogt strongly advocated planned economy on natural resource issues. In his book of 1947, *Road to Survival,* he pointed out in neo-Malthusian manner the grave consequences that would follow through the devastation of the earth's natural resources and the ever-increasing world population. The free market economy was to blame for the impending catastrophe.

> For free enterprise must bear a large share of the responsibility for devastated forests, vanishing wildlife, crippled ranges, a gulled continent, and roaring flood crests. Free enterprise – divorced from biophysical understanding and social responsibility.[69]

To Vogt, the only road to survival was an adjustment of the economic system to the laws of nature. A fundamental transformation of society was necessary, 'a revolution in Kropotkin's sense', which implied a radical change in the perception of humanity's interaction with nature. Vogt placed his hope in international planning of resources, primarily through the UN.[70]

Even though Fairfield Osborn was less critical towards free enterprise, he called for a new economic order. For him, industrialism's increasing exhaustion of non-renewable resources paired with population growth was the key problem in the 1940s. 'The exhaustion of these resources implies major, even drastic changes in the world's economy', Osborn proclaimed at UNSCCUR.[71] Borgström concurred. Charity to the starving people of the world was not enough, 'a new societal order must take shape'.[72] Thus, some of the conservationist conclusions and recommendations, such as criticism of free market economy or pleas for centralised international economic planning, distanced them from the liberal economic core of the natural resources discourse. In the United States at this time, these were certainly controversial claims. It made the conservationist vulnerable to accusations of communist sympathies. In a review of *Road to Survival*, ecologist Paul Sears worried that conservationists such as Vogt and Osborn might be accused of communism.[73]

Borgström presented a vision of the rich world acting in solidarity with the underdeveloped countries and a new ethic where the Golden Rule was the guiding moral norm for society. Borgström called this optimistic anticipation 'the only realistic action programme', but in retrospect it appears rather as a utopian programme. An ideology may well have a utopian element as its specific type of political orientation towards the future. Explicitly or implicitly it entails a view of a possible future social order that is radically different from the present. The very meaning of the word 'utopia' is 'nowhere', as it was coined by Thomas More in his book about the island that was nowhere. As Ricoeur points out, utopia thus implies a form of reflexivity, 'the ability to conceive of an empty place from which to look at ourselves'.[74] Even if Borgström's optimistic vision of a world in solidarity was far-fetched at the time, he pointed out a way to go, which would inspire like-minded conservationists and future environmentalists.

Unlike some of the new conservationists, Borgström never gave any attention to aesthetic arguments for protecting nature. For him it was solely a matter of the means of support. Preservation was not Borgström's primary concern. In fact there is a striking difference between the focus of the preservationist movements on pristine nature and Borgström's concern for how nature was best managed for the maximum common good. The important mission was to provide for this planet's needy human inhabitants. In that respect, his message was not an expression of a post-materialist perception, where nature is a place for leisure and recreation. The new ideology was not only concerned with a shift of attitude, it called for a change in the systems of production, it even involved new systems of distribution. In this sense at least, some of those involved formulated a new kind of conservationism, opposed to American and European classic wilderness preservation. It was closer to what Ramachandra

Guha and Juan Martinez-Alier label as the environmentalism of the poor, where the struggle over productive resources is at the heart of the conflict.[75] Of course, it was still concern from 'outside'. It was not a struggle for the conservationists' own daily subsistence, it was not a question of their own immediate survival.

Ecology in the middle decades of the century centred on concepts like producers and consumers, planning, management and engineering – metaphors derived from the political-economic field. The managerial ethos in the so-called New Ecology, which had emerged by the middle decades of the twentieth century, reinforced by political–economical metaphors, was applied back to society.[76] The need for ecological management of the world's natural resources not only implied the vital importance of political planning. It also promoted the idea of social engineering extended to the whole world of life. In *Our Plundered Planet*, Osborn urged for a more centralised planning to cope with the depletion of the nation's assets. He proposed a massive education campaign to convince the public of the need to restrict property rights to strike a balance in the country's natural resources.[77]

In some articles the first four themes of the ideology outlined above are expressed, but the authors do not draw political implications from them. Some merely conclude that the situation is serious or that people must be educated in these issues, but do not relate it to a political change. These articles express conservation ideas, but not the ideology. The political norms for society have to be manifest, or at least clearly latent, if the article is to be categorised as a manifestation of the *new* ideology.

Of course, previous conservation had been political. All texts, all statements have an absolute political horizon through which they must be understood. But the new conservationism had explicitly expressed political motives. That is not to say that its adherents always conceived of themselves as political agents. Borgström stressed that he was not a politician. He was merely presenting the facts.

A New Conservationism?

Was this post-war conservation ideology really new? According to historian Arthur Herrman, among others, there is a direct line of descent from the declentionist philosophies in the nineteenth century, and the Malthusians and environmental pessimists of the twentieth century.[78] However, on a closer examination of conservationist neo-Malthusians, it is clear that the kinship is quite remote. Some of them argued that the critique was not new, it had been known since the days of Malthus. The novelty was that it was now subject to public debate.

However, the contrary view seems to have been more common, indicating that many of those involved held the opinion that a shift of ideas was taking place in their own time. Sten Selander argued that 'in recent years' it had become clear that nature protection was 'the most important of all practical issues' involving the survival of humanity.[79]

According to historian of literature, Martin Kylhammar, Selander re-evaluated his conservation programme after reading Vogt. Faced with Vogt's scenario, the Swedish Conservation Society's struggle for an aesthetic, scientific and social nature protection would in the long run be meaningless.[80] Fairfield Osborn and Samuel H. Ordway in the Conservation Foundation labelled themselves 'new Conservationists' to emphasise the broader perspective compared with old-fashioned nature protection.[81] This ties in with one of the conclusions of this chapter: even though aspects of its themes had appeared earlier, this does not contradict the fact of a new post-war ideology. It is essential for the analysis of the post-war debate to realise that these themes now constituted an ideology, where the ideas supported and depended on one another and were connected with norms for society. In short: scientific evidence shows that humanity itself is endangered, since the order of nature has been violated by society's utilisation of nature. Thus, a political change toward an ecological society was needed to avoid catastrophe, where the common resources of the world household were to be planned in international cooperation. The notions of a world household and endangered humanity are perhaps the most striking expressions of the new ideology, but all five themes are intimately connected. This ideology is also essentially new in the respect that it was intimately linked to post-war discourses such as that on globalisation. The themes have been exemplified by quotations from various articles. Are they then used consistently in a specific debate, according to the analysis? Is the ideology concept applied here just a futile attempt to see a unity among agents lumped together in a mythical past by latter day environmentalism?

In the books referred to, Borgström, Osborn and Vogt clearly adhere to the ideology. A content analysis using indicator words from three public Swedish debates (1948, 1949 and 1953–4) and the proceedings from the plenary meeting at UNSCCUR 1949,[82] shows that the themes were frequently expressed, even when all allusions and merely hinted references are ignored.

The idea of a world household is the most commonly expressed theme in the articles. The political conclusions were more controversial, and often only vaguely expressed. At UNSCCUR, catastrophe empiricism was, perhaps surprisingly, little expressed. A more in-depth reading reveals, however, that sometimes the catastrophic arguments were collected from specific scientific fields that were not covered by the rather general vocabulary used for indicator words. And since it was a scientific conference, the scientific foundation for

Table 4. Conveyed New Conservation Ideology Themes

	Ideological themes				
	World household	Order of nature	Catastrophe empiricism	Endangered humanity	Ecological society
Sweden 1948–9 (9)	6	5	4	5	4
UNSCCUR 1949 (88)	32	21	13	22	15
Sweden 1953–4 (15)	10	8	7	8	6
Total (122)	48	34	24	35	25

Number of articles expressing conveyed new conservation ideology themes. The texts were scanned and searched by computer. Only the manifest message was analysed, using indicator words for each of the themes. Numbers of Contributions in respective debate are in parenthesis. Following indicator words, derived from the qualitative analysis, were used for the themes respectively: *Order of Nature*: 'balance', 'limit', 'order', 'interplay'; *Catastrophe Empiricism*: 'catastrophe' OR 'crisis' OR 'danger' OR 'extinct' OR 'threat' OR 'risk' OR 'danger' AND 'knowledge', OR 'prognos.' OR 'statistics' OR 'proof' OR 'calcul.' OR 'support' OR 'fact' OR 'figure' OR 'science'; *Endangered Humanity*: 'catastrophe', 'danger', 'extinction', 'threat', 'risk', 'danger', 'impend', 'future of' AND 'planet' OR 'world', OR 'man' OR 'civilisation'; *The World Household*: 'World' OR 'Earth' OR 'planet' OR 'glob.' AND 'household' OR 'common' OR 'care' OR 'provision' OR 'conservation' OR 'share'; *Ecological Society*: Texts coded as Order of Nature AND 'politics' OR 'regulat.' OR 'govern' OR 'societ.'.

the argument was taken for granted. Still, most contributions seem not to have perceived the population–resource crisis as catastrophic, rather more as a serious problem for the economic development of the world.

The content analysis also confirms that proponents of conservation ideas conveyed the ideology. In 14 out of 112 contributions, the structural argument is based on the outlined conservation ideology, where all five themes depend on and support one another. In four other articles, at least three of the conservation ideas were expressed.

It is problematic to compare English and Swedish material. It is of course not possible to conclude from this analysis that conservation ideology was more frequently expressed in Sweden than in the United States. Rather, it is a question of genre: one explanation might be that in a public debate it was easier to express your political views more freely, whereas at a conference you had to consider the conventions of international scientific conferences. For example, Borgström did not express any of the ideas at UNSCCUR, but all of them in an article four months earlier, when Osborn's book was published in Swedish. In radio and newspaper debates, two opposing sides, must often conservation and utilisation, are invited by an editor. Representatives of different positions are summoned to vie with one another. At UNSCCUR, most participants were appointed by their governments and a few by other organisations. The small number of articles conveying a conservation ideology reveals its marginalised role in the natural resources discourse, even though it was not completely expelled.

Jeffrey C. Ellis criticises Osborn and Vogt for seeing overpopulation as the only root cause and failing to consider the massive over-consumption of the United States. [83] It is true that there was a strong emphasis on the problems of overpopulation, but their analysis was more complex than attributing the origin of the crisis to the single factor of population growth. By contrast, Vogt emphasised the fault of free market economy and Osborn resource depletion caused by industrialisation. Even though they highlighted the issue of overpopulation, their argumentation was congruent with this new complex ideology. The emphasis on overpopulation can be explained by the controversial status of this issue which they were trying to establish on the agenda. The preparatory

Table 5. Conveyed New Conservation Ideology

	Number of articles	Articles expressing the new conservation ideology	
		n	%
Sweden 1948–9	9	4	44
Sweden 1953–4	15	5	33
UNSCCUR 1949	88	5	6
Total	122	14	8

Number of articles expressing a new conservation ideology. Articles where all five themes in Table 4 are manifest.

work of UNSCCUR shows how delicate the issue was at the time. However, later in the 1950s, the case might have been different.

The new ideology tied in closely with the preoccupations of the time, such as the new demands of capitalist production modes and mass consumption, globalisation discourse and new technological possibilities for mass destruction. These were issues that were inadequately dealt with in traditional utilisation practice as well as in old-style conservationism. They allowed the new ideology only limited success, but success all the same. The messages of the conservationists in many respects are attached to the discourse of modernisation. There are examples of a more thorough anti-modernism, but until the movement of the late 1960s they were few and had little influence. In the late 1940s, critics first expressed the themes. During the following decade they became central in the debates on natural resources. Even though opponents disagreed with the conservationists' conclusions, they had to relate to these themes. They formed essential parts of the ideological foundation of the intense environmental debates that were yet to come. Expressed as it was by several influential conservationists in unison, the new conservation ideology helped to form an understanding of a global environmental crisis.

In the critique of the utilisation of the world's natural resources a new narrative of the terms for human civilisation was declared. An ideology was formed that became essential to the worldview of the environmental movement and the formation of an environmental discourse in the 1960s.[84] This is not to say that there is a direct line from new conservationism to present-day environmentalism. There is no common origin of identical meaning or coherent identity between them. But the new conservationism is certainly one forerunner of environmentalism, one that resembles it, but still has to pass through transformations, repudiations, substitutions and displacements.[85]

As Pierre Bourdieu points out in his elaboration of Plato's concept of *doxa*, an ideology must try to close the gap between itself and social reality, into which critique could be inserted. It must try to coincide with people's conditions of living to avoid anomalies that could stir distrust. Otherwise a new ideology will appear which provides a tighter fit. Therefore social reality is reviewed and redefined by ideology, so that they will match. This process provides the appearance that reality has generated the ideology, not that it is the other way round, or that they breed together.[86] Inspired by Bourdieu, Terry Eagleton states that 'successful ideologies are often thought to render their beliefs natural and self-evident – to identify them with the "common sense" of a society so that nobody could imagine how they might ever be different'.[87] An ideology would hardly survive if it could not forge its descriptions, values and recommendations into a perceived unity. It must find support in that which can be regarded as reasonable, sound and continuously confirmed. To appear as consistent with reality, ideology needs to be legitimated by experience, common sense or some accepted institutions of knowledge; preferably all of these. Conservation ideology thus connected itself with experiences in time, such as food shortage, World War rationing and dust-bowls; with common sense, 'you cannot eat your cake and have it'. Moreover it sought its legitimisation through science, whereupon we shall turn to the scientific arms of conservationism and neo-Malthusianism.

6

On the Outskirts of Babel

Science was given a crucial role in international politics in addressing the population–resource crisis, as the UN resource conference 1949 and the endeavours toward the Green Revolution made evident. For the new conservation ideology scientific knowledge was fundamental, often with an emphasis on a new synthesis using interdisciplinary research.

Science certainly prescribed the premises in the post-war debate on resources, for the utilisation as well as for the conservation side. For both sides, science was the normative foundation on which society should be built, although they differed fundamentally on the design of the construction. In the scientific community, the dividing line between the two sides was conspicuous.

This chapter deals with the role of science in the early post-war population–resource crisis. Its purpose is twofold: it starts out with a discussion of the scientific influences on the new conservationists, and details how this was received among other researchers at the universities and in industry. Reactions in the scientific community are illustrated through the career of Borgström as a food scientist. It will try to answer why neo-Malthusians caused so much commotion, and to discern what interests they challenged in the scientific world.

The Scientific Arm of Conservationism

The emergence of the new conservation ideology owed much to scientists, particularly from such fields as ecology and geography. Ecology is sometimes described as the scientific arm of the conservation movement. In some respects this is true. Much of the rhetoric in American conservationism is derived from ecological studies. However, many of the concepts that are perceived to be derived from the field of ecology, such as the metaphor of a *balance of nature*, actually have their origin in traditional natural history.[1]

Starting out from plant physiology and gradually broadening his scope until he eventually become professor both of Food Science and Human Nutrition and of Geography, Borgström's professional career could have neatly encompassed the two main scientific influences on conservationism: ecology and geography. However, Borgström's career does not fit as conveniently as that. Although a representative transformer of the new ideology, he was more of a plant physiologist than an ecologist.

Even though ecology as a scientific practice was fairly young at this time, it was a recognisable scientific field, since its theses were organised on the lines of scientific models, and strove towards coherence and demonstrativity. It was also accepted, institutionalised and transmitted as science. Apart from the scientific field of ecology, there developed a common usage of the term 'ecology' that draws upon the connotations of the word, implying that its purpose is not to define but to associate. This approach is here called *rhetorical ecology*, since it is connected to the communication of concepts obtained from the field of ecology, rather than to its scientific practice. Rhetorical ecology attached itself to ideas derived from ecological research, such as interdependence and equilibrium in nature.

Borgström appears not to have been directly influenced by contemporary well-known ecologists. Though he referred to 920 sources in his list of references in *The Earth – Our Destiny*, Borgström only used one reference that used the word ecology in its title, Amos H. Hawley's book on *Human Ecology*.[2] Moreover, he did not use this reference in terms of ecology. Not one of the earlier and contemporary ecologists mentioned in Thomas Söderqvist's ambitious study of the emergence of Swedish ecology is quoted in *The Earth – Our Destiny*. Of the other names and works mentioned in three major American and British works on ecology [3] only three are mentioned in the references to *The Earth – Our Destiny* and none of these was used in reference to particular scientific ecological issues. The physical chemist Alfred J. Lotka's co-authored *Length of Life: A Study of the Life Table* (1936),[4] and population geneticist Raymond Pearl's *The Natural History of Population*, [5] were both mentioned in references to the introductory chapter in connection with the seriousness of human population growth. Biologist Rachel Carson's *The Sea Around Us* was quoted in a chapter dealing with the sea as a nutritional source.[6] Only once did Borgström use the term 'ecology' or its derivatives in this book. 'The information in the long run, will aim at giving humans a sound ecological orientation, that takes into consideration the demands of nature.'[7] This singular usage seems to relate to the popular, rhetorical sense of the word, rather than referring to the scientific field of ecology.

In the three Swedish public debates that confirmed the proponents of conservation ideas as conveyers of ideology (see Chapter Four), only one of the protagonists used the word *ecology*.[8] Neither in these debates nor in *The Earth – Our Destiny* does Borgström use common concepts in the scientific field of ecology, such as 'climax', 'equilibrium', 'food chain', 'stability'.[9] In contrast, Osborn and Vogt referred to these common scientific concepts.[10]

Neither does he use the following concepts that are central in Systems Ecology: 'ecosystem', 'niche', 'energy flux', 'consumer', 'producer', 'reducer' and 'decomposer'.

So, when Borgström, more than 30 years later, claims in retrospect to have embraced ecology in the late 1940s, it appears not have been with respect to the scientific field of ecology, but rather in a rhetorical way which conveyed a common understanding of ecology. In 1969, Borgström called Malthus 'the world's first ecologist', which provides us with a Borgströmian definition of ecology. Malthus was an ecologist in the sense that he saw the global causal connection across the specialised disciplines.[11] Perhaps it is symptomatic that Borgström in 1971 changed the subtitle of his 1969 book *Too Many* from 'A *Biological* Overview of Earth's Limitations' to 'An *Ecological* Overview of Earth's Limitations'.

Rather than studies in ecology, it appears to be his nutritional and demographic studies that inspired his new direction. In *Mat för miljarder* (*Food for Billions*), from 1962, he describes the crisis not as an ecological problem but as economic–demographic and nutritional.[12]

From a disciplinary point of view, economic geography became an important field for Borgström in the early 1950s. Yet, as he himself pointed out, Osborn and Vogt contributed a great deal to his worldview. He shared the basic ideas outlined by Vogt and Osborn, who on their part used major ecological authors like Charles Elton, Aldo Leopold, Raymond Pearl, J. E. Weaver, Paul B. Sears, and Fredric E. Clements. They were profoundly affected by studies in ecology. Thus, the scientific field of ecology influenced Borgström indirectly.

In the following, I will examine scientific influences on conservationists concerned with population by relating to three strands important to the emerging environmental consciousness: *Land Ethics, Ecological Equilibrium* and *The Human Species Community.*

Land Ethics

Aldo Leopold is probably the single person in the field of environmental history who has been most closely associated with the reciprocal relationship between ecology and conservation. Borgström made no references to him in *The Earth – Our Destiny,* but Vogt and Osborn relied heavily on Leopold's work.

Leopold became famous after he published his *Game Management* in 1933 and he is widely regarded as the father of wildlife management in America. In this book Leopold promoted the theory of a comprehensive scientific management of nature as a means to advance social and economic objectives. But gradually Leopold became sceptical about this drive for a controlled environment.[13]

It is not primarily to *Game Management* that conservationists such as Osborn turned. In 1933 Leopold also published a more philosophical essay entitled 'The Conservation Ethic'. Here he reasoned that the relationship between *ecology* and *economics* was not altogether harmonious. Instead of resource exploitation as a means of livelihood, he advocated a reconciliation, 'a universal symbiosis' between technological civilisation and the land. Like many conservationists, Leopold was vague about 'that new social concept toward which conservation is groping'.[14] The experience of the Dust Bowl years had led Leopold to the conclusion that humankind threatened its own existence. Through neglect of the rights of the land, an ecological catastrophe was impending. In 1947 Leopold stressed that it was necessary to teach the public an 'ecological consciousness', which emphasised that humankind is a dependent member of the biotic community.[15]

Leopold had just finished his classic essay 'The Land Ethic' when he died in 1948 while fighting a brush fire. This text stands as a landmark in the new conservationism. It brings together a biocentric ethic with a science-based ecological criticism of modern economic exploitation of nature. Besides 'The Land Ethic', the posthumously published *Sand County Almanac* (1949) contains a series of outdoor natural history essays, which reveal a disillusionment with the faith in rational management of nature, of which he himself had previously been a representative. Over-specialised scientific management was denounced: in the essay 'Natural History – The Forgotten Science' he defied the narrow-minded academic researcher. Conservation had to have a broader scientific perspective. He advocated reviving holistic out-of-doors education. The sciences taught in laboratories and universities merely served technological progress.[16] He was yet another pro-technologist turned sceptic towards academic specialisation. Humanity had to accept its role as a 'plain member and citizen' of the Earth, instead of trying to be its masters. The *Land Ethic* required humans to encompass a communitarian ethic towards all beings in nature. 'We abuse land because we regard it as a commodity belonging to us. When we see land as a community to which we belong, we may begin to use it with love and respect.'[17]

Leopold emphasised the dichotomy between agricultural practices and the ecological context. Traditional conservation felt 'no inhibition against violence, its ideology is agronomic', i.e. land use had an economic rationale, whereas the new conservation approach was inspired by 'an ecological conscience'.[18]

Vogt and Osborn shared material and references with each other. These authors also corresponded with ecologists Paul Sears, Charles Elton and G. Evelyn Hutchinson. According to Lewis in 'Progress and Apocalypse', Leopold supplied Vogt and Osborn with recent ecological thinking, whereas Vogt gave Leopold advice on editing. He also tried to persuade his publisher, Sloane, to publish Leopold's *Sand County Almanac*. In March 1947, Osborn invited both

Leopold and Vogt to a meeting at the New York Zoological Society to plan the foundation of the Conservation Foundation. Vogt, Leopold, Sears, Elton, Hutchinson and Carl Sauer all came to serve on the Conservation Foundation's advisory council.[19]

Even though Osborn and Vogt referred to Leopold in their books from 1948, Borgström first referred to him as late as 1962 in his book *Food for Billions,* by quoting *A Sand County Almanac.* However, it is not as a scientist he is using Leopold, but as 'the great nature writer of the USA'. And it is not his Land Ethic that he turns to. He is quoting Leopold on the dangers of not owning a farm, that is, when people believe that breakfast comes from the grocery store and that heat comes from the oven. Borgström used this Leopold quotation apropos of the importance of educating youth in the fundamentals of food production.[20] Vogt and Osborn were also profoundly influenced by Paul B. Sears' ecological work, especially *Deserts on the March* (1935), in which he delivers a harsh critique of prevalent land-use practices. Through an extensive international survey of desertification, Sears examined the catastrophic consequences of ecologically misunderstanding nature. Like Leopold, Sears was affected by the experience of the Dust Bowl in the Midwest, which threatened to turn the Great Plains into a barren desert.[21] Borgström for his part was influenced by the British soil scientists Graham V. Jacks and Robert O. Whyte, who in their dramatic *The Rape of the Earth: A World Survey of Soil Erosion* (1939) warned that industrial society's exploitation of the environment threatened to bring about a catastrophe for human civilisation.[22]

Ecological Equilibrium

The concept of an ideal state of nature was apparent in a holistic tradition in natural history and early ecology, characterised by phrases like 'the unity of nature', 'the chain of being', or 'balance of nature'. The idea of a balanced nature that was essentially stable dominated the greater part of nineteenth century biology and natural history. Scientists hoped to find order in the universe, and the tradition of balance of nature and economy of nature was predicated on such an order, divinely ordained or naturally engendered.[23] The works of Malthus and Darwin reinforced the ideas of earlier natural history and proposed that populations are limited by natural checks, but also that different populations are intertwined and related to other organisms as well as to the physical environment. Species populations formed communities that maintained balance.[24]

The dynamic ecology of the American ecologist Frederic E. Clements was based on plant-cover formation and its presumed progressive development or succession to climax. It was recognised by many of his contemporaries and successors as the premier theory of plant ecology. From Clements's work were

derived factors responsible for maintaining equilibrium, or for controlling populations in the absence of equilibrium. Populations were formed and replaced
until a relatively stable *climax* was reached which was maintained through
self-regulating and stable populations. Major ecologists in Great Britain and the
USA were focused on the problem of stability and how equilibrium of populations could be maintained within a community. Randomness and extinction
were not commonly regarded as possibilities.[25]

Clements's doctrine of climax as a natural ideal seems to have been well
established among new conservationists. His climax theory provided a touchstone for judging human manipulation of nature and a substantial scientific
argument for the normative order of nature. Worster points out its importance
for American environmentalists.

> Their basic assumption was that the aim of land-use policy should be to leave
> the climax as undisturbed as possible – not on account of the intrinsic value of
> virgin wilderness, but more pragmatically because it had proved itself through
> millennial vicissitudes of climate to be stable, tenacious, and marvellously well
> adapted to its habitat.[26]

As they were used to interpreting interaction among species in terms of niche
and competition, it seems reasonable that this understanding would lead to
the conclusion that, when humans expanded their environmental space, other
species would suffer. If a biotic community was changing toward a climax that
attained a state of equilibrium, to break this climax would mean to disturb the
balance. As Vogt interpreted Weaver and Clements, natural areas are in, or will
tend toward, a climax in the absence of human disturbance.[27]

In the United States, the Clementian emphasis on a progressive trend
towards climax and a stable state under the control of climate, succession and
organismic community dominated the major textbooks of plant ecology before
1950.[28] According to ecologist Robert P. McIntosh, 'Clements' organismic
dynamic theory of communities was widely accepted by many plant ecologists
and at least tacitly by animal ecologists until the 1950s.'[29]

In order to speak of a disturbance of nature, there must be an understanding of a systemic order that constitutes the normative 'state of the art'. The
normative nature idea was established in environmental debate. It was tacitly
presupposed in discussion of other issues, such as pollution. When dealing
with pollution in *Purity and Danger,* anthropologist Mary Douglas states that
it is necessary to presuppose such an order to identify matter as 'out of place'.[30]

As discussed in Chapter Five, a new moral consciousness took shape in
the early post-war years. Humankind was threatened, so the insights of ecology
must be used to restrain the powers of science-based technology. It coincided
with the shadows of the mushroom clouds of Hiroshima and Bikini. However,
it was not until 1958 that the ecological effects of atomic fallout became a

widespread concern among American scientists. In an analogy borrowed from T.H. Huxley, William Vogt compared the knowledge of ecology with that of knowing the rules of chess. If one's happiness depended on winning a game of chess, surely everyone would learn the rules.

> Yet it is a very plain and elementary truth that the life, the fortune and the happiness of every one of us do depend upon our knowing something of the rules of a game infinitely more complicated than chess. The chessboard is the world, the pieces are the phenomena of the universe and the rules of the game are what we call the laws of Nature. The player on the other side is hidden from us. We know that his play is always fair, just and patient. But we also know, to our cost, that he never overlooks a mistake or ignorance.. One who plays ill is checkmated without haste but without remorse.[31]

In this deterministic description of world order, Vogt's awesome god of ecology appears like the Old Testament Jehovah. The concept of balance of nature began to be questioned as quantitative studies of populations and communities increased. Frank Egerton states that the traditional understanding of the balance-of-nature concept assumed more or less a stability of populations in a likewise stable environment.[32] In *Animal Ecology and Evolution* (1930), Charles Elton, an Oxford University zoologist, refuted the idea of nicely balanced animal communities. 'The "balance of nature" does not exist, and perhaps never has existed.'[33] In 1927 Elton had published his first major work, *Animal Ecology.* His more immediate purpose with this 'sociology and economics of animals' was to synthesise the existing ecological knowledge into a new model of community. Elton's interest focused on the organisation and population of, as well as the distributions within, a natural community.[34] In *Road to Survival,* Vogt recommended *Animal Ecology.* He claimed it to be the 'closest thing we have to a satisfactory text on the subject'. Many of the principles it developed were applicable to 'the problems of human populations'.[35]

Elton's critique of a balance of nature as outlined in *Animal Ecology and Evolution* did not agree with Vogt's conservation ideology and neither was this book mentioned in the reading list.

Other animal ecologists defended the balance of nature concept. Warder Clyde Allee and co-authors claimed in *Principles of Animal Ecology* (1949) that 'the community maintains a certain balance, establishes a biotic order, and has a certain unity paralleling the dynamic equilibrium and organisation of other living systems'.[36]

The tension between natural balance and natural reproduction became pressing in the 1960s. The balance concept was questioned by writers on population such as Paul Ehrlich, who described the idea of a balance in respect to population size as 'demonstrably false'.[37] Borgström expressed the same notion, in a book on Malthus in 1969. He argued that Malthus was the first to conclude that all life tends to reproduce above its access to nutrition. That is the way things have been throughout history and that is the way things will remain in the future. In that sense there was no equilibrium in nature.[38] Nevertheless, Borgström continued to speak of 'nature's delicately balanced interplay' which humankind, however, threatened to jolt by its wasteful living.[39] Population stability did not just happen as a law of nature. It was something that had to be achieved. With this in mind, neo-Malthusian conservationism could rest on population ecology. According to British biologist C. D. Darlington a comparison of population control behaviour among humans and animals had far-reaching consequences. 'The preservation of a stable population with an optimum density not only avoids war, famine, and pestilence: it preserves the whole habitat.'[40] One reason for the wars, famines and pestilence facing humankind was that the basic instinct for population control adjusted to the habitat had been thrown into disarray in recent evolution.[41]

Contrary to the ecologists who inspired new conservationists such as Vogt and Osborn, the leading British plant ecologist, Arthur Tansley, rejected many of Clements's ideas in the 1950s. He wanted to bring the discipline of ecology more into line with the positivistic ideal, with strictly mechanistic and quantitative analysis. He denounced the holistic idea that a plant aggregation is more than the sum of its parts, since it resisted a reductive analysis. He tried to rid ecology of all the persistent traces of organismic philosophy. Instead of the 'obscure' analogies to social communities and 'romantic' connotations of organisms, Tansley launched the concept of *ecosystem*. He defined ecosystem as the whole system including not only the organism-complex, but also the whole complex of physical factors. He acknowledged a hierarchy of systems and saw an ecosystem as one category in a range of systems between atom and universe. According to Worster, the concept 'dovetailed nicely with the agronomic and industrial view of nature as a storehouse of exploitable material resources'. Eco-system was a key concept in the so-called New Ecology, which further merged ecology and economics in the discourse of natural resources.[42]

Many conservationists saw ecology as a counterweight to too much economic influence on politics. In the new conservationism, science was an important instrument for repudiating the capitalist exploitation of nature. While ecological studies were used by the new conservationists to criticise the dominant economic attitude, ecology as a scientific discipline was moving in the opposite direction. Ecological studies became more abstract and reductive. Drawing from the ecosystem concept, ecology turned towards the quantitative study of energy flows in nature. The emergence of this so-called 'New Ecology' began in the 1930s and gained general acceptance among ecologists in the 1960s. Many of its key concepts were derived from economics, such as 'ecological efficiency', 'producers' and 'consumers'.

Worster argues in *Nature's Economy* that the New Ecology in the mid-decades of the twentieth century was itself influenced by economic concepts. Especially, it seems to have been affected by the managerial ethos of Fordism.[43] With Fordism came the notion that direction and control by trained specialised managers were crucial to the proper ordering of our common affairs. Economic growth depended on a new politics of production, labour and distribution control and management. Economists like John Maynard Keynes argued that it was necessary to have scientific managerial strategies as well as state powers in order to stabilise capitalism.

Through his studies in the sociology and economics of animals, Elton laid the foundation for the New Ecology. According to Worster, Elton's ideas had a tremendous impact on Anglo-American ecologists. 'In Elton's account of the natural community as a simplified economy, twentieth century ecology found its single most important paradigm.'[44]

Worster argues that it is not very persuasive to explain the development of this New Ecology simply by referring to internal explanations. 'It is obvious that the rise of a bio-economic ecology owed a great deal to its larger cultural milieu.'[45] From the basis of my analysis, that is almost an understatement. This study of the scientific community starts from the assumption that science is a historically and socially situated practice. Therefore, it must be understood in relation to the contexts in which it occurs. I argue that there is a correlation between societal conditions and scientific knowledge. Scientific descriptions of nature reflect interests in society at the time they are developed. Thus, the traditional debates among historians of science on internalism and externalism deal with an arbitrary demarcation. Both politics and science are part of the same social processes. Consequently, the development of ecology in the 1950s can be seen in part as a product of the logic of capitalist accumulation, which brought about a transformation in economic production and its related modes of social and political regulation at the beginning of the twentieth century.

The Human Species Community

In the first decades of the twentieth century the concept of 'population problems' entered the vocabulary of demography, and appeared in many publications. An early demographer, Warren S. Thompson, saw population growth as a strategic political problem. In 1929 he published *Danger Spots in World Population*, in which he argued that high population densities together with limited resources were a key factor in causing war. He continued this line of thought in 1946, in *Population and Peace in the Pacific*. He warned that the large populations of China and Japan threatened the post-war possibilities for peace in East Asia. If peace was to be secured, the United States had to recognise and deal with the pressure of these increasing populations on the natural resource base.[46] The works of demographers like Thompson were important sources for Borgström's analysis in *The Earth – Our Destiny*. He also referred to other books on demography, such as the British demographer Alexander Carr-Saunders' *World Population: Past Growth and Present Trends* (1936); the German demographer Friedrich Burgdorfer's *Sterben die weissen Völker?* (1934); and *Bevolkerungsdynamik und Bevölkerungsbilanz* (1951).

As discussed in Chapter Two, demography appeared as a respected field of academic study in the United States in the 1930s and 1940s. By connecting population growth and food production with national security, experts at universities and philanthropic organisations were successful in capturing the attention of political leaders in the United States. In the late 1940s, demography was integrated into American national security planning. Until the mid 1960s, Thompson's work was reprinted over and over.

In the mid-twentieth century, population studies of species communities led to the idea of the species community of 'the family of man' in neo-Darwinian evolutionary theory. 'Population' replaced 'race' as the key object of knowledge for the science of biology. Typological taxonomies were now regarded as bad science. The tie between race and culture was rejected, and in its place a populationist evolutionary biology was on the rise.[47]

In 1946 the Population Commission was set up under ECOSOC. From 1946 to the 1960s, in its activities on population studies, the UN concentrated on the calculation and statistics of population, reports that Borgström made great use of. The FAO's first director-general, the British biologist and Nobel Peace Prize winner Lord John Boyd-Orr seems to have inspired Borgström's work as well, even though he did not mention him in his recollections of his sources of inspiration. When Boyd-Orr received the Nobel Prize Borgström wrote celebratory articles and invited him to come to Gothenburg.[48]

His early books reveal that Borgström was inspired by the biological trend in American demography, represented by the works of Pearl, Lotka and Louis Dublin, among others. Lotka had developed a mathematical theory of stable population. As mentioned, Borgström drew upon Lotka's and Dublin's co-authored book *Length of Life* (1936). The relationship between animal and human ecology was strengthened by the efforts of Pearl's demographic studies to develop a common biological law of population growth. In his early works he applied a logistic curve of growth for everything from *Drosophila* flies to *Homo sapiens*. Pearl's effort to apply conclusions from biological experiments to human society was controversial; for example, Soviet demographers considered his analogies dubious.[49] Borgström was inspired by Pearl's work and used his *The Natural History of Population* (1939) in *The Earth – Our Destiny*. The global view of the relationship between humankind and nature gathered inspiration from various fields, for example geography and geology. In the 1950s a new interdisciplinary field appeared – *human ecology* – which brought together natural and social sciences. The fundamental message was that human civilisation had to abide by both physical and moral constraints. From the late 1940s there are many examples of an emerging field of human ecology, especially coming from anthropology and geography.[50] Borgström, in his interdisciplinary approach to the population–resource issue, connects closely to the development of human ecology. In his future career as both food scientist and geographer, this link would become even more apparent.

According to one of his confidants, Gunnar Dahmén, there were 'cock-and-bull stories' that Borgström had employed a porter to work at the laboratory till late at night to speed up the completion of the dissertation. Rudebeck also heard these rumours.[51] In spite of the criticism, he received a position as university lecturer in botany a month after receiving his degree.[52] There were intense controversies over Borgström's work, with both supporters and adversaries engaged in disputes over his scientific focus, performance and conclusions. However, criticism from fellow scientists was not so much focused on his message as on the manner in which his scientific work was conducted.

A Storm in a Tin Can

Later, in the rhetoric of the environmental movement of the 1960s, Borgström was regarded as something of a martyr, who was expelled from the leadership of SIK because of hostile reactions to his message. Even today this is a common perception among many Swedish environmentalists and scientists.[53] Non-conformist critics of the techno-science system have often been opposed and even victimised by the establishment. Perhaps many see Borgström's conflicts as a parallel to their own positions, working against the current in a hostile professional environment.

Borgström was recruited in 1948 to organise and administer the Swedish Institute for Food Preservation Research (SIK). Since he had been the director of the Institute for Plant Research and Cold Storage (IVK), he was an obvious choice for this position. The Institute was jointly financed by the Swedish government and food preservation industries. The government paid for roughly two-thirds of the finances and about 50 industries, through the Foundation for Swedish Food Preservation Research, contributed the remaining one-third.[54] The Institute's mandate was to conduct research into the preservation and storage of food, as well as to gather information from outside the country, arrange educational courses and provide information and reports.

Two years on, big and powerful preservation companies were displeased with Borgström and used their influence to get him dismissed as head of the

Institute. They wanted a more direct return on their subsidies, and accused Borgström of not devoting sufficient time to tangible science projects, and of spending too much of it on public lectures on broader topics. This criticism stemmed from Borgström's numerous speeches at organisations such as local merchants' associations, housewives' clubs, men's clubs and student unions.[55] At these meetings, he often did not limit himself to the role of preserved food in the family household, but broadened the perspective to the conservation of food resources in the world household. A vivid account of one of his speeches at the annual congress of ICA (one of Sweden's largest chains of grocery stores) gives a sense of the atmosphere that surrounded Borgström. The author described him as 'a man with magnetism. He is sturdily built, somewhat stocky, always well-dressed and polished and with an air of high society.'[56] Borgström had talked about the preserved food of tomorrow in front of 'the slightly shocked Swedish grocery merchants'.

> When Professor Georg Borgström climbed down from the podium at ICA's big November congress in Stockholm there was more than one who believed themselves to be seeing a superhuman with the eye of a Cyclops just disembarked from a spaceship. The public was spellbound. The press the day after was full of plaudits. The director of the institute of preservation research, 'the Gothenburg alarm clock', had once again won one of his numerous victories on the podium.[57]

At the end of October 1953, just after *The Earth – Our Destiny* had been published and was debated in media, Borgström's public appearances were discussed at a board meeting. Knut Laurin, chairman of one of Sweden's largest packaging companies, PLM, argued that the director devoted too much time to general questions and public work.[58]

Borgström was appointed Professor by the government on 14 November 1953. The same day, the board of the Foundation expressed discontent with Borgström's many public appearances. His alleged 'propaganda', and the associated 'exaggerations and deficient reliability,' had obstructed the possibility of persuading members of the Foundation to raise their subsidies.[59] The board of SIK consisted of five government representatives and five from the Foundation. The chairman of the board, the Liberal Member of Parliament Carl S:son Schmidt discussed the matter with Borgström. He pointed out that Borgström was in the newspapers every other day, and explained to Borgström that some of the interested parties thought that Borgström did nothing but travel, lecture and write, which was of no use to the Institute. They agreed that Borgström should make a monthly report on his public appearances. The board declared that it was content with these measures.[60] However, at the end of 1954 the issue came up again. One of the board members argued that Borgström's public work, except for presentations of the company's own research, placed a strain on the Institute's operations. The chairman, however, had no objections to the speeches mentioned by Borgström in his monthly report.[61]

In accordance with his own broad interests, Borgström wanted to broaden the scope of the Institute to more general food science. This endeavour was strongly opposed by his adversaries in the Foundation and increased their hostility.[62] But it was not only his public appearances that gave him enemies within the industry. He had also aroused criticism from some enterprises in the Foundation for issuing certificates to competing companies to be used for their marketing purposes.[63] In November 1955, the board of SIK unanimously decided to advise Borgström to find another position. Two days earlier, the Foundation and the working committee of the board had held a joint deliberation concerning Borgström's position as head of SIK. Representatives from the Foundation, led by Laurin, criticised Borgström and raised the question of his employment. They also linked the issue of directorship of SIK to the terms of a new agreement between the government and the Foundation. The financial situation for SIK was tight and subsidies from the government as well as from the Foundation had to be raised. Laurin, who was chairman of the Swedish Food Preservation Research Foundation, argued that it would be difficult to gather support among the member industries for increasing their subsidies, as long as Borgström remained head of the Institute.

Even those who considered Borgström to be a good scientist and a suitable leader of the Institute now backed down and endorsed the decision. They considered it extremely difficult to achieve productive operation in the existing circumstances. Among the researchers employed at SIK, opinions on Borgström varied. Before being questioned by the committee, they discussed their respective viewpoints on Borgström's leadership. The opinions were then fairly evenly split, roughly half in favour of Borgström and half opposed to him.[64]

The industry representatives who opposed him argued that Borgström was unfit as a leader because of his role as a scientist. Laurin, argued that 'Science and propaganda do not belong together'.[65] They also questioned his scientific competence. Their criticism was supported by company-employed researchers.[66] Borgström was characterised as being negligent with facts. Even though he used a huge number of references he sometimes used them carelessly, according to Laurin. He even had doubts whether Borgström should be regarded as a scientist.[67] In an unsigned article defending the board's decision by a person 'close to the Board of the Preservation Institute', Borgström's alleged insufficient scientific competence was the main issue. The author claimed that Borgström's dissertation had been weak. As leader of IVK in Nynäshamn, he was no success, and as head of SIK he neglected research in order to make public appearances. Rather than taking an active part in research, he had been speaking around the country, for example about starvation in Asia. According to the anonymous writer, Borgström had not published any scientific work of significance since his dissertation in 1939. Because of his 'fantastic receptivity', however, he had managed to write hundreds of articles, but these were merely compilations of other scientists' work. These articles were above all a great credit to the Institute's library, according to this critic.[68]

Later, when commenting on the allegations of Borgström's lack of scientific competence, his supporters pointed at his high receptivity and his capacity to see the broad perspective. Velander, director of the Royal Swedish Academy of Engineering Sciences, who had previously been on the board of SIK, stressed that although Borgström showed a certain lack of carefulness and stringency when dealing with numbers and statistics, this was a tendency he shared with many others. In addition, statistics in the area of world population and nutrition were indeed vague. The closer you came to the borders of knowledge, the more inevitable it was that you should sometimes be wrong, Velander argued.[69]

Board member Jöran Hult, director general of the Board of Fisheries, who was in favour of Borgström, remembered from his time at Uppsala University that Borgström's dissertation had been disputed. It was a matter of fact that Borgström was a controversial name in the scientific world. But he had an outstanding ability to fill his co-workers with enthusiasm. He was also very competent in the areas Hult had been presented with. According to Hult, Borgström's ability to compile and synthesise made him highly qualified to lead the institute.[70] Hult had been one of the actors in the Swedish controversy surrounding Osborn's *The Plundered Planet* in 1949, where he was very sympathetic to its message.

Gösta Lindeberg, microbiologist at SIK from 1952 to 1956, argued that even though the criticisms of Borgström's handling of figures might be just to some extent, it was regrettable that minor errors in figures were allowed to obscure the important conclusions of Borgström's message. 'Borgström was a synthesiser and not an analyser.'[71]

Collecting statistical material was indeed one of Borgström's specialities. He had a vast acquaintance with global literature and was competent in seven foreign languages: English, French, German, Spanish, Russian as well as the Scandinavian languages, Danish and Norwegian. This enabled him to cover a very wide range of literature. Considering the huge quantity of literature that Borgström penetrated, it is not surprising that figures could be misplaced. But that was a grave fault in a quantitative scientific setting, which celebrated the experimentally skilled and exact researcher.

Borgström had indeed distanced himself from the normal science of plant physiology. From 1949 economic geography became an ever more important field for him. In fact, in 1950 Borgström applied for a position as

Associate Professor of Geography at the University of Gothenburg. The head of the Department of Geography had encouraged him to apply, since they needed teachers. Borgström was to share his time between SIK and the Department. The professor supported his application by referring to his works on 'central problems in economic geography'.[72] However, Borgström turned down the offer when he got a position as Associate Professor in Preservation Technology at Chalmers Institute of Technology in 1951.

In regard to Borgström's scientific competence, his supporters noted that he was, after all, a member of the Royal Swedish Academy of Engineering Sciences and The Royal Swedish Academy of Agriculture and Forestry. Furthermore he had been given the title professor, an appointment that was accompanied by an examination of his scientific work.[73] One of the professors on the evaluation committee who recommended him for the designation thought that his organisational skills and his extensive use of practical scientific publications well qualified him for the title professor. Another supportive evaluator (one of the participants in the radio discussion in 1948) also thought Borgström well deserved that recognition, although he wished he would be more careful with his statistics when speaking about the world's food supplies. A third argued that Borgström would hardly have been qualified for an ordinary chair, but considering his directorship of a research institute there were enough reasons to give him the appointment. Foreign Minister Östen Undén who commented on the proposal on behalf of the government, shared this opinion.[74]

Faced with the massive animosity against him, Borgström finally resigned his position as head of SIK in August 1956, and left Sweden to become Professor of Food Technology at Michigan State University. 'The Borgström Case' aroused an intense debate in the Swedish press. In this study more than 100 articles published during the fall of 1956 have been examined; including those from 1947 and 1948, a total of more than 160 articles were studied.[75]

The major newspapers in Gothenburg, both liberal, took completely different, even mutually antagonistic standpoints. *Göteborgs Handels- och Sjöfartstidning*, whose editor had been Borgström's critic back in 1953, was very critical towards Borgström's way of running SIK and he took the side of the industrial critics. Editorials spoke of the 'The problem of Georg Borgström' as well as 'The hubbub at the Preservation Institute'.[76] On the opposite side was *Göteborgs-Posten*, which fully supported him in articles and editorials with headlines like 'Monopoly Ambitions and Mr. Borgström', 'Bluff', 'Motives for Borgström's Resignation Not Clear'.[77] All in all, *Göteborgs-Posten* published more than 50 articles on the Borgström case. His supporters at the newspaper did not blame the animosity he faced on his inconvenient message. Instead, the newspaper suspected monopoly ambitions to be the main reason behind the affair: Laurin's company produced tin cans, so he wanted to get Borgström dismissed because he opposed Laurin's attempts to persuade the Institute to close down its packaging research.[78]

Laurin had indeed made an attempt to get the packaging laboratory closed, but without success, something that annoyed him a great deal. According to the scanty board minutes, Borgström had defended the packaging laboratory and concluded that closure of the packaging research facility would have to be initiated by the government, since it was regulated in the Institute's agreement with the government.[79]

Borgström claimed that of the 55 enterprises in the Foundation 48 were pro-Borgström, five indifferent and three opposed.[80] Unfortunately for him, these were the three largest companies by far. Borgström argued that these three companies could have it their way because of their dominant position, since many of the other companies in the Foundation were dependent on doing business with them.[81]

Interestingly, even Borgström at this time did not think that his message on population and conservation of resources was the real reason for the criticism against him as leader of SIK. According to Borgström, Laurin contested his leadership because he had supported the new freezing technique in Sweden. This new storage technique was against the commercial interest of Laurin's tin can packaging. This was the real reason, argued Borgström, but in the strategies advanced by his adversaries, it was his work on the world's food problems that was being used to compromise him.[82]

Göteborgs-Posten labelled Borgström 'one of the country's most outstanding scientists'.[83] In the spring of 1956, Swedish newspapers had discussed the 'brain drain' of Swedish scientists to foreign countries. Borgström became yet another Swedish scientist leaving the country in the mid 1950s. In an appeal to the government in September, 24 professors from the university cities demanded an unbiased investigation of the reasons why Borgström had been recommended to leave his directorship. They also wanted an overview of the terms of employment for qualified scientists linked to semi-governmental research institutes. 'Every emigration of a Swedish scientist is a serious national loss.'[84]

A leading liberal newspaper, *Dagens Nyheter,* thought the affair showed an astonishing softness on the part of the government representatives on the board toward the industrialists. It was remarkable that a few industries could get the government to dance to their tune. The explanation must be that the Minister of Commerce personally wished Borgström to be removed. The editorial hoped for great debate in parliament when it opened for the fall. This was heeded by Hugo Osvald, a Liberal Member of Parliament, who raised a question for the Minister of Commerce, Gunnar Lange. Osvald was a friend of Borgström's and a supporter since the days of the 'Tempest' debate in 1953. He regarded the SIK controversy as extremely serious. There were two main reasons for this. First of all, the business revealed a serious threat to the freedom of research: a scientist should not have to risk his employment if the results from his work did not satisfy some interested party. Secondly, as the petition from the 24 professors had pointed out, Sweden could not afford to export prominent scientists with international reputations.[85]

After Osvald's question in parliament, *Dagens Nyheter* demanded an investigation.[86] Borgström had previously written to the minister who had inaugurated SIK, John 'Kinna' Ericsson, and asked for his support, without success. The great turmoil that surrounded Borgström's resignation induced the Minister of Commerce to ask the board of SIK to account for the reasons for its actions against Borgström. The board answered that it did not consider it possible or appropriate to give such an explanation. However, two of the government-appointed board members gave their own explanations. The representative for the Fisheries Board stressed in his statement to the Minister that his decision was not motivated by objections to Borgström as a scientist. He stated that his decision to support the board's recommendation was based on an actual ultimatum from Laurin: either the termination must be made, or the Foundation would withdraw their subsidies. He added that it was of the greatest importance that public education on preservation matters should continue. A professor on the board stated that he thought Borgström's scientific qualifications were so great that it would be to the benefit to SIK if he had stayed. His concurrence with the decision was based solely on an understanding that the great animosity against the Director made it impossible for the Institute to carry out productive work.[87]

The Minister of Commerce, being unsatisfied with the reply of the board, appointed a Government Commission in October 1956, to write a report (SOU series) on the affair. The 270-page report, *Utredning om förhållanden vid konserveringsinstitutet (Report on Some Conditions at the Preservation Institute)*, was finished in early 1958. Forty-two persons had been interviewed, producing about 1,200 pages of transcripts. The Government Commission, including the Nobel Prize-winning professor in chemistry Hugo Theorell, found the critique against Borgström justly grounded overall. Even though the circumstances were such that Borgström's resignation was not necessary, the report found no cause to object to the industry representatives for their campaign to get him dismissed. Borgström had acted improperly when he issued commercial certificates that could be used for marketing the products of the firm receiving them. In the report, his public appearances to speak about world food problems were not a matter for criticism.

There was some formal criticism of the procedure when Borgström's leadership was questioned. It had been discussed in a joint meeting between the board and the Foundation's working committee, whereas, according to the statutes of SIK, it should be the business of the board alone to deal with the question of directorship. But the manner in which the critics had tried to get Borgström dismissed gave no cause for objection, since he had only been recommended to seek other employment. The Commission did not find sufficient reason to criticise Laurin for threatening to withdraw the subsidies.

Because of the allegations, the Commission also examined Borgström's scientific competence. The main views expressed by persons involved in the controversy have already been referred to in this chapter. The investigators had several objections in regard to the research at SIK. The published results of the experimental research at SIK during the first ten years had been quite modest. Borgström had not been engaged in any experimental research himself. But, on the other hand, it was not necessary for the Director to partake in the actual laboratory work. Borgström was acknowledged for his great effort in initiating the development of the Institute. The Commission concluded that building it up had taken most of his time in the early years of his leadership. However, Borgström's supervision of research had suffered from his activities outside SIK, especially his public work, such as authoring publications, giving speeches and lectures and attending meetings. His participation in conferences and study tours was also mentioned. According to Borgström's own records he had made 74 trips outside the country during the eight years he had been head of SIK. These activities had taken too much time from his directorship of the intended activities of the Institute. According to the investigators, more concentration on SIK's activities would probably have given better results.[88]

The report mentioned that Borgström had a tendency to overemphasise the value of his presentations, with less attention to impartial reliability. At the same time the report established that some of Borgström's qualities made him well suited for public relations work: his unusual receptivity, his working capacity, his wide reading, his vast knowledge of languages. The report concluded that it had been verified that Borgström had the required scientific competence when he was appointed Director of the Institute. However, after his doctoral thesis in 1939 he had not increased his scientific qualifications in the form of published research. The report of the Government Commission found no support for the allegations that the activities against Borgström were *solely* motivated by competitive business interests or by the monopoly aspirations of the big company representatives. Neither did their ambition to replace Borgström constitute a danger to the freedom of research, as had been suggested by the 1956 appeal of the 24 professors.[89] Borgström's appointment as professor was not fully based on his scientific qualifications, it was also motivated by his position as director of the Institute. Since his work was regulated by the board, he could not be completely independent. Thus, argued the Commission, the freedom of research was not at stake in this case.[90]

In his statement to the Government Commission, Borgström urged that it should 'stigmatise' the recklessness with which the board had accepted all kinds of spiteful and badly substantiated assertions. He also asked that the report should establish that the accusations made by *Göteborgs Handels- och Sjöfartstidning* were groundless. The newspaper had charged Borgström with mismanaging SIK for many years and, in Borgström own words, accused him of being 'a malefactor beyond comparison', when it came to economic management.[91]

The chairman of the board, Schmidt, claimed in front of the Commission that he had been given to understand at the Department of Commerce that it favoured a change of director. The Department denied the allegation. Instead it stated that there was scepticism towards Borgström in the Agricultural Ministry.[92]

Reactions to the report from the Swedish press varied. The supportive *Göteborgs-Posten* stressed in its editorial comment that the report had concluded that his resignation had not been necessary. The newspaper claimed that in the language of Government Commission reports, this meant the resignation was actually highly regrettable.[93] It also published a letter to the editor pointing out that the chairman of the unbiased Commission, Olof Söderström, had been linked to the social democratic administration for a long time. Its editorial even insinuated that the Commission might not have been altogether unbiased after all.[94] *Expressen*, a liberal tabloid, wrote with irony that for some newspapers Borgström had 'been deprived of his martyr's halo: There was no "Borgström Case"'. But, argued *Expressen,* the subject was not closed. The report of the Government Commission had left many questions unanswered and criticism of the big company representatives had only been hinted at. That the Commission omitted to mention the actions of the government representatives on the board raised questions about the freedom of research. *Expressen* also used the opportunity to criticise what it perceived as social democratic abuse of power.

> The report of the Borgström investigations is interesting reading. One does not find a single one of the suspicions that were expressed by the 24 professors repealed. On the contrary one gets yet another worrying insight into the interaction of the mandarins in the kingdom Idyllia.[95]

After the report, Borgström himself criticised the organisation of semi-government research institutes. It was harmful to separate research from the universities and create independent special institutes that are not given enough money for independent research.[96]

Göteborgs Handels- och Sjöfartstidning, on the other hand, wrote that it was not unexpected that the report concluded that it was correct to urge Borgström to seek new employment. It noted with satisfaction that the Commission had left unheeded Borgström's request that it should refute the accusations made by the newspaper. [97]

However, the Member of Parliament who had raised the question in 1956, Hugo Osvald, was not satisfied. He asked again, considering Borgström's resignation, if the state of scientific freedom was satisfactory in a semi-government research institute. Considering the evaluation of Borgström's scientific competence made by the report, he also questioned if the Government Commission had fulfilled the demand of objectivity that had to be placed on a report of a Government Commission. The Minister of Commerce remarked that the report gave the answers to Osvald's questions and that it was a thorough and well-performed investigation. Osvald was still not content with the answer and demanded that Prime Minister Tage Erlander answer the questions himself.

> In regard to the examination of scientific skill, the Minister of Commerce seems to put an 'equals' sign between scientific qualification and experimental research. He bases his argument on biased and incompetent persons. Should the Government or the Prime Minister share this view, it is a bad sign for all the research institutes in this country that are not run by the State.[98]

Osvald reiterated that he was waiting for the Prime Minister's answer on these questions, whereupon the Minister of Commerce replied that he would have to wait for quite a long time. It was not good practice to discuss individual matters in parliament and he had answered Osvald only with some hesitation.[99]

Nineteen professors from the universities of Stockholm, Uppsala, Lund and Gothenburg joined in the critique of the Commission's report and demanded an overhaul of the employment conditions of scientists serving at partly-government- financed research institutes. These were virtually the same professors who in 1956 had signed the 24 professors' petition. They argued that the Commission had based its judgment of Borgström's scientific quality less on present expert opinions than on the statements of persons whose suitability for this task could be questioned. This time the government left the petition of the 19 professors without response.[100]

A New Kind of Scientist

So, what was 'the Borgström Case'? Did a conservationist who was ahead of his time suffer from a miscarriage of justice because of his unpalatable message, or was industry justified in asking him to resign, because he simply did not do his job properly? From examination of the documents at SIK and the arguments raised in the report of the Government Commission, it seems clear that by threatening to cut down their subsidies these influential representatives for the food preservation industry got the board of SIK to urge Borgström to resign in November 1955.

Since the 1960s, it has been a common view among environmentalist that Borgström was expelled from the leadership of SIK because of hostile reactions to his message. However, such criticism of his message on population–resource issues was never explicitly expressed by his opponents in the SIK affair. The great controversy about Borgström in 1955–6 focused on his role as a scientist and leader of a research institute and did not expressly deal with his messages. His opponents stressed that a good scientist should have acquired, or at least be able to test, his conclusions himself. As one of his critics put it: 'He would not even touch a test tube.'[101] Anders Wiberg, a former board member, stated that Borgström was not his type of researcher. He would rather see a researcher of 'the quiet sort, a man who put on his white coat and devotedly attained his research goals, even if it was in a basement'.[102] This description is quite a long way from the picture of Borgström on the podium. The conclusion of the Government Commission on Borgström's scientific qualities also seems to be based on this traditional view of the scientist. Borgström was certainly not alone among conservationists in being exposed to such criticism. Even Vogt and Osborn had their scientific authority questioned. *Time Magazine* claimed that 'real scientists take a dim view of *Road to Survival*.' These scientists found little accuracy in 'Vogt's errors, prejudices, mysticism and reckless appeals to emotion'.[103]

Borgström's opinion of specialised scientific practice was bound to bestow on him criticism from within the scientific community. His critics can be divided into two groups: those who criticise him for being a propagandist, primarily representatives from industry, and those who find him too pessimistic. Both adopt the line that Borgström was not a proper scientist.

Borgström, on the other hand, emphasised the need to synthesise and present scientific knowledge to the public. In his reply to the Government Commission, he regretted that learning was not given its proper value. The food research he advocated demanded a broad overview.[104] Later, he made a point that on many occasions fishermen and farmers comprehended what he was talking about better than scientific audiences. The former had a greater understanding of the earth's resources than the scholars, who were mere specialists without an overview.[105] Borgström's conclusion was that scientific specialisation, 'the confoundedness of the Tower of Babel' must be abandoned so that a holistic perspective, 'a universal view', can be established for the future salvation of humanity.[106]

Following Luis Althusser, Foucault adopts the Freudian concept of 'displacement' on epistemological thresholds that 'suspend the continuous accumulation of knowledge, interrupt its slow development and force it to enter a new time'.[107] It was often conservationists like Borgström who took on a new, more active role than the traditional researcher. Furthermore, they were often early proponents of interdisciplinary studies. These conservationists were in many ways anticipating a new type of scientist. Borgström was in these respects caught in a *displacement* in scientific practice. A communist newspaper acknowledged the element of scientific struggle in the SIK controversy.

> Professor Borgström is a scientist of the new kind. He is a brilliant talented man with broad perspectives, who can never be accused of hiding his light under a bushel. We have not always shared his views, but have always admired his ability to quickly draw practical conclusions from his research results, not least by presenting his results to the public on the radio. Besides his outright unionist advantages he has, in spite of his youth, been one of the forerunners in Swedish science when it comes to usefully broadening the scientific debate.[108]

Science can be used as a disclosure mechanism for what is perceived as abnormal within the discourse.[109] It is important to stress that, even though science is used as a disclosure mechanism, in the environmental debate the opposite is also true. Science was also used as an instrument to criticise the discourse of natural resources, for example in catastrophe empiricism, where research reports were used to confirm the impending catastrophe resulting from prevailing practice in resource utilisation.[110]

Sociologist Steven Shapin states in *The Social History of Truth* that reliability is essential for attaining and maintaining social and cognitive order. Our knowledge of the world is dependent on our knowledge of the people who function as our sources of information and under which circumstances they can be trusted. Shapin shows how scientific trustworthiness depended on the word of the gentleman in seventeenth-century England. Just as the virtue of the gentleman guaranteed the reliability of his word, so modern science depends upon the reports of scientists. The modern scientist, like the gentleman, possesses cognitive authority by virtue of the acknowledged reliability of his word.[111]

The importance of reliability is well illustrated by the Borgström controversy. The conflict was not merely about Borgström's scientific competence and his employment; it also had consequences for his ambition to influence the cognitive system of his time. Indirectly, the struggle came to be about his mission as a public educator. What credibility would his evidence for a catastrophe have, if he acquired the reputation of being a bad scientist? Scientific trustworthiness was of the utmost importance for Borgström. He later criticised Rachel Carson's *Silent Spring* as too populist. She was not adequately authentic in her use of scientific facts. His own compilation of statistical material from around the world was intended to show that, contrary to what his critics claimed, his conclusions were founded on solid scientific investigations. But the source of information and the institutional site for Borgström's work was rather the library than the laboratory, together with journals of food technology and the mass media.

The press did not neglect the chance to attack big business as well. Borgström had stood up in defence of low prices for good quality food, for which the housewives of Sweden where grateful, but of course this pursuit had collided with the interests of big enterprises.

Some of his adversaries made a point of Borgström's being the son of a priest, who had preaching in his blood. Certainly he was affected by and learned from the language and presentation of his father's sermons. Borgström appears to have been a Christian believer, at least during some parts of his life. During his university years he wrote articles for the Lund Christian Student Union, hoping for a church revival and defending the position that it was really sensible to combine science and Christian faith.[112] Later his faith was kept in his private life. His biblical language was his rhetorical style, rather than some missionary urge. Even though his father was a low-church priest, he was several times characterised as having been brought up in a Schartauan home (a strict Lutheran sect) or in a Free Church home. Perhaps that suited the image of a doomsday prophet better.[113]

In idea analysis it is crucial to consider the relationship between a source and its subject. What intentions for an act can be ascribed to an agent? It is not possible for us to fully identify ourselves with Borgström or any other agent. Thus it is not feasible to establish, beyond a doubt, the intention of an author, since we cannot completely discern the intentions and the reactions in a language event. But since all communication is dependent on inter-subjective references, as in discourse, it is possible to give a reasonable interpretation of the meaning of a text, by relating to the context. Communication in context is the very nub of the conveyer concept. It is an attempt to analyse what is communicated by the agent, how is it communicated, and what was communicated to the receiver. It is important here that the primary aim of analysing Borgström's work is not to discern his intentions, but to try to apprehend what the text communicated in its context.

It is thus necessary to relate Borgström's work to its specific contexts. His institutional setting as well as his role varies. Utterances must be considered for their use in a specific situation so that we can understand the underlying conventions and discursive rules, and discern what they relate to culturally and historically. Ironies, manipulations and allusions are important in this respect. When Borgström writes in the last chapter of *The Hungry Planet* (1965) about winning the victory crown, the meaning can perhaps be better understood if one acknowledges Borgström's allusion to the Bible's eschatological words about winning the victory crown on judgment day.[114]

In an intellectual biography, even though it focuses on the conveying function of an agent, it might be tempting to speculate about what at heart evoked a certain standpoint. The causes of certain responses are entangled in a complex web of interactions, especially with regard to biographical material. Borgström's background, his social life, his ability to coin expressive formulations, of course helped to form his career. His Christian upbringing, for example, is reflected in a flair for biblical vocabulary, perhaps also in his advocacy for the 'Christian' Golden Rule. Personal experiences can help us explain certain events and they will thus be employed in the analysis at some points; but, because of the speculative temptations they offer, psychological profiles are used sparingly in the analysis of the debate.

At the beginning of the 1950s, a controversy emerged regarding the so-called *third position*. The climate of the Cold War caused strong anti-communist sentiment on most of the nation's editorial boards. Liberal newspapers like *Dagens Nyheter* and *Göteborgs Handels- och Sjöfartstidning* criticised the Government's policy of non-alignment. The Swedish political science professor and liberal chief editor Herbert Tingsten headed an intensive campaign in favour of Sweden joining the Atlantic Pact.[115] He criticised the Social Democratic Government for being soft on Stalinist terror. Tingsten was very critical towards political ideologies. Science should be the guiding rule of society, instead of the metaphysics and speculations of ideologies. Later he predicted the death of ideologies. They had had their day and hence would disappear. Tingsten had a huge influence on liberal debate.

Borgström was thus very keen on emphasising that he was a scientist and not an ideologist. At the age of 74, Borgström was annoyed by a journalist asking if things had gone the way he had *believed*. Borgström replied that he had never been occupied with believing, he was only seeking and conveying knowledge. Borgström emphasised that as a scientist he had only 'presented the truth'.[116]

The scientific profession held (and of course still holds) a substantial cognitive authority. This authority is of enormous value for any individual scientist, particularly one who is inclined to have opinions on society. Thus scientists have a vested interest in maintaining this authority, by guarding the boundaries of and avoiding threats to their reputation. Scientific authority is protected, even though the boundaries may change, as new practices or contents are employed over time.

As an agent, an individual scientist is participating in a scientific *form of life*. This Wittgensteinian concept emphasises the facility of professional relationships. Through training, the scientist is formed by and participates in a tradition, including laws, rules, norms, meaning and definitions. Through his practice he contributes to the continuation of the tradition. A form of life involves an agreement in the practice, not necessarily in opinions, but in the language used.[117]

Many science studies of today indicate the conventional character of these boundaries as the outcome of a social and historical context, of the strategic activities of scientists themselves. Scientific boundaries are defined and maintained by social groups who, in the words of philosopher David Bloor, 'are concerned to protect and promote their cognitive authority, intellectual hegemony, professional integrity, and whatever political and economic power they may be able to command by attaining these things'.[118]

A scientific form of life acquires and supports a tradition that postulates how the scientific work shall be conducted, what is supposed to be done and what is not. There are a number of fundamental approaches which this form of life generates and which are at the basis of scientific practice; it has distinct boundaries which stipulate what can and shall be researched. Borgström, by being on the outskirts of plant physiology and food technology, violated these basic postulates with his non-specialised, non-laboratory focus. He raised other questions to which, for him, food science could not give satisfactory answers. The communist newspaper was probably right. In his synthesising methods and strong ambition to communicate his assessments to politicians and the public, Borgström in many ways represented a new type of scientist who was unique in the food sciences, and elsewhere would become more common in years to come. These scientists, who openly communicated with politicians and attempted to influence political discourse, were targets for criticism from the traditional scientific community.

Prior to 1948 Borgström did not focus on a critique of scientific specialisation. Probably inspired by Vogt's critique of specialised technicians and his proposals for a broader conservation education coupled with Borgström's own university experiences, this came to be a main theme in his message in the 1950s. And this time the criticism from the scientific world was stunning.[119]

A magazine compared him with Gunnar Myrdal:

> The restlessness, the elegance, the broad perspectives, the lightning-fast judgments, and the quick tongue. With both of these [Myrdal and Borgström], you have always had a feeling that Sweden is far too small for these gentlemen's activities. They need European or actually global horizons to guide their activities to a fruitful outcome.[120]

As the controversy at the Preservation Institute was in its cradle this magazine writer proposed the UN or the FAO as suitable arenas for Borgström. These institutions would provide a better scope for his vast knowledge than the leadership of some 'small Swedish institution involved in internal quarrels and financial worries as well as jealously scrutinised'.[121] Instead Michigan State University became Borgström's international stage.

Land Grant Controversies

While the controversy at SIK was stirring, Borgström was looking for employment elsewhere. In the spring of 1956, Borgström wrote to an acquaintance at Michigan State University (MSU), inquiring about the possibility of a position at the university. He got a favourable response, 'Sweden's loss is our great fortune.'[122] At the beginning of fall 1956, when the dispute over Borgström's leadership of the Preservation Institute was rife in Sweden, Borgström himself went into exile in the United States. For Borgström, it was not only that the population–resource problem complex was international: the stage on which to come to terms with it was equally international. Thus, it was only natural that he would seek for a position abroad.

Recruiting Borgström probably fitted well into the plans of the President of MSU, John A. Hannah. According to Borgström's ecologist colleague, John Cantlon, the Borgström name was known to anybody who had a substantial international reputation on significant issues relating the biological and physical world to humankind. Hannah, who had a very international appetite, had been active in the Point Four Program and the role of the land grant universities in the recovery of Europe.[123]

MSU is a land grant university. In the mid-nineteenth century acreages of land were given to one university in each state, funds from which were to be used for the teaching of agriculture and mechanics or engineering. Consequently there was a tendency for the faculty to be more practically orientated, rather than purely academic. The feeling of technological optimism was rampant in the agricultural and engineering colleges of these universities. Agribusiness and the Federal Department of Agriculture had a large influence on their research, and schools of agriculture had many applied entomologists who were defenders of the pesticide business. These companies were dependent on the use of university experts who were employed to assess the effects of different fertilisers and pest control chemicals on crop pests. Chemical companies like Dow Chemical and Monsanto funded some MSU research.

Borgström accepted a full professorship in food technology in the Department of Horticulture at the College of Agriculture. At the time of Borgström's arrival, US agriculture was deeply into pushing technology to maximise crop production in particular areas, an approach that later came to be known as the *Green Revolution*. Highly bred varieties of the key food plants – rice, wheat, barley, oats and soybeans – were being produced. Breeding them to maximise yield required artificial additions of fertilisers and pesticides. According to three of Borgström's colleagues at the department, there was optimism, at that time, that food production would be no problem. 'We simply increased the amount of nitrogen fertiliser and with adequate pest control we could do everything we wanted'.[124]

On a visit in late June 1956, Borgström proposed holding seminars at the department. He suggested five different topics for his speeches, which indicates the broad scope of his interests: 'Influence of light and temperature on the stability of ascorbic acid in fruit juices', 'The role of psychrophilics in fruit and vegetable cold storage', 'Riddles in frozen food microbiology', 'Some neglected international aspects of world food problems' and 'The role of vegetable products in world diet'. Symptomatically, the head of the Department of Horticulture picked the first two. It was as a food technologist that he was of interest, not as an illuminator of world population–resource problems.[125]

Borgström came to the United States with a somewhat different objective. After he took up his position at the university, he continued transmitting the message he had begun in Sweden. Borgström kept pointing out that there were pitfalls in the drive towards narrow areas of technological development, like highly bred varieties of grains (e.g. short-stemmed wheat and stick rice varieties), as the answer to world food supplies. While they increased the yield, they demanded more fertilisers and more pesticides. On this issue, Borgström came into conflict with MSU agricultural technologists who were trying to push this new technology out to the developing nations. Robert Bandurski, one of Borgström's plant physiologist colleagues, recalls: 'he could become extremely pessimistic during the course of a lecture and his pessimism seemed to feed upon itself, and so one couldn't help but feel that there is really no hope, there is nothing we can do on this problem, George seemed always to present a new problem.' MSU had missions overseas in several countries in South America, in Southeast Asia, in Africa and in the Middle East. They aimed at replacing traditional agriculture with elements of the Green Revolution. Borgström was indicating that this might not be a good idea.[126]

His opinions aroused criticism from several quarters at MSU. In his discipline he was not regarded as a 'real' food scientist. He was also criticised by researchers in other disciplines, for example by agricultural economists. He was accused of dealing with issues in which he was not trained and therefore did not have the proper knowledge. Many scientists at state universities and land grant colleges had an important role in the realisation of the Point Four Program and in the businesses of the agricultural industries. Because of the dominant position of applied research in colleges of agriculture in land grant universities, scientists who opposed the present practice of the agricultural industry found themselves in controversy. Borgström suffered from these circumstances, but the situation was nothing like as fierce as the SIK conflict. It seems rather to have been an academic quarrel at seminars and at the dining tables of the faculty lounges.[127]

At MSU, Borgström managed to develop another entry into the university. Besides his position in the Department of Food Science, he was awarded a joint appointment with the Department of Geography in 1962. Here Borgström was allowed to be a different food scientist, with a global point of view, who was not just interested in the details of preparation and preservation of food. He was also able to focus on global population issues and their importance for the future of the world's food supply.

Together with history professor Thomas Greer, he started a senior-level credit course called 'Great Issues'. These lectures dealt with a multifaceted approach to world problems. He would focus upon water resources, land resources, population resources, public health, the military, or the economy. He emphasised that these issues constituted the framework in which major problems had to be approached rather than by the narrow methods of non-transgressional science. In 1966 and 1967 he offered public lectures on the population explosion, the world's food supply, food and the Cold War, the dilemma of Western technology, as well as on population and the struggle for resources as a cause of the tensions in the world.[128]

Over the years, Borgström seems to have been increasingly reluctant to carry his message into scientific journals. After he became Professor of Geography at Michigan State University he only published four articles and one review in geographical journals, though he had opportunities to do more. Instead he tried to reach a broader audience by writing popular books.

Borgström's interest shifted even more from a small academic audience to making his conclusions understandable to a wider readership. In the spirit of accessible science, he found it more interesting to address broader audiences than to be published in the Annals of the Association of American Geographers.[129] Quite the reverse of this trend, as we shall see in chapter eight, he became at the same time increasingly more hopeful about the ability of scientists to govern the world, in contrast to 'irresponsible' politicians.

Science and Politics in Symbiosis

The world order that emerged after the Second World War involved broad segments of the US scientific community. New demands were made that cut deeply into the contemporary view of science. At the same time, recorded expenditure in research and development in the United States rose from 0.2 per cent of the gross domestic product in 1921 to three per cent by the mid 1960s.[130] Science as a legitimating foundation for political acts strengthened in Western countries. The agenda of the natural resources debate was established in collaboration between natural scientists and politicians. The new conservationist scientists who entered this process early both benefited and suffered from it. In the early post-war years it was mainly to their advantage, since they, as experts, were given a platform in the media and in conference auditoria. This process had evolved in the 1930s when a 'science and society' movement originated in the United States, arguing that scientists should take greater responsibility for the social uses of science.[131] The communication process between politicians and scientists was clearly illustrated in the political ambition to bring about the 1949 UN conference on the world's resources. By being involved in a high priority problem on the political agenda – to avert natural resource shortages as potential nodes of conflict – scientists were involved as keepers of the post-war world order.

Ecological studies also benefited from the increasing superpower tensions. Ecology came to be tied in with defence-related research. Rachel Carson, for instance, worked in a government agency, the Bureau of Fisheries, until her bestseller *The Sea Around Us* (1951) enabled her to become a freelance science writer. The Bureau, which was at first within the Department of Commerce but later absorbed into the Fish and Wildlife Service of the Department of the Interior, was mobilised to learn more about the marine environment in case of a nuclear war, and to help devise means to exploit the oceans for food, navigation and defence.

The possibility of nuclear fall-out as a result of a nuclear war between the Soviet Union and the United States was indeed very real. In fact school children in both countries were trained how to survive a nuclear blast. Because of this, there was an interest in the behaviour of land ecosystems exposed to nuclear fall-out. Ecological and chemical research, particularly for building the necessary elaborate analytical techniques through computers and remote sensing, were supported by the US Atomic Energy Commission and the Department of Defense. The research of the famous ecologists Eugene and Thomas Odum was almost entirely supported by the Department of Energy. The former also received funding from AEC.[132] At the same time, the Department of Agriculture and the State Department's US Agency for International Development (USAID) were funding research focusing on technologies for the Green Revolution. The National Science Foundation had programmes generating broad areas of new research data. Since Borgström was looking at synthesising accessible data , his funding possibilities were limited in this respect.

Nevertheless, the USA's Cold War strategy had a profound effect on the scientific fields that relate to the new conservation ideology. As shown in Chapter Three, the land grant universities were used in Truman's Point Four Program. The Ford Foundation's strategy of linking scientific research on high crop yields and the issues of overpopulation was motivated by American geopolitics. Moreover, new academic fields appeared in the late 1940s, such as Area Studies, which synthesised multidisciplinary knowledge about a region into culture-adapted advice and assessments. The need to understand a region's culture in order to deal successfully with foreign countries was acknowledged by the Social Science Research Council. During the Second World War the need for regional specialists had been highlighted. This demand was reinforced by the challenges of the post-war world. In the advocacy for Area Studies, the inevitability of American worldwide involvement was stressed. The success of US foreign policy required more broadly prepared experts on various cultures.[133]

Borgström was not a new data generator, he was a synthesiser of data, pulling together data from international literature and putting global data sets together. The neo-Malthusian upsurge coincides with an enormous expansion in data gathering. Information was beginning to emerge which gave him an opportunity to form a global perspective on all aspects of food supply.

Neo-Malthusians used the data coming out of a wide range of different disciplines and programmes, for instance, from the International Geophysical Year (IGY) 1957–9. It was a scientific programme of international scope, with oceanographers, glaciologists, geologists and limnologists. They were all looking at geophysical phenomena. Researchers within IGY studied the physics of the ocean, the physics of the atmosphere and the linkage between the physics and chemistry of the ocean and the physics and chemistry of the atmosphere. Remote sensing techniques were also developed at this time, and computers enabled analysis with big number sets. Computerised number-crunching also provided international demographers with the necessary tools to estimate the impact of population change.[134]

In the immediate post World War II period, there was an emerging oceanographic scientific effort looking at global circulation, ocean basin circulations, circulations of minerals, salinity values in the sea. A lot of it was motivated both in the East and in the West by defence interests, because submarine warfare required a great deal of knowledge about the physics and the chemistry and even the biology of the oceans. These developments made possible a global look at ocean basins, ocean currents and circulations, with data from international studies getting better and better.

IGY was followed by the International Biological Program (IBP). It was the first major international science programme in ecology. The whole project took the form of a rolling programme, which occupied some five years of preliminary discussion and planning commencing in 1959, followed by a decade of research and publishing, 1964–74. 58 countries were directly involved in the programme and 40 others indirectly. The overall theme chosen was 'The Biological Basis of Human Welfare'. The original impetus for the IBP was the desire to obtain some of the same benefits that had accrued to the earth sciences from the IGY, such as creating international networks of collaborators, collecting data on large-scale systems, and, not the least, obtaining the attention of decision-makers. As a Swedish biologist, Borgström motivated the programme.

It was the big chance for biologists to make themselves heard and to bring sense to research policy. IBP's first general assembly in Paris 1964 resolved that the programme should contribute to 'the optimum exploitation, on a global basis, of the biological resources on which mankind is vitally dependent for its food and for many other products'. This should be done within three themes: conservation, human adaptability, and use and management.[135] The rationale behind IBP was obvious at the time of the second peak of post-war neo-Malthusian concern.

John H. Perkins argues that there were at least two tendencies towards neo-Malthusian thinking on global population–food questions. One was political, of which Thompson was a representative, linking population densities to national and international economics. One was ecological, linking population densities to resource degradation.[136] However, as I hope this book indicates, they are complexly intertwined. Worster points at this mutual relationship in his analysis of New Ecology's economic view of the natural world.

> If society and its economics shaped the New Ecologists, that influence was a two-way street; we must also ask what cultural impact their account of nature had. Modern man depends heavily on the scientist to explain what kind of world we live in, and now the ecologist's answer was: an economic one. All creatures on the earth are related to one another essentially as producers and consumers; interdependence in such a world must mean sharing a common energy income. And as part of nature, man must be considered primarily as an economic animal – he is at one with all life in a push for greater productivity.[137]

As Steven Shapin argues in *The Scientific Revolution,* there lies at the heart of modern science the paradox established in the seventeenth century.

> [T]he more a body of science is understood to be objective and disinterested, the more valuable it is as a tool in moral and political action. Conversely, the capacity of a body of knowledge to make valuable contributions to moral and political problems flows from an understanding that it was not produced and evaluated to further particular human interest.[138]

Borgström recognised this fundamental regulation. Even though he called for a change in society, to Borgström these political recommendations were conclusions based on thorough scientific research. He stressed that he was not a politician or even an environmentalist. He was merely a scientist pointing out the facts.[139]

Political acts in particular must be supported by discourses that legitimise them as normal, sound and rational. Science plays a critical role in such discourse, in legitimating not only the present order but also changes in power relations. Shapin argues that the very distinction between social and political issues on the one hand and scientific truth on the other is a product of the scientific revolution. The essence of modern natural science lies in the recognition that scientists must provide objective accounts of physical reality. They depict what *is* in the natural world, not what *ought* to be. The objects of science are separated from moral discourse. The practitioners of science are expected to free themselves from personal interest and passions when they are producing knowledge. 'The most powerful storehouse of value in our modern culture is the body of knowledge we consider to have least to do with the discourse of moral value.'[140]

Scientific change evolves with its societal context. Competing interest groups use science as a social resource. Scientific descriptions of nature are thus likely to be reflections of societal interests.[141] But science does not merely reflect interests in society. Science and society live, so to speak, in symbiosis. An ideal social state is protected by reference to absolute laws. These may be divine laws or, more common in our secularised world, the laws of nature. These laws of nature are used to sanction a moral codex.[142] If the authority on how to live our lives is to be derived from laws of nature, a great boost is given to the sciences that can most convincingly discern these laws. The science of ecology was not slow in taking advantage of this prestige. But therein lies a problem for this position: science was not supposed to propagate political norms, but ecology's prestigious academic position depended on its ability to provide the norms that could be derived from natural systems. The establishment of norms was a part of its function. Knowledge making and knowledge holding are indeed social processes. All concepts are marked 'made in culture'. Our understanding of an objective physical universe is culturally formed. That is virtually a truism, although one it is still necessary to establish. Unfortunately in these days of illusive social constructivism, it is also necessary to emphasise that it is the *concept* that is culturally formed. Even though all concepts are human made, it does not mean that what they are *trying to portray* does not exist outside culture. Of course nature is what we have defined as nature. However, this construction most often does not appear out of nowhere; knowledge cannot be regarded as unconnected to people's experiences of the natural world.

Some environmental historians stress human interaction with nature as principally depending on cultural constructions.[143] Even if some acknowledge that '[t]his is not to say that the non-human world is somehow unreal',[144] these analyses run the risk of failing to recognise that human existence is an utterly physical state. Of course, nature is socially constructed in the sense that we understand it primarily through our language, which is socially constructed. That is more or less taken for granted in the humanities and social sciences of today. But this 'social construction' is not arbitrary: the actual survival of humans has been dependent on their interaction with their environment throughout history. There is *ultimately* a material base for human cultural production, to argue otherwise might, somewhat drastically, be designated as full-belly naiveté. Nature is not merely a social construction but a product of a culture emanating from material conditions. Certainly, technologies and physical nature cannot be accounted for outside our descriptions, yet they offer resistance to our ideas and perceptions, they cannot be captured any which way. Fishing cannot, for instance, be described in terms of a cornucopia if the fishing nets are repeatedly empty.

When writing about nature it is crucial that we distinguish between two meanings of the word *nature,* meaning the physical matter that makes up our material base on this planet, and *Nature,* meaning the conceptualisation of our understanding of nature.[145] Starting from human history, these two concepts *interact.* In its broadest sense, environmental history investigates how society's coevolution with the natural environment has affected the historical process. The emphasis on the reciprocal interaction between culture and nature is an important building block of environmental history. As environmental historian Donald Worster points out: 'Its principal goal became one of deepening our understanding of how humans have been affected by their natural environment through time and, conversely, how they have affected that environment and with what results.'[146]

Economist Richard B. Norgaard uses the concept of *coevolutionary changes* to account for the feedback between social and ecological systems. Coevolutionary theories of development 'stress that everything is symmetrically related to everything else. Nothing is exogenous', as opposed to 'conventional environmental histories' that tend to depend on a deterministic relationship between a limited number of exogenous causes from outside a system being analysed and a limited number of endogenous effects within the system.[147]

As nature is physically altered it is concurrently epistemologically constructed and transformed. Concepts are employed to describe our interactions with nature. They form how we perceive nature, what function it has and how its practices should be arranged. Thus, changes in the way we interact with nature are reflected in metaphors, symbols and new concepts. Views on nature are political at heart. Raymond Williams points out in his classic essay 'Ideas of Nature': 'What is often being argued... in the idea of nature is the idea of man; and this not only generally, or in ultimate ways, but the idea of man in society, indeed the ideas of kinds of societies.'[148]

Roland Barthes urges us to 'establish Nature itself as historical'. Social codes – and thus also social oppressions – are entrenched through mythmaking about nature.[149] However, it is important to stress that to establish nature as historical does not mean that all norms understood from nature are merely the product of human volition. It is the product of a culture which is formed by understandings of certain physical and biological conditions. Or in other, almost forgotten, words: the base of the superstructure. It is our evolving *understanding* of the concept of nature that rests on history.

Barthes questions the possibility of drawing normative conclusions from a physical universe. Of course, against this position a new conservationist might have argued that if we observe that people die or suffer, and have reasons to believe this is caused by a certain human behaviour, if the situation would not occur without this behaviour – it seems fair enough to claim that the behaviour violates a natural state, meaning the situation that would be if humans had not made this particular impact.

Here it might be appropriate to stress that criticism of specific scientific practices is not the same as criticism of science per se. Some of the persuasive stories of science must be examined, but my mission here is not to turn up a postmodern nose at the possibilities scientific knowledge provides of contributing to a better understanding of the world and of its ability to make it a better place for its inhabitants. Science is used in power struggles and is associated with the prevailing discourse, but that does not imply that *all* scientific practices have to be condemned as false and oppressive.

Conservationists such as Borgström placed high hopes upon a new interdisciplinary and synthesising direction in scientific research, a hope that would only increase as scepticism grew in the 1960s toward contemporary political solutions to the population–resource crisis. Borgström applauded that, as he expressed it, 'science enters politics'. Science and technology carried a key responsibility for humanity's predicament. This was reflected in the 'newly awakened' interest in research among politicians of the world.[150] 'A common battle against starvation, disease, and misery, and above all against ignorance, requires a radical change in the goals of world science.'[151]

7

Green Revolutions

In the early 1960s, in a second peak of post-war Malthusian concern, there was a return from the optimism of the 1950s to anxiety about the world food situation. The population–resource debates of the 1960s were marked by aspects of two green revolutions: first, a shift in consciousness embodied in emerging environmentalism, in the West as well as in the Third World, and second, the high-yielding food technology called the Green Revolution.

What might appear as opposing ideas can be part of the same social process. These green revolutions were two different approaches to the population–resource crisis, but they both stemmed from the resource–security theory of the early post-war years. Though they represent two differing attitudes to technological solutions, the differences between them were not necessarily fundamental. The same problem underlay both revolutions: A population–resource crisis was looming.

The 1960s Crisis

The food crisis of 1950s did not turn out as badly as had sometimes been expected. There were modest gains in total as well as in per capita food supplies in developing nations. More and more, policymakers expected the developing nations to escape from the Malthusian dilemma through the demographic transition, where high birth and death rates are replaced by low ones. In this transition, death rates fall first, followed after a while by a reduction in the birth rate.

In the 1950s, criticism of the FAO's early reports also became more outspoken. Colin Clark, among others, argued that the FAO had exaggerated the situation.[1] Optimism flourished over the possibilities of technological development securing the world's future food supply. After World War II, food production underwent enormous development, through plant breeding, insecticides, pesticides, and storage improvements such as freezing technology. Food aid shipments from industrialised countries made up for food shortages in poorer countries. At the same time, it served to reduce food surpluses in exporting countries. The domestic agricultural sector also benefited from this aid. It created a situation in which grain became more expensive in exporting countries, but cheaper in receiving countries. As a negative consequence for the aid-receiving countries, the price cut put pressure on domestic food producers. Grain exports from the Western world to so-called developing countries rose from an average of four million tons in 1948 to around 25 million tons in 1964.[2]

The brash optimism of the 1950s, with increased gains in global food production, was soon to be challenged by disturbing signs. Rapidly declining death rates, particularly through less expensive health measures, resulted in an unprecedented population growth in the Southern Hemisphere. Many experts doubted that the decline in birth rates would come fast enough to avoid the situation where population growth would exceed the supply of natural resources. The problem became apparent in the 1960s, when the world was stricken by catastrophic famines in Asia and Africa. Children from various famine-affected areas in the media limelight became pedagogical arguments for parents to per-suade their children to eat up the food being served. 'Finish your plate – think of the children in India!' became a kitchen table mantra.

The neo-Malthusians of the 1960s had an easy time finding ammunition for their cause. The 1960s became the peak of a turnaround in global food trading patterns. Up until World War II, many Third World regions were net exporters of food. By the 1960s, they had become net importers of altogether 13 million tons annually. By 1970, their imports of food had reached 20 million tons per year.[3] The United States Department of Agriculture was pessimistic in its prognosis at the beginning of the 1960s. *The World Food Budget, 1963 and 1966*, published in 1961 added to the sense that the population–resource crisis was getting out of hand. The report concluded that in the so-called developing countries 1.9 billion people were inadequately nourished: 'In most of them, population is expanding rapidly, malnutrition is widespread and persistent, and there is no likelihood that the food problem soon will be solved.'[4] In 1963, the FAO published its third *World Food Survey*. It concluded that 60 per cent of the people in underdeveloped areas suffered from malnutrition.[5] The FAO's first World Food Congress, which met in Washington, D. C. 1963, was a sign of increased FAO activity to cope with the population–resource crisis. The conference proposed a programme for future action against food shortage. The FAO also called for similar congresses to be held periodically, which should review a survey of the world food situation in relation to population and overall development.

China became a major importer of wheat in 1961 after the agricultural failures of the *Great Leap Forward*. In 1958, the Chinese Communist Party launched this infamous campaign. It was aimed at catalysing economic and technical development in China at a vastly faster pace than hitherto. The people, according to this policy, should be more ideologically educated and domestic resources should be utilised more efficiently in a simultaneous development of industry and agriculture. The creation of people's communes and increased collectivisation, however, contributed to a decline in food production. Combined with increased food exports, with the aim of attaining capital for industrial investments, these developments led to a devastating famine. The famine that followed the Great Leap Forward is one of the worst in human history. The number of victims has been estimated at between 10 and 20 million people.[6]

South Asia was of special concern since it was one of the most populous and undernourished regions. Bad monsoon seasons for two consecutive years in 1965 and 1966 caused crop failure in this critical region. To abate a catastrophic famine in India massive grain shipments were launched, predominantly from the United States. In 1964 US Public Law 480 promoted food aid as a means to improve attitudes toward the United States and its policies. That year non-industrialised countries in the Southern Hemisphere and some countries with centrally-planned economies imported nearly 15 million tons of grain. Also, the Soviet Union became a net importer in 1963 and 1965, after being a net exporter of five million tons of grain annually in the first years of the 1960s.

In a way, the situation was useful for countries like the United States, Canada and Australia, which had increased grain production to fill the needs of war-devastated Europe and Japan. By the early 1960s, the agricultural sector had recovered enough to make them quite self-sufficient in food. In this situation, the great grain exporting countries were faced with dwindling markets and subsequent declining prices for their surplus crops. An overproducing farm sector became a difficult problem for the politicians to handle. Shipments of the surplus to needy nations made it possible to postpone lower market prices hitting the farmers. The great grain-producing countries could get rid of a large portion of their crop surpluses and thus postpone major government intervention in farming.

At the beginning of the decade, 'That Population Explosion' was on the cover of *Time* magazine: 'Long a hot topic among pundits ... the startling 20th century surge in humanity's rate of reproduction may be as fateful to history as the H-bomb and the Sputnik, but it gets less public attention.'[7] The cover story gave numerous accounts from all over the world of an overcrowded planet, where people were living on an increasingly poorer diet. It even quoted Pakistan's President Ayub Khan saying: 'If our population continues to increase as rapidly as it is doing... we will soon have nothing to eat and will all become cannibals.' The magazine called attention to the prospect that by year 2000 there would be four Asians for every European, and twice as many Americans living South of the Rio Grande as North of it. If all that was facing the growing masses was endless poverty, 'their fury may well shake the earth'. The magazine pointed at the promise of technological and scientific innovations to remedy the problem. It had done so in the past, and would most likely do it again. That ought to be food for thought for the world's pessimists. Nevertheless, the cover article concluded that the problem of population would demand not only he skill of science, but the wisdom of government and the good will of all 'men'. 'Population, as much as anything else, will determine the direction history takes.'

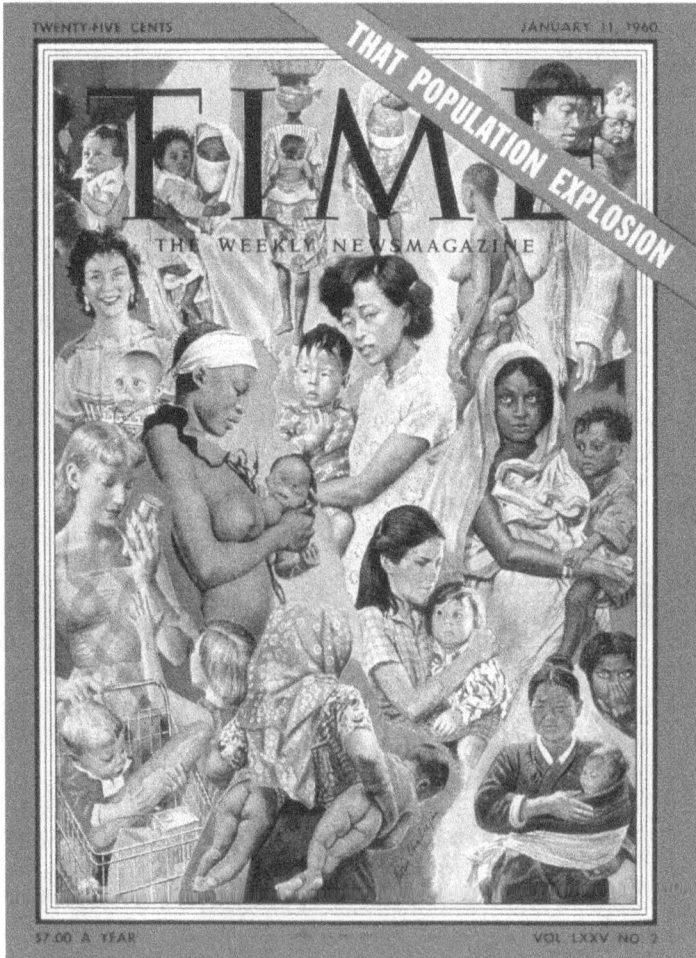

Cover of Time *Magazine, 11 January 1960*

The *Time* journalists had noticed a lack of public attention to this dramatic population growth. That was soon to change. A voluminous outpouring of literature appeared on the population–resource dilemma in the 1960s. Vogt published *People: Challenge to Survival* (1961). The same year, demographer Alfred Sauvy's presentation of population problems from Malthus to Mao Zedong was translated into English as *Fertility and Survival.* Osborn edited *Our Crowded Planet* in 1962; it was a collection of essays on population growth by several well known biologists, Marston Bates, Charles Galton Darwin, Julian Huxley, Walter Lowdermilk, Paul Sears, and Solly Zuckerman; a second edition was sponsored by the Conservation Foundation. The same year, the FAO declared a campaign against world hunger. Stewart Udall, US Secretary of the Interior in the Kennedy administration, worried in *The Quiet Crisis* (1963) that 'the best qualities in man' would 'atrophy in a standing-room-only environment'.[8] News releases from the Population Reference Bureau on current population topics from around the world increased from 231 in 1952 to 1,216 in 1960, 3,334 in 1961 and 5,725 in 1962.[9]

Environmental historian Adam Rome points out that concern for population growth became an argument for the critique of suburban sprawl and the loss of open-space areas in America: 'The open-space literature was full of references to the psychological costs of population growth.'[10] In *The Squeeze* (1960), a book about cities and space with a foreword by Fairfield Osborn, geographer Edward Higbee predicted that within the next hundred years the United States 'will breed a population that will surpass that in China today'. If metropolitan development was not changed decisively, 'it will not be long before there is standing room only in the cluttered heart of Metropolis'.[11] Harry Harrison illustrated the same theme in the science-fiction novel *Make Room, Make Room* (1966). The setting for the futuristic crime novel was New York in 1999. Some 35 million people were squeezed into a city of mass starvation, gigantic environmental destruction, energy shortage, poverty, and misery. England had become one gigantic city. In Harrison's novel, Danish people still ate on regular basis, but had a concrete wall across the border to Germany with guards shooting as soon as starving people tried to sneak in. The oil was gone, the soil stripped and eroded, the trees cut down, animals extinct. Seven billion people were fighting over whatever was left. And no one had heeded all the warning voices.[12]

In *Essays of a Humanist* (1964), Julian Huxley gives an eloquent description of the population concern of his time:

> The neo-Malthusians, supported by the progressive opinion in the Western World and by leading figures in most Asian countries, produce volumes of alarming statistics about the world population explosion and the urgent need

for birth-control, while the anti-Malthusians, supported by the two ideological blocs of Catholicism and Communism, produce equal volumes of hopeful statistics, or perhaps one should say of wishful estimates, purporting to show how the problem can be solved by science, by the exploitation of the Amazon or the Arctic, by better distribution, or even by shipping our surplus population to other planets.[13]

Huxley joined the ranks of the former. He sharply criticised the widening gap between 'the haves and the have-nots' in spite of scientific and technological efforts. He presented overpopulation as the root cause for malnutrition and resource depletion: 'Not content with destroying or squandering our resources of material things, we are beginning to destroy the resources of true enjoyment – spiritual, aesthetic, intellectual, emotional.'[14] He set his hopes on what he called the Ecological Revolution and the Humanist Revolution. But if humanity did not quickly put a halt to population growth and attain a balance between its numbers and its material resources, 'we shall be dooming our grandchildren and all their descendants, through thousands upon thousand of monotonous generations, to an extremely unpleasant and unsatisfactory existence, overworked and undernourished, overcrowded and unfulfilled.'[15]

In a famous interview in *Le Monde,* philosopher Jean-Paul Sartre declared after a world tour that the confrontation with famine had changed him profoundly. After having seen children die of hunger, he concluded that human alienation on Earth, exploitation of humans, and malnutrition had to put all metaphysical evil into the background: 'Hunger is the only thing, period.' He was surprised that world hunger, the atom threat, and the destitute of humanity did not colour all literature.[16]

In this second peak of Malthusian concern, Borgström attained international recognition. *The Hungry Planet: The Modern World at the Edge of Famine* (1965), became part of Borgström's international breakthrough. It was selected by the American Library Association as one of the fifty most important books published in 1965. It was translated into Danish, Finnish, German, Norwegian, Polish, and Spanish. In both Sweden and the United States it was published in three editions, as well as in two in Germany.[17]

Nutritional Equalisation

Borgström begins the *The Hungry Planet* with a short poem from the Nobel Prize-winning author Harry Martinson's cycle of poems, *Aniara: A Review of Man in Time and Space* (1956). The quotation sets the tone of the book, at the same time as it can be seen as his final biting statement to his opponents at the Swedish Food Preservation Institute:

For this reason I preserve what is fitting
bearing comfort's colours and resembling life.
And every time anguish patters through our ship
and dread and unease agonise our nerves,
I pass around the mima's dream preserves.[18]

In *The Hungry Planet*, Borgström introduced a *population equivalents* concept. It was based upon the idea of measuring the food consumption of livestock in terms of human intake. Such computations revealed that the United States, on top of a then current feeding burden of 195 million people, also had to provide nourishment for livestock animals which, measured in terms of their protein consumption, corresponded to 1300 million humans. The figures for Sweden were 39.2 million person equivalents, on top of its 7.5 million human beings. The purpose of this method of counting food consumption was to polemicise against economists, agricultural scientists, and geographers who claimed that the world had a food potential to sustain twelve, fifteen or twenty billion people. Counting in population equivalents, the total feeding burden of the world at that present time exceeded eighteen billion human beings.[19]

The agricultural regimes of the Netherlands and Denmark were often hailed as examples for the rest of the world of what efficient, rationalised farming could accomplish. What was forgotten, Borgström responded, was the fact that they depended on their fisheries as well as on considerable imports of feedstuff. According to Borgström, they were oversimplifying calculations which left out the livestock. Denmark imported several 'Denmarks' in fish and grain from other parts of the world, and then marketed the livestock fed on them as high value products. The system was not all that productive, because of these massive imports.[20] This example illustrates what Borgström as a non-laboratory and non-field researching scientist strove to accomplish: an analysis of the totality of global exchange.[21] He underscored the risk of looking narrowly at productivity figures and measures that would enhance productivity without looking at the broader nutritional elements. Borgström pointed out that it was possible to massively increase carbohydrate output but, in the process, there could not be a comparable protein source. Borgström distinguished between primary and secondary calories. When we eat meat, the primary calories are multiplied by between five and eight times, because essentially it took five to eight pounds of plant to make one pound of animal. Thus, the calorie gap between the 'have and the have-not' nations increased. If people in the poorer countries changed their diet from a primarily vegetarian one to a diet that included animal protein, they were going to place an enormous demand upon the world resources.[22] This is still a critical issue today: for example, Borgström's point was essentially the same conclusion as that of the World Watch Institute report *Who Will Feed China?* (1995).[23]

Here Borgström elaborated one of his most important contributions to the environmental debate: his study of the *externalities* of rationalised agriculture. Externalities, as the concept is employed by Juan Martinez-Alier, account for the shifting of uncertain social costs (or benefits) to other social groups – other classes, foreigners, or future generations.[24] The people of the luxury nations, to which Americans and Swedes obviously belonged, disposed of as many calories per day as did the 1300 million people at the opposite end of the scale. And the United States alone disposed of as much primary (plant) protein as India, China, Indonesia, and Ceylon taken together.[25] 'There is an upper class of some 450 million, out of the world's 3.5 billion, which occupies a privileged position as far as nutrition goes.'[26] Peru's fisheries were one of Borgström's striking examples, which he returned to throughout the years. Peru had the largest anchovy industry in the world. Yet the largest part of the catch of fish protein was exported to the United States and Europe as, for example, livestock and poultry feed, even though South America was one of the most critical areas in terms of protein malnutrition.[27] Fisheries had become one of Borgström's specialities. He edited a four-volume work *Fish as Food*, an overview of the knowledge on fish as a food supply. In it Borgström raised the question of the precariousness of global fisheries. Fisheries at that time were not a major problem on the agenda, since fish appeared to be an inexhaustible resource: 'Tapping of the wealth of the oceans has become an urgent need for the survival of the human race', Borgström emphasised in the first sentence of the first volume.[28]

In several books on fisheries, Borgström pointed at the enormous post-war growth of world fisheries. The world's total catch had doubled in 17 years, amounting to around 50 billion metric tons annually. The techniques and equipment for catching fish had developed in a revolutionary manner. New, rich areas for primarily ocean fishing had emerged. Especially, Borgström pointed to the dominating roles of the Soviet Union, Japan, Peru, and China. Together these countries fished almost half of the world's total catch. Despite the immense growth in fisheries, it was still a neglected source of food supply in many countries. In spite of the great promises of future development of fisheries, it could hardly be the solution to the world's food crisis. FAO experts had estimated a possible doubling of world fisheries. According to Borgström, that would hardly suffice to raise China to the present nutritional standard of Japan. Borgström's conclusion was once again the need for a planned economising of the world food supply.[29]

The patterns of the global flow of energy had been acknowledged prior to Borgström, but it was not until the 1970s that ecological economics was established as an important field of research.[30] Borgström elaborated agricultural energetics, not only to include, but also to focus on protein flows. It was a fallacy, he argued, to account *only* for calorie requirements in population calculations. Proteins, together with a number of vitamins, special fats and carbohydrates were vital in the basic diet of human beings.[31] According to Grigg in 1993, many scientists in the 1960s saw protein shortage as the main source of malnutrition, and this led to the FAO's making higher estimates of the need for protein.[32]

'We are entitled to speak of success in our fight against hunger in the world only if we can supply people's minimal protein needs.'[33]Fisheries were an indispensable source of protein for the poorer countries of the world. Borgström coined the term *fish acreage* to account for how many acres a country would need to produce the amount of protein from milk equal to that provided by fish. The figures for fish acreage showed, for example, that Japan would need one and a half times the area of its tilled land. Thus, fisheries were a neglected but vital source to supply the world's indispensable protein.[34] Borgström also forecast that the ocean was not going to be an inexhaustible supplier of protein forever, that overfishing would indeed endanger the fish resource – a depletion problem that did indeed become urgent in the 1980s. Fish acreage constituted one of the basic elements of Borgström's key concept of *ghost acreage*. It is 'the computed, non-visible acreage which a country would require as a supplement to its present visible agricultural acreage in the form of tilled land in order to be able to feed itself'.

With the *ghost acreage* concept Borgström anticipated the concept of *ecological footprints*. Today this term is used to account for the environmental consequences that a way of living produces and that sets its footprint somewhere else. The geographers Mathis Wackernagel and William E. Rees use the concept of ecological footprints to emphasise the point that urban populations are supported by land and resources from all over the world. They define the ecological footprint of an individual, city, or nation as the amount of land necessary to support its lifestyle. In a similar line of reasoning, geographer Anthony Allan uses the concept of *virtual water* to account for the amount of water necessary to produce crops. To import food is essentially the same as importing water in condensed form.[35]

The ecological consequences are often not apparent to the consumer. The other important element in the ghost acreage concept is *trade acreage,* basically imported fodder and fertilisers.[36] Here Borgström introduced a problem complex that has been acknowledged latterly in international environmental justice analysis: trade in nutrient components. As mentioned above, Borgström pointed out the Netherlands and Denmark as parasitic on the rest of the world. Even though they had a very efficient agriculture locally, they still depended on imports from the rest of the world for a variety of resources, including air and water and terrestrial products, and on the sea. So he recognised that the

Netherlands and Denmark were supported by phantom land, i.e. ghost acres, elsewhere.[37] Since then environmentalists and researchers have repeatedly pointed at the huge dependency of European farms on land elsewhere.

Making a worldwide distribution plan was not an easy task. As Martin-ez-Alier points out, all needs other than the basic biological ones are cultural constructions, so it is difficult to take them as points of reference. Felt needs are as much dependent on the consumption of other people as on one's own needs. When poor people know that they cannot consume certain products, they may perceive that they are not in need of them, a line of thought political theorist Jon Elster has characterised as *sour grapes*.[38] So Borgström argued primarily for a redistribution to meet the minimum nutritional needs based on contemporary nutritional research. To meet this need, Borgström called for 'a revolutionary programme' of 'nutritional equalisation':

> Nutritional equalisation will probably be the next step in the development of mankind. This will have far more revolutionary effects than the various strivings for equality symbolised by the French and Russian Revolutions. Historians have too frequently overlooked the economic factors which both capitalists and Marxists profess and to which they give priority as driving forces. World events are to no little degree subordinate to nutritional conditions. Human endeavour and progress depend to a considerable extent upon adequate food.[39]

Since lack of food resources had given rise to major human migrations and severe hostilities, 'the proteins have always had a key position in world economy'.[40]

One implication of the ghost acreage concept could be *autarky*, i.e. a policy of national self-sufficiency. Borgström was not directly arguing that no food or other resources should be imported. But in a world of resource shortage, if a country was not self-sufficient, it had to draw on somebody else's basic resources. And the poorer countries would have to sacrifice much-needed foodstuffs and other resources in an overpopulated world.

Borgström became a United States citizen in 1962. He was certainly no opportunist in his new home country. He criticised the 'privileged West' and disdained the American tendency to blame all mischief on communist subversion. In a radio programme commenting on a peace demonstration in Washington in 1962, he claimed that even if communism had not existed the world would still be faced with great problems. Disarmament was essential, but something more was needed. The real reasons for tensions in the world was the hunger gap between the 'have and the have-not' nations. So he urged the political leaders of the superpowers to cooperate. At this time, in early 1962, he saw some hope in John F. Kennedy's and Nikita Khrushchev's declarations of peace and cooperation.[41] Borgström's bridge-building approach in food issues continued to be the basis of his views on international politics:

The great issue of our age is not the Iron Curtain or the Bamboo Screen, but the Hunger Rampart – the enormous and constantly widening gap separating the 450 million well-nourished inhabitants of the globe from these one and a half billion who are underfed or malnourished.[42]

In the late 1960s, theorists of interdependence discussed how foreign policy-making was influenced by the combination of modernisation, resource constraints, mass democracy and international interdependence.[43] Environmentalists saw interdependence as a goal. It was a necessary condition for world affairs. Finally world leaders would realise this, and it would force a joint effort against resource depletion and pollution.[44]

However, Borgström dreaded the communist system which he saw coming, not by invasion but because of the population–resources crisis: 'We are horrified at the Chinese communes, yet we are drifting toward similar living conditions. – Mass collectivisation is on its way also, not unexpectedly, in the overpopulated parts of Western Europe and the United States.'[45] Perhaps this arousing of the communist ghost was a part of Borgström's skilful rhetoric to awaken people. Communism was certainly no alternative for him, being a liberal at heart.

At a time when centrally-planned economies and market-driven economies were at the absolute opposite ends of the spectrum, Borgström called for worldwide general planning and stated that free market economy should not be applied to resources: 'Production regulations, subsidies, tariffs, taxes and subvention purchases have long ago replaced free competition in this area – fortunately, it may be fair to add.'[46] Nevertheless, he is not always clear on how the planning should be done. A collective reading of his proposals indicate that regulations controlled by a international political system, such as the UN, was the way to accomplish nutritional equity. How should this be done? Through aid? Central distribution of resources? Economic redistribution? He is not entirely specific on practical implementation.

In his booklet published by the Swedish United Nations Association, *The Crisis of Abundance,* Borgström states that if we are not able to create a more just world order, the resource–population crisis will lead to a 'fatal global class struggle' between the nations of the world.[47] In *Too Many* he warns that overpopulation might lead to a third world war.[48]

Moon Rockets or Food?

The more precarious the situation, the more divorced from reality the solutions, in the eyes of many environmentalist neo-Malthusians. Borgström gave a number of examples of solutions suggested by scientists, which he characterised as 'one-eyed specialists'. They included melting down the enormous ice cap of the Antarctic region by atomic energy; bedrock ground into fines in order to supply nutrients to fields and at the same time create new farmland; the ocean bed warmed up by heat cables; sending masses of people to other planets. Borgström called these solutions 'scientific superstition', adding that this superstition was much more dangerous than its religious equivalent. Also, more ordinary ideas that he regarded as more realistic, such as production increases through irrigation, desalinating ocean water, farming in the tropics and fertilisers, were irresponsible if they did not consider the limits of human existence. They gave false hopes to which most people surrendered and 'sought their comfort in the superstitious belief that science and technology somehow would find some expedient to avoid the complete catastrophe, even if it was by means which were in direct conflict with the laws of nature'.[49]

The British physicist John Fremlin elaborated the possiblities of using technology to solve the problem of future population increase. In 1964, he assumed that if food and fresh water could be found to supply the world indefinitely, in 890 years some 60,000 trillion people would live on Planet Earth. By then it would be all one city. The poles, which would long since have melted down, would have been built over, as well as the evaporated oceans. This city of Earth would then have to consist of skyscrapers 2000 storeys high. Every human would have a space of seven square metres. 60,000 trillion people would be the ultimate limit to population growth. The Earth city would be too hot from the heat that human bodies produced. Even if humans could construct particularly efficient cooling machines, the heat had to be disposed of somewhere. Fremlin suggested that the heat waves could be beamed into space from a skilfully designed roof. But with 890 years of continued population growth, this roof would have to take care of a heat of 5,000 degrees C. – as hot as the surface of the Sun.[50] Fremlin's scenario was one of the most extreme. Yet it was published in a respected scientific journal. This kind of mind-boggling future scenario thrived upon the prevalent population concerns. What would happen if population growth never ceased?

Later Fremlin stated that he himself saw his forecast as improbable. Well before this would happen, we would take off to colonise new planets. Even though he was sarcastic about the neo-Malthusian technology critics, he declared in 1972 that he was concerned with population growth in the long run as a possible threat to a decent society, but there was no need to 'cry wolf'. In fact, he expected that within 80 years world population would have reached its peak as a conscious choice on an international scale. If not, there were plenty of technological solutions at hand.[51]

All through his career, Borgström saw a serious threat in a too-optimistic and unproblematised faith in the development of science and technology as the panacea for the population–resource crisis. Blind faith in technology and science was the superstition of our time and had taken the place of religious dogmatism.[52] Optimistic visions of technical solutions as the resort for humanity were nothing but utopias.[53] It was this heedlessness about the population–resource crisis that worried him.

Borgström did not write off future technical advances, but it would require enormous efforts from a humanity working in concord. The situation was grave, but not hopeless. Borgström believed that it was possible for humanity to correct the mistakes it had made.[54] Technical solutions could ease the hunger crisis, but they would be far from sufficient. The only proposal that Borgström found anything like realistic in 1964 was a 20-billion-dollar project for building fertiliser factories. Technical solutions could be achieved, but they demanded single-minded steering and careful planning.[55] He later gave some credit to the Green Revolution, although with a great deal of caution. On energy supply, Borgström was equally pessimistic. He argued that it was important to conserve energy resources since they were rapidly going to run out. He saw no solution in the development of nuclear power. He was remarkably early, at least from a Swedish standpoint, to warn of the risk of atomic energy. In 1962, he claimed: 'The use of atomic energy forces mankind to face new, even more serious threats. To dispose of the radioactive waste from the atomic reactors involves difficulties of staggering dimensions. So far, all these issues have been swept under the rug.'[56] Instead of trusting to the development of new techniques, energy consumption had to give priority to basic needs, such as food production and water treatment.[57]

As a pro-technologist turned sceptic, even disheartened, he was very critical of putting huge amounts of money into large-scale technological endeavours. Consequently, Borgström denounced the US space programme. To his question, 'Food or moon rockets?' his answer was obvious. Borgström also availed himself of the opportunity to give his old colleagues in plant physiology an eschatological flick on the nose:

> But the day of reckoning will dawn, and it is probably not so far away, when science and technology will be held responsible before mankind. Men of all nations will then become aware that the spectacular promises given by dam constructors, plant breeders, soil scientists, and chemists have not been fulfilled.[58]

Instead of dreaming of new heavens and new earths, instead of constructing moon rockets, humanity should maintain the fragile spaceship they were living on.

Early on, Borgström employed this spaceship metaphor, which was to become popular later in the 1960s. But Borgström was not the only one in 1965 to use the analogy. Adlai Stevenson, US ambassador to the UN, used the spaceship metaphor in his famous speech to ECOSOC in 1965 on joint international action on development aid. In the closing of what became his last speech, Stevenson reflected the new conservationism:

> We travel together, passengers on a little space ship, dependent upon its vulnerable reserve of air and soil; all committed for our safety to its security and

peace; preserved from annihilation only by the care, work and, I will say, love we give our fragile craft. – We cannot maintain it half fortunate, half miserable, half confident, half despairing, half slave – to the ancient enemies of mankind – half free in the liberation of resources undreamed of until this day. No craft, no crew can travel safely with such vast contradictions. On their resolution depends the survival of us all.[59]

In 1966, it was simultaneously employed by Kenneth Boulding in *The Economics of the Coming Spaceship Earth* and Barbara Ward in *Spaceship Earth* to reason that the earth must be managed as nearly as possible as a closed system. This image was soon to be reinforced by photos of the earth from space and from the moon.

A decade later, Borgström's concluding words in *The Hungry Planet* echoed Stevenson's by-then-well-known speech, but combining the modern space technology metaphor with a biblical allusion to winning the victory crown on judgement day:[60]

> The victory in the fight for world supremacy may not go to the one who has accomplished the most spectacular celestial fireworks but rather to the party that does something efficient to alleviate the distress among the peoples on earth. In reality, these unfortunates in their suffering care little if their saviour labels himself capitalist, communist, or liberal. The victory crown will go to the one who takes the lead in what today is the most essential task: to mobilise the resources of the globe – for the noble task of striking a balance and making us recognise the very obvious limitations of our own spaceship and to act accordingly.[61]

As we shall see, in Borgström's own later opinion, his call was not heeded. His trust in political democracy gradually diminished. Borgström continued his warnings with greatly increased authority. The international recognition of *The Hungry Planet* had bestowed upon him a crown of glory as an international population–resource expert.

Nuclear Annihilation or Population Suffocation?

In *Too Many: A Study of Earth's Biological Limitations*[62], Borgström followed up on his arguments in *The Hungry Planet* and updated and elaborated them further. Borgström excelled in his speciality of gathering data into neat concise tables that well illustrated the summary of results from published studies. He presented statistics for tons of cod fished, tons of corn harvested, people in particular areas, and amount of food imported, all of which were components in the dynamics of the world's food supply. As the title reveals, Borgström's main focus in this book was on the physical limits to population growth. Once again he emphasised the theme of endangered humanity – that an inevitable catastrophe was at hand if humankind continued its present practices: 'As a human race we are heading for Supreme Disaster, and the great challenge to our generation is to avert this calamity.' [63]

A major Swedish newspaper announced a series of articles on the book under the provocative headline, 'Terrifying fact: Your grandchild must starve.' The newspaper introduced the book as 'a thriller that will make Ray Bradbury's space visions seem pale'. Fifteen years on, the Earth was exhausted, the water had run out, and we must eat cockroaches.[64] In 1965, a Conservative member of parliament argued for a halt in the decrease of agricultural subsidies on account of Borgström's prognosis for the future food situation.[65] The *Endangered Humanity* theme was prevalent. Symptomatically, Borgström in this book has population growth illustrated by a nuclear mushroom cloud. In the Swedish

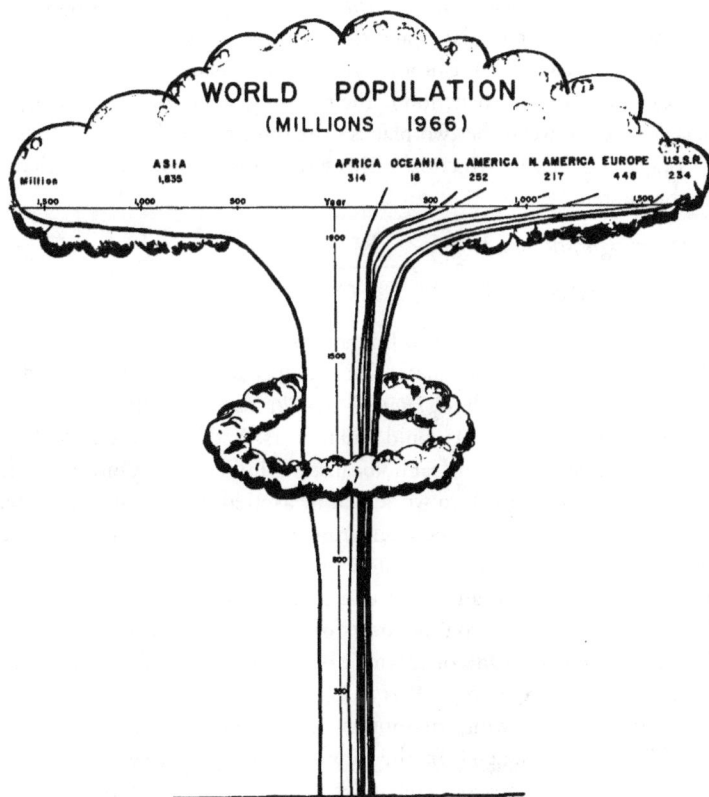

WORLD POPULATION
(MILLIONS 1966)

| | ASIA | | AFRICA | OCEANIA | L. AMERICA | N. AMERICA | EUROPE | U.S.S.R. |
| Million | 1,835 | | 314 | 16 | 252 | 217 | 448 | 234 |

Figure. 2. World population growth as illustrated by Borgström
From *Too Many: An Ecological Overview of Earth's Limitations*, (New York, Collier Books, 1971), p. x.

version of the book published in 1964, one of the subheadings was 'the population bomb', a prelude to Ehrlich's famous book with the same name.[66] This symbolic reference was probably inspired by a chapter in Vogt's *People!* (1961) called 'The Mushroom Cloud', where Vogt outlined his overpopulation apocalyptics.[67]

In the case of Borgström's population diagram, the system of signification – the nuclear holocaust – became a part of the *content* of the population–resource crisis. Through 'Duck and Cover' protection drills at schools, TV programmes on how to protect one's family, banks offering loans to people to build shelters, survival equipment being advertised, and so on, the nuclear fear came to be uppermost in the minds of most US citizens. By 1962, a majority of Americans believed that if a bomb was dropped on their city, they would be killed or injured by fallout.[68]

Roland Barthes shows in *Elements of Semiology* that each system of significations consists of two planes and the relationship between them: a plane of *expression* (E) (e.g. 'the mushroom cloud') and a plane of *content* (C) ('the human capability of self extinction'). The meaning being conveyed emerges in the *relation* (R) between the two planes ('the mushroom cloud manifests the human capability of self extinction'). This system ERC can become an element of another system:[69]

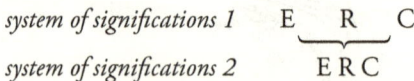

system of significations 1	E $\underbrace{\qquad R \qquad}$ C
system of significations 2	E R C

In using these semiotic references, Borgström made the feared scenario more vivid and reinforced its seriousness. The two apocalyptic scenarios could also be linked in connection with the *resource–security theory*. The struggle for scarce resources or overcrowded areas could lead to wars. And in a world locked up in Cold War power spheres, a nuclear holocaust was impending: 'Only by tackling these questions *now* can a third world war be averted. It is getting very late.'[70]

There were direct links between growing environmentalism and the anti-nuclear movement. It was in the late 1950s, almost a decade after the Bikini atom tests, that it first became clear that radioactive fallout was a significant problem. By 1958, the ecological effects of atomic fallout became a concern to American scientists. One of the members of the Committee for Nuclear Information, plant physiologist Barry Commoner eventually became a well-known leader of the growing environmental movement.[71]

With a picture taken from the famous clock on the cover of the *Bulletin of Atomic Scientists*, Borgström concludes that 'it is five minutes to twelve'.[72] The trajectory of development is unsustainable; he describes it as 'our frantic rush downwards' but rarely states what the catastrophe involves. For example, in *Överflödets kris* (*The Crisis of Abundance*) from 1966 he gives a vague quotation from the Italian author Giuseppe Tomasi di Lampedusa's novel *The Leopard*

(1959): 'Even if we do not *want* to change anything, everything will be changed.'[73] Nevertheless, in some sequences he elaborates on what the catastrophe threatens to bring about. In *The Hungry Planet* Borgström warns that 'we seem to face the alternative of nuclear annihilation or universal suffocation because of the resources–population crisis'.[74] Most of all, the catastrophe entails starvation. In *Too Many* Borgström exhorts that it is cynical to locate the catastrophe in the future. The catastrophe is already here for the two-thirds of humanity who are undernourished.[75]

Similarly, in 1969 Ehrlich predicted that 'the greatest cataclysm' in the history of humankind would descend upon 'our moribund globe' within a generation:

> It took several million years for the population to reach a total of two billion people in 1930, while a second two billion will have been added by 1975! By that time some experts feel that food shortages will have escalated the present level of world hunger and starvation in famines of unbelievable proportions. Other experts, more optimistic, think the ultimate food–population collision will not occur until the decade of the 1980's. Of course more massive famine may be avoided if other events cause a prior rise in the human death rate. [76]

Not only would famine spread worldwide. As population grew both worldwide plague and thermonuclear war were more likely. Together they made up the trio of what Ehrlich called 'potential death rate solutions' to the problem of high birth rates: 'Make no mistake about it, *the imbalance will be redressed*.'[77]

Population as Resource

Concern over a population–resource crisis caused many researchers to analyse the constraints on food in the 1960s. It attracted the attention not only of natural scientists at the agricultural universities, but also of economists and social scientists. One of the better known of these was Clifford Geertz, who in *Agricultural Involution* (1963) developed ecosystemic arguments for how development occurred in Indonesian agriculture. He argued that it was driven by population and productivity growth meeting a resource constraint, but in different ways in different parts of the country. In inner Indonesia the constraint was overcome by an intensified paddy rice production, whereas on the outer islands the area cultivated was expanded. Both these processes were shaped by specific environmental conditions, which likewise formed the respective social structures.

A Danish economist became even more famous when she translated certain arguments of Geertz and others into a general theory of development. Ester Boserup made quite a stir when she stressed the role of population growth as a driving mechanism to innovations in food production. She took the opposite

view from the neo-Malthusians. With increasing population, farming went from
an extensive agriculture to a more intensive form. Her book *The Conditions of
Agricultural Growth* (1965) got a tremendous response. Boserup was on the other
end of the scale to the neo-Malthusians, as she did not attribute starvation to
overexploitation, but rather to a lack of labour.[78] Contrary to conservation-style
neo-Malthusians, neoclassical economists argued that technological development
would offset resource constraints. The rapid rates of population growth in
the Third World had to be met by economic and technological development.
That way these countries would go through the same demographic transition
of declining population growth that the Western world had experienced in the
nineteenth and early twentieth centuries, where birth and death rates had been
sinking since the 1930s.[79]

Even though it had a different starting point, some of the Marxist
responses to the population–resource crisis led to conclusions similar to the
neoclassical. A common Marxist assumption was that the rich feared an increasing
number of poor who would compete with them for resources. As is evident in
resource–security theory, Washington also anticipated that population growth
would increase the risk of revolution. For many Third World socialists it was
apparent that the rich countries wanted to slow development in the poorer regions by imposing environmental demands that served to keep them as suppliers
of raw materials and cheap labour. Even though there were many exceptions,
such as Frantz Fanon's *The Wretched of the Earth* (1967),[80] the leading Marxist
conclusion at the time was that economic and technological development
needed to be accelerated, so that a social transformation could be achieved.[81]

In a preface to the Polish edition of *The Hungry Planet,* Professor B.
Struzek stated that the book was a valuable and insightful contribution by an
expert on an important topic. He applauded Borgström for his critique of the
enormous gap between the food standard of the rich world, foremost the United
States, and the poor world. However, the Polish professor concluded that Borgström, who spoke of a nutritional revolution, neglected the power of French
and Russian revolutionary tradition as an expeditious way to create nutritional
equity. Borgström's historical philosophical approach came in for its share of
criticism as representing bourgeois neo-Malthusianism. Perhaps dutifully, the
Polish author quoted Lenin's 'The Working Class and Neo-Malthusianism', which
attacked the wish of the bourgeoisie not to have many children, thus failing to
view the population issue in the light of the proper social theory. Nevertheless,
the preface concluded with a strong recommendation of Borgström's book,
although cautioning that it should be read with a critical mind.[82]

The Revival of Malthus

In the 1960s, child mortality in the poorer countries decreased rapidly, primarily due to access to improvements in sanitation and new medicines. Subsequently, the population bomb was ticking in the debate in the West. The American engineer and architect R. Buckminster Fuller complained in 1965 about all 'the hullabaloo about a world population explosion'.[83] According to Dale Harpstead, Borgström's agronomist colleague at MSU, this was also the sentiment at the Crop and Soil Sciences Department when he arrived in 1969.

> That was the time when we all were pessimistic about the world food. – Dr. Borgström, maybe he was even more pessimistic than the rest of us were pessimistic. Certainly it was the time we had many fears about what was going to happen in the next few years relative to the availability of food supply and the availability of protein as a critical component of diets.[84]

By 1960, the world's population had doubled once since the turn of the century, amounting to three billion. That the world would be able to sustain an additional doubling in thirty years seemed unrealistic.[85] If people were already starving now, what would a doubling of the world population in only thirty years entail?

According to *World Population Prospects: The 2000 Revision* and *World Urbanization Prospects: The 2001 Revision* from the Population Division of the Department of Economic and Social Affairs of the United Nations Secretariat,

Table 6. Future Human Population Growth Estimates, in Millions

	2000	2025
Borgström 1953	3,668	–
Borgström 1964	6,000	15,000
Borgström 1968	6,000	–
Borgström 1969	7,000	
United Nations 1998, medium projection	6,055	7,937
United Nations 1998, constant fertility extension	6,113	8, 647

Sources: Borgström, *Jorden–vårt öde* (1953), *Gränser för vår tillvaro* (1964), *Världens mat* (1968), *Flykt från verkligheten* (1969); United Nations, *World Population Prospects* (2001).

the world's human inhabitants amounted to 6,056,715 when we entered the new millennium.[86] The world population exceeded Borgström's unsustainable scenario by roughly 50 million. Still we can conclude that Borgström's millennium estimate for total world population came quite close, whereas his longer-term estimates are very high compared to recent UN estimates (see Chapter 9).

During the late 1960s, concern about rising populations and environmental deterioration increased to a new peak of Malthusian concern.[87] In *World Futures*, Sam Cole (1978) provides an overview of futurology studies from the mid-1960s and the 1970s, with *The Limits to Growth* (1972) as the most famous. He argues that many of these forecasts were variations of the Malthusian view that population threatens to outpace food supply. Certainly, the neo-Malthusian prospect had an immense influence over the population–resource debate in the 1960s. In his foreword to the American biologist Paul Ehrlich's *The Population Bomb* (1968), the Sierra Club's David Brower claimed that only in the mid-1960s did it become possible to 'question growth' and the social uses of science. In this respect the 1960s became the heyday of the population–resource debate.[88] After Borgström's *The Hungry Planet* and Philip Appleman's *The Silent Explosion* (1965), there came an outpouring of overpopulation warnings towards the end of the 1960s: William and Paul Paddock's *Famine – 1975* (1967), Arthur Hopcraft's *Born to Hunger* (1968), Paul Ehrlich's *The Population Bomb* (1968), and Garret Hardin's 'Tragedy of the Commons' (1968).

The late 1960s and early 1970s saw an upsurge in food experts, demographers and environmentalists, predicting that the coming three decades would see massive starvation and famine in what were called the Most Seriously Affected areas, i.e. parts of Africa, Asia, and Central and South America. Population growth in combination with an inadequate agriculture would not keep pace with nutritional needs. Besides the suffering of famines and starvation, growing populations would create conflicts by consuming too much food and, by making it scarce, add to the inflationary cost of food.[89]

Even UN Secretary-General U Thant expressed his deep concern for the global predicament in 1969. Although he did not wish to seem 'overdramatic', he could conclude on the information he received as Secretary-General that the situation was acute:

> '[T]he Members of the United Nations have perhaps ten years left in which to subordinate their ancient quarrels and launch a global partnership to curb the arms race, to improve the human environment, to defuse the population explosion, and to supply the required momentum to development efforts. If such a global partnership is not forged within the next decade, then I very much fear that the problems I have mentioned will have reached such staggering proportions that they will be beyond our capacity to control.[90]

In Stanley Kubrick and Arthur C. Clarke's science fiction film *2001: A Space Odyssey* (1968), the narrator gives the present circumstances after the turn of the century: 'By the year 2001, overpopulation has replaced the problem of starvation but this was ominously offset by the absolute and utter perfection of the weapon.'[91] The English physicist and novelist C. P. Snow (1905–1980) regretted in 1969 that he had avoided speaking explicitly on population issues in his earlier book *The Two Cultures* (1959). In his later novels he emphasised the seriousness of the situation: 'Perhaps in ten years, millions of people in the poor countries are going to starve to death before our very eyes. We shall see them doing so upon our television sets...'[92] The famine in Biafra became a precursor of things to come. Famine hit this province during its liberation war against Nigeria. Soils and crops were destroyed and food supplies devastated as the central government tried to force the rebels to surrender. Pictures of starving children in Biafra became yet another symbol of the horrible consequences of the destructions of resources. The emaciated children of Biafra replaced the children of India as emblems of a starving world.

The American physicist M. King Hubbert pointed at the physical limits of the present growth rate: 'To see that limits do exist, one need only to consider that if the present world population were to be doubled but 15 more times, there would be one man for each square metre on all of the land areas of the earth, including Antarctica, Greenland and the Sahara Desert. And at the present rate of growth this would require but 525 more years.'[93]

American biologist Paul Ehrlich was one of the leading voices on the 'population explosion'. Like Borgström, he was influenced early in his career by reading Osborn and Vogt. Around 1970, world population had reached over three billion and was increasing at a global rate of more than two per cent a year on average. In neo-Malthusian terms, he pointed out that if the economy expanded at a geometric rate it would eventually run up against the limits of the earth: 'A cancer is an uncontrolled multiplication of cells; the population explosion is an uncontrolled multiplication of people.'[94] The 'gunpowder of the population explosion' was the ominous fact that people under 15 years of age made up roughly 40 per cent of the population in what Ehrlich called the 'undeveloped' areas. When they came into productive age we would see the greatest baby boom of all time.[95]

Rather than claiming direct descent from Malthus, the conservation-ist-style neo-Malthusians constructed a Malthus that served their purposes. A revised Malthus gave them an intellectual grounding in the past. In the post-war population–resource debate, the Malthus scenario was enlarged by yet another dimension of population growth. Another misery was to be added to the unplanned checks predicted by Malthus: war and famines (as opposed to planned constraints on population such as Malthus' preference for sexual continence). Environmental degradation through industrialisation would put unpleasant checks on population growth. Food was not the only issue at stake in the population–resource dilemma for environmentalists concerned with the Malthusian dilemma. More people could only be accommodated through a more intensive use of land and larger consumption of the earth's resources. It would mean less room for other species. Unspoiled nature was likely to diminish through the growth of cities, breaking of new land in forest and marginal land, and extended extraction of other natural resources.[96] The Earth could not take an additional billion people living at Western standards. In the words of geographer David Pepper, 'People pollute [was] the theme of population control movements in the early 1970s inspired by Hardin and Ehrlich.'[97]

Ehrlich quickly became one of the figureheads of neo-Malthusian concern. Ehrlich's *The Population Bomb* became an immediate bestseller; it even surpassed *Silent Spring*, making it the most widely purchased environmentalist book in the 1960s.[98]

Ehrlich admitted that programmes to 'stretch the Earth's carrying capacity by increased food production could save many lives. Yet, these programmes will only provide a stay of execution unless they are accompanied by determined and successful effort at population control.'[99] In fact, he started out the prologue to *The Population Bomb* by declaring that the battle to feed humanity was already lost. During the 1970s, the world would suffer famines where hundreds of millions would starve to death, regardless of any new crash programmes.[100] A quote by Ehrlich from an interview in *Look* magazine before Earth Day 1970 became notorious: 'When you reach a point where you realise further efforts will be futile, you may as well look after yourself and your friends and enjoy what little time you have left.' With present population growth, Ehrlich concluded 'that point for me is 1972'.[101]

As mentioned in Chapter 4, Borgström was eager to dissociate himself from Malthus in the early 1950s. At that point in time, Borgström denied that he was a follower of Malthus; he wanted to separate himself from Malthus' social views. In the 1960s the tide had turned. Malthus was once again of immediate importance in the debate. Borgström's need to distance himself from Malthus was gone in *The Limitations to Our Existence*. Instead he began praising 'the clear-sighted Malthus'. Borgström commended his theories and called him a mathematician and economist and not at all a 'mediocre misled priest'. Of course, Malthus was also a priest. However, since Borgström had personal experience of being excluded by the preacher label, he obviously wanted to emphasise the other aspects of Malthus' work and stressed that he actually held a chair in economics at Cambridge.[102]

He objected to those who tried to expel their opponents by negative labelling. A denial of the obvious limits to the propagation of humanity was one serious underlying cause of the catastrophic circumstances humanity now faced. Moreover, that was not enough:

> We have not even wanted to discuss these, but instead have been occupied with the not very intelligent (and in truth not supportive to the world's progress) sport of pasting labels on supposed opponents. All kinds of clichés whirl around: neo-Malthusians, pessimists, doomsday prophets, reactionaries, and much more, and this only because attempts are made to bring the food supply discussion back to reality and to put an end to the absolutely fatal competition that is also going on, in talking oneself away from reality.[103]

Hunger was not only a social problem to Borgström, it was in essence a biological one. Humanity cannot escape Malthus's biological law. In 1969 Borgström, together with his wife, edited a selection of Malthus's writings together with a discussion around the texts. In the preface Borgström argued that he was the first to conclude that all life tends to reproduce above its access to nutrition. That is the way it has been throughout history and that is the way it will remain in the future: 'His law of population growth is a biological law.'[104] Borgström had come out of the closet and could now take the stage as a neo-Malthusian.

There are, of course, several similarities between Borgström's message and Malthus's. Both started from the thesis that population increased geometrically (1, 2, 4, 8) whereas the means of supply, at the most, could increase arithmetically (1,2,3,4). Both concluded that this could lead to a catastrophe if nothing was done. Both argued for family planning as a prerequisite to solving the population crisis. And finally, both took the position that people had a moral responsibility to solve the crisis. Everybody must be prepared to make personal sacrifices. For Malthus this implied sexual continence. Borgström did not specify the means of birth control, but it is apparent that he urged material sacrifices. In spite of the basic similarities and common underlying arguments, there was a rift between the conservative social and political message of Malthus and Borgström's environmentalist style of neo-Malthusianism. In his call for a nutritional redistribution and fairer world order, Borgström's perspective was quite different from Malthus's rather dim view of the poor.

In the same year Ehrlich rose to fame, Hardin argued in 'The Tragedy of the Commons' that it was too late to stop population growth on a voluntary basis. Zero growth of birth rate had to be accomplished through compulsory legislation.[105] Many other environmentalists objected strongly to this view, especially Barry Commoner who attacked the 'new barbarism of lifeboat ethics'.

A bitter public quarrel raged between Commoner and Ehrlich on the population-versus-pollution debate. Ehrlich put the emphasis primarily on biological constraints, whereas Commoner saw social and economic origins in the environmental crisis. The two environmentalists attacked each other's scholarship, personal character, and especially all conclusions about the root cause of the environmental crisis. In *The Closing Circle* (1971) Commoner argued that population expansion was not the primary problem. It was rather modern technology, in the hands of far too powerful multinational corporations, which was depleting nature. Behind it all lay the economic order of capitalism and colonialism. Rather than an Ehrlichian population explosion, a 'civilisation explosion' had hit the Earth.[106] In contrast, Ehrlich traced the heightening pollution and environmental degradation to population growth: 'Too many cars, too many factories, too much detergent, too much pesticide, multiplying contrails, inadequate sewage treatment plants, too little water, too much carbon dioxide – all can be traced to *too many people*.'[107]

Paul and Anne Ehrlich defined overpopulation as when an area 'can only be supported by the rapid consumption of nonrenewable resources. It must also be considered overpopulated if the activities of the population are leading to a steady deterioration of the environment.'[108] Which led them to the conclusion that '*the planet Earth as a whole, is overpopulated*'.[109]

In contrast, Barry Commoner saw the optimum population of an area as a matter of choice, political or existential:

> To determine the optimum size of the human population we need to decide first what feature of human life we wish to optimise. In the abstract, the choice might be made from among a wide range of conditions of value to human beings and involve the most complex moral, social and political questions. However, in the reality of present circumstances this choice is very considerably simplified, for the current condition of the human population is such that one value dominates all others – the survival of human society.[110]

Commoner argued that developed nations with a very limited population growth consumed more resources per capita than densely populated countries with a rapid increase in population. To put the effort merely into limiting population was to Commoner 'equivalent to attempting to save a leaking ship by lightening the load and forcing passengers overboard. One is constrained to ask if there isn't something radically wrong with the ship.'[111]

In a very critical review of *The Closing Circle*, Ehrlich and John P. Holdren in exchange accused Commoner of being too simplistic when attributing the environmental crisis to technology. They returned to Commoner's analogy of a leaking ship:

> If a leaking ship were tied up to a dock and the passengers were still swarming up the gangplank, a competent captain would keep any more from boarding while he manned the pumps and attempted to repair the leak.[112]

In the dispute with Commoner, Ehrlich together with John Holdren elaborated his population–resource theory. They introduced a formula for environmental impact (pollution). It was the product of a combination of population, affluence, and technology; the number of people, the quantity of goods people consume, and the technologies people employ to produce the goods. The compact formula was defined as I = P•A•T (Impact = Population x Affluence x Technology). Essentially, this equation stipulated that an increase in population and/or in consuming or polluting technologies would result in an increase in environmental impact.[113]

Following their critique, folk singer Peter Segeer took a mediating position between the environmentalist rivals. In a letter to the Editor of *Environment* he discarded the connection between population and pollution: Commoner had convinced him 'that technology and our private profit politics and society must be radically changed and quickly. But I'm still working hard for Zero Population Growth, because… it's a big world problem.'[114]

Limits to Growth?

The 1960s were the heyday for predictions of the future. Two reasons for the expansion of futurology can be pointed out. The organising and investment planning for welfare states demanded that politicians predict how society would appear in a few decades. The global planning of the post-war world order expanded to a long-range future. Moreover, futurology was needed to meet the growing urgency of the calls to reverse industrialism. All this criticism could not be dismissed by the political powers as merely maladjusted, conservative grumbling. It was apparent that industrialism could not manage to solve all its social problems. Its future needed to be guided, and futurology was a response to this need and a complement to the resource inventories. In 1958, sociologist Raymond Aron argued that 'we are too much obsessed by the twentieth century to spend time in speculating about the twenty-first. Long-range historical planning has gone out of fashion.' Perhaps this was typical for the 1950s, when the development and the spreading of the blessings of industrialism appeared to be relatively problem-free.[115] But in the 1960s this view was no longer prevalent. Futurology became a fashionable science. The debates on the world's resources in the late 1960s and the early 1970s were marked by a period of economic growth that was heading for recession and inflation.[116] Many reports of a warning sort were published around 1970, e.g. *The Blueprint for Survival* and the Menton Declaration in 1971. The latter warning of environmental deterioration, destruction of non-renewable resources and population growth was issued by six prominent biologists and later signed by over 2,000 scientists and public figures from 23 countries.[117]

In 1972 the Club of Rome sponsored the report *The Limits to Growth*. It got an enormous response. In the foreword the President of Potomac Associates provides the official explanations behind the project: to examine what the Club of Rome called 'the world problematique'. It combined 'the complex of problems troubling men of all nations: poverty in the midst of plenty, degradation of the environment, loss of faith in institutions, uncontrolled urban spread, insecurity of employment, alienation of youth, rejection of traditional values; and inflation and other monetary and economic disruptions'.[118] Scientists at Massachusetts Institute of Technology (MIT) used computer simulations to forecast global natural resources. The report starts out with the previously quoted statement of UN Secretary-General U Thant from 1969.

The conclusion of the MIT scientists was that a catastrophe was impending, if population growth, resource depletion and environmental degradation did not halt.[119] *Limits to Growth* is perhaps the most famous of the neo-Malthusian prospects of 1970s. The report employed the theory of exponential population growth and arithmetical increase of food supply. Human existence is determined by physical limits: if a catastrophe occurred it would be due to humans transgressing that boundary:[120]

> If the present growth trends in world population, industrialisation, pollution, food production, and resource depletion continue unchanged, the limits to growth on this planet will be reached sometime within the next one hundred years. The most probable result will be a rather sudden and uncontrollable decline in both population and industrial capacity.[121]

The Club of Rome report was criticised for methodological shortcomings, but had without a doubt a great impact on the debate. The Club of Rome was an informal group of scientists, economists, civil servants, educators, humanists, and, most notably, industrialists from large multinational companies. The report was backed by companies like Volkswagen, Fiat and Olivetti, among others. Golub and Townsend have argued that these industrialists, through this appeal for the global good, hoped to create political acceptance for sacrificing national interest to create a stable international economic environment, all in their own economic interests.[122]

Around 1970, the flowering of books on environmental dystopias provoked the Swedish atomic physicist Tor-Ragnar Gerholm to a counterblast in his book *Futurum exaktum: the technical challenge* (1972) with an optimistic account of the technological solutions for natural resource and environmental problems. Futurology had got out of hand, Gerholm maintained. His attack on the environmentalist prophets gives a vivid illustration of the sentiment in the population–resource debate in the early 1970s:

There are no bounds to the misery. We are told of an unavoidable population explosion with world wide starvation and a constantly growing gap between poor and rich people as practically natural necessary consequences. Social crisis, war and revolution is talked about, and how superpowers armed to the teeth stagger towards the precipice of total extinction.

… The blessings of industrialism are, we are now told, nothing but hollow lies. Welfare, society's glimpse of prosperity, is arrogantly preached as a crazy episode in humanity's history. Soon we will have emptied the Earth's store of natural resources and we are thus forced back down to the gray tristesse of agrarian society and threadbare destitution. Unless already before that we have been choked and poisoned in our desecrated and sick environment.[123]

The Green Revolution: a Pyrrhic victory?

The Green Revolution stood as the hallmark of a technologically optimistic approach to the population–resource crisis. India was to be the great example. In 1964, Prime Minister Jawaharlal Nehru died and was replaced by successors more favourable to Green Revolution technologies. Two events helped spur this shift. First, in the years 1965–6 and 1966–7 severe droughts significantly reduced the harvest. India was forced to import ten million tons of grain. US President Lyndon B. Johnson launched aid programmes to India in 1965–7 to ease the acute food crisis, at the same time pressing its leaders for the domestic and foreign policies desired by the United States.

Second, Borlaug's Rockefeller Foundation team in Mexico had developed new wheat seeds that could double or triple the yield. From 1966–7 to 1972–3 the area planted with the high yield varieties increased from a little over 500,000 hectares to over ten million hectares. Correspondingly, India's grain import dropped from 4.7 per cent in 1960–61 to 0.8 per cent in 1972–3.[124]

For countries like India, Mexico, or the Philippines, the Green Revolution not only held the prospect of reducing malnutrition. Agricultural products could once again become an export trade. More farm workers could be available for work in factories. For India, it would also mean that the country would not be constrained by the political pressure of American food aid. In 1970, between 10 and 15 per cent of wheat and rice fields of the Third World were planted with the new varieties of the Green Revolution. In 1983, plantings of the new varieties accounted for over half of the total crop area. By 1991, the proportion had grown to three quarters. Although the Green Revolution originated in American anxiety about the spread of communist influence, scientifically improved crops also spread in socialist countries like China and Cuba.[125]

Nevertheless, the limited success of the Green Revolution became evident in the late 1960s. The inordinate enthusiasm of people eagerly looking for a positive slant on the population–resource issue also faded somewhat. Norman Borlaug's speech when accepting the Nobel Peace Prize in 1970 is illustrative of such downgraded expectations. Defending the Green Revolution, he saw it as a change in the right direction, but he acknowledged the social and economic problems it raised. According to Borlaug none were more keenly aware of its limitations than those who started it. The Green Revolution had not brought solutions, it had merely bought some time in which solutions could be developed.[126]

Artificial fertilisers contributed to widening the gap between rich and poor farmers, among countries and within them. It gave those who could easily afford the cost of the fertilisers a competing edge over those who could not afford to use them. Until the 1970s, agriculture in the global North continued to increase its production, and poorer farms with little or no possibility of using artificial fertiliser could not compete on the world market. Within poorer countries it was mainly the large farms that could take on the additional costs. Plants that responded well to fertiliser, such as maize, replaced those that did not. Chemical fertilisers are energy-consuming to produce, as John R. McNeill puts it, '…our food is now made from oil as well as from sunlight'.

In Borgström's view, the rice and wheat of the Green Revolution did indeed ease some of the growing pressure on the world food production. However, it did not attend sufficiently to the most urgent nutritional problem – protein. The foremost reason for the severe crisis in foreign aid to the developing countries was the basic misjudgement of its nature: 'The notion that a global technical salvation army would save the world dominated the technical aid programmes of the post-war years.'[127] The ability to cope urgently with the protein supply could be decisive for the fate of the world. Borgström proposed that protein should replace the role of the gold standard in the world economy. Following Malthusian logic, the Green Revolution itself also was a factor that accelerated population growth. Sooner or later this high-yielding technology would hit the ceiling of increased yield and new productive land, he predicted. The increasing number of people in the world was accelerating the process of environmental degradation, which had already severely disturbed the balance of nature.[128]

In March 1972, the British newspaper *Observer Review* brought together Borlaug and Borgström for a 'great doom debate'. Borlaug was to represent the optimists and Borgström the pessimists in a debate over the world's food crisis. The reporter's question 'Is the world heading for a massive famine?' was dismissed by Borgström: 'How many hundreds of millions are going to suffer extreme food shortages before we recognise that the issue is here *today*?'[129] Typically for Borgström, he focused primarily on synchronic externalities. The diachronic externalities, shifting costs to future generations, were not the most urgent issue. As masses were starving now, the crisis was here, and could not be postponed until the future. As it turned out, perhaps somewhat surprisingly, Borlaug and Borgström agreed on most issues during the interview. They both concurred with the Malthusian view that merely giving away food to the poorer countries of the world would do no good in the long run. Population would just increase. Borgström claimed that it would be catastrophic to increase food production without trying 'very strictly to control population'.[130]

There was no argument between them that the Green Revolution had accomplished tremendous results. But Borgström emphasised that exceptions had been greatly exaggerated. It was simply a Band-Aid, not a final cure. The huge inputs of water and fertilisers required limited the applications of the Green Revolution. The new varieties had taken land used for other crops that were of better all-round food value for people. Moreover, the energy cost was stupendous. More energy had to be used for fertilisers, irrigation, transport etc. than actually came out as increased food. Both men predicted that fertilisers would be a major bargaining counter in the international politics of the 1970s; Borgström argued it might well be the most important issue. It was vital that cities recycled their sewage and put it back on the land. Water shortage was the most urgent issue. Borgström proclaimed that 'because of the water shortage, mankind is *now* only one or two years from starvation'.[131] Because of this, he predicted in the interview that the 1970s would see the collapse of production and distribution: 'We will do our best, but we will not be able to stop the unrest and riots and, I am to sorry say, the killings.' Borlaug agreed with Borgström. Unless they could come to grips with the population–resource crisis, democracy would disappear: 'Then total civilisation would follow.'[132] As it turned out in this interview, the differences between the two different approaches to the population–resource crisis were not immense in 1972. Both adhered to the prospect of a coming population–resource catastrophe. Their disagreement on scientific and technological solutions dealt with the possibilities for relieving the crisis, but neither of them held likely in 1972 that the crisis could actually be solved by current technology.

'Round Midnight

By the late 1960s, Borgström was widely respected in Sweden as an international authority on population–resource issues. In 1967, a major Swedish tabloid nominated him the most important Swede in the world.[133] Borgström, however, was far from uncontested. One of his fiercest critics held him to be 'a record holder' as 'the most pessimistic of pessimists'. Gunnar Alexandersson, Professor in International Economic Geography at the Stockholm School of Economics, accused Borgström of exaggerating and consciously or unconsciously distorting facts. Their dispute made the front pages in several Swedish newspapers in 1968. Alexandersson was, according to his own account, concerned that Borgström's 'exaggerations' gave rise to newspaper placards like 'All must be sterilised'. This might be dangerous, Alexandersson argued, since people might think that it was meaningless to give a few Swedish kronor to development aid. Alexandersson further accused Borgström of only presenting the highest of the UN population estimates in his statistics.

In contrast to Borgström's predictions of up to seven billion, he pointed to the predictions of Donald J. Bogue, demographer at the University of Chicago. He had forecast a world population of 4.5 billion by the year 2000.[134] Coils, contraceptive tablets, plastic condoms, and other modern preventive techniques had created the means for successful birth control all over the world. This process had been made possible by 'generous' research grants from private American foundations. All of Borgström's figures and numbers for the last fifteen years could fill many volumes of the textbook *How You Can Prove Anything with Statistics*. Alexandersson complained that Borgström's doomsday visions had been accepted as true. Young people, in particular, most often mentioned Borgström among their prophets. This emotional and militant youth believed that they helped their starving Asian brethren by fighting the police and carrying badly written placards on every occasion. Instead of playing their part in the fantastic results of the American foundations, youth listened to the views of 'false prophets' like Marx, Herbert Marcuse, and Borgström. Clearly frustrated with the radical year of 1968, the Stockholm School of Economics professor claimed, remarkably, that you 'help the poor Asians by diligently driving your Ford car filled with Esso gasoline, rather than through demonstration tom-foolery'.[135] Borgström replied that Professor Alexandersson was childish. The allegations against him were on all counts incorrect and false. Alexandersson was misinformed, and he had misconstrued Borgström's facts on the crisis of the underdeveloped countries. Anyone expressing himself as Alexandersson did could not be in full possession of his senses.[136]

Borgström predicted that world population would double in the next thirty years to seven billion. No 'agricultural miracles' in the world could cope with such development. Within ten years both politicians and the public around the world will find it 'as natural to have sterilisation after the third child as one now regards getting a vaccination'.[137] Borgström repeated his apocalyptic warning: 'It is very late – five minutes to twelve.' Borgström transferred God's warning to the Babylonian king Belshazzar to a Western world faced with world starvation: 'The Handwriting – mene, mene tekel upharsin – is clearly visible on the wall in our festive hall.'[138] In the second edition of *Too Many* he interpreted it as: 'Our days are numbered'. The prophet Daniel's translation was not referred to. Besides revealing to the terrified king that his empire would be crushed, Daniel conveyed that 'Thou art weighed in the balance, and art found wanting':[139] hardly intended literally by Borgström. Borgström focused on the unequal distribution of resources: 'The present economic order in the world leads to rich countries getting richer and the poor poorer.'[140] The Conservative newspaper, *Svenska Dagbladet*, concluded that this was one of the fundamental theses in Marxism. The newspaper had over the years been positive to Borgström's message, and the reviewer explained these leftist tendencies by Borgström's well-known bent towards exaggeration.[141]

In *Focal Points: A Global Food Strategy* (1971) Borgström claimed that the 1970s would be humanity's fateful decade. If nothing radical was done, humans would definitely lose the possibility of controlling development. The problem was not that the world was underdeveloped, but rather that it was *overdeveloped*. In the long run, population control was the ultimate basis for human survival. In a short-range perspective, 'a restructuring of world trade and a massive assault on waste and spoilage' were the most urgent and constructive measures: 'These issues will reach overwhelming proportions in the seventies, this being the last decade when we still have a chance, although slim, of saving mankind and civilisation.'[142] To Borgström, humanity had been on the brink of a full-scale catastrophe for two decades. The time for humanity was no longer five minutes to twelve. In consequence, he concluded the book with his continued warnings: 'The time is five minutes past twelve.'[143]

Of a world population of approximately 3.7 billion, some 2.5 billion were suffering from serious undernourishment. Out of 75 million new inhabitants each year, 55 million were added to the starving part of the world population. The gap was widening, and the poor countries were drowning, not only in their overpopulation but also in ever more burdensome debts. Moreover, a new type of 'imperialism' was emerging in the form of the multinational corporations, which enhanced the West's monopoly on world resources. Borgström raised a warning finger: it was an ostrich policy to believe that the poor countries would be content with this situation. But even if all present food supply were to be distributed equally to all humans, none would be sufficiently nourished. Thus a more just distribution had to be combined with a less wasteful lifestyle.

In *Focal Points* Borgström concluded that it was five minutes past twelve, and the crisis was at large. In spite of the fact that the call of the midnight hour had not been heeded in time, humankind's 'greatest moment may still lie ahead', if the crisis was faced with 'the courage of frantic determination' and attended to through a global crash programme. In many ways this was basically the same programme Borgström had been proposing since the 1950s, except that now the accent was on population control.[144] With this shifting emphasis, the antidotes for coming to terms with the population–resource crisis presented in *The Earth – Our Destiny* are elaborated in his books from the 1960s and 1970s – especially the need for a moral appraisal, for worldwide cooperative planning and distribution of resources, and for population control.

He denounced calculations that claimed that sufficiently large areas of land could be developed for cultivation to meet the pressure of population increase. Borgström called these opinions 'lofty promises and oversimplified assertions' as well as 'pie in the sky and semantic exercises'.[145] A grave responsibility had fallen on scientists. They had 'in a steady stream provided a number of recommendations for the salvation of the world from the hunger threats'.[146]

For Borgström, the naive optimists of the future instilled pessimism: 'Personally, I am seized with a deep despondency, when I daily read about all these fair promises of the future and all the panacea recommendations, completely detached from reality.'[147] He himself was neither an optimist nor a pessimist, he emphasised – he was a realist.[148] Once again, Borgström defied having labels stuck on him. His catastrophe empiricism should speak for itself. Over and over again, he resisted being categorised as a propagandist. He was merely presenting facts.

In the second edition of *Too Many* in 1971, a new chapter on 'Man and Nature on Collision Course' concluded the book. In this chapter, Borgström pointed at several of the environmental issues of the time: e.g. devastation of forested land, nuclear waste, contamination and waste of water, and, most of all, oil discharges.[149]

As the environmental movement gained momentum, the neo-Malthusian prospect was increasingly broadened. Yet, to neo-Malthusian environmentalists all the efforts against environmental degradation were not sufficient if population control was excluded. It was essential to solving the population–resource problem in the long run.

The conservationist neo-Malthusian solutions can be summed up in five essential projects:

A *new ecologically based education,* which makes the citizens of the world aware of how the Earth's resources are being depleted: 'Without a large-scale educational drive, our frantic rush downwards with a constantly accelerated speed cannot be slowed up, or, better still, switched into a smooth climb for prosperity, progress, and human betterment.'[150]

A *new economic world order,* which takes into account nutrition and public health. Withdrawal of resources has to be accounted for, not just seen as productivity. The guiding star must be better utilisation of resources. A foundation for the new economic order should be a long-term agreement to redistribute and supply their protein need to all humans. Borgström proposed a 'biological budget': 'It is high time that economists made an effort to return to the concrete level of real values in order to formulate a valid world budget – and not only in terms of nitrogen. They can no longer remain in the lofty world of abstract symbols such as dollars, roubles, and francs.'[151]

A *new technology*, that is, designed in consideration of the interplay of nature. Humanity must be freed from specialisation and grand-scale projects that are misguided and will add to the problems in the long run. This new technology should prioritise primary human needs: food, clothing, housing, and education.

A *global development programme* for strategic planning of the world's common resources. Political leaders, conscious of their responsibilities need to 'retake the reins and get the world to cooperate'.[152] Borgström saw the UN as the mutual organ for cooperation, but then it had to be universalised and must abandon its preoccupation with Western interests. *The World Household* continued to be one of Borgström's key metaphors. However, Borgström in time fully incorporated the vocabulary of globalisation: in *Focal Points,* his key metaphor became the *global* household.[153]

Population control was essential if all the other programmes above were to be achieved. Humanity was running close to the maximum number of inhabitants that the Earth could ecologically sustain. To ensure that humanity did not exceed the carrying capacity the number of humans had to be maintained, for some even decreased, by voluntary or, if necessary, compulsory population control.

Crises of Grain and Oil

From the end of World War II until the 1970s, international agricultural trade changed drastically. The industrialised market economies went from being net importers of agricultural products to being net exporters, mostly because of an enormous expansion of US crop exports. The European import level remained quite stable. Simultaneously, taken together the non-industrialised countries in the South became net importers of foodstuffs.

The fear of an impending worldwide famine in the 1960s induced expansion of wheat production in the major exporting countries. As surpluses grew, ultimately grain production began to decrease in the late 1960s.[155] Optimism began to rise among policymakers. Prices were declining due to the large surplus of grain. As a response, the Nixon administration even decided to hold land out of production in the early 1970s. Food and fertilisers were cheaper, surpluses mounted, and the production capacity of the major grain producers was unprecedented and needed to be restrained. As a result of the Green Revolution, production levels rose in countries such as India. Food scientists and even demographers began to express high hopes. For example Donald J. Bogue found it doubtful whether a total net food shortage for the entire earth would ever develop: 'Given the present capacity of the earth for food production, and the potential for additional food production if modern technology were more fully employed, the human race clearly has within its grasp the capacity to chase hunger from the earth – within a decade or two.'[156]

Then came a new period of food crisis from 1972 to 1974. Grain reserves decreased to a post-war low in 1973. Prices of grain increased fourfold. And above all, almost half a million people were reported starving in Bangladesh, Southeast Asia, and the Sahel region of Africa.

After a 20-year period of surpluses and low grain prices, world food production fell in 1972. It was off 35 million tons in relation to the previous annual increase of 25 million tons. The drastic drop was caused by major crop failures in the Soviet Union, South Asia, and North America. The Soviet Union had experienced dramatic crop failures in the past, for example in 1963 and 1965. In contrast to previous shortfalls when livestock grain consumption had been reduced, the Soviet Union tried to make up for the deficit by importing enormous quantities of grain. It was able to acquire grain from United States at the low 1972 market prices. Prices soon rose dramatically. Grain reserves were further reduced by large demands from western Europe, Japan, China, and many countries in the global South. Altogether grain exports rose by 36 million tons from the two previous years. Grain stocks fell rapidly. Wheat prices

Table 7. Changes in Net Import and Exports of Grain, in Millions of Metric Tons[154]

	1934–38	1948–52	1960	1966	1973
North America	+5	+23	+39	+59	+88
Latin America	+9	+1	0	+5	-4
Western Europe	-24	-22	-25	-27	-21
USSR and Eastern Europe	+5	–	0	-4	-27
Africa	+1	0	-2	-7	-4
Asia	+1	-6	-17	-34	-39
Australia and New Zealand	+3	+3	+6	+8	+7

rose from US$60 in 1972 to US$200 per ton in 1974. Simultaneously, rice prices increased from US$130 to more than US$500 per ton. However, the devaluation of the dollar stimulated further import of grain from the United States, in spite of the price hike. In the major grain producing countries, the United States and Canada, the high prices encouraged a further increase in grain acreage, and grain prices began to decline in spring 1974. Then the worst growing season in 25 years struck the 'breadbasket of the world' – the United States.[157]

Several factors impinged on the 1972–4 food crisis. A tremendous population increase in developing regions was accompanied by dramatic shifts in weather patterns, such as extreme drought and monsoon rains, that hit agriculture in particularly vulnerable regions. At the same time the grain stocks of the exporting countries declined, and fish were being depleted in parts of the sea, especially the Peruvian anchovy catch. In the richer countries, demand increased because consumption per capita was rising significantly. On top of these factors came economic changes, particularly the devaluation of the US dollar and rising oil prices. A devalued US dollar made it possible to purchase more of the USA's surpluses. Because of this, the Soviet Union was able to purchase vast amounts of wheat in a relatively short period of time, which also accelerated the crisis.

In the midst of the grain crisis came another resource crisis. In 1973, the Organization of Petroleum Exporting Countries (OPEC) increased the price of oil by limiting production. Oil was not only the basis for the mechanised agriculture vital for the Green Revolution; it was needed in the energy-consuming chemical fertiliser industry, so production became considerably more costly. To make things worse, the fertiliser industry had decreased its surplus since the mid-1960s. Prices increased from between US$50 and US$75 per ton in 1972 to between US$300 and US$400 in 1974.[158] The relationship and the importance of the specific factors in the 1972–4 food crisis remain disputed. Nevertheless, the list points at a many-faceted and complex background to the crisis.[159]

From 1945 until the early 1970s, US food surpluses had been a significant factor for world food security. The massive food aid to India during its drought crisis of 1965–6 is one example. Many policymakers in the United States urged that the country should take advantage of the fact that the superpower had become the 'bread basket of the world, and use food as an instrument to influence its foreign policy interests'. The House of Representatives held a hearing on the 'Use of U.S. Food Resources for Diplomatic Purposes'. In the mid-1970s, President Gerald Ford publicly suggested that the United States could play the food card to counterbalance the oil card of the OPEC nations. Secretary of Agriculture Earl Butz was quoted in *Business Week* 1975 saying, 'In the long run, agripower has to be more important than petropower.'[160]

The food crisis of 1972–4 changed international food relief policy. An institutional gap was exposed, with drought, floods and famine and a turbulent international cereal market. Several new agencies tried to rise to the occasion; International Emergency Food Reserve (a joint effort by the World Food Programme and FAO) was established to provide collective emergency food aid. The FAO's Global Information and Early Warning System should provide warnings of areas at risk. The Consultative Group on International Agricultural Research (CGIAR), established in 1971, supervised research funding for food crops and livestock. The organisation saw a rapid increase in funding in the 1970s from US$50 million to $250 million in 1980.[161] The World Food Council was set up in 1977. Within FAO, the Committee on World Food Security was to provide reviews of the world food situation.

During the 1972–4 food crisis, as many as half a million people may have died in the African Sahel region. Many of the poor countries could not compete on the weakened food market, and the situation got worse due to low food reserves in the industrialised countries. The 1972–4 crisis made evident that the resource dilemma was to a large extent a question of purchasing power. The inequality of the distribution of food became apparent. Whereas richer countries such as the Soviet Union and Japan imported food throughout the crisis, poor countries like Bangladesh could not afford to import the food that was needed. The Soviet Union even imported grain to be able to maintain their livestock. The developed nations could even find it profitable to discourage grain production, whereas some poorer nations could neither produce nor purchase the food they needed.[162]

The crisis further promoted plans for a World Food Conference, which was held in Rome in 1974. At the conference, delegates from the South demanded that rich industrialised countries should guarantee a level of food reserve, which could be used to meet crisis situations in the poorer countries but would also serve to stabilise market price fluctuations.[163] The conference gave widespread recognition to the new policy concept of food security. Initially the concept of food security highlighted the need to ensure sufficient production of food supplies and stabilise the international flow.

Crisis of Interdependence

With the dramatic resource developments in the early 1970s, interdependence theorists pointed at the world's finite natural resources as crucial factors in international relations.[164] One author called it 'the crisis of interdependence',[165] The global South could demonstrate that they could use the scarce resources as instruments to promote a new international economic order, and the North could do likewise to stop it.[166]

In December 1967, the Swedish delegation to the UN introduced the idea of an international environmental conference to the plenary session of the General Assembly. Sweden sought recognition that the environment was not the sole important transnational issue; these efforts were also linked to the country's bridge-building role in the Cold War world. The cross-sectoral character of environmental issues could help to tear down barriers in the sectoral and rigid UN system. It was hoped that the environment, as an issue of global concern, could also serve to strengthen a United Nations strained by tensions between East and West and struggling with the aftermath of decolonisation.[167]

Yet international security policies were not the whole story. Environmental awareness was at the time fairly high in Sweden. During the mid-1960s the protest against the further exploitation of unexploited rivers turned conservation into a nationwide popular movement. Additionally, following the tremendous impact of Rachel Carson's *Silent Spring* (first published in Swedish in 1963), Swedish scientists successfully managed to direct public attention to the serious domestic environmental consequences of mercury poisoning and acidification. Influential scholars had effectively argued that a growing world population and accelerating environmental degradation in the near future would present crucial political difficulties to all world governments.[168] The warnings evidently did not leave policymakers indifferent. Collectively, these domestic and international problems found a resonance in the Swedish domestic political sphere that prompted a Swedish desire to bring environmental issues onto the international agenda.[169]

The 1960s had hosted a number of international conferences that elaborated the themes from the Lake Success conferences, but with a slightly changing emphasis from resources to environment. The United Nations Conference on the Application of Science and Technology for the Benefit of the Less-Developed Areas, in Geneva, February 1963 was something of a sequel to the UNSCCUR conference in 1949. At the end of 1965, Lyndon B. Johnson followed the line of Roosevelt and Truman and called for a White House Conference on International Cooperation. It focused on the connection between international development programmes and a looming environmental crisis. The Council of Europe sponsored the European Conservation Year in 1970, and the Economic Commission for Europe held a symposium the following year on Problems Relating to Environment.[170]

From June 5 to 17, 1972, the Royal Opera House in Stockholm hosted the United Nations Conference on the Human Environment. The conference was organised around five sets of issues (besides the organisational matters): human settlements, natural resources, pollution, educational, social and cultural aspects of environmental issues, and environment and development. Even though one reviewer of *Focal Points* urged that the book should form the basis for hosting the 1972 Stockholm conference, environmental neo-Malthusians had no direct influence on the agenda of the conference.[171] Since one object was to unite the

UN around a common cause, controversial subjects, like population control or disputed economic development programmes, were not major agenda items.

Comparing the agenda of the Stockholm Conference 1972 with Lake Success, it is clear that there had been changes both in attitudes and in institutional relationships in regard to the earth's resources. The most striking differences were the active and independent approaches from Third World delegates, and that the whole focus had turned more toward political and social factors. The devotion to technical and economic solutions was not as dominant, compared to UNSCCUR.[172]

At the Stockholm Conference, Third World representatives expressed the suspicion that Western environmentalism could contain veiled neo-imperialism. Their countries' economic growth was to be constrained so they would continue to be subordinate suppliers of raw materials and consumers of Western industrial commodities. India's Prime Minister Indira Gandhi saw poverty as the greatest polluter, and for this she held the wealthy countries responsible:

> Many of the affluent countries of today have reached their present affluence by their domination over other races and countries, the exploitation of their own masses and own natural resources. They got a head start through sheer ruthlessness, undisturbed by feelings of compassion or by abstract theories of freedom, equality, or justice.[173]

This critique was fomented by socialist ideologists, who saw in capitalism the root cause of imperialism and environmental degradation. To avert this criticism, development had been made one of the main topics at the conference. In the Swedish Prime Minister Olof Palme's address to the conference, representing the host country, he underscored the importance of the Declaration to focus on development needs along the environmental challenges. Borgström was not involved in the conference, but following Borgström Palme declared that it was an inescapable fact that each individual in the industrialised countries draws, on the average, 30 times more heavily on the limited resources of the earth than his fellow man in the developing countries. He concluded that these facts raised the question of more equal distributions between countries and within countries.[174]

To overcome the rift between the particular environmental focus of the North and the concerns of the poorer countries, indeed to avoid a complete boycott of non-alignment within the Group of 77, the agenda needed to be readdressed. The preparatory work and the Stockholm Conference itself became something of a matchmaker for an attempted union of environment and development. It spawned the notion that environmental protection and economic development were intrinsically linked. Not only were they supposed to be possible to achieve simultaneously, but also continued economic development was seen as the 'only answer' to most environmental problems.[175] This spadework on the hypothesis of sustainable development was quite contrary to the 'limits to growth' solutions of neo-Malthusian environmentalists.

The Lifeboat or the Termitary

In *Brave New World Revisited* (1958), Aldous Huxley described human societies as becoming more and more like the hive or the ant heap. The process of civilisation had transformed primitive packs into a crude and mechanical analogue of the social insects' organic communities. 'At the present time the pressures of over-population and technological change are accelerating this process. The termitary has come to seem a realisable and even, in some eyes, a desirable ideal.'[176]

The title of the book refers to his re-examination of *Brave New World* (1932), where he portrayed the sophisticated social control and dehumanising effects that could follow scientific and technological advances. A quarter of century later, population growth had made him a great deal more pessimistic than when he wrote his famous dystopian novel. Huxley argued that many of the fictional descriptions had come uncomfortably close to reality. The means of government control and propaganda had increased, and scientists could even control the genetic code of life itself. An overcrowded world would likely drive the poorer countries to totalitarian regimes (at that time probably communism). Then, Huxley foresaw, the industrialised world would find itself cut off from the resources their industries and wealth depended on. The highly advanced technology that permitted the rich countries to have a much larger population than their local resources could sustain would break down, and the nations of the world would find themselves in a precarious situation. In this prospect, the increasing powers of central governments 'may come to be used in the spirit of totalitarian dictatorship', because a permanent crisis would justify a permanent control of all things and all people by the agencies of the central government: 'And permanent crisis is what we have to expect in a world in which overpopulation is producing a state of things in which dictatorship and Communist auspices become almost inevitable.'[177]

In the spirit of Malthus, Huxley concluded that 'in any race between human numbers and natural resources, time is against us'.[178] So, Huxley ends his revisit of *Brave New World* urging us, while there is still freedom in the world, to resist the forces of overpopulation and over-organisation and the totalitarian society that would follow from them. Huxley died five years later. Had he lived to follow the direction of some neo-Malthusian proposals of the late 1960s, he would have seen de-humanising theories of population concern growing even closer to his predictions.

In *Famine 1975! America's Decision: Who Will Survive?* (1967) William and

Paul Paddock advocated a triage approach from military medicine, according to which those little hurt should take care of themselves, the hopeless cases should be allowed to die, and efforts should be directed toward those where aid would make a difference between life and death. They distinguished a 'can't be saved' group, which should not receive any aid. This group included, among others, India and the Philippines.[179] Garret Hardin, one of the most controversial of the environmental neo-Malthusians, argued that zero population growth must be accomplished through compulsory legislation: 'Freedom to breed will bring ruin to all'[180] With 'The Tragedy of the Commons' (1968) he coined a new analytical concept in social sciences. If the world is one big commons where the food is shared equally, we are all doomed, according to Hardin.

Evidently there was a Malthusian fear of an uncontrolled growth of masses of poor. The President of Algeria, Houri Bumédienne, was quoted in *Washington Post* 1977, raising the spectre of population growth as means of bringing pressure for economic reforms: 'No quantity of atomic bombs could stem the tide of billions... who will some day leave the poor southern part of the world to erupt into the relatively accessible spaces of the rich Northern Hemisphere looking for survival.'[181]

'Lifeboat ethics' was a grim response to such scenarios. It implied that it was better that millions of people perished, than that all humans should be headed toward total catastrophe. Hardin used the lifeboat analogy in a notorious article in 1974. Death rates had declined drastically in the 1940s and 1950s, whereas birth rates only declined marginally. Thus, some populations grew much faster than their food supplies. Giving food aid would only promote an unsustainable situation: 'More food means more babies.'[182] In *The Limits of Altruism* (1977), Hardin advocated a more 'tough-minded' approach to countries, such as India, that had exceeded their carrying capacity. The edited volume *Lifeboat Ethics: The Moral Dilemmas of World Hunger,* elaborated the theories in relation to the world food crises following the oil and grain crises of 1972–4.[183]

Ehrlich, who formed the Zero Population Growth organisation, advocated constraints on reproduction internationally as well as domestically in the USA. At home, population control would be accomplished 'by compulsion if voluntary methods fail'. Coercion? He was asked when discussing sterilisation of men in India with more than two children: 'Perhaps, but coercion in a good cause.'[184] Internationally, he urged US politicians to use the nation's superpower status as a pressure to achieve population control: 'We must use our political power to push other countries into programmes which combine agricultural development and population control.'[185] Even though he was far from Hardin's harsh solutions, Borgström predicted that within ten years both politicians and the public around the world would find it 'as natural to have sterilisation after the third child as one now regards getting a vaccination'.[186]

By 1972, Borgström was a well-established authority on population–resource issues, although still controversial in this position. As mentioned, the 1960s signalled his breakthrough as a public figure, as overpopulation became a key issue in the environmental debate. According to an interview in 1967, Borgström himself regarded 1965 as a turning point, with the exceptional reception of *The Hungry Planet*.[187]

In the early 1970s, Borgström received official reparation in Sweden. The government granted money for a personal chair as visiting professor at the Centre for Interdisciplinary Studies of the Human Condition at the University of Gothenburg. Representatives from the Centre tried to get the Minister of Education's personal support for a chair for Borgström. According to Emin Tengström, head of the department, one of their main arguments was that it was a shame for Sweden that one of the earliest environmentalists had been thrown out of the country.[188] Surely, it was an effective argument at the time of the Stockholm Conference on the Human Environment in 1972. In 1980, he achieved his ultimate recognition in the Swedish scientific community, when he was elected to the Royal Swedish Academy of Sciences.

So, what influence did a conservationist neo-Malthusian like Borgström

Borgström Receiving the J.A. Wahlberg Gold Medal from HM King Carl XVI Gustaf in 1974, 'in recognition of his extensive research on the food situation in the world'.

have in the media, the environmental movement, politics, and science? Borgström had been something of a media celebrity ever since the intense debates
in the 1950s and the great SIK turmoil. When a Gothenburg newspaper in a
front-page feature wrote about Borgström's critique of space-travel, it recalled
for its readers that Borgström had been constantly appearing on newspaper
placards for the preceding six years.[189]

Borgström had been harshly criticised ever since the 1950s for his
pessimistic descriptions. The newspaper which, in all reviews and editorial
comments on Borgström's first radio appearance, and through all his books,
had been favourable to his message, concluded that he had a tendency to
exaggerate. At the same time, the author allowed, it was difficult to dispute
that overall developments had proved his gloomy predictions right.[190] Among
Swedish environmentalists, he was celebrated as a pioneer, the man who 'created
the modern environmental debate in Sweden'.[191] He was indeed important for
the environmental movement. It had no solid knowledge base. As a political
movement, it needed science-based sources to prove its point. Borgström's
population–resource message became important in this regard. He became a
touchstone on which to found one's argument. One of the early leading Swedish
environmentalists in the 1960s, Rolf Edberg, called him 'The Swedish Cassandra
Voice'.[192] Borgström also came to influence many concerned Swedish scientists.[193]
Borgström had a reputation in many newspapers as the international expert who
had been forced from Sweden by a rigid establishment. In *Göteborgs-Posten* he
was regarded as one of the scientists who became inconvenient to the Swedish
establishment.[194] An article in *Svenska Dagbladet* widened the scope of Christ's
words and claimed that no-one is a prophet in his own country. Borgström saw
a parallel between himself and messengers in the time of the ancient Chinese
dynasties: 'The Chinese emperors in old times had a reputation for executing
messengers who arrived with bad tidings. Figuratively this is still done, that is
what I and many other tellers of the truth have experienced.'[195]

With this message Borgström achieved an unquestionable significance
as a public educator. In his role as a rehabilitated and internationally recognised
authority, he became of great symbolic significance for an environmental movement struggling to gain a hearing. In the institutionalisation of social movements,
cognitive positions become associated with specific persons. Sociologists Ron
Eyerman and Andrew Jamison point out that 'established intellectuals' play an
important role in the initial phase of a social movement.[196] Borgström attained
a position linked to the knowledge production of the environmental movement.
His position could be described as a *symbolic representative*. He was an ideological representative of a movement to which he did not belong himself: he
was the bold forerunner. Borgström was also a source of inspiration for radical
students. A sociological study of a demonstration in 1968 showed that many of

the demonstrators mentioned Borgström as one of the sources of inspiration, although some politically more radical authors were more widely read.[197]

Hartvig Sætra claimed that 'all politics has changed after Borgström'. In his book *Den økopolitiske socialisme (Eco-political Socialism)* from 1973, Sætra explained what he meant by this statement. He did not argue that Borgström was a great political thinker. His epoch-making achievement was that he had distinctly shown that the resources of the earth were limited and that he had asserted that this understanding must guide all political decision-making.[198] In 1979, the Norwegian journal *Gyldendals aktuelle magasin* wrote that few people had marked Norwegian public debate in the 1960s and early 1970s to such an extent as Georg Borgström: 'One spoke for a long time of before and after Borgström.'[199]

The American ecologist George Woodwell argues that Borgström had an important role in the transformation of environmentalism:

> Borgström and others came through with detailed analysis of these particular segments of that series of problems. I thought it was a pretty powerful time, because there weren't too many people that were involved in thinking about it and you could make a mark. If you had a good story, people noticed. And Borgström had a good story.[200]

However, the main aim of this study has not been to measure the degree of influence of an individual. It is as a conveyer of ideas that he can give us a better understanding of the population–resource crisis.

What imprint did he make as a conveyer of a new conservation ideology in the science community? According to *Science Citation Index,* the only one of his books that was widely referred to by other scientists was his work on fisheries, *Fish and Food.* His books on the general population–resource problem received far less recognition among fellow scientists. Among those who quoted his population–resource publications in scientific journals were environmentalists concerned with population–resource issues, such as Ehrlich and Lappé.[201]

In social science journals, however, his books on general population–resource issues seem to have been more widely used. According to *Social Citation Index* from 1966 to 1972, roughly two-thirds of the 56 entries quoted *Hungry Planet, Too Many* or some other population–resource publication, whereas the remaining third mostly referred to his works on fisheries.[202] Thus, it seems as if his general discussion of world food issues was not particularly recognised in scientific journals. It was the public media debate that was his major arena for those questions. Perhaps that was one reason for his growing lack of interest in writing for scientific journals. In many ways Borgström was an early representative of a new type of scientist, promoting interdisciplinary studies and taking on a more active role communicating through the mass media with politicians and the public. Though contested at first, he met a growing recognition as a scientist. In 1967, he was elected to the American Society for the Advancement of Science and to the World Academy of Art and Science. The latter had its roots in the Pugwash movement and was devoted to global issues.

Borgström appears to have become more and more sceptical during the 1970s towards what politics could accomplish. In *Focal Points* (1971) he stated that it was 'depressing, to say the least, to think how world politics for a quarter-century discussed hunger and poverty but nonetheless only made sporadic efforts to cope with these realities in an effective manner'. Instead he put increasingly higher hopes on the scientist. Scientists needed to take over from irresponsible politicians. The universities must take on their responsibility for society. A great concentration on interdisciplinary operations was necessary, if life on earth was to be saved. By 1979, he had reached the conclusion that humanity's fate could not be left to 'politicians, charlatans and story-tellers'.[203] Borgström, who himself was a regional member of parliament for the Liberal Party in the 1940s, gradually lost all faith in the political system and politicians' willingness or ability to respond to the world population–resource crisis.

By the 1970s, Borgström's view on scientists had taken a quite surprising turn. After having spent so much of his professional life criticising his fellow scientists for being too narrowly specialised and indifferent to the issues of survival, he saw them as the hope for the future. Borgström had been accepted by the scientific establishment; and realising that he lacked support from the politicians, he came to place his hopes on the rule of experts as if on platonic philosopher kings.

In contrast, Barry Commoner argued in *The Closing Circle* that 'the balancing of social judgment against cost should be made by every citizen and not left to the experts'.[204] Neo-Malthusian conservationists have been accused of seeing population growth as the only root cause of the predicament. It is a fair critique of some writings, especially in the voluminous flora of Malthusian concern in the 1960s. But for many, the population–resource crisis was not confined solely to a matter of too many people. Borgström's call for nutritional equity is one strong case against the generalisation that neo-Malthusian conservationists had one-track minds. Lester Brown also argued that fairer distribution was essential in combating hunger: 'It is hard to see how there can be any meaningful modernisation of food production in Latin America and Africa south of the Sahara unless land is registered, deeded, and distributed more equitably.' Brown wanted to move beyond the Malthusian dilemma. It was not only a food–population problem, but also an employment-population dilemma. 'Feeding the increased numbers of people will not be easy, but it is likely to prove much more manageable than providing jobs.'[205]

The Limits to Growth authors pointed at a correlation between population growth and inequity. As a fixed resource had to be distributed among more people, the equality of distribution would suffer. Population and capital growth had to be limited to avoid the lifeboat ethics of a struggle over resources in an overcrowded, over-consuming world: 'Equal sharing becomes social suicide if the average amount available per person is not enough to maintain life.'[206] Thus, population growth had to be curbed in the name of equity. To halt the exponential growth of resource depletion, economist Herman E. Daly argued that it was necessary to switch to a steady-state economy. Inequality of resource distribution was a key issue: '... the important issue of the stationary state will be distribution, not production. ... The stationary state would make fewer demands on our environmental resources, but much greater demands on our moral resources.'[207] Paul Ehrlich, too, shifted his ground from the simplistic attribution of environmental crisis primarily to population, as expounded in *The Population Bomb,* to the more complex relationship expressed in the formula I = P•A•T that he devised along with Holdren.

In 1971, Frances Moore Lappé created quite a stir with her widely read book, *Diet for a Small Planet*, in which she pointed at the high economic, social, and ecological costs of a meat-centred diet. Contrary to prevailing convictions that meat-rich diets were critical to our health, Lappé argued that a vegetarian diet surely could provide sufficient protein. So, it was fully possible to decrease the resources and land used for livestock, which would allow the world's agricultural resources to suffice for a healthy diet for everyone on the planet. The policies of the big international financial institutions had not only failed to reverse world hunger, but through their policies, they had institutionalised it. Not only did she link consumption, environmental destruction and international policy with the food crisis, the book also included recipes for vegetarian cooking as a practical help to start living the message. The book sold more than three million copies and was translated into French, German, Japanese, Spanish, and Swedish.[208] In 1975, Lappé founded the Institute for Food and Development Policy, better known by its later name, Food First. Lappé linked the lack of real democracy in the world with deepening poverty and increased environmental degradation. With increased democratic participation by the world's poor in global policy making, food security could be achieved.[209]

It does not take much effort to find separate statements that fit into the simplistic view of one-track neo-Malthusianism. Nevertheless, on the whole, most environmentalists portray a more complex relationship of the elements in the population–resource crisis. Then again, probably the majority of people had not read most of the relevant books and articles, but instead constructed their opinions on the debate from one-liners in the media.

I argued earlier that views of nature are political at heart. They reflect views of humans in society. Borgström appears to have become pessimistic about the earth's carrying capacity because he became pessimistic about human ability to cope with the laws of vulnerable nature. In the opinion of some these neo-Malthusian environmentalists, Nature is so vulnerable to misjudgements that it must be left to experts to govern it. Democracy simply does not stimulate action that is responsible enough. Such anti-democratic conclusions, together with harsh recommendations for population control expressed by some of the neo-Malthusians, eventually gave the whole genre a bad reputation. Together with a continued growth in food production, this contributed to the decline of neo-Malthusianism.

Decline of Declensionism

While apocalyptic warnings were being trumpeted around the world in the early 1970s, the population growth rate had already started to decline, a trend that became increasingly obvious during the 1990s. In 1976, the FAO concluded that since 1952 the rate of food production increases in the developing regions had been, on average, 0.4 per cent annually. Only seven countries, predominantly in Africa, still faced serious food shortages. In contrast, the FAO pointed to the evidence that 75 developing countries had improved their conditions in the post-war period.[210]

The adversaries of the population bomb were encouraged. An editorial in the conservative *Wall Street Journal* could hardly refrain from gloating over the decreasing concern for population growth:

> It seems to be harder and harder to keep a crisis going, even when a lot people have a vested interest in stirring up public fears. The latest crisis to face the risk of public boredom is the population crisis, which once had even higher billing than the energy crisis, the ozone crisis, the law of the seas crisis, or what have you.[211]

A year later, Herman Kahn and co-authors claimed that 'The overpopulation worries and alarmist exhortations of the 1960s and 1970s may well be regarded as an amusing episode in human history.'[212]

When the breakthrough for environmental policy and the environmental movement came in the latter half of 1980s, neo-Malthusianism had gone out of fashion. For sure, the neo-Malthusian arguments could still be heard, but they certainly were not at the top of the agenda. Malthusian concerns simply did not fit in environmental discourse.

In a polemic article, indirectly advocating zero-population growth for the United States, Roy Beck and Leon Kolankiewicz describe how the US environmental movement abandoned the population issue. Whereas it had been the linchpin at the time of Earth Day 1970, by the late 1990s it was off the agenda for the prominent figures of the environmental movement.[213]

There are probably several reasons for the decline in environmentalists' interest. In the light of the environmental movement's focus in the 1980s and 1990s, two reasons stand out in particular. First, since fertility rates dropped below zero in the 1970s at the latest in most Western countries, population stabilisation became solely an issue of immigration restrictions. Harvey argued in 1974 that the projection of a neo-Malthusian view in politics at the time appeared to invite repression at home and neo-colonial policies abroad.[214] The social and racial connotations were far from the ideology of the greater part of the environmental movement. In addition, abortion and contraceptive policies were controversial political issues that environmental organisations thought better to avoid if they wanted to attain the broadest possible support. Second, analogous to Ehrlich's and Holdren's formula, consumption and technology, especially in the affluent countries, stood out as more important in the impact equation than the population size of poorer countries.

More than two decades after the first conference, many of those who attended the second World Food Summit in 1996 concluded that the proportion of undernourished people had fallen from 38 per cent in 1969/71 to 20 per cent in 1990/92 according to the FAO. World food production had outpaced population growth; the combination of new technology, more intensive agriculture, with massive irrigation, pesticides, herbicides, and fertilisers as well as a closer integration of markets sustained the growth in production, in many ways belying the more pessimistic forecasts of 20 years previously.[215]

After 1974, famine became almost confined to conflict situations, where considerable political and logistical difficulties hampered access. According to the FAO, the proportion of people living in countries with an inadequate supply of food has in the last 30 years dropped from 56 per cent to 10 per cent. Even though these statistics are not hard data, they clearly reveal a trend. However, excluded from this positive development are some parts of South Asia and particularly African countries of the sub-Sahara. Per capita food production did not increase in the most highly indebted, low-income countries. Drought-related food crises particularly affected people living on pastoral land in marginal environments in Africa, such as parts of Sudan and Kenya.

At a global level, things seemed to be going quite well. Since the 1960s, the world had experienced an unprecedented increase in global food production. As of 2001, we had almost a third more food per person on average, compared with 1961. At the same time, prices have gone down by 40 per cent. The Green Revolution's fast growing and high yielding crops made up an important part of this harvest increase. Food increased and population growth slowed.

In 1998, the United Nations announced the 'Day of Six Billion', scheduled for 16 June 1999. [216] However, the pace of population growth was slower than expected, so this special occasion had to be postponed for four months. All through the 1990s, the United Nations Population Division had to revise its projected growth rate downward.

Year 2001, however, was an exception. The population division had to raise its 2000 middle scenario for the global population in year 2050, from a projected 8.9 billion to 9.3 billion. The somewhat higher fertility estimated for a number of populous countries (e.g. Bangladesh, India, and Nigeria) accounted for almost a third of the increase. The largest share of the higher prognosis stemmed from higher future fertility levels projected for the 16 developing countries whose fertility had not yet shown signs of a sustained decline. Nevertheless, the total fertility of the world was expected to decline from 2.82 children per woman in 2000 to 2.15 children per woman in 2050. In the same period, life expectancy is expected to increase from 65 years to 76 years. As a consequence, the population growth rate would drop from 1.35 per cent per year in 2000 to 0.47 per cent per year in 2050.[217] We shall return to the recent figures in the final chapter.

In spite of these trends, it appeared at the turn of the millennium that the technology optimists had declared their triumph too early. Malthus was not properly buried even by this time. And the gravediggers made up a quite unexpected company: the former allies of the technology optimist of the 1970s – the high-tech food industry.

8

The Return of Neo-Malthusianism

Global food production increased enormously in the last four decades of the twentieth century. In spite of a doubling of the world population, the amount of kilocalories that we consume on average rose from 2,000 to 2,800 per day between 1962 and 1999. At the same time, the growth rate of the global population decreased, and continues to do so.[1] Nevertheless, from the late 1990s neo-Malthusian warnings that world population growth threatens to outstrip the food supply in the long run echoed the population debates of the late 1960s and early 1970s. This time they were highlighted in the official reports of international institutions, and not least, in the public relations output of the big plant breeding corporations. Why then are many recent official prognoses variations or developments of neo-Malthusian concern?

The Ghost of Malthus Continues to Haunt

Grave warnings of a population–resource crisis have often recurred, in spite of an enormous increase in yield and declining population growth rates. Now they even appear in the official publications of international institutions like the UN, FAO, CGIAR, and the World Bank. With diminishing resources and an additional three billion people by 2050, all in poorer countries, we are warned that resources simply will not suffice. In spite of a tremendous development of new biological techniques in recent decades, at the turn of the millennium, FAO estimated that 842 million people were subject to undernourishment.[2]

On the Day of Six Billion 1999, the UN estimated that hunger and its related consequences extinguished 24,000 lives every day – one human being every 3.6 seconds. Even within developed countries, food insecurity was once again acknowledged. The FAO report *The State of Food Insecurity in the World* in the same year estimated that more than 30 million people were chronically undernourished in the industrialised world. They were particularly to be found in the former eastern bloc countries. However, even the United States government attached a Food Security Supplement to its annual Current Population Survey. The Supplement asked questions such as: 'In the last 12 months did you or other adults in your household ever not eat for a whole day because there wasn't enough money for food?' In 1999, the results of the survey indicated that 4.2 million households in the United States experienced some hunger for at least part of the year. Households suffering from severe hunger, that is, where children were involved or adults were more seriously affected, amounted to around 800,000.[3]

UN estimates for food insecurity, when people live with hunger or fear of starvation, indicate that in the period 1997–9, 815 million people were undernourished in the world. Some 777 million of these were in the developing countries, 27 million in transition countries and 11 million in the industrialised countries. In 1992, the World Food Summit decided to cut the number of undernourished by half by the year 2015. In fact, there was a slowdown in the reduction of undernourished in the world. For the developing countries, 2001 figures showed a decrease of 39 million since 1992 and an average annual decrease of about six million people. To accomplish the World Food Summit goal would require an average annual decrease of 22 million, far above that level.[4]

Only a third of the developing countries recorded a decrease in their numbers of undernourished between 1990 and 1999. In these countries the number fell by 116 million people. In the other developing countries the people who are undernourished increased by 77 million. Because several large countries, including China, Indonesia, Thailand, and Nigeria, managed to reduce the number undernourished, their reduction outweighed the increase in the less populated, but numerically larger group of countries. Thus, the net reduction was 39 million. Yet in most of the developing countries the number of undernourished increased considerably.[5]

The proportion of undernourished fell in the majority of developing countries. However, in many of these countries the fall coincided with a rise in absolute numbers. *The State of Food Insecurity of the World 2001* concludes: 'The decrease in the proportion of undernourished in these countries has not been sufficient to offset the effect of population growth. Continuing rapid rises in the number of mouths to feed imply further difficulties in meeting the World Food Summit target.'[6]

In addition, we were likely to have an additional three billion people feeding upon the Earth.[7] The World Bank's annual report for 1999 stated that global food production must double in the next 35 years to meet future demands caused by population growth and an expected as well as much needed rise in nutritional standards. At the same time, between five and six million hectares of agricultural land was being destroyed each year as a result of soil degradation, through soil erosion, nutrition leakage and desalination. Other experts calculated even higher numbers. Comprehensive surveys of the world's natural resources and ecosystems in *World Resources Report*, biannually jointly published by the World Resources Institute, United Nations Development Programme, United Nations Environment Programme and the World Bank, pointed to a stagnation in the increase of food production, primarily due to post-harvest losses, soil degradation and irrigation problems. At the same time, unsustainable environmental trends were augmented: collapsing fisheries, decreased forest, global warming and vanishing species.[8]

It was not only environmentalists who warned of an impending food crisis. Experts and policymakers associated with the Green Revolution concurred. In the report *Food in the 21st Century*, published by CGIAR, Mahendra Shah and Maurice Strong raised the alarm: 'As the new millennium begins, the world faces another food crisis that is just as dangerous – but much more complex – than the one it confronted thirty years ago.'[9]

However, whereas environmentalists took the serious situation as an argument for caution about technological development, the industry and many experts of CGIAR or FAO used it as an argument for new biological technologies, which many influential environmental groups regarded with scepticism. They put their hope in the hands of the researchers, who through biotechnology and other means were to accomplish a new and more ecologically sound Green Revolution.[10]

Feeding the Multitude

'Africa needs GM crops to survive' was the alarming headline on BBC World News in May 2000.[11] Similar examples are manifold. One of Sweden's experts on genetically modified (GM) crops, Professor Kristina Glimmelius, also seized on the catastrophe rhetoric. She warned that if we refrain from using gene technology in agriculture 'half or large parts of the world' run the risk of 'starving to death'.[12] It sounds like the Doomsday debate all over again, except the conclusion is rather different.

Neo-Malthusian warnings have attained discursive prominence in times when new large-scale technological solutions have been promoted globally. This was true of the resource debates of the late 1940, leading up to the United Nations Conference on the Conservation and Utilisation of Natural Resources 1949 and Truman's Point Four Program as well as the plant breeding endeavours of the Rockefeller and Ford Foundations. The apocalyptic debates of the 1960s and early 1970s coincided with the breakthrough of the Green Revolution. Of course, as the previous accounts in this book have made evident, the promotion of technological solutions is not the only reason for the discursive position of Malthusian concerns. Economic factors, national security policies, severe climate, population density, media coverage, communications and, not least, real experienced starvation are all some of the interacting factors behind the peaks of Malthusian concern. Technology development is yet another explanation for Malthusian concern attaining a discursive position, especially as food insecurity in poor countries has become the premier rhetorical argument of the big plant breeding corporations. One of their obvious goals is to make the rich world's public opinion more positive towards GM crops.

As this chapter was written, US authorities claimed that a row over genetically modified food was threatening to derail efforts to help twelve million people across southern Africa who were facing a critical food shortage. The United Nations relief aid for this region turned out to contain genetically modified organisms from the largest donor, the United States. Zimbabwe and Zambia in particular aroused frustration among US aid officials by turning away thousands of tons of maize in the summer of 2002, even though the countries could face famine in the month of September. Zambian officials expressed concern that the food could contaminate local agriculture.[13] Critics argued that this was just an attempt of the United States to force a less sceptical policy towards the GM crops in the interest of its own agricultural industry. GM-sceptical Friends of the Earth accused the US government and the biotech lobby of using the critical situation in southern Africa to score GM propaganda points.[14]

The food industry joins the long line of Malthusian concern. When biotechnology efforts took off at Monsanto and other corporations in the early 1980s, there was hardly any consideration for the poor and starving people of the world. The research was directed towards crops for western markets, crops that could generate a large return on investment. Twenty years later, even though the lion's share of the research was still going to the profitable crops, the research had slightly changed; but the rhetoric had changed much more. As science reporter Daniel Charles put it: 'A visitor from another planet eavesdropping on defenders of genetic engineering during the summer of 2000 might have come to the conclusion that it was a technology developed mainly to feed the world's poor and malnourished.'[15]

Indeed, some of Monsanto's public relations material even gave the impression that world food shortage had been the prime motivation all along: 'Since the early 1980s, Monsanto Company has researched the possibilities of plant biotechnology for improving the world's food supply.'[16] However, none of the booklets or reports of Monsanto from the 1980s available at the company's headquarters at St Louis support this more recent self-image.

When Robert Shapiro took over as CEO of Monsanto in 1995, he authorised a conference for Monsanto employees on global environmental trends. There the ecological catastrophe scenario was presented to the audience, with a world population consuming ever more energy, soil, water, and biological diversity. Company leaders also convened with Amory Lovins, the well-known American environmentalist and green capitalism proponent. Clearly this was an inspiration. At the company meeting where Shapiro laid out the 'world improving' arguments for Monsanto's GM business, employees garlanded their company nametags around the neck of the CEO, as a token of their support.[17]

Many commercial producers claim that GM crops can solve world food problems. At present, great expectations are tied to future achievements in gene technology that will make it possible to modify plants, so they can, for example, produce more biomass per unit of water, a technique that would pre-empt the rapidly deepening water crisis. It is hoped more food, with better composition of nutrients, can be grown on less land so that more could be used for other purposes such as wildlife habitat, or on more marginal land, such as arid lands. Soil erosion could be halted and topsoil renewed if ploughing could be replaced by perennial crops or crops that do not depend on eradicating competing crops before they are planted.[18] However, the first GM crops on a large commercial scale were only planted in 1996; so GM crops are still a relatively new technology, with most of the promises yet to be proven.

In a classic Malthusian manner, Monsanto's public relations material proclaimed: 'A fast-growing world population ... will inevitably outstrip our capacity to produce enough food to meet our needs.' [19] The description of the problem is indeed familiar. The overall valuation is, at least rhetorically, in much the same environmental style as the neo-Malthusians. Yet the recommendations for action are new. 'World population is soaring, yet the amount of arable land available for food production is diminishing. New agricultural technology has never been more urgently needed.'[20]

From the mid-1990s, environmental and food security arguments became Monsanto's prime public relations arguments. Full-page ads in leading international newspapers played the humanitarian and moral cards:

Worrying about starving future generations won't feed them. Biotechnology will.[21]

The International Food Information Council likewise stressed world hunger in their 'Communication Tenets for Consumer Acceptance of Food Biotechnology', prepared in 1997 for 'opinion leaders' charged with communication of food biotechnology to the public.[22]

As mentioned, it was not only from the plant-breeding corporations that voiced high hopes about GM crops as the cure for food insecurity. The International Food Policy Research Institute in Washington, as well as several experts and politicians in the global South, argued that the poor people of this world cannot disregard the potential of gene technology. The health and ecological risks of GM crops are subordinate to the risks of not getting any food at all, according to some proponents.

Particularly in Asia, people rely heavily on a few stable grains, primarily rice. The diet contains little beta-carotene, the substance that supplies the body with vitamin A. The deficiency causes millions of pregnant women to suffer haemorrhages that can result in miscarriages; hundreds of thousands of children go blind, and millions are impaired in their mental and physical development. 'Golden Rice' was bred to help overcome vitamin A deficiency, by adding genes that produce beta-carotene in the rice. When the first modest results of successful manipulation of the rice were presented in the leading scientific journal *Science* in early 2000, the proponents of biotechnology celebrated Golden Rice,[23] which became the *pièce de résistance* for the potential of genetic engineering, or more appropriately the *shewbread*, since it was yet to be introduced to the market.

Food Safety *vs.* Food Security

Once again we are facing a conflict about techno-scientific solutions to world hunger. Genetic engineering has aroused fear and hostility in many countries. Many environmental organisations strongly criticise genetic modification of organisms. Will the striving for *food security* – access at all times for all humans to sufficient food to live a long and healthy life – threaten our *food safety* – that the food we consume will be safe for our health?

There is considerable public distrust and criticism towards both modern agriculture and science. It is argued that the techniques merely support the development of large-scale, industrialised and non-sustainable society, that the environmental risks are not sufficiently known, thereby implying ethical problems in the use of GM techniques on crops. Consumer organisations, environmental organisations, and a wide range of political parties in Europe have criticised the development and implementation of genetic engineering in agriculture. It has become evident that the formal political and administrative process of creating legal regulation of genetic engineering must, in order to gain the necessary legitimacy, establish a new framework for communication and interaction with groups such as consumers and environmentalists.

In this context, food security has become one of the key rhetorical arguments for GM crops used by the multinational plant-breeding corporations. Thus the public concern of global food distribution has gained new relevance in the light of the increased utilisation of genetic engineering. The inevitable role and just cause of the big biotechnological corporations like Monsanto and Novartis in developing the greater good for humankind is a crucial part of the discourse of GM crops.

The biotechnology question is multi-dimensioned. It involves issues such as nutritional composition; whether genetically engineered crops are ecologically harmful; whether biotechnology is beneficial to certain kinds of agricultural practices. Another related set of issues is what kind of economic and social system is promoted by the currently dominant uses of biotechnology. If genetic modification turns out to be ecologically harmful, it will surely affect food safety in the long run. However, biotechnology currently appears mainly to be a matter of whether the agricultural systems that are promoted by biotechnology are beneficial or not to food security.

Critics of the present use of genetic engineering point to the pitfalls of attempting to persuade the big corporations to take responsibility for the needs of the poor for public relations reasons. The risk is that the messages become merely cosmetic and only support a discourse about GM crops – potentially a counterproductive effect on food security.

In the 1980s, the FAO widened the concept of food security to include a third point: People exposed to risk of starvation should have access to available supplies. The world food problem is, by this definition, not synonymous with world hunger, immediate famine or malnutrition. Long-term food security is in this view inextricably intertwined with solutions to issues such as debt, unemployment, energy use, environmental degradation, and political security – as well as population. The World Food Summit thus provided a broad definition of the concept: 'food security, at the individual, household, national, regional and global levels is achieved when all people, at all times, have physical and economic access to sufficient, safe and nutritious food to meet their dietary needs and food preferences for an active and healthy life'. The Summit noted that poverty is 'a major cause of food insecurity' but recognised also that 'conflict, terrorism, corruption and environmental degradation also contribute significantly to food insecurity'.[24]

Some proponents of GM crops claim that they will be beneficial for the agriculture-dependent economies of poor countries.[25] Quite to the contrary, many critics argue that the livelihood of the 90 per cent of the Third World population that still draws its support from agriculture, is threatened through Technical Intellectual Property Rights, patents on genetically modified organisms (GMOs), future plans for Genetic Use Restriction Technology (so called terminator crops) and economic structures that favour the large-scale monoculture of present GM crop varieties. Here, another kind of environmentalist reasoning is brought to the fore, one that emphasises social and ecological vulnerability, rather than natural resource constrains. Will the gains in food production be worth the PR victory of a few big multinational corporations? Will it serve to enhance an ultimate corporate vertical integration, where a few actors control the whole chain from gene to loaf, which might be counterproductive to food security?[26]

Today, it is only the big corporations like Monsanto, Pioneer, and Novartis that have the capacity to develop this resource-demanding technology. One of India's best-known environmentalists, Vandana Shiva, has warned about the monoculture that the practices of these companies bring about, in her opinion.[27] An imminent risk is that the demand for profit will counteract the fight against undernourishment, foremost by patenting of living organisms or standardisation that threatens diversity in agriculture. Is it realistic to persuade these multinational corporations to take social and ecological considerations into account, other than for limited PR purposes, when there is no money in developing GM crops for financially weak groups?

Shiva argues that the assumption of substantial equivalence is the single most important problem in a socially and ecologically responsible evolution of biotechnology. These corporations say their genetically modified organisms are exactly like nature made them. RoundUp Ready Soya is just like ordinary Soya, while Bt Cotton and Bt Canola are no different from ordinary cotton and canola. When it comes to responsibility for any interactions that this organism has, either in the ecosystem or for our health, they say that the organism is completely natural, she argues; labelling and segregation is unnecessary. But when it comes to property rights, they claim novelty for the same thing. It is their invention, their property, and anyone using it should pay. This is 'ontological schizophrenia', in Shiva's words. The same corporations are literally controlling the regulating and science system, which in Shiva's argument really turns a contrived engineered definition of equivalence into a problem.[28]

Shiva argues that we have a contest between democratic control over food and agriculture and science and technology, on the one hand, and 'dictatorial control' on the other. The livelihood of the 90 per cent of the Third World who still depend upon agriculture is threatened through intellectual property rights or abolition of the traditional right of saving seeds. With today's GM crop developments, Shiva sees this as a deliberate destruction of alternatives.[29]

Ethiopian scientist Tewolde Gebre Egziabher, winner of the Right Livelihood Award in 2000, warned of the uncertainty that will remain for a long time regarding the ecological consequences of GM crops. 'We are tampering with the foundations of life. We must wait long enough – or face the consequences. If we ever find that GM technology would bring us major benefits in years to come, then let's look at it. But you have to wait as long as it takes to sort out the problems – a few generations perhaps.'[30]

In the toxic battle over GM crops, proponents of the technology place the moral responsibility on those who oppose or are reluctant, especially Friends of the Earth and Greenpeace. Ingo Potrykus condemned this 'radical' GMO opposition: 'My view is that those who delay the responsible exploitation of golden rice have to take responsibility for the unnecessary deaths and blindness of millions of poor people.'[31] In *Designer Food* (2002), a book praised by Borlaug, Gregory E. Pence called destruction of fields planted with GM crops 'ecoterrorism': 'Such "direct action" should be seen for what it is: ecofascism, which, if it sweeps up millions more behind it, could become really dangerous.'[32]

The Need for Modified Expectations

Gene technology was obviously one important factor behind the new peaking of Malthusian concern. Philosopher Isabel Stengers, among others, provided another complementary explanation. As policy making increasingly becomes a domain for experts and transnational capital, elected politicians are more and more confined to an administrative scope of action. In this process, nature and food increasingly become the domain of the politicians. Here democratic institutions and regulations are still expected to play a role.[33]

Is the food crisis a population issue? Is the food supply insufficient because we are too many on this planet or because resources are too few? Not at present. The tragic fact is that the food could suffice today. Conflicts and, even more importantly, insufficient purchasing power are the primary causes of today's food crisis. The gap between the rich world and the poor grew constantly wider since the population debates of the 1960s. World trade increased fifteen-fold between 1960 and 2000, and global per capita incomes doubled. In spite of this, the gap between the richest fifth and the poorest fifth became three times as wide in these 40 years. In 2000, the richest fifth accounted for nearly 86 per cent of total private consumption. This took place in a world where half of the population lived on less than two US dollars a day. Such inequalities not only cause fierce global tensions, but as a hundred ministers of environment concluded in the Malmö Ministerial Declaration of 2000, 'the burden of poverty on a large proportion of the Earth's inhabitants, counterpoised against excessive and wasteful consumption and inefficient resource use' perpetuates 'the vicious circle of environmental degradation and increasing poverty'.[34]

In the Millennium Declaration adopted by the UN General Assembly in 2000, member states resolved to halve the number of persons who live on less than one dollar a day, suffer from hunger, and do not have access to safe drinking water. It would have required approximately an additional US$50 billion a year just to implement the goals of the Millennium Declaration.[35]

As so often when the solutions at hand seem difficult or impossible, it is easy to put our hopes in miracles. Genetic modification often appears as the wonder cure that will render economic and social reforms superfluous.

Are the efforts over GM crops addressing the right issue? The FAO was not clear which way to proceed. The report *The State of Food Insecurity of the World* (2001) suggested: 'Given population growth, reversing the trend requires either faster growth in per capita food availability or more equitable access to food – or a combination of both'. [36] Yet economist Amartya Sen has argued that production, to a large extent, is driven by demand. What farmers will produce food that they cannot be paid for? Inversely, if demand for beef, flowers, or golf courses increases, land and water resources will tend to be used for these purposes. It does not matter what supervariations gene technological development can accomplish; food is above all produced in relation to purchasing power. And it is difficult to see how purchasing power in poorer countries can be accomplished without systematic development efforts and debt relief, alleviation of poverty, and changes in unsustainable and unfair patterns of production and consumption. [37]

The food could suffice. The reduction of poverty in developing countries is a far more effective, and perhaps also more cost-effective means to reduce the numbers of undernourished people. Still, considering the current stagnation of yield increase, would it even be possible within an equitable world order to sufficiently and sustainably feed the additional three billion expected by 2050, without genetic engineering?

The ordained role and just cause of the big biotechnology companies in furthering the greater good for humankind is a crucial part of the GM discourse. Their role is seen as inevitable, even necessary, and it is absurd to question it. Development Economist Michael Lipton has suggested the strategy of harnessing the need of the GM corporations for a better public image, and so persuading them to collaborate in targeting genetic modification plant science on the needs of the poor in the developing world. [38]

It is possible that the dominating corporations can be persuaded by public opinion to use at least a part of their capacity to develop gene technology for poor consumers. However, there is a risk that these goodwill efforts will enhance a system that in itself is a great risk with respect to food safety. If it works, public opinion in the rich world will be more positive towards the benefits of genetic modification; most likely, it will also bring about a more favourable attitude towards the dominance and power of the big plant-breeding corporations. As mentioned, critics question if it is worth it. Will the small gains justify a PR victory for Technical Intellectual Property Rights and GMO patents? The public relations effort might do some good, but it would also support a GM discourse that in the long run is potentially counterproductive to food security – at least if that obscures the need for social reform.

Publicly funded and interdisciplinary research into the social and ecological risks and benefits of GM crops – on a scale that can match the corporations' initiatives – would require an enormous political effort and a vast amount of taxpayers' money. Yet projects such as the Human Genome Project show that great public spending measures can be possible. Two decades ago, US President Bill Clinton declared that we had learned the language in which God created the world, while Britain's Prime Minister Tony Blair smiled out from a video screen behind him. In this project, business interest eventually cooperated with corporation interests, but on more equal terms. To borrow President Clinton's vocabulary: Intellectual Property Rights is not the language in which God created the world or even genetic diversity. If the predicament of food security is as serious as the international organisations point out, GM crops are quite as deserving of public funding as the Human Genome Project.

However, some analysts, such as the influential British Panos Institute warned that a preoccupation with GM crops risked diverting research effort and financial resources away from attending to agricultural needs that were of more pressing interest to the poor and food insecure: 'a common argument made against the endeavours to feed the world with GM crops is that there are cheaper, lower-tech solutions already available to some of the problems of poorer farmers, which have not yet been tried properly'.[39] With the future challenges to global food security, the expectations of gene technology have to be seriously assessed, as a complement to poverty reduction, along with various measures to eliminate food insecurity. Alternatives need to be preserved as minimum conditions for freedom in society, in Shiva's words, 'as a real test for whether or not what you are getting is an improvement or just a rip-off'.[40]

Green Evolutions

The area of crop plantations with GM traits has increased more than a hundred-fold globally, from 1.66 million hectares (ha) in 1996 when these crops were first sown on a large scale, to 185.6 million ha in 2020. That year, GM traits accounted for almost half (47.4 per cent) of global plantings of soybeans, maize/corn, cotton and canola, which are the four main commercialised GM crops. Nevertheless, the conclusion from the first edition of this book still holds. Even if genetically modified crops may be needed in the future to feed a growing world population, conventional techniques could currently provide the capacity to deliver sufficiently high yields to meet the requirements of a nutritious diet for the world population, despite there being an additional two billion people to feed.[41]

Today, food insecurity still primarily results from inefficiency, conflicts, accessibility and purchasing power impaired by income disparities. Roughly two-thirds of the world's agricultural land is used for livestock grazing on meadows and pastures, while the remaining third is used for crops.[42] Meat, aquaculture, eggs and dairy supply 37 per cent of the global population's intake of protein and 18 per cent of calories.[43] Further, the FAO (2019) estimates that 14 per cent of the world's food is lost between harvest and sale at stores and other markets.[44] On top of that, UNEP calculates that another 17 per cent of the world's food is wasted in household, food services, and retail. Combined, the loss and waste of food could have fed 1.26 billion people according to the FAO.[45]

Moreover, while the trend in increased production of the most critical crops is inadequate for keeping up with the anticipated future demand for a healthy and nutritious diet for all, the UN anticipates the global human population to reach ten billion over the next two decades.[46] On top of that come the challenges of a warming world.[47] The World Resource Institute has estimated the world will face a 56 per cent gap between the crop calories need in 2050 compared to the food produced in 2010, unless productivity rises. This translates into an agricultural land gap compared to 2010 of 593 million hectares, or almost twice the size of India. At the same time, Greenhouse Gas emissions will continue to mount even under the most optimistic assumptions of current efforts to decarbonise societies.[48] Hence, the persistent Malthusian dilemma remains a key argument for GM crops, maintaining that 'world leaders and scientists need to be worried about feeding humanity into the future and to act on the use of all available technologies'.[49] Since the first edition of this book, gene editing, such as CRISPR/cas 9, has materialised as an alternative, transgenic-free, modification. This could allow for genes to be changed more easily than using recombinant DNA procedures. As such, it is now put forward as a more accessible technology that can help to feed the world.[50]

The prospects that genetic editing should be able to avoid the political economy dependency risks of transgenic modification for smallholder farmers in low- and middle-income countries can be summarised in six main arguments: The technology 1) is relatively cheap and thus affordable to vastly more actors than solely the multinational crop companies; 2) requires less scientific expertise; 3) is user-friendly as it does not require extensive expertise or practice; 4) involves lower regulatory requirements, enabling small businesses to enter and compete in markets; 5) involves fewer intellectual property rights, at least in non-profit research; and 6) allows smallholder farmers to save seeds for crops in the following year.[51] For these reasons, gene-editing technologies are seen, by their proponents, as being able to boost plant and animal breeding, specifically in low- and middle-income countries, and thus counter food insecurity.

However, there remains some uncertainty about how these novel technologies will be regulated through internationally agreed frameworks, such as the Cartagena Protocol on Biosafety to the Convention on Biological Diversity. While the FAO considers gene editing to be one of the strategically important technologies for food security, the organisation points out the regulatory challenges.[52] Examining the democratisation of CRISPR for agricultural use and ultimately feeding the world, Maywa Montenegro de Wit concludes that, while genetic editing has the potential to 'fundamentally reshape the political economy of seed ... the flow of value from land to lab in plant biotechnology remains extractive – an accumulation of knowledge and materials from local communities and landscapes as genome editors seek further resources to "improve"'.[53] To ensure the democratisation of CRISPR, a social contract of the public interest of smallholder farmers in low- and middle-income countries will need to be maintained with open source and commons-based intellectual property rights' non-proprietary models for sharing and using seeds.[54] How to balance the need to stimulate research and development in food systems, with the imperative not to lock small-holder farmers into dependency of the big corporations remains a critical question. Here universities – who hold most of the patents for CRISPR – can play a key role through social licensing.[55]

Expectations for genetic editing fuel mounting calls for a new Green Revolution.[56] Indian Prime Minister Narendra Modi and former Microsoft CEO Bill Gates are among the many who argue that the food crises necessitate a 'Second Green Revolution'.[57] Faced with a growing world population, the effects of climate change in diminishing the area of new arable land to cultivate, and land competition between food and energy, new agricultural technologies should once again come to the rescue. Like Malthusianism, the idea of a green revolution is powerful.

But what if there never was a first green *revolution?* Examining the evidence, Roger Pielke Jr. and I find it more appropriate to talk about a 'mythology of the green revolution'.[58] This is 'a story' about how an impending widespread famine was averted thanks to 'technological innovations' that boosted crop yields, making it possible to feed the rapidly growing population in developing continents. 'The fact that the world did not experience a global famine in the 1970s is cited as evidence in support of the narrative.'[59] In particular, the averted famine in India is taken as proof. However, after the 1967 regional drought, evidence rather points to an increase in cultivated land area and favourable weather phenomena as critical factors behind the surge in food production at a time when the new technologies were introduced.[60]

Malnutrition was, and remains, one of humanity's most persistent challenges. However, there was not an unprecedented global famine in the 1960s. The world had experienced even direr famines before. One of the reasons why apocalyptic hunger visions caught on among those in political and economic power was that the environmentalist warnings aligned well with the technological 'quick fix' narrative. Yet, rather than providing a rapid silver-bullet intervention, the Green Revolution was the accelerated outcome of incremental agricultural productivity gains over decades, resulting from continuous innovation and intensification, and new land being brought into production. So, rather than a Green Revolution, the world has experienced a '*Green Evolution*' during the twentieth century.[61] Evenson and Gollin distinguish between the 'early Green Revolution' and the 'late Green Revolution' to acknowledge that the crop yield data indicated that there was not an unequalled one-time production surge in the late 1960s, but rather a recurring increase in productivity growth.[62]

When reviewing the conditions for accelerated increase of grain crops in smallholder production around the world – often labelled green revolutions – Dorward et al. identify a combination of policies and measures that need to be in place: 'appropriate and high-yielding agricultural technologies; local markets offering stable output prices that provide reasonable returns to investment in "improved" technologies; seasonal finance for the purchase of inputs; reasonably secure and equitable access to land, with attractive returns for operators (whether tenants or owners); and infrastructure to support input, output and financial markets'.[63] In our examination of the myth-building of the Green Revolution, Pielke and I argue that such 'conditions are influenced by geopolitics, market development, local social, economic and environmental conditions, but also national government investments in research and development, infrastructure and extension services as well as government support, such as price support, guaranteed produce procurement and credit subsidies'.[64]

The lack of sufficient and adequate healthy and nutritious food for every human being is caused by inefficiency, waste, conflicts, and, in recent years, the effects of a warming world. However, two decades after the first edition of this book, lack of purchasing power remains the most critical driver of food insecurity.[65]

9

Crisis? What Crisis?

Proponents of Malthusian-style environmentalism have repeatedly emphasised that 'time proved us right'. Technology has eradicated neither environmental degradation nor human malnutrition. On the other side of the debate, opponents concluded that 'as we can see, they were wrong' and civilisation had not come to an end, and over time each human being has more food per capita on a global average. In the last decade, the number of pointing fingers seems to have increased, especially since it became apparent that the growth rate of the world's population is declining. In the second part of this final chapter I will discuss how the population–resource crises were framed and whether the postwar neo-Malthusians were right or wrong. But first, I will draw together some of the themes of conservationist neo-Malthusianism concern in the post-war years.

The Malthusian Legacy

Malthusianism left more than a very deep imprint on post-war environmentalism. The concerns were not limited merely to a few 'green' pessimists; they also made their mark on international relations and international cooperation. Post-war conservationists were part of a broad international concern about potential population–resource crises.

The framing of the population–resource crisis in Europe and North America was largely shaped by the new world order that emerged after World War II. Four developments can be highlighted. First of all consider the demographic changes: owing to spectacular developments in medicine and hygiene, death rates fell rapidly – most notably in the Southern Hemisphere. This trend led to remarkable increases in world population growth rates. Second, the new world order involved a regeneration of domains of interest for the new superpowers. The post-war era also marked a turning point in American foreign policy. The United States abandoned its traditional non-intervention policy and fully entered the international arena as a superpower. Third, a transformation of the political economy created a decisive boom in economic growth built on mass production and mass consumption. The capitalist accumulation mode expanded to a global mass market. In this new situation, shortage of natural resources featured high on the agenda of international politics, the scientific community, and the media. Fourth, physical degradation became apparent. Memories of the dust bowl in the American Midwest in the 1930s were revived by new warnings of soil erosion, oil shortages, and alarm bells regarding pollution and contamination by DDT, mercury, sulphur and other pollutants.

What kinds of solutions to this impending crisis can humankind find? The analysis of the process of communication between scientific communities and the political system indicates that the population–resource crisis was presented as a scientific, rather than a political or economic problem. However, the examination of the planning of the United Nations Conference on the Utilisation and Conservation of Resources in 1949 and its connection to Truman's Point Four Program reveals that it was indeed very much a geopolitical issue. A major impetus behind the globalisation of the natural resource discourse was the desire to solve contradictions in the post-war world order. By manifesting the global extent of resource problems, the political and social advantages in natural resources that were held by different people and classes the world over could be neutralised. The increasingly intimate communication between scientists and politicians the world over clearly left its imprint on the natural resources debate.

Critical environmentalists could benefit from the post-war situation in three ways. First, the priority of the issues on the political agenda legitimised their framing of the problem. Their ideas largely went along with the modern globalisation agenda. Second, the esteemed position of science in prescribing premises for policies gave authority to the critics, who were predominantly trained scientists. Science was the normative foundation for policy. Third, the often dramatic condemnation by the critics of prevailing optimism about resource utilisation and progress made it interesting to feature them in the media. The traditional style of protection of nature was challenged by a new conservation ideology. In the post-war years, a new global view of humankind's relationship with nature emerged, forming an ideological foundation for Western post-war environmental criticism.

The description of the reality, goal valuations and recommendations for action of the new conservation ideology can be outlined in five analytical themes:

The order of nature: An ecologically ideal state of nature was threatened by the prevalent resource utilisation. Nature had an intrinsic order, in equilibrium or not, that might collapse if manipulated. The root cause of the world's dilemma was that humanity has neglected this longstanding message from natural history: humans had not realised that they were a link in nature's great chain. The unity of the world implied both human and ecological interdependencies. Natural resources issues had to be addressed based on the ecological discernment that everything on earth was interrelated and interdependent.

Catastrophe empiricism: Scientific facts could predict the calamities; research reports replaced doomsday prophecies. Many conservationists increased the credibility of their forewarnings by supporting them with statistical material. For a long time environmentalists, like Borgström, warned that it would soon be too late for humankind – it was 'five minutes to twelve'. This apocalyptic notion served a rhetorical purpose. It served to make people aware of a problem or a threat. This did not mean that the threat was not regarded as real, but the main purpose of rhetorical apocalyptics was to be a driving force. Even when the clock advanced to 'five minutes past twelve', there was still a 'slim' chance of saving humankind and civilisation.

Endangered humanity: In the light of the population–resource crisis, the survival of humankind became the overshadowing question for many conservationists. Not only nuclear armaments, but also material welfare became a threat to civilisation. The provision and ultimately the fate of humankind came into focus. Scarcities of resources were no longer mere local, surveyable problems, but an acute and complex threat to the survival of humankind. Conservation became anthropocentric in the very essence of the word. To protect nature was not only a question of endangered animals or biotas; of its own accord humanity itself had become an endangered species – *Homo incestus*.

The world household: The world must be regarded as an entity and the utilisation of its resources planned through international cooperation. Global interdependence was not only an ecological and economic fact, but also a desired political goal. The metaphor of a 'world household' embodied some essential parts of the critical debate on natural resources, since it included global, economic, and conservation connotations. No part of the world remained unaffected by what happened in other countries and continents. As Borgström encapsulated the world household metaphor: 'a sounder economising is probably an unavoidable road for the well-being of the whole of humanity'.

The ecological society: A political critique was formulated demanding that the economy should be adjusted to the order of nature and the understanding that the world needed to be governed as a household. Criticism against the present political order was mostly reformatory in its scope, but demands for radical changes in political economy also appeared, where the threats towards nature were seen not as an aberration of the socio-economic order, but as a direct consequence of it.[1]

The critique of the utilisation of the world's natural resources manifested a new narrative of the terms for human civilisation. It formed the basis for a new conservation ideology underpinning the environmental movement and the formation of an environmental discourse in the 1960s. Many scientists came to embrace the ideas of the new conservation focus and took an active part in the process of reconsidering knowledge. Neo-Malthusian environmentalists like Vogt, Osborn, and Borgström vigorously conveyed their ideas to decision-makers, scientific communities, and the public. They came to set the stage for the neo-Malthusian heyday of the 1960s.

The debate on natural resources is part of a continued modernisation of the world economy. In many ways, the message of the new conservationists served a modernisation discourse well, for instance in their promotion of a rational international planning of resources. A contemporary view, which has survived to the present day, is that the message of the post-war conservationists was reactive, a protest, trying to halt development. Yet in promoting the modernisation of production, many conservationists were rather formative, a part of the avant-garde of a modernisation invoked by progressive politicians and industrialists. Even though the very foundation of capitalist consumer society was attacked by many leading conservationists, some of the new conservation impulses served as a major influence on the modernisation of the economy. New consumption demands were brought to the fore that eventually generated new modes of production. Modern technology that made production more resource-efficient and less harmful in its residues was promoted. The population–resource debate went to the heart of the question whether social and economic development and environmental protection could be achieved simultaneously. Confronted by growing pollution and a constantly more depleted world, many people became sceptics. The limits to growth indeed constituted the cornerstone of neo-Malthusian environmentalism.

In the early post-war years, one can identify a diffraction in the natural resource discourse. Certainly, the concepts of *utilisation* and *conservation* were not theoretically incompatible. In the discourse, however, they came to symbolise two radically different approaches, where utilisation was gradually getting the upper hand. With the escalation in the Cold War, the utilisation of natural resources became an increasingly important factor for the aspirations of the superpowers. In a world marked by competition for world hegemony, the advocates of a globally planned economy became voices crying in the wilderness. The Truman administration retreated from the commonwealth conservation of the New Deal era. Moreover, in a scientific society which surfed on a spirit of the age dominated by optimistic faith in the technical–scientific system's ability to solve humanity's crises, those who were distrustful and pessimistic towards the specialisation of normal science were dismissed as out-of-date luddites. In this atmosphere, pro-technologists turned sceptics were dismissed as backsliders.[1]

In Sweden, the neo-Malthusian framing of the problems was, at first, widely regarded as accurate. However, the solutions – and even more so the rejection of mainstream *solutions by progress*, aroused resentment. Science prescribed the premises in the post-war debates on resources for those who emphasised utilisation, as well as for those who advocated conservation. For both sides, science was the normative foundation on which society should be built, although the construction designs differed fundamentally. In the scientific community, the dividing line between the two sides was conspicuous. The conflict was epitomised in the intense controversies over Borgström's work, where both supporters and detractors engaged in disputes over his focus and his conclusions. However, in the mid-1950s the critique from fellow scientists was not so much focused on his message as on the manner in which his scientific work was conducted. Being on the outskirts of his discipline, advocating interdisciplinary research and, on top of that, being associated with a propagandist mission, Borgström was not regarded as a real scientist by his opponents.

However, two can play the same game. Borgström made great efforts to prove that he was presenting only bare facts from thorough scientific investigations. At the same time, he criticised over-specialised science for lacking a broad overview. The global issues of providing resources for humanity demanded an interdisciplinary approach and a holistic perspective. Borgström's pessimism was criticised, as well as his data-gathering, but not his most radical critique against the present economic order. His call for 'a revolutionary programme' for a redistribution toward nutritional equity was a non-issue for his critics. In the late 1960s the criticism of industrialism made a significant imprint on the public debate. The ambivalence of industrial development was revealed, an apprehension long overdue, which had been obscured by the economic success of the post-war West. The 1950s are often characterised as the climax era of confidence in the automatic progress of industrial growth. From a 1970s or even 1980s point of view, this might have been true. However, since the 1990s, confidence in industrial progress in its new, less ugly and less visibly polluting guise has been undergoing a revival. Today, it is heralded as an intrinsic part of a green economy in mainstream climate action and at international sustainable development summits.[2]

The neo-Malthusian warnings were, of course, part of the 1960s wave of critique, both affected by it and reinforcing it. The widespread recognition of catastrophic population scenarios in the 1960s mirrored a wider scepticism about inevitable progress. It is important to keep in mind that for most population-concerned conservationists the civilisation critique was not made of the same stuff as radical environmentalism, such as Deep Ecology, which was more defiant of modernism. The critique focuses on *some* of the manifestations of the project of modernity. It took a rather Habermasian approach. The modernity project had not failed: it needed to be corrected. To Borgström, the superstition of his time bore the hallmarks of modernity: science and technology. So the process of enlightenment had to be carried on. Science and technology had to be given their right proportions, and most of all, they had to be guided by a generalist and interdisciplinary global view.

However, the global outlook did not stop at appeals for international regulations, foreign aid, and a liberal anti-racism. The realisation of nutritional equity demanded radical changes in modern economic exchange. It was, in my mind, one of the most important contributions of the neo-Malthusian conservationists to the formation of an environmental consciousness in the 1960s. They called into question the international socio-economic basis of Western consumption and pointed at the rich world's ecological dependence on resources and people in other parts of the world.

The total planetary catastrophe never came; the global famine never hit. So was there never any crisis? Were conservationist neo-Malthusians just as misguided in their Malthusianism, as Malthus had been in 1798? So far, the Malthusian prediction, that population growth will outstrip resources in the long run, has been historically false, at least on a global scale.

Neo-Malthusians, as well as their technology-optimistic counterparts, were engaged in constructing a crisis from the 1950s to the 1970s. Both sides selected facts from the material reality and put them together to form either a state of crisis or a state of reassurance.

By putting so much emphasis on population growth, neo-Malthusian framing of the crisis was flawed – in retrospect, perhaps even harmful. It diverted attention from more serious problems of production and consumption. However, many neo-Malthusian conservationists pointed not only to population growth, but also to distribution inequalities. As the environmental debates gained momentum, production and consumption increasingly added to the neo-Malthusian critique. Since humankind seemed to be too populous already, it was deeply immoral to further destroy the supply situation and to take more than one's share from the global household.

Were the Neo-Malthusians Right or Wrong?

This book has tried to understand post-war neo-Malthusian concern and its upsurge in a time of profound changes in demography, capitalism, resource availability, technology, security policy, public health, mental and material glo-balisation, environmental change, green awareness, and the like. The purpose has not been to conduct a critique of the neo-Malthusians or their adversaries, or to pass a verdict on them.

Still, the question of whether they were right or wrong lingers through-out the years. As both neo-Malthusian and cornucopian predictions often used the turn of the millennium as reference year, it became something of a day, of reckoning, sparking lively debates as to whether the neo-Malthusians were right or wrong. Perhaps it was not so much a debate, as a gloating over the false pre-dictions of 'the prophets of doom'. At the new millennium, Georg Borgström's old adversary from the 1960s, physics professor Tor-Ragnar Gerholm, a Swedish Julian Simon equivalent, argued that time had proved him right. Humanity's plight of survival was perhaps, after all, nothing but a sort of obscenity literature for intellectuals.[23] Nowadays, he claimed, one cannot understand how people could ever take the doomsday prophecies of Borgström and his like seriously.

The allegations call for an examination: Were the neo-Malthusians right or wrong? To answer the question, we have to examine several strands of environmentalist Malthusian concern by returning to four specific areas: the prognoses of population growth, catastrophe scenarios, nutritional equity, and the earth's carrying capacity.

Prognoses of Population Growth

How many people would inhabit the earth by the year 2000, according to Borgström's estimates? In 1953, he calculated that we would number almost 3.7 billion at the turn of the new millennium.[4] During the 1960s, there were improvements in population statistics, and in that period his prognosis ranged between six and seven billion – the lower estimate being right on target in the light of present UN numbers.

From a longer-term perspective, however, he was more pessimistic than today's forecasters. In 1964, he estimated that if trends were maintained, there would be up to 15 billion of us by the year 2025. The growth rate, however, has been decreasing ever since the 1960s, a trend that has been increasingly apparent in recent decades. Since the first edition of this book in 2003, the world's population has continued to grow, rising by almost a quarter. The 'Day of Eight Billion' was marked on 15 November 2022. Yet, the pace is slowing. At the peak in the second half of the 1960s, the world population was increasing by 2.1 per cent per year. In 2020, the growth rate had fallen below one per cent and it is expected to continue to fall. In the medium variant the global population is projected to grow to around 8.5 billion in 2030, 9.7 billion in 2050 and 10.4 billion in 2100 in the UN middle scenario.[5]

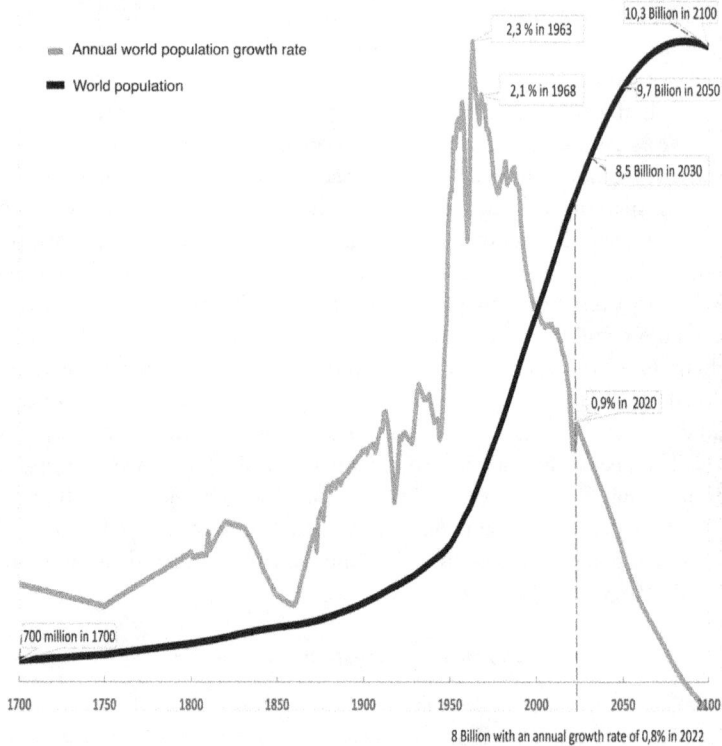

Legend:
- Annual world population growth rate
- World population

Labels on figure:
- 2,3 % in 1963
- 2,1 % in 1968
- 10,3 Billion in 2100
- 9,7 Billion in 2050
- 8,5 Billion in 2030
- 0,9% in 2020
- 700 million in 1700
- 8 Billion with an annual growth rate of 0,8% in 2022

Figure 3. World population growth 1700–2100. World population in billion and annual global growth rate.[6]

The UN population projections hinge on uncertain factors. They build on estimates of the range of plausible future trends in fertility, mortality and international migration in different places around the world as well as 'optimistic' assumptions about the progress of socio-economic development, health and gender equality.[7] A critical question is how a warming world, increased tensions or slowed economic output, will affect these assumptions. As the economic effects of climate change and loss of biodiversity are expected to hit the poor the hardest, it may well contribute to a slowdown of the expected demographic transition. Again, the global gaze can obscure the prevailing disparities between regions. While all but one of the continents are expected to see declining populations, more than half of the population increase up to 2050 will occur in sub-Saharan Africa, with over one billion new inhabitants expected.

We must not forget that the technology optimists were also wrong in their population forecasting. In the late 1960s demographer Donald J. Bogue predicted a world population of 4.5 billion at the new millennium, with a growth rate at zero per cent (or easily within the capacity of its expanding economy to support). Using Bogue, Gerholm, the notorious critic of prophets of doom, found it hard to imagine in 1972 that the world population by year 2000 would exceed 5.5. billion, the UN's lower estimate.[38] Over and over again in the 1960s, the American engineer and architect, R. Buckminster Fuller, who devoted much of his writing to arguing that technology could save the world, predicted an end to humanity's problems before the turn of the century: 'Humanity's mastery of vast, inanimate, inexhaustible energy sources and the accelerated doing more with less of sea, air, and space technology has proven Malthus to be wrong. Comprehensive physical and economic success for humanity may now be accomplished in one-fourth of a century.'[4] Few would agree that such successes have been accomplished for all human kind Considering the long-term consequences of many environmental problems like climate change, deforestation, soil degradation, and loss of biodiversity, it is not within our reach for the foreseeable future.[9]

With the growing world population and rising incomes in low- and middle-income countries, the *World Resource Report* anticipates that food demand will surge by 50 per cent from 2010 levels to 2050. Moreover, animal-based diets may increase by almost 70 per cent.[10] This will happen as climate change has an increasingly negative effect on food security, nutrition and micro-nutrient sufficiencies in all scenarios considered by the Intergovernmental Panel on Climate Change (IPCC). While global crop productivity may increase as lower temperature regions become warmer, agricultural production in areas already struggling the most with food insecurity will suffer the worst effects. Nutritional quality is expected to decline, as pests and diseases, and the frequency, intensity and severity of extreme weather events, increase. Cereal prices in 2050 could increase by between one and 29 per cent. An additional one to 183 million people are at risk of hunger.

The variations in estimates are enormous, as the number of people who will be affected will depend on how the world succeeds with the other factors behind food security discussed in this chapter. Nonetheless, all the evidence points to climate change being yet another difficult stressor to food security. Areas in sub-Saharan Africa, South Asia, Central and South America and Small Island states are particularly vulnerable. And the expected need for carbon sinks to reach the Paris temperature goals will restrict opportunities for clearing new land areas for agricultural production.[11]

Biodiversity is critical for safeguarding food production in the future. For example, more than 75 per cent of agricultural crops around the world are dependent on pollinators. Faced with the staggering loss of species around the world, the International Science-Policy Platform on Biodiversity and Ecosystem Services (IPBES) warn of an unprecedented extinction rate, threating a million species. So, yet another severe threat to food security is looming. International market demand, changes in demography, urbanisation and climate change accelerate drivers of biodiversity loss, such as harmful land-use practices, pollution, the spread of invasive species and overharvesting.[12]

Most of the world's inhabitants are still waiting for the arrival of the 'economic success' envisioned by the cornucopian antagonists of neo-Malthusianism. The fact is that finding predictions gone wrong among both neo-Malthusians and their adversaries is like shooting sitting ducks. As Arthur C. Clarke's maxim states: 'The future is not what it used to be'.

Most neo-Malthusian prognoses from the 1960s onwards for how many people there would be by the year 2000 were fairly accurate. They usually followed UN statistics. It is the longer-term prognoses that differ drastically from today's estimates, primarily because they did not foresee the demographic transition at the end of the twentieth century. The suggestion that there could possibly be as many as 15 billion of us by 2025 was absurd to them anyhow. By then we would have hit the limits for what the earth could sustain biologically. Yes, feeding even six or seven billion was impossible without utter misery for us all, according to the neo-Malthuisians.

So they got it wrong in two respects: food production increases and population prognoses for time spans longer than three decades. It was possible to *produce* food for a population of six billion. Yet, as for our ability to properly feed all human beings at the birth of the new millennium, they were right in their forecasts – even though the reason is not that we are too many, but that that we are still beset with too much inequality, ineffectiveness and violent conflicts.

Faced with exponential growth charts of world populations in the 1960s and 1970s, it is not hard to see how one could be frightened. One would have had to be a true believer in agricultural and technological ingenuity not to be. The major error was not to foresee that population growth could level off. In that shortcoming, they were in a very strong company indeed; and the technology-optimist adversaries, for their part, missed the inequity of resource distribution and environmental degradation that followed industrialised agriculture.

Catastrophe Scenarios

What then, would follow the third Horseman of the Apocalypse, the messenger of Famine on the black charger? Borgström warned the Swedes in 1965 that their grandchildren would starve. (Since I was born around that time, he was talking about my own children.) However, not many Swedish children go hungry today. For those who do, it certainly is not because of general food shortage, but for social and economic reasons. Others warned of a worldwide famine in the 1970s. Ehrlich referred to the optimistic prognosis that dated 'the greatest cataclysm' in the history of humankind at some point in the 1980s. The 'natural' balance between birth rate and death rate would be restored by famine, plague, and/or nuclear war.

Several conservationists predicted a coming class struggle for resources, which also might lead to the Third World War. The dark mushroom clouds of the Cold War had left their mark on the so-called 'prophets of doom'. In the scenario where total catastrophe could be avoided, the end of civilised society was still drawing near as humans were being added by the billions. To several involved in the debate, including UN Secretary-General U Thant, the 1970s were the Decade of Fate, the last chance, if ever so small, to save humanity and civilisation.

The world reached six billion, and just over two decades later eight billion, without a complete catastrophe, Third World War or permanent worldwide famine. The dystopias did not meet the deadline. So was the population–resource crisis solved?

In the new millennium, warnings of a threatened civilisation continue to resonate. After travelling the 'frontlines of the green revolution', journalist Joel K. Bourne resorted to the Malthusian silver bullet in his award-winning book *The End of Plenty: The Race to Feed a Crowded World*: 'Of course, the most beneficial thing humanity could do is to show more restraint in the bedroom'.[13]

Scientific papers address the neo-Malthusian concerns in relation to, e.g., sub-Saharan Africa,[14] climate change,[15] environmental boundaries,[16] fisheries,[17] trade constraints,[18] and consumption and affluent life styles.[19] The entire Agenda 2030 is at risk, according to South African geographer Bopaki Phogole and ecologist Kowiyou Yessoufou: 'The ongoing exponential growth of human population poses a risk to sustainable development goals (SDGs). Unless we understand the drivers of this growth and inform policy development accordingly, SDGs would remain a dream.'[20]

Limiting population growth is not, however, on the table in the international climate negotiations. It would simply be too controversial for the world's states to agree on. It is, indeed, one of the most divisive topics. The International Negotiations Survey gauges policy preferences among participants at the Conference of Parties (COP) to the United Nations Framework Convention on Climate Change (UNFCCC). The respondents are from most countries of the world. The sample is roughly split between negotiators as well as other government representatives and non-state observers at the meetings. When asked to rank the best ways to tackle climate change, 30 per cent firmly disagreed that population control was an effective response. However, even though population measures were not even on the negotiation agenda, 19 per cent clearly agreed. Population growth apparently remains a concern for many participants in global environmental politics. Compared to other solutions discussed at the negotiations, it was clearly the most controversial, followed by market mechanisms. (Fig. 4).

Effectiveness of Measures for Tackling Climate Change

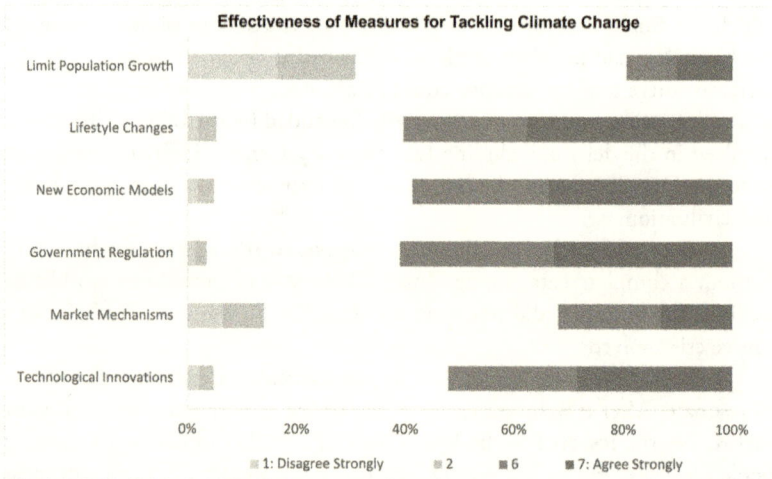

Figure 4. UNFCCC COP18-21 and 24-25 respondents' perceptions of the most effective measures to tackle change, ranging from disagree (1) to agree (7) (n= 3953).

In the wake of the food price crises of 2007–2008 and 2010–2012, the founder of World Watch Institute Lester Brown, who has been active in the population debates since the 1970s, raised the prospects of food shortages bringing down civilisations. As water shortages, soil degradation and global warming amplify food scarcity and drive up prices, poorer states would be plunged into chaos. As a consequence, these fragile states would threaten world order by exporting terrorism, illegal drugs, diseases and refugees to the richer countries. The warnings echo the Malthusian story, that the poorer masses will threaten stability of the rich. Yet again, the image of a looming threat to Western civilisation from the densely populated poorer parts of Africa and Asia is deployed to scare the affluent into action. The World Economic Forum's World Risk Report warn of 'geopolitically motivated food-supply disruptions' as greenhouse gases warm a world already tense with conflicts and looming trade wars. The 2019 report gives a dire outlook: 'Domestically, rationing might be needed. Hoarding and theft could undermine the social order.'[21]

While scarcity alone is unlikely to lead to large-scale violent conflicts, as biological resources make up only a smaller part of a state's war-making capacity, geopolitical conflicts over scarce resources are integral to the struggle for power in human civilisations.[22] Food has been a geopolitical weapon or a way of waging war throughout history, from salting the soils in the Punic Wars between Rome and Carthage[23] to the Russian Federation seizing and destroying agricultural machinery, fertiliser, seeds and fuel stocks in Ukraine.[24] In peacetime too, food has been used as a geopolitical tool, as in Truman's Point Four programme, and the US State Department's Green Revolution strategies and the wheat crises of the early 1970s. These are examples of food securitisation: from the territorial notion of food as a zero-sum competition between states to ideas of universal human security based on positive-sum international cooperation. Throughout the neo-Malthusian debates and political strategies covered in this book, we see examples of the tensions and co-existence of two articulations of food security: one geopolitical and one individual-centred. As peace researcher Jiayi Zhou has shown, the struggle between these two enunciations of food security lingers throughout the post-war period until today.[25]

While the civilisational warnings still linger today, some environmental neo-Malthusians in the 1970s started to turn to the collective imperative to respond to the individual needs, emphasising the ongoing individual catastrophes for the many millions of hungry people. We should not need a total planetary catastrophe or the collapse of Western civilisation to take action: it ought to be a moral obligation to respond to the suffering of our fellow humans. Over the course of many years Borgström warned, time and time again, that the clock stood at 'five minutes to twelve'. And time went by. Consequently, he ends *Focal Points* (1971) by concluding that the time was now at 'five minutes past twelve'. The bell had already tolled. It was cynical, argued Borgström, to fix the catastrophe in the future. It was already here for the two-thirds of humanity that was malnourished. And this leads us to one of the more important contributions of some of the population–resource concerned environmentalists – the call for nutritional equity.

Nutritional Equity

In their concern about resource shortages in the poorer regions, environmentalists focused on externalities: the shifting of costs in modern world agriculture. To the neo-classical externalities were added the shifting of social and ecological costs to other classes, to foreigners and to future generations. The analysis of social and ecological externalities has since been developed as one of the cornerstones of environmental justice. Thus, in this area, they made a lasting contribution to green ideology. However, in the analysis of externalities, the environmentalists moved away from the neo-Malthusian dilemma, to point towards problems inherent in the economic order. It was not population growth that was at fault, but the present mode of capitalism as well as communism. In other words, the main importance of conservation-style neo-Malthusianism was not Malthusianism, but its analysis of unsustainable depletion and inequalities in resource distribution.

The Peruvian fishery was at the time one of the most striking examples of unjust nutritional distribution. Despite a critical shortage of protein according to the FAO, the lion's share of the gigantic catches of fish protein became feedstuff for animals in the USA and Europe. To elucidate the resources consumption the rich world demanded, Borgström coined the concept of *ghost acreage*. This was the non-visible amount of land abroad that was needed for a country to feed itself besides its own visible acreage, the actual farmland in the country. Many population–resource debaters criticised the putative high productivity of agriculture in countries such as the Netherlands and Denmark. They were to a large extent 'parasites' on the rest of the world, especially on the South. Their high productivity was dependent on import of resources from other parts of the world, such as energy, feedstuff and fertilisers.

The concept of ghost acreage anticipated today's frequently used concept of *ecological footprint*. Today's ecological economists have criticised neo-classical economics for not taking into account ecological costs and energy and material flows. In this respect, at least some neo-Malthusian environmentalists questioned the socio-economic basis for the rich world's consumption, by pointing to the dependency on resources and labour in the poorer parts of the world. The idea of the ecological footprint has been criticised as a call for autarky, as well as for being too simplistic. Yet, it is not necessarily a call for policies of self-sufficiency or objective measurement of environmental impacts, but rather could function as a pedagogical, heuristic concept to point at inequalities of resource distribution. In the early post-war world, food self-sufficiency was an important national security issue. Later, the ability to grow one's own food was no longer as important; the crucial factor was rather the ability to purchase food in a world market. Radical environmentalists emphatically argued that more of the same was no longer good enough. Technological innovation could only ease the situation somewhat. Borgström, for one, called for 'a revolutionary programme' of nutritional equity. But to fully solve the crisis, radical changes in society were necessary. For a long time, the profound redistributional calls made by some environmentalist neo-Malthusians deviated from the mainstream sustainable development discourse in international environmental governance.

The traditional sustainable development hypothesis rests on three main suppositions. First, species and ecosystems can be resources for development. Second, when striving to raise standards of living, industrialisation will take a heavy toll on the environment. Once countries reach a certain standard, they can afford to take environmental considerations into account. Third, growth generates technological innovations, which can be more resource-efficient and less polluting. In the early post-war decades, such ideas were hotly debated in environmental governance.[26] For population–resource conservationists it was as distortion of the facts; the hypothesis of sustainable development that economic growth and environmental protection could be combined in the long run was still to be proven on a global scale. Even though increased consumer pressure and political concerns have pushed industry in some parts of the world into less polluting and less wasteful production by the turn of the millennium, the magnitude of consumption continued to take a heavy toll on the environment. According to the *World Resources Report 2000–2001*, waste volume, soil degradation, carbon dioxide emissions, and deforestation were increasing[27] – and this is to name but a few pressing environmental problems. At the same time, economic and social development for the poor was struggling. Global per capita incomes had doubled since 1960. In spite of this, the gap between the richest fifth and the poorest fifth had become three times wider in 40 years. The richest fifth accounted for nearly 86 per cent of total private consumption, while at the new millennium half of the world's population lived on less than two US dollars a day.[28]

Since then, poverty has been on the decline, though the gap between the richest and the poorest continues to grow. In 2015, the World Bank estimated that 736 million people were living in extreme poverty, which was a drop of more than 60 per cent compared to the 1,895 million people in in 1990. So, while the world population increased by almost 30 per cent, the number of people living in extreme poverty fell from 36 per cent to 10 per cent. Since then, progress has slackened, from an average of 1.1 per cent to 0.6 per cent annually. This is mainly due to extreme poverty that is increasingly concentrated in sub-Saharan regions where per capita income is growing slowly.[29] The *World Inequality Report* 2022 estimates that the richest 10 per cent of the global population earn 52 per cent of total income and own 76 per cent of all wealth, while the poorest half of the global population accounts for 8.5 per cent of the income and only two per cent of the wealth.[30] The partial success in reducing extreme poverty is very uneven.

The average wealth of the poorest half has grown by 3.7 per cent per annum since 1995, the middle 40 per cent has grown at a rate of 3.8 per cent, while richest tenth has grown at 3 per cent. However, the very richest in the world continued to increase their wealth at an even higher pace, of four per cent for the top thousandth. Over the past 30 years, women's share of income has only slightly increased.[31] Geographically, the number of poor people in East Asia, the Pacific and in South Asia has decreased, while the amount of people living in extreme poverty in sub-Saharan Africa has seen the opposite trend, with extreme poverty increasingly being concentrated in fragile states and areas plagued by conflicts.[32]

While more than 600 million people were able to leave poverty between 2006 and 2016, mainly because of the economic transition in China and India, the hungry of this world were reduced by only 120 million over the same decade. The number of undernourished people now exceeds the proportion living in extreme poverty, which is a reminder that eradicating hunger is not only about purchasing power, but also about conflicts, droughts, flooding, failing transport logistics and geopolitical strategies.

After hunger declining for decades, progress halted after 2014. In 2021, between 702 and 828 million people faced hunger, corresponding to between 8.9 and 10.5 per cent of the world population. This is an increase of roughly 180 million since the launch in 2015 of the 2030 Agenda on Sustainable Development, with its goal of halving the number of hungry by 2030. While more than 80 per cent of this increase happened since the COVID-19 pandemic struck the world, the number of hungry had been on the rise even before 2019. The COVID-19 pandemic left one in three people moderately or severely food insecure in 2021. Only two out of seven nutritional targets in the 2030 Agenda are showing improvement: exclusive breastfeeding and the prevention of stunting among children under five years of age.

However, since the UN Conference on Sustainable Development in 2012 (Rio +20), calls for societal transformations involving deep technological, economic, political, social, cultural and environmental changes have mounted from international organisations and in national decision-making arenas around the world. The need for profound societal transformations in response to climate change and unsustainable trajectories is underscored in the 2030 Agenda and the assessments of the IPCC and IPBES, among many others. Such declarations would have encouraged the hearts of many environmental neo-Malthusians, although they would have commented on the lack of population control in the equation. There is no consensus in the scientific literature yet of what such transformations entail and how they can be achieved. The calls span from reform of the agricultural and energy sectors to restructuring the world economy.[33] The Sharm El-Sheikh Climate Implementation Summit Declaration concluded from the COP27 food security roundtable that the 'transformation of the food systems is a cornerstone in combating climate change including regenerative agricultural practices, reduced trade restrictions and changes in consumption and diet patterns, as well as looking into alternatives for proteins'.[34]

Interdependence among the countries and regions of the world was seen as crucial to solving the global resource crisis among most population–resource environmentalists, which emphasised metaphors such as the 'world household', 'spaceship Earth' and the 'global village'. In this respect, their message is highly relevant, as well as a morally compelling reason for an equitable distribution of the world's resources. Throughout the post-war period it has been commonly argued that a universalist resource planning is in the direct self-interest of the rich nations. Ever since the beginning of the Cold War, scarcity of foreign natural resources and a lack of development have been linked to domestic security and foreign policy making. Since the end of the Cold War, there has been a growing movement to redefine national security to include environmental, natural resource related, and population issues. Following the terrorist attacks on 11 September 2011, British Chancellor of the Exchequer Gordon Brown and economist Jeffrey Sachs, among others, have called for a 'new Marshall Plan' to fight hopelessness and despair in the poorest countries of the world. In the run-up to the UN World Summit on Sustainable Development in Johannesburg in 2002, a new 'global deal' or 'global partnership' was envisioned. So-called developing countries would initiate institutional reforms and increase spending on the needs of the poor, while the rich countries would open up domestic market access, increase aid, stimulate foreign investments and grant debt relief. The call of several neo-Malthusians and other environmentalists for a global development programme[35] continues to echo in updated and more comprehensive plans for nutritional equity. Calls for global plans for pro-equity nutritional distribution go to the heart of achieving Sustainable Development Goal 2: halving hunger in the world.[36]

Homer-Dixon differentiates between supply driven, demand driven and structural scarcities, which he explains using the pie metaphor. Demand-induced scarcity is when the pie is shrinking in quantity or quality, so that there is not enough for everybody around the table. Supply is scarce when demand increases as more people gather around the table (or when they each need a larger piece of the pie to be fulfilled). Structural scarcity arises when some grab a larger share of the pie, leaving smaller, insufficient, slices of the pie to share. Food supply scarcities are thus when the land fails to deliver sufficient quantity or quality of food. Demand-induced scarcities are the result of increased consumption, either because of increased per capita demand or more people. Structural aspects account for the uneven distribution of and access to food resources. Homer-Dixon notes that 'neo-Malthusians and economic optimists accent supply-induced and demand-induced scarcities, while generally overlooking the political economy of resource distribution'.[37] As this study demonstrates, this was not true for many environmental neo-Malthusians.

International trade has to some extent relieved regions where resources are constrained, whether through lack of supply or unattainable demand. Trade has become an essential cornerstone in the international food system and is indispensable for countries with agricultural constraints, such as countries in North Africa and the Middle East. Between 1986 and 2009, trading of food calories on the international market more than doubled. In 2014, almost one quarter of food was traded internationally.[38] With changes in diets for a growing world population and climate change impacting harvests over the world, the role of trade in food security is only expected to increase.[39] With the growing importance of trade, structural scarcity and the political economy distribution will be even more critical for nutritional equity across and within countries.

The challenge of supplying a growing world population made it necessary to safeguard everybody's needs. The Club of Rome's report saw a correlation between population growth and inequity: 'As the number of people over whom a fixed resource must be distributed increases, the equality of distribution decreases.' Thus, population growth had to be curbed in the name of equality. 'Lifeboat' Malthusians had quite the opposite take on equity. The crisis was constructed as if it were already too late to save all humanity – a select few had better take care of their own survival.

The neo-Malthusians relied heavily on scientific findings and figures from official organisations, which in many cases proved them wrong as science moved on. For example, according to Grigg, many nutrition scientists as well as the FAO overestimated the need for protein and thus exaggerated the protein shortage in the world, whereas today the FAO's official policy is that a diet that supplies enough calories usually has sufficient protein content.[40] So, when Borgström was wrong it was not so much bad science that made him wrong, as his pessimistic view on what nature could endure and what human ingenuity could accomplish when it comes to technological solutions. His pessimism on human ingenuity concerning nutritional and economic equity, on the other hand, has thus far proven him right. While the transformation of the global food systems over the last 50 years – from rural toward industrialised – has provided more affordable diets for many, it has subsequently resulted in many negative outcomes for nutritional quality of diets, environment, inclusion and equity.[41]

The Earth's Carrying Capacity

The Malthiusian predictions about the earth's carrying capacity have so far been wrong. No agricultural miracles were going to produce enough food for a population of six or seven billion, they warned. Today there could be enough food globally. No worldwide famine has yet descended upon humanity.

In 1953, Borgström expected the human population to be almost 3.7 billion people at the dawn of the new millennium. In 1969, he pointed out that – with present population growth – there would be around six billion people in 1999.[42] It seemed unrealistic to Borgström that it would be possible to sustain such a population. According to the UN's Population Division there were 6,056,715 human inhabitants in the world at the dawn of the new millennium. The 'Day of Six Billion' was observed by the UN on 12 October 1999. Since then, another two billion have been added.

Some may argue that this proves Borgström wrong. The post-war population–resource crisis was solved. The world reached six billion without a complete catastrophe or permanent worldwide famine. Global food production had risen remarkably over the past 30 years, according to *World Resources Report 1998–99*. Not only had three billion more people been supported, but also food supply, counted in calories per capita, rose from 2000 a day in 1962 to 2500 in 1995.[43] Since 1961, the global average of food available for each person has increased more than 30 per cent, in part due to an 800 per cent increase in the use of nitrogen fertilisers and doubling of water resources used for irrigation.[44] With rising incomes in the world, the consumption of meat and other animal products has surged, increasing the pressure on croplands and rangelands.[45] Food trade increasingly became an essential part of the international food system. Countries' dependency on trade for the food-sufficiency increased substantially since the 1990s.[46]

If he had lived to confront these figures, Borgström would probably have questioned – faced with the famines and destitution of the 1990s – whether the world truly could be said to support even its present population. Some 800 million people, 200 million of them children, suffered from chronic malnutrition.[47] And while environmentalists have been proclaiming his message of the need for a fairer world order, the gap between the rich and the poor countries had constantly been growing wider, despite an economic boom in several developing countries. The dilemma pointed out by the equity-emphasising neo-Malthusians is still urgently waiting for its solution.

In 1960, at the height of the 'population explosion' debate, world population amounted to three billion, and the global growth rate was 2 per cent (2.4 in less developed countries). The annual additions were about 58 million. Over the following 30 years, the momentum of population growth had slowed. At the turn of the millennium, the world population had just passed 6 billion, growing at an annual rate of 1.23 per cent (1.48 in less developed countries), but still the absolute numbers, 77 million people per year, were higher than 30 years before. Even though the global growth rate had dropped below one per cent in 2022, that year the world still added 78 million people.[48]

The drastic drop in growth rates and demographic turnaround, means that the dependency rate will increase. That is, fewer people of productive age will support an ageing population. As fewer people will work to extract resources as they become increasingly scarce, some researchers see a new Malthusian dilemma appearing. The ageing population cannot be sufficiently sustained, as they are too many in relation to the ability to provide goods and services in a resource-constrained world, with proportionally an ever-shrinking work force to extract the resources.[49]

Whatever the size of the future world population, 90 per cent of people will be in today's developing countries. Even though the world has experienced

Chapter 9

a tremendous increase in food production since the 1960s, the yields of the major crops have reached a 'yield stagnation' and are rising more slowly now. The distribution of food continues to be the greatest problem. Moreover, post-harvest losses, soil degradation from erosion and poor irrigation jeopardise food production in many regions.[50] As the human population continues to grow, the impossible question of how many people the earth can support remains unsolved.[51]

The Nature of the Crises

Is the title of this book right at all? Were there actually any population–food crises? Were the crises really induced by population growth? Would it not be more correct to designate them as simply food crises? As this book has tried to show, and as many environmentalists have argued from time to time, the perceived resource dilemmas of the world were not merely a matter of population growth. The cause of concern had several factors, such as capitalist as well as socialist economic modes of production, waste, reckless industrialisation, greed, and the like. The title of this book was chosen because it focuses on perceptions of crises which were not necessarily solely caused by population growth, but were interlinked with it.

Malthusianism left a deep imprint on post-war environmentalism. That is not to say that many environmentalists did not object to the Malthusian message. The population-versus-pollution debate visualised a split in the views of the root causes of environmental degradation.

Over the years, Malthusian scarcity has developed within environmentalism into a fivefold complex: population increase, consumption increase, environmental effects, geopolitical strategies and unequal distribution of resources. The population–resource crisis became not only a matter of food security. Besides the constraints on feeding a growing world population, environmentalists pointed towards increased pollution, resource depletion, species extinction, shrinking wilderness, violent conflicts and a more inhuman society. Yet the last-named threat can rebound on those environmentalists who advocated severe population control or totalitarian societies, and certainly on the few outspoken voices that pleaded for lifeboat ethics.

At the 1996 World Food Summit in Rome, many delegates dismissed rigid Malthusians who considered the answer to world food problems to be exclusively a combination of rigorous population control and massive efforts to produce more food in areas of high potential, disregarding poverty reduction as a strategy for food security.[52] This description of a two-track Malthusianism might apply to some neo-Malthusians, but certainly not to all. Many environmentalists combined a call for population control and environmental protection with closing the social and economic gaps between the have nations and the have-not nations.

For environmentalists the population-resource dilemma was not only a matter of food security. In relation to environmental issues it was also perceived as a threat to other natural resources and not least to wildlife. Two new factors became increasingly important with environmental neo-Malthusianism: over-consumption and pollution. For these environmentalists it was a fallacy only to count heads and not to focus on the demand on resources per individual.

Still the Malthusian quandary seems to linger on. We are still presented with more or less simplistic solutions to the population–resource challenge. Since the mid-1990s, GM crops, as the backbone of the calls for a new Green Revolution, have often been promoted as such a single solution to food shortage. Yet today we are faced with what Amartya Sen calls a 'boom famine'; there is starvation even though there is no real food shortage.[53] As long as purchasing power is not sufficiently dealt with, the tech-fix neo-Malthusians are addressing the wrong crisis. Biological resources will not, on their own, suffice to meet expected population increase and demand.

According to present food security discourse, traditional technology improvements will not suffice. The Green Revolution's grand old man, Norman Borlaug, laughed at the suggestions that organic food could feed the world.[54] Something else has to be done, in this view. Biological process has to be altered. The GM rhetoric is congruent with the Malthusian view that conventional technology will not suffice to keep up with population growth in the long run. Malthus wanted to tamper with human biological reproduction, GM proponents with biological reproduction of plants. One form of biological reproduction has to be halted, or another enhanced. Nature's inability to provide enough nutrients to keep up with human breeding is to blame. When proponents of transgenic crop modification label environmentalists as 'gloom-and-doom neo-Malthusians',[55] it is often a mirror reflection of their own rhetoric. The Malthusian dilemma is basically the same as it was 200 years ago, except for a crucial ethical implication: For Malthus the poor were to be blamed for the dilemma; for the vast majority of today's neo-Malthusians, be they environmentalists or GM crop supporters, the poor and hungry are to be aided.

In a way, the neo-Malthusianism of the 1960s and 1970s seemed better empirically grounded than that of today. Then, a global food shortage was a manifest dilemma. In 1963, the FAO estimated that 60 per cent of the population in the so-called underdeveloped world were suffering from malnutrition. It was certainly not far-fetched or unrealistic to conclude that the food available simply did not suffice. Even the founding father of the Green Revolution, Borlaug, expected that contemporary technology would not solve the crisis at the beginning of the 1970s. To him it just bought some time. Today, food shortages are rather local or regional dilemmas. It is an accepted fact that at present there is enough food for the present population, even for the over 800 million living in food insecurity. It is the future supply that is at stake. The expected moment when food shortage actually becomes primarily a production problem in absolute terms is all in the years to come.

Presented with a new panacea for food security, it is wise to heed Commoner's warning about all kinds of simplistic solutions to population–resource dilemmas:

> Confronted by a situation as complex as the environment and its vast array of living inhabitants, we are likely ... to attempt to reduce it in our minds to a set of separate, simple events in hope that the sum will somehow picture the whole. The existence of the environmental crisis warns us that this is an illusory hope.[56]

Thirty years later, organisations like the FAO and CGIAR emphasised this broader focus on the population–resource dilemma, for example in *Dialogue on Water, Food and Environment*. In a joint project of ten major international organisations, dealing with water resources, environmental conservation and health, wants to broaden the focus beyond a narrow one-issue approach to look at food and environmental security combined. The problem was not our capacity to produce enough food for the expected needs to come – the crux of the problem is to do it without spoiling the environment.[57]

The turn of the millennium saw a finger-pointing debate between environmental neo-Malthusians and cornucopian technological optimists on the nature of the food-population crisis. Today, the conundrum remains how we can sustain 10 billion people with healthy diets while safeguarding the environment and the climate. This is a challenge far more complex than maximising agricultural productivity or reducing the rate of new-born children on Earth. It is now apparent that there is no silver bullet to achieve global food security and nutritional equity. There is a general realisation that responses to fight food insecurity need to be mindful of the local context while addressing the food system – from farm to fork – where production, financing, processing, trade, transport, markets, and consumption are interacting components in complex international web.[58] The dividing line today is not between different silver bullet solutions, but rather goes between those who assume that the need to 'optimize across a far more complex landscape of production, environmental, and social justice outcomes'[59] can be achieved through a reformation of the food system and those who argue that it requires deeper transformations. The dominant approach centres around reforming the system by enhancing an agricultural productivity that is resilient to climate change, continue the international integration of food markets, incentivising private investments, capitalising on corporate initiatives.

In essence, it builds on the successes of industrial agriculture over the past 50 years, while being mindful of its local conditions and negative environmental and socio-economic effects.[60]

Critics point to the recurring failure to make substantial progress on eradicating hunger, despite technological innovations and a halting, but relative, progress on reducing poverty globally. To truly provide the conditions for eradicating hunger would require deep transformation that involves profound changes, such as a rethinking of the socio-technical innovation efforts, restructuring of the political economy as well as how we value and consume food. The societal transformations imperative at the heart of the 2030 Agenda's headline 'transforming our world' has given voice to calls for more radical changes in the political economy, such as FAO's High Level Panel of Experts on Food Security and Nutrition of the Committee on World Food Security: 'Policies that promote a radical transformation of food systems need to be empowering, equitable, regenerative, productive, prosperous and must boldly reshape the underlying principles from production to consumption.' Such calls to address unequal exchange within and across countries through economic redistribution are aligned with environmental neo-Malthusians calls for nutritional equity.

Societal transformations require practical, political, and personal change.[61] New innovative practices and technologies, such as regenerative farming, new crop varieties, digital farming[62] and Artificial Intelligence,[63] can potentially address the intertwined crises of food insecurity, climate change and biodiversity loss. Political decisions can ensure market access, economic redistribution and poverty elevation. Socio-cultural aspects influence our dietary preferences, how we value food nature, and how we perceive our fellow humans around the world.

So we may conclude that many of the population-concerned environmentalists have been wrong in many details and assumptions. Neo-Malthusianism in its simplest form, with population growth as the single root cause of the resource shortage, had not made a convincing case by the beginning of the twenty-first century, a time when it would be too late to avoid the worldwide catastrophe according to most post-war neo-Malthusian predictions. Compulsory population control never became inevitable. However, the notorious technology-optimists have not got it all right either. The complex problematique of environmental population–resource concern, with increasing consumption, environmental degradation, unequal resource distribution, short term profits, waste, pollution in combination with population growth – has not yet found an ecologically sustainable solution.

Malthusian concern has so far been misplaced. Even the most rapid population growth in human history has not outstripped food supply, although it has come at a price that conservationists warned about: social costs, environmental degradation, and loss of biodiversity. But the total global catastrophe has not yet descended upon us. The lifeboat-ethic neo-Malthusians seem to have sunk mercifully into oblivion.

The purpose of population-concerned conservationists does not seem to have been, primarily, to make exact predictions about the future. Rather, through rhetorical catastrophe empiricism, they have striven to achieve a change in the contemporary population policy and ultimately the international food systems and international economic order. To some extent these conservationist succeed, as equitable access to notorious food is enshrined in the 2030 Agenda and the calls for reforming food systems increasingly resonates in international organisations. Yet, in spite of an increased recognition in words, little happens in practice. Currently, food inequality is on the rise. The call of equity-emphasising neo-Malthusians for a fairer distribution of resources and nutrition remains unfulfilled after half a century. It is surely ironic that, even when showing optimism, they seem to have been mistaken. Many neo-Malthusian environmentalists put their hopes in a new morality of nutritional equity within the world household. In that respect they have regrettably been wrong – so far.

Notes

Chapter 1. Crises of Population and Resources

1. Throughout this book, the term population–resource has been shown thus (with a dash) rather than population-resource (hyphenated) to indicate that the crisis or concern is not a matter of population as a resource, but a complex problem of population growth and its effects on resources.

2. David Grigg, *The World Food Problem*, 2nd edn (Oxford, Blackwell, 1999 (1993)), pp. 5–55.

3. Thomas Robert Malthus, *The Works of Thomas Robert Malthus. Vol. 1, An Essay on the Principle of Population* (London, Pickering and Chatto, 1986 (1798)), p. 4.

4. Malthus, *Essay on the Principle of Population*, ch. 1.

5. Cf. Göran B. Nilsson, 'Om det fortfarande behovet av källkritik', *Historisk Tidskrift*, 2 (1973), pp. 173–211; Rolf Torstendahl, *Introduktion till historieforskningen: Historia som vetenskap* (Stockholm, Natur och Kultur, 1978 (1971)), pp. 89–103; Arne Jarrick and Johan Söderberg, *Praktisk historieteori* (University of Stockholm, 1993), pp. 131–4.

6. Bernt Skovdahl, 'Idéhistoria och källkritik', in Lennart Olausson (ed.), *Idéhistoriens egenart: Teori- och metodfrågor inom idéhistorien* (Stockholm, Symposion, 1994), pp. 35–52.

7. The first time a Swedish book title is mentioned, an English translation of the Swedish title is given in parentheses. To facilitate the reading for non-Swedish readers, the English translation will be used when referring to the book subsequently.

Chapter 2. A New World Order

1. D. Gale Johnson, *World Food Problems and Prospects*, Washington, DC, American Enterprise Institute for Public Policy Research, 1975, p. 12; David Norman Balaam, 'The political economy of international food production and distribution' (Dissertation, University of California, Santa Barbara, 1978), p. 24.

2.   John R. McNeill, *Something New Under the Sun: An Environmental History of the Twentieth-century World* (New York, W.W. Norton & Company, 2000), p. 44.

3.   McNeill, *Something New Under the Sun*, pp. 48–9; William B. Meyer, *Human Impact on the Earth* (New York, Cambridge University Press, 1996), p. 77.

4.   Dudley Dillard, *Economic Development of the North Atlantic Community: Historical Introduction to Modern Economics* (Swedish edn, Malmö, Liber, 1985), pp. 556–8; Stephen E. Ambrose, *Rise to Globalism: American Foreign Policy since 1938*, 4th edn (New York, Penguin, 1985), pp. XIV–XVI; Lynn Boyd Hinds and Theodore Otto Windt, *The Cold War as Rhetoric: The Beginnings, 1945–1950*, (New York, Praeger, 1991), p. 2.

5.   George Woodbridge, *UNRRA: The History of the United Nations Relief and Rehabilitation Administration* (New York, Columbia University Press, 1950), Vol. 1, pp. 138–9, 231–2, 371–2, 416–17.

6.   United Nations, ECE, *Economic Survey of Europe* (1947), p. 11; United Nations, ECAFE, *Economic Survey of Asia and the Far East* (1948), p. 49.

7.   United Nations Interim Commission on Food and Agriculture, 'Facts about FAO' 11 September 1945, General File, Harry S. Truman Library (HSTL).

8.   McNeill, *Something New Under the Sun*, pp. 23, 25.

9.   FAO, *World Food Survey* (Washington, DC, 1946).

10. Melvyn P. Leffler, *A Preponderance of Power: National Security, the Truman Administration and the Cold War* (Stanford, CA, Stanford University Press, 1992), p. 6.

11. Leffler, *Preponderance of Power*, p. 7; Bengt Owe Birgersson, Stig Hadenius, Björn Molin, Hans Wieslander, *Sverige efter 1900: en modern politisk historia* (Stockholm, Bonniers, 1984), p. 344.

12. Leffler, *Preponderance of Power*, p. 7.

13. *Ibid.*, pp. 7–8.

14. Leffler, *Preponderance of Power, passim*; Randall B. Woods and Howard Jones, *Dawning of the Cold War: The United States' Quest for Order* (Athens, GA, 1991), pp. 133–52, pp. 97; David McCoullough, *Truman*, (New York, Simon and Schuster, 1992), p. 731.

15. John H. Perkins, 'The Rockefeller Foundation and the Green Revolution, 1941–1956', *Agriculture and Human Values*, 7 (1990), pp. 7–9; Woods and Jones, *Dawning of the Cold War*, p. 97; McCoullough, *Truman*, p. 731; Clifton Wharton, interview by author, New York, 31 October 1995.

16. John H. Perkins, *Geopolitics and the Green Revolution: Wheat, Genes and the Cold War* (Oxford, Oxford University Press, 1997), ch. 6.

17. Giovanni Arrighi, *The Long Twentieth Century: Money, Power and the Origins of Our Times* (London, Verso, 1994), pp. 27, 29; Thomas J. McCormick, *America's Half-Century: United States Foreign Policy in the Cold War and After* (Baltimore, Johns Hopkins University Press, 1995).

18.   Joshua S. Goldstein and David P. Rapkin, 'After insularity: hegemony and the future world order', *Futures*, 23 (1991), pp. 935–59; Arrighi, *Long Twentieth Century*, ch. 4.

19.   Angus Maddison, *Phases of Capitalist Development* (Oxford, Oxford University Press, 1982), pp. 39–41.

20.   Arrighi, *Long Twentieth Century*, ch. 1.

21.   *Ibid.*, p. 298.

22.   David Harvey, *The Condition of Postmodernity* (Cambridge, MA, Blackwell, 1990), pp. 132–3.

23.   Alfred D. Chandler, *The Visible Hand: The Managerial Revolution in American Business* (Cambridge, MA, Belknap, 1977), pp. 79–376.

24.   Harvey, *Condition of Postmodernity*, pp. 125–7; Maddison, *Phases of Capitalist Development*, p. 26; Robert Boyer, *The Regulation School: A Critical Introduction* (New York, Columbia University Press, 1989), pp. 73–5, 86–7.

25.   Harvey, *Condition of Postmodernity*, pp. 125–7; Maddison, *Phases of Capitalist Development*, p. 26; Boyer, *Regulation School*, pp. 73–5.

26.   Arrighi, *Long Twentieth Century*, p. 2; Boyer, *Regulation School*, pp. 85–7.

27.   Fernand Braudel, *Civilization and Capitalism: 15th–18th Century*, Vol. 2, *The Wheels of Commerce* (London, Collins, 1982 (1979)), pp. 223–30, 554; Cf. Arrighi, *Long Twentieth Century*, p. 10.

28.   McCormick, *America's Half-Century*, p. 99.

29.   Clayton R. Koppes, 'Environmental policy and American liberalism: the Department of the Interior, 1933–1953', in Kendall E. Bailes (ed.), *Environmental History* (Lanham, MD, University Press of America, 1985), p. 440; Roderick Nash, *Wilderness and the American Mind*, 3rd edn (New Haven, Yale University Press, 1982), p. 204.

30.   Harvey, *Condition of Postmodernity*, p. 135; Richard B. Norgaard, *Development Betrayed: The End of Progress and a Coevolutionary Revisioning of the Future* (London, Routledge, 1994), p. 44.

31.   Harvey, *Condition of Postmodernity*, p. 136.

32.   Arrighi, *Long Twentieth Century*, pp. 295–6.

33.   The indices in Maddison's index of volume of world exports refer to special exports and exclude re-exports of merchandise and services (with a few exceptions).

34.   Maddison, *Phases of Capitalist Development*, p. 128; Arrighi, *Long Twentieth Century*, p. 128.

35.   Arrighi, *Long Twentieth Century*, p. 66.

36.   Truman to John G. Winant 4 September 1946, OF85.DD, UNSCURR, HSTL; *Proceedings of the United Nations Scientific Conference on the Conservation and Utilization of Resources. 17 August–6 September 1949, Lake Success, New York*. Vol. 1, p. vii.

37. Gifford Pinchot to Franklin D. Roosevelt, 17 January 1940, in Edgar B. Nixon, (ed.). *Franklin D. Roosevelt and Conservation 1911–1945*, Vol. 2 (Hyde Park, NY, Franklin D. Roosevelt Library, 1957), p. 971.

38. Carroll Pursell, 'Conservation, environmentalism, and the engineers: the progressive era and the recent past', in Kendall E. Bailes (ed.), *Environmental History* (Lanham, MD, University Press of America, 1985), pp. 176–91; Cf. Char Miller, *Gifford Pinchot and the Making of Modern Environmentalism* (Washington, DC, Island Press/Shearwater Books, 2001).

39. Donald Worster. *Nature's Economy: A History of Ecological Ideas*, 2nd edn, Cambridge, Cambridge University Press, 1994, p. 266.

40. Samuel P. Hays, 'From conservation to environment: environmental politics in the United States since World War II', in Bailes, *Environmental History*, p. 199.

41. Nash, *Wilderness and the American Mind*, pp. 67–73; Alfred Runte, *National Parks: The American Experience* (Lincoln, University of Nebraska Press, 1979), pp. 11–72; William Beinart and Peter A. Coates, *Environment and History: The Taming of Nature in the USA and South Africa* (London, Routledge, 1995), pp. 74–5; John Ise, *Our National Park Policy: A Critical History* (Baltimore, Johns Hopkins Press, 1962), p. 154; Björn-Ola Linnér, 'Naturen som minnesmärke', in Annika Alzén and Johan Hedrén (eds), *Kulturarvets natur* (Stockholm, Symposion, 1998), pp. 51–83.

42. Hays, 'From conservation to environment' pp. 142–3; Carolyn Merchant, *The Death of Nature* (San Francisco, Harper & Row, 1989), p. 100; Robert P. McIntosh, *The Background of Ecology: Concept and Theory* (Cambridge, Cambridge University Press, 1985), p. 294.

43. Beinart and Coates, *Environment and History*, pp. 76–8.

44. Donald Worster, *The Dust Bowl: The Southern Plains in the 1930s* (New York, Oxford University Press, 1982), pp. 212–13.

45. Nash, *Wilderness and the American Mind*, p. 204.

46. Pinchot to Roosevelt, 29 August 1944, 'Proposal for an International Conference on Conservation', in Nixon, *Roosevelt and Conservation*, pp. 1125, 1126.

47. Roosevelt to Pinchot, 24 October 1944; Roosevelt to Cordell Hull, 24 October 1944, in Nixon, *Roosevelt and Conservation*, pp. 1132, 1133.

48. Edward R. Stettinius to Roosevelt, 10 November 1944, in Nixon, *Roosevelt and Conservation*, pp. 1137, 1138. The conflict between the separate organisations within the UN and its conferences linger on in the UN system. The same arguments were posed against the plans for the 1972 UN Conference on the Human Environment in Stockholm, Sweden, 1972.

49. Roosevelt to Stettinius, 22 November 1944, in Nixon, *Roosevelt and Conservation*, p. 1142. The President added, 'When I say short space of time, I mean a hundred years but that is short in these times.'

50. Stettinius to Roosevelt, 16 December 1944, in Nixon, *Roosevelt and Conservation*, p. 1145.

51. Pinchot to Roosevelt, 22 January 1945, in Nixon, *Roosevelt and Conservation*, p. 1154; Pinchot to William D. Hassett, 17 April 1945, Papers of Harry S. Truman, President's Secretary's Files, HSTL.

52. Hinds and Windt, *The Cold War as Rhetoric*, p. 8.

53. Arrighi, *Long Twentieth Century*, p. 97.

54. Daniel Yergin, *Shattered Peace: The Origins of the Cold War and the Nation Security State* (Boston, Houghton Mifflin, 1977), p. 59.

55. Pinchot to Roosevelt, 10 April 1945, in Nixon, *Roosevelt and Conservation*, p. 1170.

56. William L. Clayton to Stettenius, 17 April 1945, 'Proposed Conservation Conference', in Nixon, *Roosevelt and Conservation*, pp. 1171, 1172.

57. Leffler, *Preponderance of Power*, pp. 30–49; Hinds and Windt, *The Cold War as Rhetoric*, p. 83.

58. Pinchot to William D. Hassett, 17 April 1945, Hassett: 'Memorandum for Mr. Connelly', 28 April 1945, Papers of Harry S. Truman, President's Secretary's Files, HSTL; Nixon, *Roosevelt and Conservation*, pp. 647–8.

59. Ickes to Truman, 31 May 1945, Papers of Harry S. Truman, President's Secretary's Files, HSTL.

60. Matthew J. Connelly to Pinchot, 15 May 1945; OF85.DD, UNSCURR.

61. Pinchot to Truman, 12 May 1945, OF85.DD, UNSCURR, HSTL; Truman to Ickes 6 June 1945; Samuel I. Rosenman, 'Memorandum for the President' 4 June 1945, Papers of Harry S. Truman, President's Secretary's Files, HSTL.

62. Confidential report from Clayton to Robert P Patterson, Secretary of War, James Forrestal, Secretary of the Navy, Harold L. Ickes, Secretary of the Interior, 2 November 1945, Office files of the assistant Secretary of State, HSTL.

63. Conference for the Establishment of the International Union for the Protection of Nature 30 September–7 October 1948, 'General Information', UNA; Alfred Barthelmess, *Walt – Umwelt des Menschen: Dokumente zu einer Problemgeschichte von Naturschutz, Landschaftspflege und Humanökologie* (Freiburg, Alber, 1972), pp. 121–8; Hugo Conwentz, *Über nationalen und internationalen Naturschutz: Rede bei der Internationalen Naturschutzkonferenz in Bern am 18. November 1913* (Lepzig, Verlag von Quelle & Meyer, 1914); Nash, *Wilderness and the American Mind*, p. 358; Björn-Ola Linnér and Ulrik Lohm, 'Hugo Conwentz', *Linköpings Biblioteks Hand-lingar* (Linköping, 1995), pp. 123–7; Kirkpatrick Dorsey, *Dawn of Conservation Diplomacy: U.S.–Canadian Wildlife Protection Treaties in the Progressive Era* (Seattle, University of Washington Press, 1998).

64. Lynton Keith Caldwell, *International Environmental Policy: Emergence and Dimensions*, 3rd edn (Durham, Duke University Press, 1996), p. 34.

65. Nash, *Wilderness and the American Mind*, p. 359.

66. *Ibid.*, p. 360.

67. *Ibid*, p. 361.

Chapter 3. Conservation and Containment

1. Truman: Memorandum for Ickes, 21 November 1945, 'US Mission to the UN', HSTL; Pinchot to Matthew J. Connelly, 15 May 1945, OF85.DD, UNSCURR, HSTL.

2. Melvyn P. Leffler, *A Preponderance of Power: National Security, the Truman Administration and the Cold War* (Stanford, CA, Stanford University Press, 1992), pp. 73–81; Stephen E. Ambrose, *Rise to Globalism: American Foreign Policy since 1938*, 4th edn (New York, Penguin, 1985), pp. 74–8; Randall B. Woods and Howard Jones, *Dawning of the Cold War: The United States' Quest for Order* (Athens, GA, 1991), pp. 98–9.

3. Woods and Jones, *Dawning of the Cold War*, ch. 4; Leffler, *Preponderance of Power*, pp. 142–7.

4. Sallie Pisani, *The CIA and the Marshall Plan* (Lawrence, University Press of Kansas, 1991), p. 121.

5. Clayton to Truman, 3 September 1946; Henry Wallace to Truman, 4 September 1946, OF85.DD, UNSCURR, HSTL.

6. Interoffice Memorandum, 28 October 1946, Rag. 2, United Nations Archives (UNA), New York.

7. L. Eustace to Lie, 10 July 1947, Rag. 2, UNA.

8. Canadian Secretary of State to Lie, 17 February 1947, Rag. 2, UNA.

9. *Proceedings of the United Nations Scientific Conference on the Conservation and Utilization of Resources. 17 August–6 September 1949, Lake Success, New York*, Vol. 1 p. vi; ECOSOC resolution 28 March 1947, Document E/404, UNA.

10. Nils Dahlbeck, interview by author, Göteborg, Sweden, 26 April, 1994.

11. E.N. Van Klefferv, 15 March 1947, Rag. 2, UNA.

12. *Proceedings* Vol. 1, p. viii.

13. *Proceedings*, Vol. 1, p. viii.

14. Lie to participating UN member nations, 11 October 1948, ECA 9/06/AJVT, UNA.

15. John H. Perkins, 'The rhetoric of population and its consequences', Paper presented at the meeting of the American Society for Environmental History, Baltimore, 6–9 March 1997.

16. Franz Schurmann, *The Logic of World Power: An Inquiry into the Origins, Currents, and Contradictions of World Politics* (New York, Pantheon, 1974), p. 402; Giovanni Arrighi, *The Long Twentieth Century: Money, Power and the Origins of Our Times* (London, Verso, 1994), p. 276.

17. Schurmann, *Logic of World Power*, p. 67.

18. Arrighi, *Long Twentieth Century*, p. 66.

19. Schurmann, *Logic of World Power*, p. 68.

20. Modernity and modernisation are used in a wide sense in this book, referring to the modes of social life, production and organisation that merged in Europe from about approximately the sixteenth century.

21. Philip Lowe and Jane Goyder, *Environmental Groups in Politics* (London, Allen and Unwin, 1983), p. 35; Philip Lowe, 'Values and institutions in the history of British nature conservation', in A. Warren and F. Goldsmith (eds), *Conservation in Perspective*,(Chichester, Wiley, 1983), pp. 329–50.

22. Jeffrey C. Ellis, 'When green was pink: environmental dissent in Cold War America' (Dissertation, University of California, Davis, 1995), ch. 2.

23. William Vogt, *Road to Survival* (London, Victor Gollancz, 1949 (1948)), pp. 129–46, 264.

24. *Ibid.*, p. 279.

25. *Ibid.*, p. 114.

26. Christopher Lewis, 'Progress and apocalypse: science and the end of the modern world', (Dissertation, University of Minnesota, 1991), pp. 102, 105.

27. Lewis, 'Progress and apocalypse', p. 132.

28. Fairfeld Osborn, *Our Plundered Planet* (Boston, Little, Brown and Company 1948), *passim.*

29. Osborn, *Our Plundered Planet*, p. 108.

30. *Ibid.*

31. David Goldblatt, *Social Theory and the Environment* (Cambridge, Polity Press, 1996), pp. 28–9.

32. In 1956 IUPN changed its name to the International Union for the Conservation of Nature and Natural Resources (IUCN).

33. *Final Resolutions of the International Conference for the Protection of Nature, Brunnen, June 28th–July 3rd, 1947* (Basel, Swiss League for the Protection of Nature, 1947), pp. 15–17; Roderick Nash, *Wilderness and the American Mind*, 3rd edn (New Haven, Yale University Press, 1982), p. 361.

34. 'Conference for the Establishment of the International Union for the Protection of Nature 30 September–7 October 1948: General Information', UNA; Dahlbeck, interview by author; Nils Dahlbeck, letter to author 16 April 1995.

35. Russell. J. Dalton, *The Green Rainbow: Environmental Groups in Western Europe* (New Haven, Yale University Press, 1994), p. 34.

36. International Union for the Conservation of Nature and Natural Resources, *1973 IUCN Yearbook* (Morges, Switzerland, 1974), pp. 17–21.

37. *International Technical Conference on the Protection of Nature. Proceedings and Papers* (Paris, 1950), p. vii.

38. Dalton, *Green Rainbow*, p. 45; Johan Hedrén, *Miljöpolitikens natur* (Linköping, Linköping Studies in Art and Science, 1994, Dissertation), pp. 48–50; Thomas Hillmo and Ulrik Lohm, 'Nature's ombudsmen: the evolution of environmental representation in Sweden', *Environment and History*, 3:1 (1997), pp. 19–29; Björn-Ola Linnér and Ulrik Lohm 'Administering Nature Conservation in

Sweden during a Century: From Conwentz and Back', *Jahrbüch für europäische Verwaltungsgeschichte*, 11 (Baden-Baden, Nomos, 1999), pp. 307–34; Lars J. Lundgren, *Miljöpolitik på längden och tvären: Några synpunkter på svensk miljövård under 1900-talet* (Solna, Naturvårdsverket, 1989), pp. 39–50.

39. Roosevelt to Pinchot, 24 October 1944, in Edgar B. Nixon (ed.), *Franklin D. Roosevelt and Conservation 1911–1945*, Vol. 2 (Hyde Park, NY, Franklin D. Roosevelt Library, 1957), p. 1132.

40. Truman to Julius A. Krug, 27 August 1947, Krug Files, HSTL; Lie to George C. Marshall, 2 December 1947, UNA.

41. 'Memorandum Summary of Comments on the Provisional Agenda of the United Nations Scientific Conference on the Conservation and Utilization of Resources by Members of the Interdepartmental Technical Committee and the Advisory Committee on American Participation', 1948; 'Advisory Committee on the United Nations Scientific Conference on the Conservation and Utilization of Resources, Third session', 16 December 1947, UNA.

42. 'Where is Man? A mid-century appraisal', *Time Magazine*, 53:15 (11 April 1949), pp. 27–30.

43. *Ibid.*, p. 30.

44. 'Memorandum Summary'.

45. Michel Foucault, *Archeology of Knowledge* (New York, Pantheon, 1972), pp. 65–6.

46. Public Papers of the Presidents of the United States, *Harry S. Truman: Containing the Public Messages, Speeches, and Statements of the President, 1949* (Washington, United States Printing Office, 1964), pp. 114–16; *The Oxford English Dictionary*, 2nd edn (Oxford, Clarendon Press, 1989) has President Truman's 'Point Four' speech as its first recorded entry of 'underdeveloped' in this sense. See also Leffler, *Preponderance of Power*, pp. 266; David McCoullough, *Truman* (New York, Simon and Schuster, 1992), pp. 730, Harry S. Truman, *Memoirs of Harry S. Truman: The Years of Trail and Hope, 1946–52* (New York, Da Capo, 1956), p. 236.

47. Public Papers of the Presidents of the United States, *Harry S. Truman*, p. 115.

48. *Ibid.*

49. Public Papers of the Presidents of the United States, *Harry S. Truman*, pp. 112–14.

50. 'The imponderable resources', *New York Times*, 22 January 1949; McCoullough, *Truman*, p. 73.

51. John A. Hannah, letter to Harry S. Truman, 4 February 1949, Harry S. Truman, letter to John A. Hannah, 14 February 1949, Papers of Harry S. Truman, President's Secretary's Files, HSTL; Richard Niehoff, *John A. Hannah: Versatile Administrator and Distinguished Public Servant* (Lanham, MD, University Press of America, 1989), pp. 215–17; Clifton Wharton, interview by author, New York, 31 October 1995.

52. Truman to Dean Acheson, 6 April 1949, Acheson Files, HSTL.

53. Laurens van der Post, *Venture to the Interior* (London, Hogarth Press, 1952), p. xi.

54. McCoullough, *Truman*, p. 731.

55. Walter A. McDougall, *Promised Land, Crusader State: The American Encounter with the World Since 1776* (New York, Houghton Mifflin, 1997), pp 181.

56. Joseph Marion Jones, *The Fifteen Weeks* (New York, Harcourt Brace, 1955), pp. 262–3.

57. James P. Warburg, 'Four primary questions' and Chester Bowles, 'Why Point Four is needed', *New York Times Magazine*, 13 May 1951; Marvin F. Plake 'A practical program', *Far East Advertiser*, May 1951; John Kenneth Galbraith, 'Hurdles to be jumped', *Commentary*, Sept. 1950; Harlod R. Isaacs, 'Legacy of imperialism'; in Walter M. Daniels, *The Point Four Program*, (New York, Wilson, 1951), pp. 24–30, 34–8, 38–42, 47–53. Italics in original.

58. William Vogt, *People! Challenge to Survival* (London, Victor Gollancz, 1961 (1960)), p. 168; Lewis, 'Progress and apocalypse', pp. 108–9.

59. McDougall, *Promised Land*, ch. 8.

60. Trygve Lie, 'Introductory address', in *Proceedings*, Vol. I, p. 5.

61. *Proceedings*, Vol. 1 p. xxiii.

62. Andrei Gromyko to Trygve Lie, 15 June 1948, Rag. 2, UNA.

63. Interoffice Memorandum, 16 October 1946, UNA.

64. 'UNSCCUR information program', Interoffice Memorandum, 11 October 1949, UNA.

65. Lie, 'Introductory address'.

66. *Ibid.*

67. Julius A. Krug, *Proceedings*, Vol. 1, p.7.

68. Fairfeld Osborn, 'World resources situation', in *Proceedings*, Vol. I, p. 12.

69. R.D. Lewis, 'The influence of cropping systems on sustained production, soil management and conservation', in *Proceedings*, Vol. V, p.231; Charles E. Kellogg, 'Modern soil science', *American Scientist*, 36:4 (October 1948), p. 517.

70. Carmelia Bryce Pinchot, in *Proceedings*, Vol. I, pp. ix, 318.

71. Herbert Broadley, 'Critical shortage of food', in *Proceedings*, Vol. I, pp. 30–34; Colin Clark, 'World resources and the world population', in *Proceedings*, Vol. I, pp. 15–28.

72. D.N. Wadia, 'Metals in relation to living standards', in *Proceedings*, Vol. I, pp. 113–17.

73. Vijaya Lakshmi Pandit, in *Proceedings*, Vol. I, p. 424.

74. Detlev Bronk, in *Proceedings*, Vol. I, p. 3.

75. Michael Graham, in *Proceedings*, Vol. I, p. 411.

76. *Ibid.*

77. *Proceedings*, Vol. I, p. 13.

78. See Chapter 5, Table 4: Conveyed New Conservation Ideology Themes, 'World Household'.

79. James Thorn, in *Proceedings*, Vol. I, p. 425.

80. *Proceedings*, Vol. I, pp. ix, 27–53; *International Technical Conference on the Protection of Nature. Proceedings and Papers* (Paris, 1950), pp. 1–13; Dahlbeck, interview by author.

81. *International Technical Conference*, pp. ix, 129–69.

82. *Proceedings*, e.g. Osborn, 'World resources situation'; Emmanuel de Martonne, 'Interdependence of resources', Vol. I, p. 55; Starker A. Leopold, 'Ecological aspects of deer production on forest land', Vol. VII, p. 207.

83. *International Technical Conference*, p. ix.

84. *Ibid.*, pp. 192–294.

85. *Ibid.*, p. ix.

86. *Ibid.*, p. vii.

87. Fredric Jameson, *The Political Unconscious: Narrative as a Socially Symbolic Act* (Ithaca, NY, Cornell University Press, 1981), pp. 20, 79; Clifford Geertz, *Interpretation of Cultures: Selected Essays* (New York, Basic Books, 1973), Ch. 8.

88. Ulrich Beck, *What is Globalization?* (Malden, MT, Polity Press, 2000), ch. 2; Fredric Jameson, 'Preface' and 'Notes on globalization as a philosophical issue', in Fredric Jameson and Masao Miyoshi (eds), *The Cultures of Globalization*, (Durham, NC, Duke University Press, 1998), pp. xi–xvii, 54–77.

89. Michel Foucault, 'The discourse on language', appendix to *Archeology of Knowledge* (New York, Pantheon, 1972), p. 219.

90. Wolfgang Sachs, 'Global ecology and the shadow of "development"', in Wolfgang Sachs (ed.) *Global Ecology: A New Arena of Political Conflict* (London, Zed Books, 1993), p. 4.

91. Ernest Gellner, *Nations and Nationalism* (Oxford, Blackwell, 1983), p.39.

92. David Harvey, *The Condition of Postmodernity* (Cambridge, MA, Blackwell, 1990), pp. 139–40.

93. Leffler, *Preponderance of Power*, p. 9.

94. Leland M. Goodrich, *The United Nations in a Changing World* (New York, Colombia University Press, 1974), pp. 47–8.

95. Arrighi, *Long Twentieth Century*, p. 97.

96. Swedish Parliament, *1966 års revisionsberättelser*, 2 saml., 1967, pp. 10, 114.

97. William Beinart and Peter A. Coates, *Environment and History: The Taming of Nature in the USA and South Africa* (London, Routledge, 1995), pp. 81–4.

98. Paul Ricoeur, *Interpretation Theory: Discourse and the Surplus of Meaning* (Fort Worth, Texas Christian University Press, 1976), p. 60; Jan-Ivar Lindén, 'Metaforen – en ricoeurisation', *Res Publica*, 9 (1987), p. 144.

99. Lindén, 'Metaforen', p. 154.

100. Paul Ricoeur, *The Rule of the Metaphor* (London, University of Toronto Press, 1978), pp. 194–8; Ricoeur, *Interpretation Theory*, pp. 50–65.

101. *The Oxford English Dictionary*, 2nd edn (Oxford, Clarendon Press 1989), p. 960, 'Underdeveloped'.

102. Quoted from Yves Lacoste, *Contre les anti-tiers-mondistes et contre certains tiers-mondists* (Paris, Éditions la Découverte, 1985), p. 68.

103. Leffler, *Preponderance of Power*, p. 9.

104. *Ibid.*, pp. 323–41.

105. John H. Perkins, 'The Rockefeller Foundation and the Green Revolution, 1941–1956', *Agriculture and Human Values*, 7 (1990), pp. 9–10.

106. Perkins, 'The rhetoric of population', p. 10.

107. Karl T. Compton to Chester I Barnard, quoted in Perkins, 'The Rockefeller Foundation', p. 11.

108. *Partners in Progress*, Report to the President by the International Development Advisory Board, Papers of Harry S. Truman, March 1951, Official File, HSTL.

109. David Goldblatt, *Social Theory and the Environment* (Cambridge, Polity Press, 1996), ch. 1; John Opie, *Nature's Nation: An Environmental History of the United States* (Forth Worth, Harcourt Brace, 1998), p. 263.

110. Eisenhower's televised speech on foreign aid, 1957 May 21, quoted from Peter W. Rodman, *More Precious Than Peace: The Cold War and the Struggle for the Third World* (New York, Charles Scribner's Sons, 1994), p. 66.

111. Samuel P. Hays, 'From conservation to environment: environmental politics in the United States since World War II', in Kendall E. Bailes (ed.), *Environmental History* (Lanham MD, University Press of America, 1985), pp. 221.

112. 'A study of mankind's future', *New York Times*, 17 August 1952.

113. Karl Sax, *Standing Room Only: The Challenge of Overpopulation* (Boston, 1955).

114. Frederik Pohl and C.M. Kornbluth, *The Space Merchants* (New York, Walker & Co., 1953 (1952)), pp. 155–6.

115. Dalton, *Green Rainbow*, pp. 33–4.

116. John Kenneth Galbraith, *The Affluent Society* (New York, Mentor, 1958).

Chapter 4. Neo-Malthusianism in Harvest Time

1. When making an individual person the focus of a study, as in this chapter, there are several ways to pursue. One is to focus on a psychological life story, emphasising personal characteristics, family affairs, etc. Another possibility is to start from an 'economic' conception of the person including, for example, rational choice. Or one can choose to regard the person as an *agent*, indicating that the person acts on a mandate. This approach emphasises how the individual as an agent is linked to culture, discourses, collective representations, traditions, etc. It is the latter trait that has been chosen for this study.

2. 'Storm i en konservburk', *Nutid*, 19 (1955), p. 45. Translations from Swedish to English are made by the author unless otherwise stated.

3. Hartvig Sætra, *Den økopolitiske socialismen* (Oslo, Pax, 1973), p. 38.

4. 'Den gröna vågen', *Göteborgs Handels- och Sjöfartstidning* 1972 June 15.

5. Rolf Edberg, *Spillran av ett moln* (Stockholm, Norstedt, 1966), p. 141; Cf. Hans Palmstierna, *Plundring, svält, förgiftning* (Stockholm, Rabén & Sjögren, 1967), p. 49; Björn Gillberg, *Mordet på framtiden: en uppgörelse med den politiska och ekonomiska kortsiktigheten* (Stockholm, Wahlström & Widstrand, 1973), pp. 27.

6. 'Vi behöver väckarklockor', *ICA-kuriren*, 1996, 18, p. 43.

7. *Social Sciences Citation Index: An International Multidisciplinary Index to the Literature of the Social, Behavioral and Related Sciences* (Philadelphia, Institute for Scientific Information, PA, 1966–70, 1971–75): 'Borgström, Georg'.

8. Leif Lewin, *Planhushållningsdebatten* (Stockholm, Almqvist & Wiksell, 1967), pp. 180–85.

9. Tage Erlander, *Tage Erlander, 1940–49* (Stockholm, Tidens Förlag, 1973), pp. 280–81.

10. Lewin, *Planhushållningsdebatten*, p. 217; Gunnar Myrdal, *Varning för fredsoptimism* (Stockholm, 1944), p. 217.

11. *Ibid.*, p. 7.

12. *Ibid.*, pp. 204–14.

13. Bengt Birgersson, Owe Stig Hadenius, Björn Molin, Hans Wieslander, *Sverige efter 1900: en modern politisk historia* (Stockholm, Bonniers, 1984), p. 187.

14. Lewin, *Planhushållningsdebatten*, p. 262.

15. Lennart Jörberg, *Den svenska ekonomiska utvecklingen 1861–1983* (Lund, Ekonomisk-historiska föreningen, 1984), p. 45, Birgersson et al., *Sverige efter 1900*, p. 187.

16. Official Statistics of Sweden, *Vital Statistics 1941–1950* (Stockholm, Central Bureau of Statistics, 1955), p. 2.

17. Sten Carlsson, *Den sociala omgrupperingen i Sverige efter 1866* (Uppsala, Samhälle och riksdag, 1966), p. 281.

18. Birgersson et al., *Sverige efter 1900*, p. 191.

19. Cf. Johnny Wijk, *Svarta börsen: samhällslojalitet i kris: livsmedelsransoneringarna och den illegala handeln i Sverige 1940–1949* (Stockholm, Almqvist & Wiksell International, 1992).

20. 1944 års Socialdemokratiska partiprogram, § 4.

21. *Arbetarrörelsens efterkrigsprogram*, pp. 55–64; *Morgontidningen*, 15 December 1945; *Vi*, 6 (1946).

22. Lewin, *Planhushållningsdebatten*, p. 263.

23. *Ibid.*, pp. 307–8.

24. Birgersson et al., *Sverige efter 1900*, pp. 181–2.

25. Lewin, *Planhushållningsdebatten*, pp. 161–3.

26. Birgersson et al., *Sverige efter 1900*, pp. 189–97; Lewin, *Planhushållningsdebatten*, p. 101.

27. Statens offentliga utredningar (SOU) 1947: 14, p. 263; Thomas Jonter, *Socialiseringen som kom av sig: Sverige, oljan och USAs planer på en ny ekonomisk världsording 1945–1949* (Stockholm, Carlssons, 1994), pp. 54–61.

28. Lewin, *Planhushållningsdebatten*, pp. 331–47; Birgersson et al., *Sverige efter 1900*, p. 189.

29. Protocols of the Swedish Parliament, FK 480119.

30. Lewin, *Planhushållningsdebatten*, pp. 331–5, 340–42.

31. Cf. Alf W. Johansson, 'Socialiseringen som kom av sig' (rew.), *Historisk Tidskrift*, 1996, 1, pp. 198–206; 'Varför gav socialdemokraterna upp planhushållningspolitiken', *Historisk Tidskrift*, 1997, 3, pp. 445–8; Thomas Jonter, 'Genmäle till Alf W. Johansson', *Historisk Tidskrift*, 1996, 1, pp. 150–58; 'Svar på Alf W. Johanssons genmäle', *Historisk Tidskrift*, 1997, 3, pp. 449–51.

32. Thomas Söderqvist, *The Ecologists: From Merry Naturalists to Saviours of the Nation* (Stockholm, Almqvist & Wiksell International, 1986), pp. 92, 107, 155.

33. *Ibid.*, pp. 92, 107, 155.

34. In 1939, 2,484 students attended Lund university and the Society for Senior Lecturers gathered around 70 members.

35. See *Arbetet*, 7 March 1939; *Lunds Dagblad*, 7 March 1939; *Sydsvenska Dagbladet*, 7 March 1939.

36. Georg Borgström, 'Naturvetare', *Meddelanden från Lunds Kristliga Studentförbund*, VIII, 1 (1932), pp. 3–5; 'Naturvetenskap och kristendom', *Meddelanden från Lunds Kristliga Studentförbund*, X, 2 (1934), pp. 13–14; 'Fotoperiodism: Dagslängdens inflytande på växtvärlden' *Nordisk Familjeboks Månadskrönika*, February 1938, pp. 101–8; 'Nyare rön angående frölösa frukter. Kenokarpi och partenokarpi', *Nordisk Familjeboks Månadskrönika*, May 1938, pp. 325–6; 'Etylenproblemet inom växtfysiologin', *Nordisk Familjeboks Månadskrönika*, February 1939, pp. 94–100; Vera Borgström, interview by author, Göteborg, Sweden, 26 April 1994.

37. In Swedish: 'prov utan värde'.

38. Borgström, 'Större kunskaper i politiska frågor önskvärda', *Skånska Dagbladet*, 4 December 1935.

39. Borgström, letter to Dahmén, 8 August 1951, BF, CHS.

40. 'Hormondusch stimulerar tillväxten av plantor', *Göteborgs Tidning*, 5 March 1941; 'Bättre gröda med hormoner', *Dagens Nyheter*, 2 March 1941.

41. Borgström, *Gränser för vår tillvaro* (Stockholm, LTs Förlag, 1964), p. 267.

42. Borgström, 'Kampen om livet', *Reformatorn*, November 1940, pp. 6–7, 16.

43. Institutet för Växtforskning och Kyllagring.

44. Borgström, letter to Dahmén, 29 March 1942, BF, CHS.

45. Borgström, 'Om några händelser och personer som har haft inflytande på min forskning och världssyn', BF, CHS; Borgström, 'Vi måste fortsätta kriget mot sjukdom och svält', *Nynäshamns-Posten*, 26 November 1946.

46. 'Farmarradio i Uruguay', *Svenska Morgonbladet*, 16 August 1946.

47.   'Där litteraturdiskussion inleder affärssamtal', *Nynäshamns-Posten*, 12 August 1946; 'Sydamerika beundrar svensk socialmedicin', *Göteborgs Morgonpost*, 12 August 1946.

48.   Björn-Ola Linnér, 'Naturen som minnesmärke', in Annika Alzén and Johan Hedrén (eds), *Kulturarvets natur* (Stockholm, Symposion, 1998), pp. 51–83; Sverker Sörlin, 'Hembygden mellan historia och framtid', *Västerbotten*, 1984, 1, pp. 71–2.

49.   Borgström, 'Tal på midsommarfesten 1943', BF, CHS.

50.   *Ibid.*

51.   *Hörde Ni?*, II, 1949, p. 23.

52.   Borgström, 'Räcker maten?', Lecture on Swedish Radio, 20 December 1948, reproduced in *Hörde Ni?*, II, 1949; pp. 23–7.

53.   Borgström, 'Världens livsmedelsförsörjning', *Göteborgs Handels- och Sjöfartstidning*, 17 December 1948.

54.   'Biffar slöseri med energi, råkost kan rädda världen', *Expressen*, 21 December 1948.

55.   Swedish Radio, 21 December 1948. Debate between Georg Borgström, Edy Velander, Sten Wahlund and Åke Åkerman, reproduced in *Hörde Ni?*, II, 1949, pp. 128–33.

56.   Borgström, 'Ett dystert världsperspektiv', *Gotlands Allehanda*, 31 December 1948.

57.   Torsten Thurén, *Medier i blåsväder: Den svenska radion och televisionen som samhällsbevarare och samhällskritiker* (Stockholm, Etermedierna i Sverige, 1997), pp. 41–63, 104–6; Orvar Löfgren, 'Medierna i nationsbygget', in Ulf Hannerz (ed.), *Medier och kultur* (Stockholm, Carlssons, 1997), pp. 85–120.

58.   'Hur reagerar', *Göteborgs Handels- och Sjöfartstidning*, 21 December 1948.

59.   'Medvetandets tröskel', *Svenska Dagbladet*, 21 December 1948.

60.   'Större än julskinkan', *Norrländska Socialdemokraten*, 23 December 1948; See also '…en god vilja', *Arbetet*, 24 December 1948.

61.   'Maten i världsperspektiv', *Nerikes Allehanda*, 22 December 1948; 'Knockout på knockout', *Dagens Nyheter*, 21 December 1948; 'Större än julskinkan', *Norrländska Socialdemokraten*, 23 December 1948; 'Ur radions repertoar', *Arbetaren*, 27 December 1948.

62.   E.g. 'Hur länge räcker maten', *Gotlänningen*, 21 December 1948; 'Den fjärde försvarsgrenen', *Tiden*, 22 December 1948; 'Räcker maten åt alla', *Jämtlands Tidning*, 10 January 1949; 'Världssvält eller överproduktion', *Svenska Morgonposten*, 17 January 1949; 'Jordbruk för export', *Göteborgs Morgonpost*, 18 January 1949; 'Till Dagskrönikan', *Norrbottens Kuriren*, 31 January 1949.

63.   *Göteborg Morgonpost*, 18 January 1949.

64.   'Hur länge räcker maten', *Gotlänningen*, 21 December 1948; 'Världssvält eller överproduktion', *Svenska Morgonposten*, 17 January 1949; 'Livsmedelsbrist', *Sydsvenska Dagbladet*, 4 April 1949; Erik Grenbäck, 'Världssvält – överproduktion', *RFL-tidningen*, 1949, 1.

65. Lewin, *Planhushållningsdebatten*, p. 338; Åke Andersson, *Staten och jordbruket – en studie med utgångspunkt i rationaliserngs politiken för jordbruket i Sverige*, (Uppsala, SLU, Inst. för ekonomi, 1997), pp. 69–116.

66. 'Världens livsmedelsförsörjning', *Göteborgs Handels- och Sjöfartstidning*, 17 December 1948.

67. Borgström, letter to Mogens Jul, 2 May 1949, Rag 2, UNA.

68. Jul, letter to Herbert Greene, 25 May 1949; Greene, letter to Alfred J. Van Tassel, 26 May 1949, Rag 2, UNA.

69. Borgström, 'Preservation of Perishable Foods', *Proceedings of the United Nations Scientific Conference on the Conservation and Utilization of Resources. 17 August–6 September 1949, Lake Success, New York*, Vol VI, pp. 370–74.

70. Borgström, 'Om några händelser och personer'.

71. E.g. *Proceedings*, Vol I, pp. 262–75, 317; *International Technical Conference on the Protection of Nature. Proceedings and Papers* (Paris, 1950), pp.192–294.

72. George Perkins Marsh, *Man and Nature: Physical Geography as Modified by Human Action*, ed. David Lowenthal (Cambridge, MA, Belknap Press, 1965); Borgström, 'Om några händelser och personer'.

73. Vogt, letter to Osborn, 11 November 1953, CHS.

74. Thomas Hillmo and Ulrik Lohm, 'Nature's Ombudsmen: The Evolution of Environmental Representation in Sweden', *Environment and History*, 3:1 (1997), pp. 19–29.

75. Ulla Isaksson and Erik Hjalmar Linder, *Elin Wägner 1922–1949: Dotter av moder jord* (Stockholm, Bonniers, 1980), pp. 244, 257–9).

76. Lennart Lundqvist, 'Miljövårdförvaltning och politisk struktur', (Dissertation, Uppsala, 1971), pp. 26–7; Desirée Haraldsson, 'Skydda vår natur' (Dissertation, Lund, 1987), p. 205; Martin Kylhammar, *Den okände Sten Selander: En borgerlig intellektuell* (Stockholm, Akademeja, 1990), pp. 99–125; Björn Segrell, *Den attraktiva kusten: synsätt, konflikter och landskapsutnyttjande* (Linköping, Linköping Studies in Art and Sciences, 1995), pp. 62–3.

77. Förslag till Naturskyddslag m. m.: Betänkande avgivet av Naturskyddsutredningen, SOU 1951:5, p. 70.

78. Lundqvist, 'Miljövårdförvaltning', p. 27.

79. *Ibid.*, p. 43; see, for example, Lorentz Bolin, *Biologernas kamp mot svälten* (Stockholm, Geberts, 1945).

80. Sten Selander, 'Modernt Naturskydd', *Svenska Dagbladet*, 30 May 1949.

81. The title of the Swedish translation is *Vår plundrade planet*.

82. 'Livsmedelsbrist och jordförstöring', *Samtid och Framtid*, no. 5, 1949, p. 239.

83. *Ibid.*

84. 'Den utplundrade jorden', *Svenska Dagbladet*, 30 May 1949; 'Sandstormen i Skåne', *Göteborgs Morgonpost*, 25 April 1949; 'Erosionen människans fiende nr. 1 – Förstör 1/5 av USA:s åkerareal', *Ny Tid*, 28 February 1949.

85. Bill in the Swedish Parliament, FK, Sam Norup et al 'angående åtgärder i prisreglerande syfte på jordbrukets område', 1949: 415.

86. Borgström, 'Livsmedelsbrist och jordförstöring', *Samtid och Framtid*, no. 5, 1949, pp. 240.

87. 'Dystert bokslut', *Norrländska Socialdemokraten*, 6 September 1949. See also 'Planhushållning', *Morgontidningen*, 6 September 1949.

88. Bertil Ohlin, 'Politisk propaganda och socialisering', *Tiden*, 1946, pp. 245–6; Lewin, *Planhushållningsdebatten*, pp. 317–18.

89. Borgström, *Jorden–vårt öde: Kan en permanent världshunger avvärjas?* (Stockholm, Forum, 1953), p. 148.

90. Borgström, letter to Dahmén, 15 October 1949, BF, CHS.

91. *Ibid.*

92. Borgström, 'Världens livsmedelsförsörjning', *Göteborgs Handels- och Sjöfartstidning*, 17 December 1948.

93. Myrdal, *Varning*, p. 392.

94. Informationsbyrån för Mellanfolkligt samarbete.

95. Världssamling för fred.

96. Samarbetskommittén för Demokratisk Uppbyggnad.

97. Örjan Appelqvist, *Världsintressets advokat: Gunnar Myrdal och den svenska efterkrigsplaneringen 1944–1945,*(University of Gothenburg, Department of Political Science, 1997).

98. Fredrika Björklund, 'Samförstånd under oenighet: Svensk säkerhetspolitisk debatt under kalla kriget' (Dissertation, Uppsala, 1992), ch. 4; Ole Elgström, *En jämförelse mellan svensk och dansk parlamentarisk utrikesdebatt 1962–1978* (Lund, Studentlitteratur, 1982), pp. 42–4; Eric Noréen, *Brobygge eller blockbildning? De norska och svenska utrikesledningarnas säkerhetspolitiska föreställningar 1945–1948* (Stockholm, Carlssons, 1994), pp. 221–8.

99. Cay Sevón, *Visionen om Europa: Svensk neutralitet och europeisk återuppbygnad 1945–1948* (Helsinki, Suomen historiallinen seura, 1995), p. 130.

100. Björklund, 'Samförstånd', *passim.*

101. *Ibid.*, p. 132.

102 *Ibid.*, p. 47.

103. Krister Wahlbäck, *The Roots of Swedish Neutrality* (Stockholm, Swedish Institute, 1986), pp. 76–80; Noréen, *Brobygge eller blockbildning?*, pp. 229–32; Daniel Viklund, *Neutralitetsdebatten: Tro, vetande och illusioner* (Stockholm, Norstedts, 1989), pp. 52–6.

104. Alf W. Johansson, 'Den svenska socialdemokratin och fascismen på trettiotalet: några reflexioner', in *Utrikespolitik och historia* (Stockholm, Militärhistoriska förlaget, 1987), pp. 98–9.

105. Bo Huldt, 'Svensk nedrustnings- och säkerhetspolitik från tjugotal till åttiotal', in Bo Hugemark (ed.) *Neutralitet och försvar: Perspektiv på svensk säkerhetspolitik 1809–1985* (Stockholm, Militärhistoriska förlaget, 1986), p. 186; Björklund,

'Samförstånd', pp. 36; Wilhelm Agrell, *Alliansfrihet och atombomber: kontinuitet och förändringar i den svenska försvarsdoktrinen från 1945 till 1982* (Stockholm, LiberFörlag, 1985), p. 280.

106. *Ibid.*

107. Folke Isaksson, quoted from Tomas Forser and Per Arne Tjäder, *Tredje ståndpunkten: en debatt från det kalla krigets dagar* (Staffanstorp, Cavefors, 1972), p. 90; Alf W. Johansson, *Herbert Tingsten och det kalla kriget: Antikommunism och liberalism i Dagens Nyheter, 1946–1952* (Stockholm, Tiden, 1995), ch. 13; cf. Anders Frenander, 'Debattens vågor: om politisk-ideologiska frågor i efterkrigstidens svenska kulturdebatt' (Dissertation, Göteborg, 1998).

108. Alf W. Johansson, *Herbert Tingsten*, pp. 182–95.

109. Borgström, 'Europa i historiens vågskål', Sveriges Radio, 29 June 1953; 'Jordens befolkningsexplosion', Sveriges Radio, 13 July 1953; 'Den vilda naturens undergång', Sveriges Radio 20 July 1953; 'Den västerländska teknikens dilemma', Sveriges Radio 3 August 1953.

110. Borgström, *Jorden–vårt öde*, p. 3.

111. *Ibid.*, p. 4.

112. *Ibid.*, p. 53.

113. *Ibid.*, pp. 72–5.

114. *Vattnet i farozonen: vattenfrågans läge i Sverige* (Stockholm, Water Committe of the Royal Academy of Engineering, 1956).

115. Borgström, *Jorden–vårt öde*, pp. 87, 126, 242.

116. *Ibid.*, pp. 380–81.

117. *Ibid.*, p. 81.

118. *Ibid.*, pp. 395–400.

119. Borgström, *Gränser för vår tillvaro* (Stockholm, LTs Förlag, 1964), p. 372.

120. Borgström, *Jorden–vårt öde*, p. 400.

121. 'Svält', *Ny Tid*, 17 July 1953.

122. Borgström, *The Hungry Planet* (New York, Macmillan, 1965), pp. 25, 56.

123. Cf. Gösta Netzén, 'Jorden – Vårt öde'; *Arbetet*, 20 October 1953; Ivar Petterson, 'Kapplöpningen mot världssvälten', *Stockholms-Tidningen*, 14 October 1953; Åke Gullander, 'Kan jorden föda oss?', *RLF-tidningen* 1953, 47; Halvdan Åstrand, 'Blir svälten vårt öde?', *Jordbrukarnas Föreningsblad*, 31 October 1953; Lars Holmberg, 'Skall svälten segra', *Sydsvenska Dagbladet*, 24 October 1953; Waldemar Svensson, 'Brist eller överflöd?', *Expressen*, 26 October 1953; Gunnar Svärdson, 'Urvalet är vårt öde', *Expressen*, 29 October 1953.

124. Åstrand, 'Blir svälten vårt öde?'; 'Svar till Gullander', *RLF-tidningen* 1953, 47.

125. Åstrand, 'Blir svälten vårt öde?'.

126. Borgström, 'Om några händelser och personer'.

127. Cf. Knut Pettersson, 'Den undernärda världen', *Göteborgs Handels- och sjöfartstidning*, 1953 November 17; I. Es, 'Georg Borgström: jorden – vårt öde',

Medlemdblad för biologilärarnas förening, 1 (1954); Netzén, 'Jorden – Vårt öde'; *Arbetet*, 20 October 1953; Åstrand, 'Blir svälten vårt öde?'; 'Svar till Gullander', *RLF-tidningen* 1953: 47.

128. Borgström, *Jorden–vårt öde,*, p. 3.

129. *Ibid.*, pp. 7, 8, 17, 29, 145, 146, 222, 223.

130. Vogt, letters to Borgström, 9 July 1952, 29 July 1953, CHS.

131. Sten Selander, 'Mänsklighetens framtid', *Svenska Dagbladet*, 14 November 1953; Åke Gullander, 'Kan jorden föda oss?', *RLF-tidningen*, 1953, 47.

132. Gunnar Helén, letter to Borgström, 23 November 1954; Magnus Fahlström, 'De oförenliga experterna', *Stockholms-Tidningen*, 18 December 1953.

133. 'Svält', *Ny Tid*, 17 July 1953.

134. 'Docentens skräckmålning', *Arbetartidningen*, 17 July 1953; 'Borgströms skräck-propaganda', *Arbetartidningen*, 17 October 1953.

135. 'Överbefolkningsteorierna igen', *Ny Dag*, 20 October 1953; 'Hört i radio', *Norr-skensflamman*, 30 June 1953.

136. 'Förkunnelse värre än ruskig på reklammöte', *Arbetaretidningen*, 23 September 1953.

136. Knut Pettersson, 'Den undernärda världen', *Göteborgs Handels- och sjöfartstidning*, 17 November 1953. *Arbetaretidningen* portrayed Borgström with the caption: 'Assisted by first custodian Kurt Skogström at Lorensberg, Associate Professor Georg Borgström helps humanity another step closer to the catastrophe he is prophesying.'

137. Borgström, 'Om några händelser och personer'; Borgström, 'Answer to *Expressen*', BF, CHS; Greta Borgström, interview by author.

138. Selander, 'Mänsklighetens framtid'.

139. *Ibid.*

140. Vogt, *Road to Survival*, pp. 272–3.

141. Foucault, 'The Discourse on Language', appendix to *Archeology of Knowledge* (New York, Pantheon, 1972), pp. 224–5; Foucault, *Archeology of Knowledge*, p. 50

142. Palmstierna, *Plundring, svält, förgiftning*, p. 56.

143. Jeffrey C. Ellis, 'On the search of a root cause: essentialist tendencies in environmental discourse', in W. Cronon (ed.), *Uncommon Ground: Toward Reinventing Nature* (New York, W.W. Norton, 1995), *passim*.

144. Bill in the Swedish Parliament, FK, 1958: 157, by Erik Arrhén and Yngve Nilsson, 'angående befolkningsfrågan'.

145. E.g. 'Frischhaltung von Fischen in Skandinavien und anderen Ländern', *Kälte-technik*, 2:5, (1950), pp. 106–12; 'Fisheries and world food problems', address at FAO Meeting on herring technology, held in Bergen, Norway, 24–29 September, 1951; 'L'industrie de la conserve et ses problèmes actuels de recherche', *Revue de la Conserve*, November 1951, pp. 30–34; 'Que é a anchova da Scandinávia?', *Conservas de Peixe*, 6:68 (1951), p. 61; Borgström and R. Marcuse, 'Probleme des Fettverderbs: Zusammender Bericht über ein skandinavisches Symposium',

Fette und Seifen, 55:8 (1953), pp. 545–8; Borgström, 'Preservation of Fruit Juices by Sterilization, Filtration, Chemical Preservatives, etc.', in Donald K. Tressler and Maynard A Joslyn, *The Chemistry and Technology of Fruit and Vegetable Juice Production* (New York, AVI Publishing Co., 1954), pp. 180–218; 'Problemas de actualidad en la ciencia de conservación de alimentos', *Revista Tecnica Informacion Conservera*, 11:12 (1954), pp. 4–11; 'Microbiological Problems of Frozen Food Products', in *Advances in Food Research*, Vol. VI (New York, Academic Press, 1955), pp. 163–230.

146. Borgström, 'European aspects of overpopulation: Balance between resources and population', *Proceedings of the 5th International Conference of Planned Parenthood, Aug. 17–22, 1953* (Stockholm, 1954). Vogt, who was national director of the Planned Parenthood Federation of America, also delivered an address on 'Population problems.'

147. Borgström, 'Il rifornimento viveri dell'Europa', *Umana, Panorama di vita contemporanea*, 4:7–8 (1955), pp. 11–15.

148. Cf. Ron Eyerman, *Between Culture and Politics: Intellectuals in Modern Society* (Cambridge, 1997), p. 4; Håkan Thörn, *Modernitet, sociologi och social rörelser*, (Göteborg, Kompendiet, 1997), pp. 154–9.

Chapter 5. A New Conservation Ideology

1. Ludwig Wittgenstein, *Philosophical Investigations* (Oxford, Blackwell, 1953), § 67; Terry Eagleton, *Ideology: An Introduction*, London, Verso, 1991, p. 193.

2. Stefan Björklund, *Politisk teori* (Stockholm, Aldus, 1976), *passim*; Eagleton, *Ideology*, ch. 1; Sven-Eric Liedman 'Om ideologier', in Sven-Eric Liedman and Ingemar Nilsson, *Om ideologi och ideologianalys* (Göteborg, Arachne, 1989), pp. 7–45.

3. Martin Seliger, *Ideology and Politics* (London, Allen & Unwin, 1976), p. 11.

4. Eagleton, *Ideology*, p. 6.

5. *Ibid.*, p. 202.

6. Paul Ricoeur, *Lectures on Ideology and Utopia*, edited by George H. Taylor (New York, Columbia University Press, 1986), p. 1.

7. Ricoeur, *Lectures*, pp. 1–17.

8. Eagleton, *Ideology*, pp. 193–220; István Mészáros, *The Power of Ideology* (New York, New York University Press, 1989), p. 10.

9. Jorge Larrain, *The Concept of Ideology* (London, Hutchinson, 1979), p. 110.

10. *International Technical Conference on the Protection of Nature. Proceedings and Papers* (Paris, 1950), pp. 177–89.

11. E.g. Fairfeld Osborn, 'World resource situation', in *Proceedings of the United Nations Scientific Conference on the Conservation and Utilization of Resources. 17 August–6 September 1949, Lake Success, New York*, Vol. I, p. 12.; Emmanuel de Martonne, 'Interdependence of resources', *Proceedings*, Vol. I, p. 55; Starker Leopold, 'Ecological aspects of deer production on forest land', *Proceedings*, Vol.

VII, p. 207; Raymond Furon, 'Protection of natural resources: education and propaganda', *Proceedings*, vol. I, p. 289.

12. 'Laxen användes som gödsel på åkrarna – nu är den slut: Människans ingrepp i naturen rubbar jämvikten', *Norrlandsfolket*, 3 March 1949; Gunnar Beskow, 'Livsmedelsbrist och jordförstöring', *Samtid och Framtid*, no. 5, 1949, p. 246; Jöran Hult, 'Livsmedelsbrist och jordförstöring', *Samtid och Framtid*, no. 5, 1949, p. 248.

13. Fairfield Osborn, *Our Plundered Planet* (Boston, Little, Brown and Company, 1948), *passim*.

14. Paul Ricoeur, *Interpretation Theory: Discourse and the Surplus of Meaning* (Fort Worth, Texas Christian University Press, 1976), pp. 185–6.

15. Johan Hedrén, *Miljöpolitikens natur* (Linköping, Linköping Studies in Art and Science, 1994), pp. 151–65.

16. Clarence J. Glacken, *Traces on the Rhodian Shore: Nature and Culture from Ancient Times to the End of the Eighteenth Century*, (Berkeley, CA, University of California Press, 1990 (1967)), pp. 3, 391, and *passim*.

17. Frank N. Egerton, 'Changing Concepts of the Balance of Nature', *The Quarterly Review of Biology*, 48 (June 1973), pp. 343–7.

18. *Ibid*. See also 'Ecological Equilibrium', Chapter 6.

19. 'Mänskligheten kanar snart i utförsbacke', *Göteborgs Handels- och Sjöfartstidning*, 31 August 1949; 'Folkmängsökningen världens undergång', *Morgontidningen*, 6 September 1949; 'Naturtillgångarna förbrukas snabbt', *Svenska Dagbladet*, 31 August 1949, 'Befolkningsökningen mest oroande faktor', *Lunds Dagblad*, 4 September 1949; 'Räcka naturtillgångarna?', *Sydsvenska Dagbladet*, 2 September 1949.

20. Osborn, 'World resource situation', p. 13.

21. Heinz Theisen, 'Katastrophenstimmung und freiheitliche Demokratie', (Dissertation, Bonn, 1984), p. 1.

22. 'Laxen användes som gödsel på åkrarna', *Norrlandsfolket*, 3 March 1949. In the article Borgström's title is *docent* which here is translated as 'associate professor'. See also 'Mänskligheten kanar snart i utförsbacke', *Göteborgs Handels- och Sjöfartstidning*, 31 August 1949.

23. 'Hört i Radio: Räcker maten?', *Sydsvenska Dagbladet*, 21 December 1948.

24. Christopher Lewis, 'Progress and apocalypse: science and the end of the modern world', (Dissertation, 2 vols, University of Minnesota, 1991), chapters 7–8.

25. Micael Barkun, 'Divided apocalypse: thinking about the end in contemporary America', *Soundings*, 66 (1983), pp. 257–80.

26. Lewis, 'Progress and apocalypse', pp. 4, 9.

27. Aldo Leopold 'Ecology and politics', quoted from Lewis, 'Progress and apocalypse', p. 70; William Vogt, *Road to Survival* (London, Victor Gollancz, 1949 (1948)), p. 78, Osborn, *Our Plundered Planet*, p. 17; Georg Borgström, *Jorden–vårt öde: Kan en permanent världshunger avvärjas?* (Stockholm, Forum, 1953), p. 400; Osvald, 'Livsmedelsbrist och jordförstöring', *Samtid och Framtid*, no. 5, 1949, p. 251.

28. Klaus Vondung, *Die Apocalypse in Deutschland* (Munich, DTV, 1988), p. 251.
29. Borgström, *Jorden–vårt öde*, p. 400.
30. Quoted from Lewis, 'Progress and apocalypse', p. 100.
31. Frank Kermode, *The Sense of an Ending: Studies in the Theory of Fiction* (New York, 1967), p. 96.
32. Johan Asplund, *Teorier om Framtiden* (Stockholm, LiberFörlag, 1979), pp. 160–61.
33. Hannah Arendt, *Die verborgene Tradition. Acht Essays* (Frankfurt, Suhrkamp, 1976), pp. 96–7; Theisen, 'Katastrophenstimmung', p. 2.
34. Borgström, 'Answer to *Expressen*', BF, CHS.
35. Beskow, 'Livsmedelsbrist och jordförstöring', p. 246; Torsten Magnusson, 'Landsbygdens avfolkning sedd mot folkförsörjningens bakgrund', *Göteborgs Posten*, 21 February 1949; Torsten Lagerberg, 'Livsmedelsbrist och jordförstöring', *Samtid och Framtid*, no. 5, 1949, p. 249; 'Försörjningskris', *Dagen*, 5 December 1949; 'Samarbete enda sättet att hindra livsmedelsbrist', *Örebro Kuriren*, 20 February 1949.
36. I. F. Clarke, *The Pattern of Expectation* (London, Jonathan Cape, 1979), p. 292.
37. Warren W. Wagar, *Terminal Visions: The Literature of Last Things*, (Bloomington, Indiana UP, 1982), pp. 24, 27, 100.
38. 'A Study of Mankind's Future', *New York Times*, 17 August 1952.
39. Borgström, *Jorden–vårt öde*, p. 400.
40. Harrison Smith, 'What shall we do to be saved?', *The Saturday Review of Literature*, 35 (21 August 1948), p. 20.
41. Vogt, *Road to Survival*, p. 17.
42. Aldo Leopold 'Ecology and politics', quoted from Lewis, 'Progress and apocalypse', p. 70.
43. William Laurence, 'Population outgrows food: scientists warn the World', *The New York Times*, 15 July 1948.
44. Lewis, 'Progress and apocalypse', p. 88.
45. Borgström, 'Naturskyddet och livsmedelsförsörjningen', *Sveriges Natur*, 3 (1954), p. 26.
46. Earl Parker Hanson, 'Mankind need not starve', *Nation*, 169 (12 November 1949), p. 464. Reprinted in Walter M. Daniels (ed.), *The Point Four Program*, New York, Wilson, 1951.
47. 'Juldagen: att vilja vara med', *Sveriges Radio*, 25 December 1949, The National Archive of Recorded Sound and Moving Images, Stockholm; 'Världshushållets dilemma', *Göteborgs Handels- och sjöfartstidning*, 22 November 1949; 'Större än julskinkan', *Norrländska Socialdemokraten*, 28 December 1948. In addition to the quotes used in the following outline of the new conservation ideology, its representativeness will be checked against a quantitative word analysis. It follows upon the outline under the heading 'A New Conservationism?'
48. *Proceedings*, Vol. 1, p. 12.

49. Borgström, 'Världshushållets dilemma', *Göteborgs Handels- och Sjöfartstidning*, 22 November 1949; 'Jordbruk för export', *Göteborgs Morgonpost*, 28 December 1948; 'Större än julskinkan', *Norrländska Socialdemokraten*, 23 December 1948; 'Räcker Maten', lecture on Swedish Radio, 21 December 1948, reproduced in *Hörde Ni?*, II, 1949, pp. 23–7.

50. Borgström, 'Frihet från nöd vägen till fred. Årets fredspristagare Lord John Boyd-Orr presenteras', *Vi*, 22 October 1949.

51. *Nynäshamnsposten*, 20 December 1949; Osvald, 'Livsmedelsbrist och jordförstöring', p. 250.

52. Hult, 'Livsmedelsbrist och jordförstöring', pp. 248–9; cf. Beskow, 'Livsmedelsbrist och jordförstöring', pp. 246–8; Osvald, 'Livsmedelsbrist och jordförstöring', pp. 249–50; 'Hur skall jorden kunna försörja sin växande befolkning? Det dagliga brödet människans aktuellaste ödesfråga', *Nynäshamnsposten*, 20 December 1949; Waldemar Svensson, 'En fråga om energi', *Stockholms-Tidningen*, 24 February 1954; Åke Gullander, 'Skogens resurser', *Stockholms-Tidningen*, 7 January 1954; *Nynäshamnsposten*, 20 December 1949; Osvald, 'Livsmedelsbrist och jordförstöring', p. 250.

53. Borgström, 'Om några händelser och personer som har haft inflytande på min forskning och världssyn', BF, CHS; cf. 'Vi måste fortsätta kriget mot sjukdom och svält', *Nynäshamnsposten*, 26 November 1946.; 'När vindruvorna mognade på Södertörns kuster', *Nynäshamnsposten*, 13 April 1948.

54. *The Oxford English Dictionary,* 2nd edn, (Oxford, Clarendon Press, 1989), 'Global'.

55. Donna J. Haraway, *Primate Visions: Gender, Race and Nature in the World of Modern Science*, (New York, Routledge, 1989), pp. 197–203; Haraway, 'Universal Donors in a Vampire Culture', in William Cronon (ed.), *Uncommon Ground: Toward Reinventing Nature* (New York, W.W. Norton, 1995), p. 343.

56. Osborn, *Our Plundered Planet*, p. 25.

57. Peter J. Taylor and Frederick H. Buttel, 'How do we know we have global environmental problems? Science and the globalization of environmental discourse', *Geoforum*, 23:3 (1992), p. 409; Wolfgang Sachs, 'Global ecology and the shadow of "development"', in Wolfgang Sachs (ed.) *Global Ecology: A New Arena of Political Conflict* (London, Zed Books, 1993), pp. 3–21.

58. Björn-Ola Linnér and Henrik Selin, 'Sustainable development and globalization: the Stockholm legacy', paper presented at the Nature and Culture Seminar, University of Kansas, 2 February 2002.

59. Maarten Hajer and Frank Fischer, 'Beyond global discourse: the rediscovery of culture in environmental politics', in M. Hajer and F. Fischer (eds), *Living With Nature: Environmental Politics as Cultural Discourse*, Oxford, Oxford University Press, 1999, p. 9.

60. Georg Lukács, *History and Class Consciousness: Studies in Marxist Dialectics* (London, 1983), pp. 202–6.

61. See e.g. David Harvey, *Justice, Nature and the Geography of Difference* (Oxford, Blackwell, 1996); Wolfgang Sachs, 'Global ecology and the shadow of "devel-

opment"', in Wolfgang Sachs (ed.) *Global Ecology: A New Arena of Political Conflict*, London, Zed Books, 1993, pp. 3–21; Peter J. Taylor and Frederick H. Buttel, 'How do we know we have global environmental problems? Science and the globalization of environmental discourse', *Geoforum*, 23:3 (1992); Ulrich Beck, *What is Globalization?* (Malden, MT, Polity Press, 2000), ch. 2; Frederic Jameson, 'Preface' and 'Notes on globalization as a philosophical issue', in Frederic Jameson and Masao Miyoshi (eds), *The Cultures of Globalization* (Durham, NC, Duke University Press, 1998), pp. xi–xvii, 54–77; Ramachandra Guha and Juan Martinez-Alier, *Varieties of Environmentalism: Essays North and South* (London, Earthscan, 1997).

62. Björn-Ola Linnér and Henrik Selin, 'The quest for sustainability: the legacy of the Stockholm Conference 1972', paper presented at the International Studies Association, Portland, OR, 1 March 2003.

63. Borgström, 'Räcker maten'; Borgström. 'Livsmedelsbrist och jordförstöring', *Samtid och Framtid*, no. 5, 1949; Jan Magnus Fahlström, 'Överflödet geografi – eller hungerns', *Stockholms-Tidningen*, 19 December 1953; *International Technical Conference*, pp. ix, 15–181.

64. *International Technic al Conference*, pp. ix, 129–69.

65. *Ibid.*, p. ix.

66. Beskow, 'Livsmedelsbrist och jordförstöring', p. 247; Hult, 'Livsmedelsbrist och jordförstöring', pp. 248–9, Osvald, 'Livsmedelsbrist och jordförstöring', pp. 250–53.

67. Beskow, 'Livsmedelsbrist och jordförstöring', pp. 246; Hult, 'Livsmedelsbrist och jordförstöring', pp. 248; Osvald, 'Livsmedelsbrist och jordförstöring', pp. 249.

68. Jeffrey C. Ellis, 'When green was pink: environmental dissent in Cold War America' (Dissertation, University of California, Davis, 1995), ch. 2.

69. Vogt, *Road to Survival*, p. 133.

70. *Ibid.*, p. 283. The Russian anarchist and geographer Prince Pjotr Kropotkin saw the solidarity and cooperation between humans and the collective as the driving force in history. He proposed a conscious social revolution against the domination and exploitation of nature as well as other humans. David Pepper, *The Roots of Modern Environmentalism* (London, Routledge, 1989), pp. 188–93; Sverker Sörlin, *Naturkontraktet: Om naturumgängets idéhistoria* (Stockholm, Carlssons, 1991), pp. 215–17.

71. Osborn, 'World resource situation', p. 13.

72. Borgström, *Jorden – vårt öde*, p. 399.

73. Lewis, 'Progress and apocalypse', p. 132.

74. Ricoeur, *Lectures on Ideology and Utopia*, p. 15.

75. Guha and Martinez-Alier, *Varieties of Environmentalism*, pp. 16–21, 92–108.

76. Robert Gottlieb, *Forcing the Spring* (Washington, DC, Island Press, 1993), p. 37; Donald Worster, *Nature's Economy: A History of Ecological Ideas*, 2nd edn (Cambridge, Cambridge University Press, 1994), p. 293. See also 'System Ecology', Chapter 6.

77. Osborn, *Our Plundered Planet*, pp. 196–8.

78. Arthur Herman, *The Idea of Decline in Western History* (New York, The Free Press, 1996), pp. 400–440.

79. Sten Selander, 'Modernt Naturskydd', *Svenska Dagbladet*, 30 May 1949.

80. Martin Kylhammar, *Den okände Sten Selander: En borgerlig intellektuell* (Stockholm, Akademeja, 1990), p. 189.

81. Gottlieb, *Forcing the Spring*, p. 37. Whether Ordway would subscribe to the New Conservation Ideology outlined in this book has not been examined. It should be noted that he tried to reconcile capitalism with conservation in *Resources and the American Dream* (1954).

82. Debate between Georg Borgström, Edy Velander, Sten Wahlund and Åke Åkerman, Swedish Radio, 21 December 1948, reproduced in *Hörde Ni?*, II (1949), pp. 128–33; 'Livsmedelsbrist och jordförstöring', *Samtid och Framtid*, no. 5 1949; 'Svält på jorden?', Debate in *Stockholms-Tidningen*, 18 December 1953, 19 December 1953, 22 December 1953, 23 December 1953, 30 December 1953, 2 January 1954, 7 January 1954, 9 January 1954, 15 January 1954, 5 February 1954, 9 February 1954, 25 February 1954, 26 February 1954, 9 March 1954; *Proceedings*, Vols I and VI. The ITCPN proceedings were not scanned for a quantitative word analysis. About half of the articles were in French, which made them less suited for a comparable quantitative analysis. And a large number of the contributions were only presented as short summaries, so the actual presentation contexts of the indicator words were thus unavailable for analysis.

83. Jeffrey C. Ellis, 'On the search of a root cause: essentialist tendencies in environmental discourse', in W. Cronon (ed.), *Uncommon Ground: Toward Reinventing Nature* (New York, W.W. Norton, 1995), p. 259.

84. Hedrén, *Miljöpolitikens natur*, ch. 2–6.

85. On the difference between 'origin' and 'descent' in the history of ideas see Michel Foucault, 'Nietzsche, genealogy, history', in *Language, Counter-Memory, Practice: Selected Essays and Interviews* (Ithaca, NY, Cornell University Press, 1977), pp. 146, 151.

86. Eagleton, *Ideology*, p. 58.

87. Pierre Bourdieu, *Outline of a Theory of Practice* (Cambridge, Cambridge University Press, 1977), pp. 164–71; Pierre Bourdieu and Terry Eagleton, 'Doxa and common life: an interview', in Slavoj Zizek, *Mapping Ideology* (Verso, London, 1997 (1994)), pp. 265–77.

Chapter 6. On the Outskirts of Babel

1. Clarence J. Glacken, *Traces on the Rhodian Shore: Nature and Culture from Ancient Times to the End of the Eighteenth Century* (Berkeley, CA, University of California Press, 1990 (1967)), *passim*; Frank N. Egerton, 'Changing Concepts of the Balance of Nature', *The Quarterly Review of Biology*, 48 (June 1973), p. 322. See chapter 5, 'The order of nature'.

2.   Amos H. Hawley, *Human Ecology: A Theory of Community Structure* (New York, The Ronald Press Company, 1950).

3.   Donald Worster, *Nature's Economy: A History of Ecological Ideas*, 2nd edn (Cambridge, Cambridge University Press, 1994); Robert P. McIntosh, *The Background of Ecology: Concept and Theory*, (Cambridge, Cambridge University Press, 1985); Peter J. Bowler, *The Environmental Sciences* (New York, Norton, 1993 (1992)).

4.   Louis I. Dublin, Alfred J. Lotka, Mortimer Spiegelman, *Length of Life: A Study of the Life Table* (New York, Ronald Press, 1936); Borgström, *Jorden – vårt Öde*, ch. 1; Borgström, List of references to *Jorden – vårt Öde*, BF, CVH.

5.   Raymond Pearl, *The Natural History of Population* (New York, Oxford University Press, 1939); Borgström, *Jorden – vårt Öde*, ch. 1; Borgström, List of references.

6.   Rachel Carson, *The Sea around Us* (New York, Oxford University Press, 1951); Borgström *Jorden – vårt Öde*, ch. 10; Borgström, List of references.

7.   Borgström, *Jorden – vårt Öde*, p. 126.

8.   Borgström, *Jorden – vårt Öde*; 'Räcker maten?', lecture on Swedish Radio, 20 December 1948, reproduced in *Hörde Ni?*, II (1949), pp. 23–7; debate between Georg Borgström, Edy Velander, Sten Wahlund and Åke Åkerman, Swedish Radio, 21 December 1948, reproduced in *Hörde Ni?*, II (1949), pp. 128–33; 'Livsmedelsbrist och jordförstöring', *Samtid och Framtid*, no. 5, 1949; 'Svält på jorden?' *Stockholms-Tidningen*, 30 December 1953; Borgström, 'Preservation of perishable foods', *Proceedings of the United Nations Scientific Conference on the Conservation and Utilization of Resources. 17 August–6 September 1949, Lake Success, New York*, Vol. VI,, pp. 370–74.

9.   These concepts were checked against the following scanned texts of Borgström: 'Räcker Maten'; 'Livsmedelsbrist och jordförstöring'; 'Svält på jorden?'.

10.   Fairfield Osborn, *Our Plundered Planet* (Boston, Little, Brown and Company, 1948), *passim*; William Vogt, *Road to Survival* (London, Victor Gollancz, 1949 (1948)), *passim*.

11.   Georg Borgström and Greta Borgström (eds), *Malthus – Om befolkningsfrågan* (Stockholm, LTs Förlag, 1969), p. 7.

12.   Georg Borgström, *Mat för miljarder* (Stockholm, LTs Förlag, 1962), p. 10.

13.   Aldo Leopold, *Game Management* (New York, 1933), pp. viii, 3, 20–21, 396; Worster, *Nature's Economy*, pp. 271–4; Roderick Nash, *Wilderness and the American Mind*, 3rd edn, (New Haven, Yale University Press, 1982), ch. 11.

14.   Leopold, 'The conservation ethic', *Journal of Forestry*, 31 (October 1933), pp. 634–43; Worster, *Nature's Economy*, p. 285.

15.   Leopold, 'The ecological consciousness', *Bulletin of the Garden Club of America*, 46 (1947), p. 49; Nash, *Wilderness and the American Mind*, p. 196.

16.   Leopold, *Sand County Almanack, and Sketches Here and There* (New York, Oxford University Press, 1949), pp. 124–7, 162–3, 190, 202–10; Worster, *Nature's Economy*, pp. 286–7.

17.   Leopold, *Sand County Almanack*, p. viii.

18.   *Ibid.*, pp. 207–10.

19. Chritopher Lewis, 'Progress and apocalypse: science and the end of the modern world', (Dissertation, 2 vols, University of Minnesota, 1991), pp. 70–72.
20. Borgström, *Mat för miljarder* (Stockholm, LTs Förlag, 1962), p. 262.
21. Paul B. Sears, *Deserts on the March*, 2nd edn (Norman, University of Oklahoma Press, 1947 (1935)), *passim*.
22. Graham V. Jacks and Robert O. Whyte, *The Rape of the Earth: A World Survey of Soil Erosion* (London, Faber & Faber, 1939).
23. McIntosh, *Background of Ecology*, p. 267; Frank N. Egerton, 'Changing Concepts of the Balance of Nature', *The Quarterly Review of Biology*, 48 (June 1973), p. 322.
24. McIntosh, *Background of Ecology*, p. 71.
25. *Ibid.*, pp. 79–99; Egerton, 'Changing Concepts', pp. 322–47; Worster, *Nature's Economy*, ch. 11.
26. Worster, *Nature's Economy*, p. 234.
27. Vogt, *Road to Survival*, pp. 87–93.
28. McIntosh, *Background of Ecology*, p. 82.
29. *Ibid.*, p. 264.
30. Mary Douglas, *Purity and Danger: An Analysis of the Concepts of Pollution and Taboo* (London, Routledge, 1966), pp. 35–40.
31. Vogt, *Road to Survival*, p. 274.
32. Egerton, 'Changing Concepts', pp. 322–47.
33. Charles Elton, *Animal Ecology and Evolution* (Oxford, 1930), p. 17.
34. Elton, *Animal Ecology* (London, 1967, (1927)), pp. vii–viii.
35. Vogt, *Road to Survival*, p. 301.
36. Warder Clyde Allee *et al.*, *Principles of Animal Ecology* (Saunders, Philadelphia, 1949), p. 728.
37. Paul Erlich and L.C. Birch, ' The "balance of nature" and "population control"', *The American Naturalist*, 101:918 (1967), pp. 97–107.
38. Georg Borgström, *Too Many: A Study of Earth's Biological Limitations* (New York, Macmillan, 1969), p. 201.
39. E.g. Georg Borgström, *Too Many: An Ecological Overview of Earth's Linitations* (New York, Collier Books, 1971), p. 367.
40. Cyril Dean Darlington, *The Evolution of Man and Society* (New York, 1969), p. 60.
41. Darlington, *Evolution*, pp. 59–61.
42. Worster, 1994, pp. 301–4; Frank Benjamin Golley, *A History of the Ecosystem Concept in Ecology: More than the Sum of the Parts,* Yale University Press, New Haven, 1993, pp. 33–4.
43. See 'The Tranformation of the World Economy', Chapter 2.
44. Worster, *Nature's Economy*, p. 295. Worster does not himself refer to the concept of Fordism.
45. *Ibid.*, p. 312.

46. John H. Perkins, 'The rhetoric of population and its consequences', Paper presented at the meeting of the American Society for Environmental History, Baltimore, 6–9 March 1997.

47. Donna J. Haraway, *Primate Visions: Gender, Race and Nature in the World of Modern Science* (New York, Routledge, 1989), pp. 197–203; 'Universal donors in a vampire culture', in W. Cronon (ed.), *Uncommon Ground: Toward Reinventing Nature* (New York, W.W. Norton, 1995), p. 343.

48. Borgström, 'Frihet från nöd vägen till fred. Årets fredspristagare Lord John Boyd-Orr presenteras', *Vi*, 22 October 1949; Letter to John Boyd-Orr, 1949 October 20.

49. McIntosh, *Background of Ecology*, pp. 190, 303; Bowler, *Environmental Sciences*, pp. 531–2, 537; Worster, *Nature's Economy*, pp. 374–5; Dmitry Shelestov, *Demography in the Mirror of History* (Moscow, Progress Publishers, 1987), p. 65.

50. Worster, *Nature's Economy*, pp. 351–2.

51. Gunnar Dahmén, interview by author ,Stockholm, 9 May 1994; Gustaf Rudebeck, interview by author, 30 May 1998, Lund, Sweden.

52. The Swedish academic title is 'docent', corresponding in academic esteem to the American position of 'associate professor'.

53. Cf. Björn Gillberg, *Mordet på framtiden: en uppgörelse med den politiska och ekonomiska kortsiktigheten* (Stockholm, Wahlström & Widstrand, 1973), pp. 27–35, 'Godmorgon världen', Swedish Radio, 11 August 2002.

54. In Swedish, 'Stiftelsen Svensk Konserveringsforskning'.

55. Birger Drake, memorandum, PBD; *Utredning om förhållanden vid konserveringsinstitutet*, Reports of the Government Commissions, 'SOU series', SOU 1958:3.

56. 'Storm i en konservburk', *Nutid*, 19 (1955), p. 45.

57. *Ibid.*, p. 44.

58. Protocol, the Board of SIK, 26 October 1953.

59. SOU 1958:3, p. 49.

60. Protocol, the Board of SIK, 17 December 1953; SOU 1958:3, pp. 47–8.

61. Protocol, Working committee of SIK's board, 29 December 1955.

62. SOU 1958:3, pp. 58–88, 112.

63. SOU 1958:3, pp. 50–54.

64. 'Vissas inställningar till vissa saker' (Certain peoples' attitude toward certain things), 14 December 1956, PBD.

65. SOU 1958:3, p. 98.

66. E.g. Findus research director Karl-Evert Flinck and Bertil Hylmö. The latter had himself applied for the position as SIK director in 1948, but wished to keep it secret (as did Borgström); Protocol, the Board of SIK, 1947 April 16.

67. SOU 1958:3, p. 159.

68. 'Baksidan av Borgströmaffären', *Aftonbladet*, 24 November 1956.

69. SOU 1958:3, pp. 154–5.

70. *Ibid.*, pp. 155–6.

71. *Ibid.*, p. 156; Gösta Lindeberg, interview by author, Uppsala, 9 February 1995.

72. Fredrik Engqvist to Rektorsämbetet at Göteborgs högskola, 1950 December 15, BF, CHS.

73. 'Hans avgång icke nödvändig', *Göteborgs-Posten*, 11 January 1958.

74. SOU 1958:3, pp. 151–54, 156.

75. The newspapers studied are: *Aftonbladet, Arbetet, Dagens Nyheter, Göteborgs Handels- och Sjöfartstidning, Göteborgs-Posten, Göteborgs–Tidningen, Ny Tid, RLF-tidningen, Skånska Dagbladet, Stockholms-Tidningen, Svenska Dagbladet, Sydsvenska Dagbladet,* as well as articles mentioned in SOU 1958:3.

76. 'Problemet Georg Borgström', *Göteborgs Handels- och Sjöfartstidning*, 24 July 1956; 'Oväsendet kring konserveringsinstitutet'. *Göteborgs Handels- och Sjöfartstidning*, 27 July 1956.

77. E.g. 'Monopolsträvanden och hr. Borgström', 25 July 1956; 'Bluff', 26 July 1956; 'Ny Laurin bluff', 27 July 1956; 'Motiven för Borgströms avgång inte klarlagda', 11 October 1956.

78. 'Monopolsträvanden och hr. Borgström', *Göteborgs-Posten*, 25 July 1956.

79. Protocol, the Board of SIK, 21 January 1955; SOU 1958:3, pp. 42–3.

80. The three companies were Åkerlund and Rausing, Findus and PLM.

81. SOU 1958:3, pp. 150–51.

82. Protocol, information meeting between Borgström and the heads of SIK's research departments, 5 September 1956.

83. 'Storm i konservburk', *Göteborgs-Posten*, 11 January 1958.

84. SOU 1958:3, p. 140.

85. Första kammarens protokoll, nr. 25, 'Interpellation ang. professorn G. Borgströms avgång från Institutet för konserveringsforskning', pp. 8–9.

86. 'Fallet Borgström', *Dagens Nyheter*, 13 August 1956.

87. Statements by the board of SIK, 'Herr Statsrådet och Chefen för Handelsdepartementet', Göteborg, 17 October 1956; 'Särskilt yttrande av herr Hult', 'Tillägg av herr Adler', Göteborg 16 October 1956, PBD.

88. SOU 1958:3, pp. 223–30, Borgström, Preliminär visumansökan, 1956, CHS.

89. SOU 1958:3, pp. 215–42, *passim*.

90. *Ibid.*, pp. 85–6, 105, 223–5.

91. *Ibid.*, pp. 212–14.

92. *Ibid.*, p. 235.

93. 'Hans avgång icke nödvänding', *Göteborgs-Posten*, 11 January 1958.

94. Erik L. Mangus, 'Besynnerlig Borgström utredning', *Göteborgs-Posten*, 1 March 1958; 'Den förutseende hr Lange', *Göteborgs-Posten*, 29 March 1958.

95. 'Borgström', *Expressen*, 14 January 1958.

96. 'Professor Borgström: 'Nya institut med för få forskare kardinalfel i näringsvetenskapen', *Dagens Nyheter*, 14 January 1958.

97. 'Icke oväntat', *Göteborgs Handels- och Sjöfartstidning*, 11 January 1958.

98. Protocol of the Swedish Parliament, FK, nr. 11, 'Interpellation ang. vissa spörsmål i samband med professorn G. Borgströms avgång från Institutet för konserveringsforskning', 1958, pp. 40–44.

99. *Ibid.*

100. 'Professorer begär översyn av anställningsförhållanden', *Dagens Nyheter*, 16 September 1958; cf. *Aftonbladet*, 16 September 1958; *Expressen*, 16 September 1958; *Göteborgs-Tidningen*, 17 September 1958; *Göteborgs-Posten*, 17 September 1958, 'Professorerna fick nej i regeringen', *Göteborgs-Posten*, 25 October 1958.

101. Bertil Hylmö, interview by author, Askersund, Sweden, 9 March 1995.

102. SOU 1958:3, p. 159.

103. 'Eat Hearty', *Time*, 8 November 1948, p. 28.

104. SOU 1958:3, pp. 159–60.

105. Borgström, 'Om några händelser och personer som har haft inflytande på min forskning och världssyn', BF, CHS; Borgström, 'Answer to *Expressen*', BF, CHS; Greta Borgström, interview by author, Göteborg, Sweden, 27 April 1994.

106. Borgström, *Jorden – vårt Öde*, p. 398.

107. Michel Foucault, *Archeology of Knowledge* (New York, Pantheon, 1972), p. 6; Thomas Flynn, 'Foucault's mapping of history', in Gary Gutting (ed.), *The Cambridge Companion to Foucault* (Cambridge, Cambridge University Press, 1994), p. 36.

108. *Arbetartidningen*, 21 October 1956.

109. Foucault, 'The Discourse on Language', appendix to *Archeology of Knowledge*, *passim*.

110. See chapter 5, 'Catastrophe Empiricism'.

111. Steven Shapin, *A Social History of Truth: Civility and Science in Seventeenth-Century England* (Chicago, University of Chicago Press, 1994), pp. 409–18.

112. 'Naturvetare', *Meddelanden från Lunds Kristliga Studentförbund*, VIII:1 (1932), pp. 3–5; 'Naturvetenskap och kristendom', *Meddelanden från Lunds Kristliga Studentförbund*, X:2 (1934), pp. 13–14.

113. 'Professor Borgström (den viktigaste svensken i världen) varnar mänskligheten: Svältkatastrof om tio år', *Expressen* 28 January 1967; Borgström, 'Answer to *Expressen*'.

114. E.g. I Peter 5:4. In the King James version, St Peter's 'victory crown' is translated as 'crown of glory'.

115. Alf W. Johansson, 1995, pp. 182–95.

116. Bernt Skovdahl, *Tingsten, Totalitarismen, och ideologierna*, Symposion, Stockholm, 1992, pp. 42–7; Alf W. Johansson *Herbert Tingsten och det kalla kriget: Antikommunism och liberalism i Dagens Nyheter, 1946–1952* (Stockholm, Tiden, 1995), pp. 23–7; Herbert Tingsten, *Från idéer till idyll: den lyckliga demokratin* (Stockholm, Bonnier, 1966), p. 24; Borgström, 'Answer to *Expressen*'; Borgström, *Jorden – vårt Öde*, p. 330.

117. Ludwig Wittgenstein, *Philosophical Investigations* (Oxford, Blackwell, 1953), § 241; Barry Barnes, David Bloor and John Henry, *Scientific Knowledge: A Sociological Analysis* (London, Athlone Press, 1996), p. 116.

118. Barnes et al., *Scientific Knowledge*, p. 168.

119. Cf. Vogt, *Road to Survival*, pp. 272–3.

120. 'Storm i en konservburk', *Nutid*, 19 (1955), p. 45.

121. *Ibid.*

122. F. W. Fabian, letter to Borgström, 4 February 1956; H.B. Tukey, letters to Borgström, 6 February 1956, 2 April 195; Borgström to Tukey, 5 March 1956.

123. Hannah, letter to Harry S. Truman, 4 February 1949; Truman, letter to John A. Hannah, 14 February 1949; Richard Niehoff, *John A. Hannah: Versatile Administrator and Distinguished Public Servant* (Lanham, MD, University Press of America, 1989), pp. 215–17; Paul Dressel, *College to University: The Hannah Years at Michigan State, 1935–1969* (East Lansing, Michigan State University Publications, 1987); Lyle Blair and Madison Kuhn, *A Short History of Michigan State* (East Lansing MI, Michigan State College, 1955). Clifton Wharton, interview by author, New York, 31 October 1995. See chapter 3, 'Truman's Point Four Program'.

124. Interviews by author, East Lansing, MI: Bob Bandurski, 5 October 1995; Glenn Johnsson, 11 October 1995; John Cantlon 9 October 1995.

125. Borgström to Tukey, 5 March 1956; Tukey to Borgström, 2 April 1956.

126. John Cantlon, interview by author.

127. 'Discussion Group on World Food Problems', 6 May 1959, MSUAHC; 'Substance of Comments made by Dr. Georg Borgström in Interview', May 1959, MSUAHC; 'Protein, Calories and Democracy – A Global Dilemma', Luncheon address, 4 December 1961; 'Global "Food Gap" Widens, Threatens Human Survival', *Lansing State Journal*, 12 August 1962; Borgström, 'Back to Reality', *Food Technology*, May 1965, pp. 71–3; Bob Bandurski, Glenn Johnsson and John Cantlon, interviews by author; Georg Woodwell, interview by author, Woods Hole, MA, 23 October 1995; Lawrence Sommers, interview by author, East Lansing, MI, 11 October 1995.

128. 'Data on Georg Borgström', MSUAHC.

129. Borgström, Comprehensive Bibliography, CHS; Lawrence Sommers, interview by author; Dough Richardson, interview by author, Washington DC, 10 March 1997.

130. Angus Maddison, *Phases of Capitalist Development* (Oxford, Oxford University Press, 1982), p. 41.

131. Peter Kuznik, *Beyond the Laboratory: Scientists as Political Activists in the 1930s America* (Chicago, Chicago University Press, 1987), p. 38.

132. Frank B. Golley, *A History of the Ecosystem Concept in Ecology: More than the Sum of the Parts* (New Haven, Yale University Press, 1993), pp. 72–4.

133. Immanuel Wallerstein, 'The unintended consequences of Cold War area studies', in Noam Chomsky et al., *The Cold War and the University* (New York, The New Press, 1997), pp. 171–238.

134. Bowler, *Environmental Sciences*, p. 394.

135. Golley, *History of the Ecosystem Concept*, p. 111; Frank W. Blair, *Big Biology: the US/IBP*, (Stroudsburg, PA, Hutchinson & Ross, 1979); Chunglin Kwa, 'Representations of nature mediating between ecology and science policy: the case of the International Biological Programme', *Social Studies of Science*, 17 (1987), pp. 413–42; Worster, *Nature's Economy*; E.B. Worthington (ed.), *The evolution of IBP* (Cambridge, Cambridge University Press, 1975).

136. Perkins, 'The rhetoric of population'.

137. Worster, *Nature's Economy*, p. 314.

138. Steven Shapin, *The Scientific Revolution* (Chicago, University of Chicago Press, 1996), p. 164.

139. Borgström, 'Answer to *Expressen*'.

140. Shapin, *Scientific Revolution*, pp. 162–4; Foucault, *Archeology of Knowledge*, p. 216.

141. Shapin, *Scientific Revolution*, pp. 8–14; Shapin, *Social History of Truth*, 408–17; David Bloor, *Knowledge and Social Imagery*, 2nd edn (Chicago, University of Chicago Press, 1991); Barnes et al., *Scientific Knowledge*.

142. Douglas, *Purity and Danger*, p. 3.

143. See for example: William Cronon (ed.) *Uncommon Ground: Toward Reinventing Nature* (New York, W.W. Norton, 1995).

144. William Cronon, 'Introduction: in search of nature', in *Uncommon Ground*, pp. 23–56.

145. Hans Fink, 'Humanøkologins naturbegrep', *Humanekologi*, 3/4 (1993), pp. 5–15; Roland Barthes, *Mythologies* (London, Paladin, 1973), p. 108; Niel Evernden, *The Social Creation of Nature* (Baltimore, Johns Hopkins University Press, 1992), pp.ix–xiii, 57–71.

146. Donald Worster, 'Appendix: Doing Environmental History' in D. Worster (ed.) *The Ends of the Earth* (Cambridge, Cambridge University Press, 1988), pp. 290–91.

147. Richard B. Norgaard, *Development Betrayed: The End of Progress and a Coevolutionary Revisioning of the Future* (London, Routledge, 1994), p. 35.

148. Raymond Williams, *Problems in Materialism and Culture* (London, Verso, 1980), pp. 70–71, 78.

149. Barthes, *Mythologies*, p. 108.

150. Georg Borgström, *The Hungry Planet* (New York, Macmillan, 1965), p. 465.

151. *Ibid.*, p. 474.

Chapter 7. Green Revolutions

1. Colin Clark, quoted in M.K. Bennett, *The World's Food* (New York, Harper, 1954).

2. David Norman Balaam, 'The political economy of international food production and distribution' (Dissertation, University of California, Santa Barbara, 1978), p. 26.
3. Thomas Poleman, 'World food: a perspective', *Science,* 188 (May 1975), pp. 561–8.
4. United States Department of Agriculture, *The World Food Budget, 1963 and 1966,* USDA Economic Research Service, October 1961, p. 5.
5. FAO, *Third World Food Survey* (Rome, FAO, 1963).
6. A. J. Jowett, 'China: the demographic disaster', in J. I. Clarke *et al.* (eds), *Population and Disaster,* (Oxford, Basil Blackwell, 1989).
7. 'Population', *Time Magazine,* January 11 1960, pp. 19–22.
8. The Danish, Finnish, and Norwegian editions were translated from the Swedish edition. Vogt, *People! Challenge to Survival* (London, Victor Gollancz, 1961 (1960)); Alfred Sauvy, *Fertility and Survival: Population Problems from Malthus to Mao Tse-tung* (New York, Criterion, 1961); Fairfield Osborn (ed.), *Our Crowded Planet: Essays on the Pressures of Population* (London, Doubleday, 1962); *Food for Life, Food for Thought: The World Must Eat* (New York, Study Guide Series, 1962); Stewart Udall, *The Quiet Crisis* (New York, Holt, 1963).
9   '1960: the world rediscovers Malthus', in Garret Hardin (ed.), *Population, Evolution and Birth Control: A Collage of Controversial Readings* (San Francisco, W.H. Freeman, 1964), pp. 46–7.
10. Adam Rome, *The Bulldozer in the Countryside: Suburban Sprawl and the Rise of American Environmentalism* (Cambridge, Cambridge University Press, 2001), p. 142.
11. Edward Higbee, *The Squeeze: Cities Without Space* (New York, Morrow, 1960). Quoted in Rome, *Bulldozer in the Countryside,* p. 143.
12. Harry Harrison, *Make Room, Make Room* (New York, Doubleday, 1966), *passim.*
13. Julian Huxley, *Essays of a Humanist* (London, Chatto & Windus, 1964), p. 241.
14. *Ibid.,* p. 244.
15. *Ibid.,* 1964, p. 245.
16. Jean-Paul Sartre, interview in *Le Monde,* translated and reproduced in *Encounter,* June 1964.
17. *The Hungry Planet* (New York, Macmillan, 1965) was essentially a translation of his 1962 Swedish book, *Mat för Miljarder* (*Food for Billions*), which in turn was a compilation of his lectures on Swedish radio from the mid-1950s and 1960–61.
18. Harry Martinson, *Aniara: A Review of Man in Time and Space,* translated into English by Stephen Klass and Leif Sjöberg (Södra Sanby, Vekerum Förlag, 1991), p. 37. In Martinson's poem, the Mima is a hypersensitive instrument conveying knowledge to the lost travellers aboard the spaceship Aniara.
19. Georg Borgström, *The Hungry Planet* (New York, Macmillan, 1965), pp. 7–26; cf. Borgström, 'The human biosphere and its biological and chemical limitations', in

Mortimer P. Starr (ed.), *Global Impacts of Applied Microbiology* (New York, John Wiley & Sons, 1964).

20. Borgström, *The Hungry Planet*, pp. 4–37.

21. *Ibid.*, pp. 25–6; Borgström, *Brännpunkter* (Stockholm, Trevi, 1971), pp. 234, 238.

22. Borgström, *The Hungry Planet*, p. 28.

23. Lester R. Brown, *Who Will Feed China? Wake-up Call for a Small Planet* (New York, W.W. Norton, 1995).

24. Juan Martinez-Alier, *Ecological Economics: Energy, Environment and Society* (Oxford, Blackwell 1993 (1987)), pp. iv–v, 179–81.

25. Borgström, *The Hungry Planet*, p. 43.

26. *Ibid.*, p. 29.

27. *Ibid.*, pp. 281–2; Borgström, *Brännpunkter*, pp. 235–8; 'Spaceship Earth: are we really in danger?', *Observer Review*, 5 March 1972.

28. Georg Borgström (ed.), *Fish as Food*, 4 vols, (New York, Academic Press, 1961–65), vol. I, p. viii.

29. Borgström, *Fish as Food*; Georg Borgström, *Revolution i världsfisket*, (Stockholm, LTs Förlag, 1966); Georg Borgström and A.J. Heighway (eds), *Atlantic Ocean Fisheries* (London, Fishing News, 1962); Georg Borgström, *Japan's World Success in Fishing* (London, Fishing News, 1964), *passim*.

30. Martinez-Alier, *Ecological Economics*.

31. Borgström, *The Hungry Planet*, pp. 27–8.

32. David Grigg, *The World Food Problem*, 2nd edn, (Oxford, Blackwell, 1999 (1993)), p. 268; Göran Djurfeldt, *Mera mat: att brödföda en växande befolkning* (Lund, Arkiv, 2001), p. 29.

33. Borgström, *The Hungry Planet*, p. 33.

34. *Ibid.*, pp. 31–9; Borgström, 'Fish in world nutrition', in *Fish as Food*, Vol. II, ch. 7.

35. Mathis Wackernagel and William E. Rees, *Our Ecological Footprint: Reducing Human Impact on the Earth* (Philadelphia, PA, New Society Publishers, 1996), pp. 7–30.

36. Borgström, *The Hungry Planet*, pp. 70–86; Borgström, *Brännpunkter*, pp. 310–12.

37. George Woodwell, interview by author, Woods Hole, MA, 23 October 1995.

38. Martinez-Alier, *Ecological Economics*, pp. 232–3.

39. Borgström, *The Hungry Planet*, p. 51.

40. *Ibid.*, p. 51.

41. Borgström, 'View Point', radio discussion with Thomas Greer, 18 February 1962, Michigan State Radio Network, Voice Library, Michigan State University; Borgström, *Brännpunkter*, p. 337.

42. Borgström, *The Hungry Planet*, p. xii.

43. Richard N. Cooper, *The Economics of Interdependence: Economic Policy in the Atlantic Community* (New York, McGraw-Hill, 1968); Robert O. Keohane and Joseph S. Nye, *Power and Interdependence: World Politics in Transition* (Boston, Little, Brown, 1977); Edward L. Morse, 'The politics of interdependence', *International Organization*, 23 (1969), p. 318; Richard Rosecrance and A. Stein, 'Interdependence: myth or reality?', *International Organization*, 35 (1973), pp. 553–60; Oran R. Young, 'Interdependencies in world politics', *International Journal*, 24 (1968–9), pp. 726–50.

44. E.g. Lester Brown, *The Interdepence of Nations* (New York, Foreign Policy Association, 1972); Paul Ehrlich and Anne Ehrlich, *Population, Resources, Environment: Issues in Human Ecology* (San Francisco, W.H. Freeman, 1970); Alvin Toffler, *Future Shock* (New York, Random House, 1970).

45. Borgström, *The Hungry Planet*, p. xviii.

46. *Ibid.*, p. 71.

47. Borgström, *Överflödets kris* (Stockholm, Stockholms FN-förening, 1966), p. 12

48. Georg Borgström, *Too Many: A Study of Earth's Biological Limitations* (New York, Macmillan, 1969), p. 23.

49. Borgström, *Gränser för vår tillvaro* (Stockholm, LTs Förlag, 1964), p. 269.

50. John H. Fremlin, 'How many people can the world support?', *New Scientist*, no. 415, 29 October 1964, p. 285; cf. John H. Fremlin, *Be Fruitful and Multiply: Life at the Limits of Population*, London, Rupert Hart-Davis, 1972, chapters 6–7.

51. Fremlin, *Be Fruitful and Multiply*, pp. vii–x, 104, 157–72.

52. Borgström, *Mat för miljarder* (Stockholm, LTs Förlag, 1962), pp. 277–82.

53. Borgström, *Gränser för vår tillvaro*, p. 248.

54. Borgström, *Överflödets kris* (Stockholm, Stockholms FN-förening, 1966), pp. 17–18.

55. Borgström, *Gränser för vår tillvaro*, pp. 17–24, 269.

56. Borgström, *The Hungry Planet*, p. 443; cf. Borgström, *Mat för miljarder*, p. 273; Jonas Anshelm, 'Bland trollkarlar och demoner: Om kärnkraftsdiskursen i Sverige under 1950-talet', *Vest*, 9:1 (1996), pp. 17–29

57. Borgström, *Jorden–vårt öde: Kan en permanent världshunger avvärjas?* (Stockholm, Forum, 1953), p. 38; Borgström, *The Hungry Planet*, p. 440; Borgström, *Focal Points: A Global Food Strategy* (New York, Macmillan: 1971), pp. 191–2.

58. Borgström, *The Hungry Planet*, p. 468.

59. Adlai Stevenson, 'Strengthening the international development institutions', *The Papers of Adlai E. Stevenson: Vol. 8, Ambassador to the United Nations, 1961–1965* (Boston, Little, Brown, 1979), p. 828; Richard B. Norgaard, *Development Betrayed: The End of Progress and a Coevolutionary Revisioning of the Future* (London, Routledge, 1994), p. 204; J.Y. Garb, 'The use and misuse of the Whole Earth image', *Whole Earth Review*, March 1985, pp. 18–25.

60. E.g. I Peter 5:4, Revelation 3:11. In the King James version, Peter's 'victory crown' is translated 'crown of glory.'

61. Borgström, *The Hungry Planet*, p. 474.

62. Georg Borgström's *Too Many: A Study of Earth's Biological Limitations* (New York, Macmillan, 1969) was to a large extent a compilation and elaboration of Swedish radio lectures broadcast between 1961 and 1963, together with some lectures given in the United States and some printed articles. In it, Borgström continued to elaborate his warnings of the resource–population crisis as the greatest threat to humanity's future. It is basically a translation of his Swedish book *Gränser för vår tillvaro* (*Limitations to our Existence*). However, *Too Many* has a different epilogue from *Limitations to our Existence*. It was published in five Swedish and two English editions and was translated into Danish, Norwegian, and Finnish.

63. Borgström, *Brännpunkter* (Stockholm, Trevi, 1971), p. 340.

64. 'Ohyggliga fakta: Ditt barnbarn måste hungra', *Aftonbladet*, 8 September 1964; 'Om femton år är allt slut!', *Aftonbladet*, 9 September 1964; 'Världsproblemet ingen vågar tänka: Vattnet tar slut', *Aftonbladet*, 10 September 1964; Sista reserven för en svältande jord: Vi måste äta kackerlackor', *Aftonbladet*, 11 September 1964.

65. 'Debatt vid remiss av statsverkspropositionen', *AK protokoll*, no. 4, 1965, pp. 39–42.

66. Borgström, *Gränser för vår tillvaro*, p. 253.

67. Vogt, *People!*, ch. 3.

68. Spencer R. Weart, *Nuclear Fear: A History of Images* (Cambridge, MA, Harvard University Press, 1988), pp. 132–3, 253–8.

69. Roland Barthes, *Elements of Semiology* (New York, Hill and Wang, 1995 (1964)), pp. 35–42, 89–98.

70. Borgström, *The Hungry Planet*, p. xix.

71. Donald Worster, *Nature's Economy: A History of Ecological Ideas*, 2nd edn (Cambridge, Cambridge University Press, 1994), pp. 346–7.

72. Borgström, *The Hungry Planet*, p. viii.

73. *Ibid.*; cf. Borgström, *Världens mat* (Stockholm, Lindblads, 1968), p. 357; Borgström, *Focal Points*, p. 258; Borgström, *Brännpunkter*, p. 236.

74. Borgström, *The Hungry Planet*, p. viii.

75. Borgström, *Gränser för vår tillvaro*, pp. 240, 271.

76. Paul Ehrlich, 'Eco-catastrophe', reprinted in Ralph S. Clem *et al.* (eds), *No Room for Man* (Totowa, NJ, Littlefield, Adams, & Co., 1970).

77. *Ibid.*

78. Clifford Geertz, *Agricultural Involution: The Process of Ecological Change in Indonesia* (Berkeley, University of California Press, 1963); Ester Boserup, *The Conditions of Agricultural Growth: The Economics of Agrarian Change under Population Change* (London, Allen & Unwin, 1965); Norgaard, *Development Betrayed*, p. 199; Janken Myrdal, 'Miljökrisens roll i historien', *Historisk Tidskrift*, 2 (1997), pp. 268–9.

79. Norgaard, *Development Betrayed*, pp. 53–4.

80. Frantz Fanon, *The Wretched of the Earth* (Harmondsworth, Penguin, 1967).

81. Norgaard, *Development Betrayed*, p. 54.

82. Borgström, *Glodujaca Planeta* (Warsaw, Panstwowe Wydawnictwo Rolnicze i Lesne, 1971), pp. 7–17.

83. R. Buckminster Fuller, 'How to maintain man as a success in the universe' (1965), in R. Buckminster Fuller, *Utopia or Oblivion: The Prospects for Humanity* (Toronto, Bantam Books, 1969), p. 250.

84. Dale Harpsteadt, interview by author, East Lansing, MI, 6 October 1995.

85. Borgström, *Brännpunkter*, p. 318; David Brower, 'Preface', in Paul R. Ehrlich, *The Population Bomb* (New York, Ballantine, 1968).

86. Population Division of the Department of Economic and Social Affairs of the United Nations Secretariat, *World Population Prospects: The 2000 Revision and World Urbanization Prospects: The 2001 Revision*, http://esa.un.org/unpp, 3 January 2003.

87. Sam Cole, 'The global future debate 1965–1976', in Christopher Freeman and Marie Jahoda (eds), *World Futures: The Great Debate* (London, Robertson, 1978), p. 23.

88. Brower, 'Preface'.

89. Lester Brown, 'The fuel that makes inflation soar: people – more people – cause scarcities the world over', *Los Angeles Times*, 28 March 1976.

90. U Thant (1969), quoted in Donella H. Meadows *et al.*, *The Limits to Growth: A Report for the Conservation Club of Rome's Project on the Predicament of Mankind* (New York, Universe books, 1972), p. 17; Cf. *Public Papers of the Secretaries-general of the United Nations: Vol. 8, U Thant, 1968–1971* (New York, Columbia University Press, 1977), pp. 274–82, 310–13, 408–12.

91. Stanley Kubrick and Arthur C. Clarke, *2001: A Space Odyssey*, Burbank, CA, Metro-Goldwyn-Mayer/Warner Home Video 1999 (1968).

92. C. P. Snow, *The State of Siege*, Scribner, New York, 1971, (1969), pp.19–20.

93. M. King Hubbert, *Resources and Man* (San Francisco, National Academy of Sciences and National Research Council, Freeman, 1969).

94. Paul R. Ehrlich, *The Population Bomb* (New York, Ballantine, 1968).

95. *Ibid.*, p. 28.

96. Study of Critical Environmental Problems, *Man's Impact on the Global Environment: Assessment and Recommendations for Action*, Report of the Study of Critical Environmental Problems (Cambridge, MA, 1970).

97. David Pepper, *The Roots of Modern Environmentalism* (London, Routledge, 1989), p. 100.

98. Roy Beck and Leon Kolankiewicz (2000), 'The environmental movement's retreat from advocating U.S. population stabilization (1970–1998): a first draft history', in Otis L. Graham Jr. (ed.), *Environmental Politics and Policy, 1960s–1990s* (University Park, PA, Pennsylvania State UP, 2000), p.124; Christopher Lewis, 'Progress and apocalypse: science and the end of the modern world', (Dissertation, 2 vols, University of Minnesota, 1991), p. 272.

99. Ehrlich, *Population Bomb*, p. xi.

100. *Ibid.*
101. 'Ecology's angry lobbyist: Dr. Paul Ehrlich argues that the chief cause of pollution is overpopulation', *Look*, 21 April 1970, pp. 42–4.
102. Borgström, *Gränser för vår tillvaro*, p. 258.
103. *Ibid.*, pp. 259–60.
104. Georg Borgström and Greta Borgström (eds), *Malthus – Om befolkningsfrågan* (Stockholm, LTs Förlag, 1969), p. 201.
105. Garrett Hardin, 'The tragedy of the commons', *Science*, 162 (1968), pp. 1243–48.
106. Barry Commoner, *The Closing Circle: Nature, Man, and Technology* (New York, 1971), p. 114 and *passim*; Michael Egan provides a very informative analysis of the controversy between Commoner and Ehrlich in 'The new Jeremiads: science, information, and environmentalism in the Commoner–Ehrlich debate', Paper presented at the American Society for Environmental History annual meeting, Denver, 2002; Pepper, *Roots of Modern Environmentalism*, pp. 20–21.
107. Ehrlich, *Population Bomb*, pp. 66–7.
108. Ehrlich and Ehrlich, *Population, Resources, Environment*, p. 201.
109. *Ibid.*
110. Barry Commoner, 'Survival in the environmental–population crisis', in S. Fred Singer (ed.), *Is There an Optimum Level of Population?* (New York, 1971), pp. 97–8.
111. Barry Commoner, *The Closing Circle*, p. 255.
112. Paul Ehrlich and John P. Holdren, 'Dispute', *Environment*, 14, April 1972, p. 31.
113. Paul Ehrlich, 'Impact of population growth', *Science*, 171 (1971), pp. 1212–17.
114. Pete Seeger, '*The Closing Circle*: readers comment', *Environment*, 14, June 1972, p. 40.
115. *Ibid.*
116. Cole, 'Global future debate', p. 9; Thomas J. McCormick, *America's Half-Century: United States Foreign Policy in the Cold War and After* (Baltimore, Johns Hopkins University Press, 1995 (1989)), p. 99; Giovanni Arrighi, *The Long Twentieth Century: Money, Power and the Origins of Our Times* (London, Verso, 1994), pp. 229–308; Robert Boyer, *The Regulation School: A Critical Introduction* (New York, Columbia University Press, 1989), pp. xiii–ii.
117. Editors of *The Ecologist, A Blueprint for Survival*, (Harmondsworth, 1972).
118. Meadows *et al.*, *Limits to Growth*, p. 10.
119. *Ibid.*, *passim*.
120. Cole, 'Global future debate', p. 11.
121. Meadows *et al.*, *Limits to Growth*, p. 23
122. R. Golub and J. Townsend, 'Malthus, multinationals and the Club of Rome', *Social Studies of Science*, 7 (1997), pp. 202–22.
123. Tor-Ragnar Gerholm, *Futurum exaktum: den tekniska utmaningen* (Stockholm, Aldus/Bonnier, 1972), pp. 6–7.

124. John H. Perkins, *Geopolitics and the Green Revolution: Wheat, Genes and the Cold War* (Oxford, Oxford University Press, 1997), p. 244.

125. World Resources Institute, 1996, p. 226; Mostafa K. Tolba (ed.) *The World Environment, 1972–1992: Two Decades of Challenge* (London, UNEP/Chapman & Hall, 1992), p. 296.

126. Norman Borlaug, 'The Green Revolution: peace and humanity', in *The Nobel Prizes, Presentations Biography and Lectures* (Stockholm, Almqvist & Wiksell, 1970), pp. 226–45; 'Spaceship Earth: are we really in danger?', *Observer Review*, 5 March 1972; see also 'Two experts see world headed for starvation', *The Sunday News*, Detroit, 30 April 1972; 'Can our World escape starvation?', *The State Journal*, 23 April 1972.

127. Borgström, *Brännpunkter*, pp. 232–3.

128. Borgström, *Focal Points: A Global Food Strategy* (New York, Macmillan: 1971), pp. 172–201, 231–8.

129. 'Spaceship Earth: are we really in danger?', *Observer Review*, 5 March 1972. Borgström apparently liked the interview, and distributed it to friends such as Gunnar Jarring.

130. *Ibid.*

131. *Ibid.* See also Borgström, *Focal Points*, pp. 172–201.

132. *Ibid.*

133. 'Professor Georg Borgström (den viktigaste svensken i världen) varnar mänskligheten', *Expressen*, 28 January 1967.

134. Cf. Donald J. Bogue, 'The prospects for world population control' (1966), reprinted in Bogue, *Principles of Demography* (New York, 1969), pp. 828–35.

135. 'Jordbruksrevolution i Asien', *Svenska Dagbladet*, 30 July 1968; 'Nytt ris får genomgripande sociala följder: Världens folkökning under kontroll 1990', *Sydsvenska Dagbladet*, 25 August 1968; Gunnar Alexandersson, 'Dagens u-länder morgondagens massmarknader', *Industriförbundets tidskrift*, 9 (1968), pp. 16–22; 'Professorsord', *Dagens Nyheter*, 15 July 1968; 'Borgström anklagas: Överdriver', *Arbetet*, 19 November 1968; 'Alexandersson: Borgströms siffror gamla', *Svenska Dagbladet*, 24 November 1968; Alexandersson, 'Speglingar av befolkningsfrågan', *Svenska Dagbladet*, 12 May 1969; Jan-Olof Drangert, 'Asiens jordbruksproblem', *Svenska Dagbladet*, 10 August 1968.

136. 'Svenska professorer i bitter strid om världens framtid', *Aftonbladet*, 17 August 1968; Borgström, 'Herr Alexanderssons vårdslöshet med fakta', reply to *Arbetet*, BF, CHS.

137. Borgström, *Too Many* (1969), p. 31.

138. *Ibid.*, p. 125; Borgström, *Brännpunkter*, p. 370.

139. Daniel, 5:27 King James version.

140. Borgström, *Too Many* (1969), p. 49.

141. Tom Leander, 'U-hjälpens småsmulor', *Svenska Dagbladet*, 26 March 1969.

142. Borgström, *Focal Points*, pp. 10, 258.

143. *Ibid.*, p. 258.

144. *Ibid.*, pp. 244–58.

145. Borgström, *Brännpunkter*, p. 313.

146. Borgström, *Gränser för vår tillvaro*, p. 267.

147. *Ibid.*, p. 265.

148. Borgström, 'Answer to Expressen'.

149. Borgström, *Brännpunkter*, pp. 341–65. This chapter concluded the book in *Brännpunkter*, the Swedish edition of *Focal Points*. In the USA it was added to the second edition of *Too Many* (1971), but it was excluded from the English edition of *Focal Points*.

150. Borgström, *Gränser för vår tillvaro*, p. 270; Borgström, *The Hungry Planet*, p. xx.

151. Borgström, *The Hungry Planet*, p. 68; Borgström, *Gränser för vår tillvaro*, pp. 247–8, 270; Borgström, *Too Many* (1969), pp. 20–21.

152. Borgström, *Too Many* (1969), p. 20.

153. Borgström, *Gränser för vår tillvaro*, p. 270; Borgström, *Too Many* (1969), p. 20.

154. Plus sign denotes net exports; minus sign denotes net imports. Figures for 1973 are estimates.

155. Balaam, 'Political economy', p. 33.

156. Bogue, *Principles of Demography*.

157. Balaam, 'Political economy', pp. 59–61.

158. *Ibid.*, p. 61.

159. *Ibid.*, p. 33; D. Gale Johnson, *World Food Problems and Prospects* (Washington, DC, American Enterprise Institute for Public Policy Research, 1975); Poleman, 'World Food'; Fred Sanderson, *The Great Food Fumble* (Washington, DC, The Brookings Institution, 1975).

160. United States House of Representatives, Committee on International Relations, *Use of U.S. Food Resources for Diplomatic Purposes – An Examination of the Issues* (Washington, DC, US Government Printing Office, 1977); Emma Rothschild, 'Food politics', *Foreign Affairs*, 54:2 (1976); William Schneider, *Food, Foreign Policy, and Raw Materials Cartels* (New York, Crane, Russak & Co., 1976); 'U.S. food power: ultimate weapon in world politics?' *Business Week*, 15 December 1975; Balaam, 'Political economy', p. 6.

161. ODI Briefing Paper, 1994 (3), September 1994.

162. Rothschild, 'Food politics', pp. 285–307.

163. United Nations, 'Assessment of the world food situation: present and future', E/Conf. 65/3, United Nations World Food Conference, November 1974, UNA.

164. Richard N. Cooper, *Economics of Interdependence*; Morse, 'Politics of interdependence'; Young, 'Interdependencies in world politics'.

165. Roger Hansen, 'The "crisis of interdependence": where do we go from here?', in *The U.S. and the World Development: Agenda for Action* (Praeger, New York, 1976), pp. 43–8.

276 *Notes to Chapter 7*

166. Keohane and Nye, *Power and Interdependence*; Rosecrance and Stein, 'Interdependence: myth or reality?'.
167. Björn-Ola Linnér and Henrik Selin, 'The quest for sustainability: the legacy of the Stockholm Conference 1972', paper presented at the International Studies Association, Portland, OR, 1 March 2003.
168. E.g. Rolf Edberg, Hans Palmstierna, Erik Dahmén, and Georg Borgström
169. Björn-Ola Linnér and Henrik Selin, 'Sustainable development and globalization: the Stockholm legacy', paper presented at the Nature and Culture Seminar, University of Kansas, 2 February 2002.
170. Lynton Keith Caldwell, *International Environmental Policy: From the Twentieth to the Twenty-first Century*, 3rd edn (Durham, NC, Duke University Press, 1996), pp. 53–6.
171. Bengt Torbrink, 'Min jord, din jord eller vår jord?', *Göteborgs-Posten*, 18 October 1971.
172. *Report of the United Nations Conference on the Human Environment: Stockholm, 5–16 June 1972*, United Nations, A/CONF: 48/14/Rev.1, pp. 36–67.
173. 'What happened at Stockholm: a special report', *Science and Public Affairs: Bulletin of the Atomic Scientists*, 28 (1972), p. 36.
174. Olof Palme, 'Speech by the Prime Minister at the plenary session of the UN Conference on the Human Environment; 6th June', in *Documents on Swedish Foreign Policy 1972*, New Series I:C:22, (Stockholm, Royal Ministry for Foreign Affairs, 1973), pp. 48–53.
175. Henrik Selin and Björn-Ola Linnér, 'The thirty-year quest for global sustainability: a historical look at the 1972 Stockholm conference and beyond', Harvard University, Belfer Center for Science and International Affairs, Discussion Paper, forthcoming 2003.
176. Aldous Huxley, *Brave New World Revisited* (London, Chatto & Windus, 1958), p. 33.
177. *Ibid.*, p. 15–16.
178. *Ibid.*, p. 172.
179. William and Paul Paddock, *Famine – 1975! America's Decision: Who will Survive?* (Boston, Little, Brown and Company, 1967).
180. Hardin, 'Tragedy of the commons', p. 1248.
181. Houri Bumédienne, quoted in *Washington Post*, 17 July 1977.
182. Garrett Hardin, 'Living on a lifeboat', *Bioscience*, 24 (1974), pp. 561–8.
183. George R. Lucas Jr and Thomas W. Ogletree (eds), *Lifeboat Ethics: The Moral Dilemmas of World Hunger* (New York, Harper & Row, 1976).
184. Ehrlich, *The Population Bomb*, pp. 165–6.
185. *Ibid.*, p. xi.
186. Borgström, *Too Many* (1969), p. 31.
187. 'Professor Georg Borgström (den viktigaste svensken i världen) varnar mänskligheten', *Expressen*, 28 January 1967.

188. Emin Tengström, interview by author, Göteborg, 27 April 1994. Borgström received the J.A. Wahlberg Gold Medal from His Majesty King Carl XVI Gustaf in 1974. He was awarded the medal by the Swedish Society for Anthropology and Geography 'in recognition of his extensive research on the food situation in the world'.

189. 'Svensk USA-professor om rymdmiljarder: Vad farao skall vi på månen att göra?', *Göteborgs Tidningen*, 23 August 1962.

190. Tom Selander, 'Katastrofhotet', *Svenska Dagbladet*, 31 October 1971.

191. 'Den gröna vågen', *Göteborgs Handels- och Sjöfartstidning*, 15 June 1972.

192. Rolf Edberg, *Spillran av ett moln: anteckningar i färdaboken* (Stockholm, Norstedt, 1966), p. 141; Palmstierna, 1967, p. 49; Björn Gillberg, *Mordet på framtiden: en uppgörelse med den politiska och ekonomiska kortsiktigheten* (Stockholm, Wahlström & Widstrand, 1973), pp. 27–33.

193. Carl-Göran Hedén, interview by author, Stockholm, 8 June 1994.

194. Bengt Torbrink, 'Min jord, din jord eller vår jord?', *Göteborgs-Posten*, 18 October 1971.

195. Borgström, 'Answer to *Expressen*', BF, CHS.

196. Ron Eyerman and Andrew Jamison, *Social Movements: A Cognitive Approach* (Cambridge, Polity Press, 1991), p. 98; Håkan Thörn, *Modernitet, sociologi och sociala rörelser* (Göteborg, Kompendiet, 1997), pp. 156–7.

197. Svante Lundberg, Sven-Axel Månsson, Hans Welander, *Demonstranter: En sociologisk studie* (Stockholm, PAN/Norstedts, 1970); 'Analys av demonstrant: Moralisk plikt att delta', *Dagens Nyheter*, 16 August 1969.

198. Hartvig Sætra, *Den økopolitiske socialismen* (Oslo, Pax, 1973), p. 38.

199. 'Georg Borgström revisited', *Gyldendals aktuelle magasin*, no. 2, 1979.

200. George Woodwell, interview by author, Woods Hole, MA 1995 October 23.

201. *Science Citation Index: An International Disciplinary Index to Literature of Science*, Philadelphia, Institute for Scientific Information, 1947–54, 1955–64, 1965–69, 1970–74, 'Borgström, G.'; Ehrlich, 'Population and panaceas: a technological perspective', *Bioscience*, 19 (1969), pp. 1065–71; Ehrlich, 'Impact of Population Growth'; Frances M. Lappé, 'The politics of protein', *America's Biological Teachers*, 35 (1973), pp. 254–9.

202. *Social Sciences Citation Index: An International Multidisciplinary Index to the Literature of the Social, Behavioral and Related Sciences*, Philadelphia, Institute for Scientific Information, PA, 1966–70, 1971–75: 'Borgström, G.'

203. Borgström, 'Balansakt för ekologer och ekonomer', *Göteborgsposten*, 14 March 1979.

204. Commoner, *The Closing Circle*, p. 56.

205. Lester Brown, *Seeds of Change: the Green Revolution and Development in the 1970's*, (New York, Praeger, 1970), pp. 112, 121–2.

206. Meadows *et al.*, *Limits to Growth*, p.178.

207. Herman E. Daly, 'Toward a stationary-state economy', in John Harte and Robert Socolow (eds), *The Patient Earth* (New York, Holt, Rinehart, and Winston, 1971), p. 236–7.

208. Frances Moore Lappé, *Diet for a Small Planet*, revised edn (New York, Ballantine Books, 1975 (1971)).

209. Frances Moore Lappé and Joseph Collins, *Food First: Beyond the Myth of Scarcity* (Boston, Houghton-Mifflin, 1977).

210. The World Food Council, *Assessment of the World Food Situation and Outlook*, WFC/17/Rev. 1, 7 June 1976.

211. Editorial, *Wall Street Journal*, 24 October 1975.

212. Herman Kahn, William Brown and Leon Martel, *The Next 200 Years: A Scenario for America and the World* (London, Associated Business Programmes, 1977).

213. Beck and Kolankiewicz, 'The environmental movement's retreat', p. 123–51; cf. T. Michael Maher, 'How and why journalists avoid the population–enviroment connection', *Population and Environment*, 18:4 (1997).

214. David Harvey, 'Population, resources and the ideology of science', *Economic Geography*, 50 (1974), pp. 256–77.

215. FAO, *Rome Declaration on World Food Security and World Food Summit Plan of Action, World Food Summit, 13–17 November 1996* (Rome, 1996).

216. United Nations Population Fund, *The State of World Population 1998*, E/31,000/1998 (New York, 1998), p. 1.

217. Population Division of the Department of Economic and Social Affairs of the United Nations Secretariat. *World Population Prospects: The 2000 Revision*, ESA/P/WP.165, 2001, pp. 7–8, 13.

Chapter 8. The Return of Neo-Malthusianism

1. World Resource Institute, *World Resources 1998–99: A Guide to the Global Environment* (New York, Oxford University Press, 1998), pp. 152–3; FAO, *The State of Food Insecurity in the World 2001* (Rome, FAO, 2001), ch. 1.

2. FAO, *The State of Food Insecurity in the World 2003, Monitoring Progress Towards the World Food Summit and Millennium Development Goals* (Rome, FAO, 2003).

3. FAO, *The State of Food Insecurity in the World 2001*, p. 2. The survey estimated the households and not the number of individuals.

4. FAO, *The State of Food Insecurity in the World 1999* (Rome, FAO, 1999), p. 15.

5. FAO, *The State of Food Insecurity in the World 2001*, pp. 2–11.

6. *Ibid.*, p. 2.

7. Population Division of the Department of Economic and Social Affairs of the United Nations Secretariat, *World Population Prospects: The 2000 Revision*, ESA/P/WP.165, 2001.

8. World Bank, *World Development Report 1999/2000: Entering the 21st Century* (New York, Oxford University Press, 2001); World Resources Institute, *World Resources 2000–2001: People and Ecosystems* (New York, Oxford University Press, 2000), *passim*.

9. Mahendra Shah and Maurice Strong, *Food in the 21st Century: from Science to Sustainable Agriculture* (Washington, DC, CGIAR, 1999), p. 9.

10. G.J. Persley and M.M. Lantin (eds), *Agricultural Biotechnology and the Poor* (Washington, DC, CGIAR, 2000), *passim*.

11. BBC World News, 'Africa "needs GM crops to survive"', 14 May 2002.

12. 'Kunskapens krona', Swedish Television Channel 1, 20 July 2002, statement by Kristina Glimmelius.

13. BBC World News, 'Zimbabwe turns away US food aid', 31 May 2002; 'Zimbabwe urged to take GM grain', 24 July 2002; 'Zambia turns down GM aid', 17 August 2002.

14. E.g. Friends of the Earth, 'Zambian GM food aid decision highlights global problems', Press Release, http://www.foe.co.uk/pubsinfo/infoteam/press-rel/2002/20020901103634.html, 1 September 2002.

15. Daniel Charles, *Lords of the Harvest: Biotech, Big Money, and the Future of Food* (Cambridge, MA, Perseus Publishing, 2001), p. 262.

16. Monsanto, 'Biotechnology: A promise for the future' (St Louis, MO, Monsanto, 1996).

17. Charles F. Barton, Director of Public Affairs at Monsanto, interview by author, St Louis, MO, 6 May 2002; Charles, *Lords of the Harvest*, p. 222.

18. Fulfilling our pledge, 2000–2001 report' (St Louis, MO, Monsanto, 2001); 'Biotechnology: feeding our future', 'A world of food and agriculture: biotechnology benefits', 'Biotechnology: solutions for tomorrow's world', 'Sustainability: seeds for thought', 'The promise of plant biotechnology', booklets, (St Louis, MO, Monsanto, undated). Cf. International Food Information Council Foundation, 'Food biotechnology benefits and products', 'The environment', leaflets (1999); Charles, *Lords of the Harvest*, ch. 17.

19. Monsanto, 'Conservation tillage: how new farming practices promise a better world', booklet (St Louis, MO, Monsanto, 2001).

20. Monsanto, 'The promise of plant biotechnology'.

21. Charles, *Lords of the Harvest*, p. 222.

22. The International Food Information Council, 'Communication tenets for consumer acceptance of food biotechnology', memorandum, 1997.

23. Charles, *Lords of the Harvest*, pp. 262–64.

24. FAO, *Rome Declaration on World Food Security and World Food Summit Plan of Action*, World Food Summit, *13–17 November 1996* (Rome, 1996).

25. G.J. Persley and M.M. Lantin (eds), *Agricultural Biotechnology and the Poor* (Washington, DC, CGIAR, 2000), *passim*; Michael Lipton, 'Reviving global poverty reduction: what role for genetically modified plants?', CGIAR Crawford Lectures (Washington DC, CGIAR, 1999).

26. Vandana Shiva and Ingunn Moser (eds), *Biopolitics: A Feminist and Ecological Reader on Biotechnology* (London, Zed Books, 1995); Gerald Nelson and C. Nelson, *Genetically Modified Organisms in Agriculture: Economics and Politics* (San Diego, Academic Press, 2001); United Nations Development Programme, *Human Development Report: Consumption for Human Development* (New York, 1998); L.A. Jackson, *The Journal of World Intellectual Property*, 3 (2000), pp. 825–48; O. Das, *The Journal of World Intellectual Property*, 3 (2000), pp. 577–88.

27. Vandana Shiva, 'A civil society perspective', in Birgitta Rydhagen and Carin Dackman (eds), *Proceedings of Dolly and the Bean: Understanding Biotechnology in Broader Contexts, International conference, Luleå, 19–21 January 1999* (Luleå, Sweden, Luleå Univ. of Technology, 2000), pp. 42–50.

28. *Ibid.*

29. *Ibid.*

30. Tewolde Gebre Egziabher, quoted in Panos Institute, *Food for All: Can Hunger be Halved?* (London, Panos Institute, 2001), p. 26.

31. Ingo Potrykus, quoted in Annika Nilsson, *Genetically Modified Crops: Why? Why Not? Report from an International Conference in Stockholm, May 14–15, 2001* (Stockholm, Royal Swedish Academy of Agriculture and Forestry, 2002), p. 52.

32. Gregory E. Pence, *Designer Food: Mutant Harvest or Breadbasket of the World?* (Lanham, MD, Rowman & Littlefield, 2002), p. 141.

33. Bruno Latour, 'Guerre des mondes–offres de paix', in Bruno Latour, *Das Parlament der Dinge: Für eine politische Ökologie* (Frankfurt, Suhrkamp, 2001); Isabelle Stengers, Cosmopolitiques, 1–7 (Paris, La Découverte, 1997).

34. United Nations Environment Programme, *Malmö Ministerial Declaration* (Nairobi, UNEP, 2000).

35. United Nations, *United Nations Millennium Declaration*, 55/2 (New York, United Nations).

36. FAO, *The State of Food Insecurity in the World 2001*, p. 6.

37. Amartya Sen, *Inequality Reexamined* (Oxford, Oxford University Press, 1992), *passim*; Björn-Ola Linnér and Jan Lundqvist, 'Ny strategi för världens vatten', *Göteborgs-Posten*, 22 January 2000.

38. Lipton, 'Reviving global poverty reduction'.

39. Panos Institute, *Food for All*, pp. 26–7.

40. Shiva, 'A civil society perspective', p. 50.

41. Leed T. Hickey, Amber N. Hafeez, Hannah Robinson, Scott A. Jackson, Soraya C.M. Leal-Bertioli, Mark Tester, Caixia Gao et al., 'Breeding crops to feed 10 billion', *Nature Biotechnology*, 37:7 (2019), p. 744.

42. FAO, *Food and Agriculture Statistics* (FAO, 2020) http://www.fao.org/food-agriculture-statistics/en/ (Accessed 29 June 2020).

43. Joseph Poore and Thomas Nemecek, 'Reducing food's environmental impacts through producers and consumers', *Science* (2018), pp. 987–92.

44. FAO, *The State of Food and Agriculture 2019. Moving Forward on Food Loss and Waste Reduction* (Rome, FAO, 2019).

45. UNEP, *Food Waste Index Report 2021* (Nairobi, UNEP, 2021).

46. Population Division of the Department of Economic and Social Affairs, *World Population Prospects: The 2022 Revision*, https://population.un.org/wpp/ (Accessed 28 November 2022).

47. Xin-Zhong Liang, You Wu, Robert G. Chambers, Daniel L. Schmoldt et al., 'Determining climate effects on US total agricultural productivity', *Proceedings of the National Academy of Sciences of the United States of America*, 114:12 (2017) pp. 2285–2292.

48. Tim Searchinger, Richard Waite, Craig Hanson, Janet Ranganathan, Patrice Dumas and Emily Matthews, *SYNTHESIS REPORT:Creating a Sustainable Food Future: A Menu of Solutions to Feed Nearly 10 Billion People by 2050* (World Resources Institute, 2018).

49. Tadesse Fikre Teferra, 'Should we still worry about the safety of GMO foods? Why and why not? A review', *Food Science & Nutrition*, 9:9 (2021), p. 5324; c.f. Deepak K. Ray, Navin Ramankutty, Nathaniel D. Mueller, Paul C. West and Jonathan A. Foley, 'Recent patterns of crop yield growth and stagnation', *Nature Communications*, 3:1 (2012); Deepak K. Ray, Nathaniel D. Mueller, Paul C. West and Jonathan A. Foley, 'Yield trends are insufficient to double global crop production by 2050', *PLOS ONE*, 8:6 (2013).

50. National Academies of Sciences, Engineering, and Medicine, *Science Breakthroughs to Advance Food and Agricultural Research by 2030* (Washington, DC, NASEM, 2019).

51. Maywa Montenegro de Wit, 'Democratizing CRISPR? Stories, practices, and politics of science and governance on the agricultural gene editing frontier', *Elementa: Science of the Anthropocene*, 8:9 (2020).

52. FAO, *Strategic Framework 2022–2031* (Rome, FAO, 2021); Kevin V. Pixley, Jose B. Falck-Zepeda, Robert L. Paarlberg, Peter W. B. Phillips, Inez H. Slamet-Loedin, Kanwarpal S. Dhugga, Hugo Campos and Neal Gutterson, 'Genome-edited crops for improved food security of smallholder farmers', *Nature Genetics*, 54:4 (2022).

53. Montenegro de Wit, 'Democratizing CRISPR?', pp.12, 22.

54. Montenegro de Wit, 'Democratizing CRISPR?'.

55. Nature. Editorial, 'License CRISPR patents for free to share gene editing globally', *Nature*, 597:152 (2021).

56. Emily Waltz, 'Asexual crops whet industry appetite' *Nature Biotechnology*, 37:2 (2019), pp. 109–10.

57. Times of India, 'Modi Presses for Second Green Revolution in Bihar', *Times of India*, 2011, http://timesofindia.indiatimes.com/city/patna/Modi-presses-for-second-green-revolution-in-Bihar/articleshow/7612745.cms

58. Roger Pielke and Björn-Ola Linnér, 'From Green Revolution to green evolution: A critique of the political myth of averted famine', *Minerva*, 57:3 (2019).

59. *Ibid.*

60. Pielke and Linnér, 'From Green Revolution to green evolution'; Nick Cullather, *The Hungry World: America's Cold War Battle against Poverty in Asia* (Cambridge, MA, Harvard University Press, 2010).

61. Pielke and Linnér, 'From Green Revolution to green evolution', p. 286. Cf. Walter P. Falcon, 'The Green Revolution: Generations of problems', *American Journal of Agricultural Economics*, 52:5 (1970), p. 700.

62. Robert E. Evenson and Douglas Gollin, 'Assessing the impact of the Green Revolution, 1960 to 2000', *Science* 300:5620 (2003), pp. 758–62.

63. Andrew Dorward, Shenggen Fan, Jonathan Kydd, Hans Lofgren, Jamie Morrison, Colin Poulton et al., 'Institutions and policies for pro-poor agricultural growth', *Development Policy Review*, 22:16, p. 613.

64. Pielke and Linnér, 'From Green Revolution to green evolution'.

65. Jean Drèze and Amartya Sen, *Hunger and Public Action* (Oxford, Oxford University Press, 1991); FAO and WFP, Monitoring Food Security in Countries with Conflict Situations: A Joint FAO/WFP Update for the United Nations Security Council (FAO/WFP, 2018). (Accessed 15 December 2018).

Chapter 9. Crisis? What Crisis?

1. Jeffrey C. Ellis, 'When green was pink: environmental dissent in Cold War America' (Dissertation, University of California, Davis, 1995), ch. 2.

2. John Dryzek, *The Politics of the Earth: Environmental Discourses* (3rd ed.) (Oxford, Oxford University Press, 2013; Karin Bäckstrand and Eva Lövbrand, 'The road to Paris: Contending climate governance discourses in the post-Copenhagen era', *Journal of Environmental Policy & Planning*, 21:5 (2019), pp. 519–32.

3. Tor-Ragnar Gerholm, 'Domedagsporr för intellektuella', Moderna Tider, December 1999/January 2000, pp. 20–3.

4. Georg Borgström, *Jorden–vårt öde: Kan en permanent världshunger avvärjas?* (Stockholm, Forum, 1953), p. 7; Georg Borgström, *Brännpunkter* (Stockholm, Trevi, 1971), p. 318.

5. Population Division of the Department of Economic and Social Affairs of the United Nations Secretariat, *World Population Prospects 2022: Summary of Results*. UN DESA/POP/2021/TR/NO. 3. (New York, 2022).

6. Our World in Data. *Future Population Growth*, https://ourworldindata.org/future-population-growth (Accessed 23 January 2020); Population Division of the

Department of Economic and Social Affairs of the United Nations Secretariat, *World Population Prospects 2022.*

7. Population Division of the Department of Economic and Social Affairs of the United Nations Secretariat, *World Population Prospects 2022*, p. 32

8. Tor-Ragnar Gerholm, *Futurum Exaktum: The Technical Challenge* (Stockholm, Aldus/Bonnier, 1972),pp. 29–30.

9. R. Buckminster Fuller, *Utopia or Oblivion: The Prospects for Humanity* (Toronto, Bantam Books, 1969), p. 394.

10. Tim Searchinger, Richard Waite, Craig Hanson, Janet Ranganathan et al., *World Resources Report: Creating a Sustainable Food Future* (World Resource Institute, 2018).

11. Cheikh Mbow, Cynthia Rosenzweig, Luis G. Barioni , Tim G. Benton et al., '2019: Food Security', in Priyadarshi R. Shukla, Jim Skea, Eduardo C. Buendia, Valérie Masson-Delmotte et al. (eds), *Climate Change And Land: An IPCC Special Report On Climate Change, Desertification, Land Degradation, Sustainable Land Management, Food Security, And Greenhouse Gas Fluxes In Terrestrial Ecosystems* (Cambridge, UK, and New York, Cambridge University Press, 2021); E. Lisa F. Schipper, Aromar Revi, Benjamin L. Preston, Edward. R. Carr, et al., 'Climate resilient development pathways', in Hans-Otto Pörtner, Debra C. Roberts, Melinda M.B. Tignor, Elvira S. Poloczanska et al., (eds), *Climate Change 2022: Impacts, Adaptation and Vulnerability. Contribution of Working Group II to the Sixth Assessment Report of the Intergovernmental Panel on Climate Change* (Cambridge, UK, and New York, Cambridge University Press, 2022).

12. FAO, *The State of the World's Biodiversity for Food and Agriculture*, J. Bélanger and D. Pilling (eds) (Rome, FAO Commission on Genetic Resources for Food and Agriculture Assessments, 2019); IPBES, *Global Assessment Report on Biodiversity and Ecosystem Services of The Intergovernmental Science-Policy Platform on Biodiversity and Ecosystem Services,* Eduardo S. Brondizio, Josef Settele, Sandra Díaz, and Hien T. Ngo (eds) (Bonn, IPBES Secretariat, Germany, 2019)

13. Joel K. Bourne Jr, *The End of Plenty: The Race to Feed A Crowded World* (London, Scribe, 2015), p. 305.

14. Mauricio Lima and Sebastián Abades, 'Malthusian factors as proximal drivers of human population crisis at Sub-Saharan Africa', *Frontiers in Ecology and Evolution*, 3 (2015); Malcolm Potts, Courtney Henderson and Martha Campbell, 'The Sahel: A Malthusian challenge?' *Environmental and Resource Economics*, 55 (2013), pp. 501–512; I.I.C. Nwokoro and Samuel O. Dekolo, 'Land use change and environmental sustainability: The case of Lagos metropolis', *WIT Transactions on Ecology and the Environment*, 155 (2012), pp. 157–167.

15. Lucas Bretschger, 'Malthus in the light of climate change', *European Economic Review*, 127 (2020).

16. Navin Ramankutty, Zia Mehrabi, Katharina Waha, Larissa Jarvis, Claire Kremen, Mario Herrero and Loren H. Rieseberg, 'Trends in global agricultural land use: Implications for environmental health and food security', *Annual Review of Plant*

Biology, 69 (2018), pp. 789–815; James A. Brander, 'Viewpoint: Sustainability: Malthus revisited?', *Canadian Journal of Economics*, 40:1 (2007), pp. 1–38.

17.   Elena M. Finkbeiner, Nathan J. Bennett, Timothy H. Frawley et al., 'Reconstructing overfishing: Moving beyond Malthus for effective and equitable solutions', *Fish and Fisheries*, 18 (2017), pp. 1180–1191.

18.   Samir Suweis, Joel A. Carr, Amos Maritan, Andrea Rinaldoc and Paolo D'Odorico, 'Resilience and reactivity of global food security', *Proceedings of the National Academy of Sciences of the United States of America*, 112:22 (2015), pp. 6902–6907.

19.   Patrick Collins, 'Population growth the scapegoat? Rethinking the Neo-Malthusian debate', *Energy and Environment*, 13:3 (2002), pp. 401–422.

20.   Bopaki Phogole and Kowiyou Yessoufou, 'Biodiversity and economy but not social factors predict human population dynamics in South Africa', *Sustainability*, 14 (2022).

21.   World Economic Forum, *The Global Risks Report 2019*, 14th edition (Geneva, WEF, 2019).

22.   Thomas F. Homer-Dixon, *Environment, Scarcity, and Violence* (Princeton, Princeton University Press, 1999).

23.   John Keegan, *A History of Warfare* (New York, Alfred A. Knopf, 1993); Alain Clément and Riccardo Soliani, 'The food weapon: Milestones in the history of a concept (17th–19th centuries)', in Yukihiro Ikeda and Annalisa Rosselli (eds), *War in the History of Economic Thought: Economists and the Question of War* (1st ed.) (London, Routledge, 2017); James C. Scott, *Against the Grain: A Deep History of the Earliest States* (New Haven, Yale University Press, 2017).

24.   Caitlin Welsh, Joseph S. Bermudez Jr., Jennifer Jun and Emma Dodd, 'Spotlight on damage to Ukraine's agricultural infrastructure since Russia's invasion', *Commentary* (Center for Strategic and International Studies, 15 June 2022.) https://www.csis.org/analysis/spotlight-damage-ukraines-agricultural-infrastructure-russias-invasion (Accessed 20 January 2023).

25.   Jiayi Zhou, *Producing Food, Security, and the Geopolitical Subject* (Dissertation, Linköping University, Faculty of Arts and Sciences, Linköping University Electronic Press, 2022).

26.   Björn-Ola Linnér and Henrik Selin, 'The United Nations Conference on Sustainable Development: Forty years in the making', *Environment and Planning. C: Government and Policy*, 31:6 (2013), pp. 971–987.

27.   World Resource Institute, *World Resources 2000–2001: People and Ecosystems* (New York, Oxford UP, 2000), *passim*.

28.   World Resources Institute, *World Resources 1998–99: A Guide to the Global Environment* (New York, Oxford University Press, 1998), pp. 144–9.

29.   World Bank, *Poverty and Shared Prosperity 2022: Correcting Course* (Washington, DC, World Bank, 2022).

30.   Lucas Chancel, Thomas Piketty, Emmanuel Saez, Gabriel Zucman et al. *World Inequality Report 2022* (World Inequality Lab wir2022.wid.world, 2021).

31.   *Ibid.*

32. World Bank, *Poverty and Shared Prosperity 2018: Piecing Together the Poverty Puzzle* (Washington, DC, World Bank, 2018).

33. Victoria Wibeck, Björn-Ola Linnér, Melisa Alves, Therese Asplund et al., 'Stories of transformation: A cross-country focus group study on sustainable development and societal change', *Sustainability*, 11 (2019), p. 2427; Schipper, Revi, Preston, Carr et al. 'Climate resilient development pathways'.

34. UNFCCC, *Sharm El-Sheikh Climate Implementation Summit Declaration COP27 Presidency Summary Outcomes, The Sharm El-Sheikh Climate Implementation Summit, 6–20 November 2022* (Sharm El-Sheikh, Eygpt, 2022).

35. Georg Borgström, 'Hälsa och Hunger – livsmedelsförsörjningens globala dilemma', *Nordisk Medicin*, 51 (1966), pp. 1493–1524.

36. Global Nutrition Report, *Global Nutrition Report: Stronger Commitments for Greater Action* (Bristol, UK, Development Initiatives, 2022)

37. Homer-Dixon, *Environment, Scarcity, and Violence*, p. 48.

38. Paolo D'Odorico, Joel A. Carr, Francesco Laio, Luca Ridolfi and Stefano Vandoni, 'Feeding humanity through global food trade', *Earth's Future* (2014), pp.458–469.

39. *Ibid.*; Johanna Hedlund, Henrik Carlsen, Simon Croft, Chris West et al., 'Impacts of climate change on global food trade networks', *Environmental Research Letters*, 17: 124040 (2022).

40. David Grigg, *The World Food Problem*, 2nd edn, (Oxford, Blackwell, 1999 (1993)), p. 268; Göran Djurfeldt, *Mera mat: att brödföda en växande befolkning* (Lund, Arkiv, 2001), p. 29.

41. Ramya Ambikapathi, Kate R. Schneider, Benjamin Davis, Mario Herrerom et al., 'Global food systems transitions have enabled affordable diets but had less favourable outcomes for nutrition, environmental health, inclusion and equity', *Nature Food*, 3 (2022), pp. 764–779.

42. Georg Borgström, *Jorden–vårt öde: Kan en permanent världshunger avvärjas?* (Stockholm, Forum, 1953), p. 7; Borgström, *Brännpunkter* (Stockholm, Trevi, 1971), p. 318.

43. World Resources Institute, *World Resources 1998–99*, pp. 152–3.

44. Mbow, Rosenzweig, Barioni, Benton, et al., '2019: Food Security'.

45. M.A. Keyzer, M.D. Merbis, I.F.P.W Pavel and C.F.A van Wesenbeeck, 'Diet shifts towards meat and the effects on cereal use: Can we feed the animals in 2030?' *Ecological Economics*, 55 (2005), pp.187–202; Emily S. Cassidy, Paul C. West, James S. Gerber and Jonathan A. Foley, 'Redefining agricultural yields: From tonnes to people nourished per hectare', *Environmental Research Letters*, 8: 034015 (2013).

46. Marianela Fader, Dieter Gerten, Michael Krause, Wolfgang Lucht and Wolfgang Cramer, 'Spatial decoupling of agricultural production and consumption: Quantifying dependences of countries on food imports due to domestic land and water constraints', *Environmental Research Letters*, 8:014046 (2013).

47. World Resources Institute, *World Resources 1998–99*, pp. 152–3.

48.   Population Division of the Department of Economic and Social Affairs of the United Nations Secretariat, *World Population Prospects: The 2000 Revision and World Urbanization Prospects: The 2001 Revision*, http://esa.un.org/unpp, 3 January 2003; Population Division, *World Population Prospects: The 2000 Revision, Volume III, Analytical Report*, ST/ESA/SER.A/200, ch. 5; The World Bank, Population Growth (Annual %), https://data.worldbank.org/indicator/SP.POP.GROW (Accessed 25 January 2023).

49.   Pedro Naso, Bruno Lanz and Tim Swanson, 'The return of Malthus? Resource constraints in an era of declining population growth', *European Economic Review*, 128:103499 (2020).

50.   World Resources Institute, *World Resources 1998–99*, pp. 152–60.

51.   United Nations Population Fund, *The State of World Population 1998*, E/31,000/ 1998 (New York, 1998), pp. 1–34; United Nations Development Programme, *Human Development Report: Consumption for Human Development* (New York, 1998), *passim*; Joel E. Cohen, *How Many People Can the Earth Support?* (New York, W.W. Norton & Company, 1995); Cohen, 'How many people can the Earth support?', *The Science*, November/December, 1995.

52.   FAO, *Rome Declaration on World Food Security and World Food Summit Plan of Action, World Food Summit, 13–17 November 1996* (Rome, FAO, 1996).

53.   Amartya Sen, *Poverty and Famines: An Essay on Entitlement and Deprivation* (Oxford, Clarendon, 1981), *passim*.

54.   Gregory E. Pence, *Designer Food: Mutant Harvest or Breadbasket of the World?* (Lanham, MD, Rowman & Littlefield, 2002), p. 6.

55.   *Ibid.*, p. 144.

56.   Barry Commoner, *The Closing Circle: Nature, Man, and Technology* (New York, 1971), p. 21

57.   The project *Dialogue on Water, Food and Environment* involves the following organisations: FAO, International Federation of Agricultural Producers, Global Water Partnership, International Commission on Irrigation and Drainage, IUCN, International Water Management Institute, UNEP, WHO, World Water Council, World Wide Fund for Nature.

58.   Karin Eliasson, Lotten Wiréhn, Tina-Simone Neset and Björn-Ola Linnér, 'Transformations towards sustainable food systems: contrasting Swedish practitioner perspectives with the European Commission's Farm to Fork Strategy', *Sustainability Science*, 17 (2022), pp. 2411–2425.

59.   H. Charles J. Godfray , John R. Beddington, Ian R. Crute, Lawrence Haddad et al. 'Food security: The challenge of feeding 9 billion people', *Science,* 327:5967 (2010), pp. 812–818.

60.   Jennifer Clapp, *Food* (3rd ed.) (Cambridge, Polity Press, 2020).

61.   Karen O'Brien, 'Is the 1.5° C target possible? Exploring the three spheres of transformation', *Current Opinion in Environmental Sustainability*, 31 (2018), pp. 153–160.

62.   Warren Purcell, Thomas Neubauer and Kevin Mallinger, 'Digital twins in agriculture: challenges and opportunities for environmental sustainability', *Current Opinion in Environmental Sustainability*, 61 (2023); Maria C. Annosi, Federica Brunetta, Francesa Capo and Laurens Heideveld, 'Digitalization in the agri-food industry: The relationship between technology and sustainable development', *Management Decision*, 58:8 (2020), pp. 1737–1757.

63.   Garima Singh, Anamika Singh and Gurjit Kaur, 'Chapter 16 – Role of artificial intelligence and the internet of things in agriculture', in Gurjit Kaur, Pradeep Tomar and Marcus Tanque (eds), *Artificial Intelligence to Solve Pervasive Internet of Things Issues* (Elsevier, 2021), pp. 317–330.

Abbreviations

BF	Borgström File
CGIAR	The Consultative Group on International Agricultural Research
CHS	Centre for History of Science, Royal Academy of Sciences, Stockholm, Sweden
FAO	Food and Agriculture Organization of the United Nations
GATT	General Agreement on Tariffs and Trade
GM	Genetically modified
GMO	Genetically modified organisms
HSTL	Harry S. Truman Library, Independence, MO
IBP	International Biological Program
IGY	The International Geophysical Year
IMF	International Monetary Fund
ITCPN	International Technical Conference on the Protection of Nature
IUCN	International Union for the Conservation of Nature and Natural Resources
IUPN	International Union for the Protection of Nature
IVK	Institute for Plant Research and Cold Storage
MSU	Michigan State University
MIT	Massachusetts Institute of Technology
MSUAHC	Michigan State University Archives and Historical Collections
OEEC	Organisation for European Economic Cooperation
OPEC	Organization of Petroleum Exporting Countries
PBD	Papers of Birger Drake, Gothenburg, Sweden
SIK	The Swedish Institute for Food Preservation Research
SOU	Statens offentliga utredningar (Swedish official reports series)
UNA	United Nations Archives
UNESCO	United Nations Educational, Scientific, and Cultural Organization
UNSCCUR	United Nations Scientific Conference on the Conservation and Utilization of Resources
USAID	United States Agency for International Development

References

Archives

Centre for History of Science, Royal Academy of Sciences, Stockholm, Sweden
Department of Public Affairs, Monsanto, St Louis, MO
Harry S. Truman Library, Independence, MO
Michigan State University Archives and Historical Collections, East Lansing, MI
Papers of Birger Drake, Gothenburg, Sweden
The Library of the Swedish Institute for Food Preservation Research, Gothenburg, Sweden
The Manuscript Department at Lund University Library, Lund, Sweden
The National Archive of Recorded Sound and Moving Images, Stockholm, Sweden
United Nations Archives, New York, NY

Newspapers, Magazines and Radio

Aftonbladet
Arbetaren
Arbetartidningen
Arbetet
BBC News World
Business Week
Dagen
Dagens Nyheter
Encounter
Expressen
Gotlänningen
Gyldendals Aktuelle Magasin
Göteborgs Handels- och Sjöfartstidning
Göteborgs Morgonpost
Göteborgs Tidning
Göteborgs Tidningen

Göteborgs-Posten
Hörde Ni?
ICA-kuriren
Jämtlands Tidning
Lansing State Journal
Look
Lunds Dagblad
Michigan State Radio Network
Morgontidningen
Nerikes Allehanda
New York Times
Norrbottens Kuriren
Norrlandsfolket
Norrländska Socialdemokraten
Norrskensflamman
Nutid
Ny Dag
Ny Tid
Nynäshamns-Posten
Observer Review
RLF-tidningen
Samtid och Framtid
Science and Public Affairs: Bulletin of the Atomic Scientists
Skånska Dagbladet
Stockholms Tidningen
Svenska Dagbladet
Svenska Morgonbladet
Svenska Morgonposten
Swedish Radio
Sydsvenska Dagbladet
The Sunday News, Detroit
Tiden
Time Magazine
Wall Street Journal
Washington Post
Vi
Örebro Kuriren

Interviews made by the author

Bandurski, Robert, 5 October 1995, East Lansing, MI

Barton, Charles F., 6 May 2002, St Louis, MO

Borgström, Greta, 27 April 1994, Göteborg, Sweden

Borgström, Vera, 26 April 1994, Göteborg, Sweden

Cantlon, John, 9 October 1995, East Lansing, MI

Dahlbeck, Nils, 26 April 1994, Göteborg, Sweden

Dahmén, Gunnar, 9 May 1994, Stockholm

Downs, Charles, 10 October 1995, East Lansing, MI

Drake, Birger, 15 May 1997, Göteborg, Sweden

Flinck, Karl-Evert, 24 September 1997, Linköping, Sweden

Harpsteadt, Dale, 6 October 1995, East Lansing, MI

Hedén, Carl-Göran, 8 June 1994, Stockholm

Hylmö, Bertil, 9 March 1995, Askersund, Sweden

Jarring, Gunnar, 10 August 1995, Viken, Sweden

Johnsson, Glenn, 11 October 1995, East Lansing, MI

Kylin, Anders, 2 January 1995, Lund, Sweden

Lindeberg, Gösta, 9 February 1995, Uppsala, Sweden

Richardson, Dough, 10 March 1997, Washington DC

Rudebeck, Gustaf, 30 May 1998, Lund, Sweden

Salemka, Linda, 11 October 1995, East Lansing, MI

Sommers, Lawrence, 11 October 1995, East Lansing, MI

Tengström, Emin, 27 April 1994 Göteborg, Sweden

Wharton, Clifton, 31 October 1995, New York, NY

Woodwell, George, 23 October 1995, Woods Hole, MA

Literature and Published Sources

1944 års Socialdemokratiska partiprogram, Stockholm, 1944

Agrell, Wilhelm. *Alliansfrihet och atombomber: kontinuitet och förändring i den svenska försvarsdoktrinen från 1945 till 1982*, LiberFörlag, Stockholm, 1985

Alexandersson, Gunnar. 'Dagens u-länder morgondagens massmarknader', *Industri-förbundets tidskrift*, 9 (1968)

Alexandersson, Gunnar. 'Speglingar av befolkningsfrågan', *Svenska Dagbladet*, 12 May 1969

Allee, Warder Clyde, A. E. Emerson, O. Park, T. Park, K. P. Schmidt. *Principles of Animal Ecology*, Philadelphia, Saunders, 1949

Ambikapathi, Ramya, Kate R. Schneider, Benjamin Davis, Mario Herrerom et al. 'Global food systems transitions have enabled affordable diets but had less favourable outcomes for nutrition, environmental health, inclusion and equity'. *Nature Food*, 3 (2022), pp. 764–779

Ambrose, Stephen E. *Rise to Globalism: American Foreign Policy since 1938* (4th edn), New York, Penguin, 1985

Andersson, Åke. *Staten och jordbruket – en studie med utgångspunkt i rationaliserngs politi-ken för jordbruket i Sverige*, Uppsala, SLU, Inst. för ekonomi, 1997

Annosi, Maria C., Federica Brunetta, Francesa Capo and Laurens Heideveld. 'Digi-talization in the agri-food industry: The relationship between technology and sustainable development'. *Management Decision*, 58:8 (2020), pp. 1737–1757

Anshelm, Jonas. 'Bland trollkarlar och demoner: Om kärnkraftsdiskursen i Sverige under 1950-talet', *Vest*, 9:1 (1996)

Anshelm, Jonas. *Förnuftets brytpunkt: Om teknikkritiken i PC Jersilds författarskap*, Stockholm, Bon-niers, 1990

Appelqvist, Örjan. *Världsintressets advokat: Gunnar Myrdal och den svenska efterkrig-splane-ringen 1944–1945*, University of Gothenburg, Department of Political Science, 1997

Arbetarrörelsens efterkrigsprogram: de 27 punkterna med motivering, Stockholm, 1945

Arendt, Hannah. *Die verborgene Tradition. Acht Essays*, Frankfurt, Suhrkamp, 1976

Arrighi, Giovanni. *The Long Twentieth Century: Money, Power and the Origins of Our Times*, London, Verso, 1994

Asplund, Johan. *Teorier om framtiden*, Stockholm, LiberFörlag, 1979

Åstrand, Halvdan. 'Blir svälten vårt öde?', *Jordbrukarnas Föreningsblad*, 31 October 1953

Åstrand, Halvdan. 'Svar till Gullander', *RLF-tidningen*, 47 (1953)

Balaam, David Norman. 'The political economy of international food production and distribution' (Dissertation, University of California, Santa Barbara, 1978)

Barkun, Micael. 'Divided apocalypse: thinking about the end in contemporary America', *Soundings*, 66 (1983)

Barnes, Barry, David Bloor and John Henry. *Scientific Knowledge: A Sociological Analysis*, London, Athlone, 1996

Barthelmess, Alfred. *Walt – Umwelt des Menschen: Dokumente zu einer Problemgeschichte von Naturschutz, Landschaftspflege und Humanökologie*, Freiburg, Alber, 1972

Barthes, Roland. *Mythologies*, London, Paladin, 1973 (1963)

Barthes, Roland. *Elements of Semiology*, New York, Hill and Wang, 1995 (1964)

Beck, Roy and Leon Kolankiewicz. 'The environmental movement's retreat from advo-cating U.S. population stabilization (1970–1998): a first draft history', in Otis L. Graham Jr. (ed.), *Environmental Politics and Policy, 1960s–1990s*, University Park, PA, Pennsylvania State UP, 2000

Beck, Ulrich. *What is Globalization?*, Malden, MT, Polity Press, 2000

Beinart, William, and Peter A. Coates. *Environment and History: The Taming of Nature in the USA and South Africa*, London, Routledge, 1995

Bennett, M.K. *The World's Food*, New York, Harper, 1954

Beskow, Gunnar. 'Livsmedelsbrist och jordförstöring', *Samtid och Framtid*, no. 5, 1949

Bill in the Swedish Parliament, FK, Sam Norup et al. 'angående åtgärder i pris-reglerande syfte på jordbrukets område', 1949: 415

Bill in the Swedish Parliament, FK, Erik Arrhén and Yngve Nilsson. 'angående befolkningsfrågan', 1958: 157

Bill in the Swedish Parliament, FK, Sven Nyman et al. 'angående nya metoder att framställa näringsmedel', 1967: 47

Bill in the Swedish Parliament, FK, Yngve Holmberg et al. 'angående den svenska hjälpen till U-länderna', 1967: 479

Bill in the Swedish Parliament, AK, Nils G. Hanson. 'om en global samordning på biståndsverksamhetens område', 1967: 483

Bill in the Swedish Parliament, AK, Gunnar Hedlund and Bertil Ohlin. 'angående det svenska biståndet till U-länderna', 1967: 484

Birgersson, Bengt Owe Stig Hadenius, Björn Molin, Hans Wieslander. *Sverige efter 1900: en modern politisk historia*, Stockholm, Bonniers, 1984

Björck, Ingela. 'Georg Borgström varnar åter i ny bok: Krafttag krävs mot folkökning: Civilsationen är inte odödlig', *Sydsvenska Dagbladet*, 14 October 1971

Björklund, Fredrika. 'Samförstånd under oenighet: Svensk säkerhetspolitisk debatt under kalla kriget' (Dissertation, Uppsala, 1992)

Björklund, Stefan. *Politisk teori*, Stockholm, Aldus, 1976

Blair, Frank W. *Big Biology: The US/IBP*, Stroudsburg, PA, Hutchinson & Ross, 1979

Blair, Lyle, and Madison Kuhn. *A Short History of Michigan State*, East Lansing MI, Michigan State College, 1955

Bloor, David. *Knowledge and Social Imagery* (2nd edn), Chicago, University of Chicago Press, 1991

Bogue, Donald J. *Principles of Demography*, New York, 1969

Bolin, Lorentz. *Biologernas kamp mot svälten*, Stockholm, Gebers, 1945

Borgström, Georg. 'Naturvetare', *Meddelanden från Lunds Kristliga Studentförbund*, VIII, 1 (1932), pp. 3–5

Borgström, Georg. 'Naturvetenskap och kristendom', *Meddelanden från Lunds Kristliga Studentförbund*, X, 2 (1934) pp. 13–14

Borgström, Georg. 'Större kunskaper i politiska frågor önskvärda', *Skånska Dagbladet*, 4 December 1935

Borgström, Georg. 'Fotoperiodism: Dagslängdens inflytande på växtvärlden', *Nordisk Familjeboks Månadskrönika*, February 1938, pp. 101–8

Borgström, Georg. 'Nyare rön angående frölösa frukter. Kenokarpi och partenokarpi', *Nordisk Familjeboks Månadskrönika*, May 1938, pp. 325–6

Borgström, Georg. 'Transverse reactions in plants: outlines of a new interpretation of the significance of growth hormones for life processes in plants' (Dissertation, G.W.K. Gleerup, Lund, 1939)

Borgström, Georg. 'Etylenproblemet inom växtfysiologin', *Nordisk Familjeboks Månads-krönika*, February 1939

Borgström, Georg. 'Kampen om livet', *Reformatorn*, November 1940, pp. 6–7, 16

Borgström, Georg. 'Vi måste fortsätta kriget mot sjukdom och svält', *Nynäshamns-Posten*, 26 November 1946

Borgström, Georg. 'Ett dystert världsperspektiv', *Gotlands Allehanda* 31 December 1948

Borgström, Georg. 'Räcker maten?', lecture on Swedish Radio, 20 December 1948, reproduced in *Hörde Ni?*, II, 1949, pp. 23–7

Borgström, Georg. 'Världens livsmedelsförsörjning', *Göteborgs Handels- och Sjöfarts-tidning*, 17 December 1948

Borgström, Georg. 'Frihet från nöd vägen till fred. Årets fredspristagare Lord John Boyd Orr presenteras', *Vi*, 22 October 1949

Borgström, Georg. 'Livsmedelsbrist och jordförstöring', *Samtid och Framtid*, no. 5, 1949

Borgström, Georg. 'Preservation of perishable foods', *Proceedings of the United Nations Scientific Conference on the Conservation and Utilization of Resources. 17 August–6 September 1949, Lake Success, New York*, Vol. VI, 1949, pp. 370–74

Borgström, Georg. 'Världshushållets dilemma', *Göteborgs Handels- och Sjöfartstidning*, 22 November 1949

Borgström, Georg. 'Frischhaltung von Fischen in Skandinavien und anderen Ländern', *Kältetechnik*, 2:5 (1950), pp. 106–12

Borgström, Georg. 'L'industrie de la conserve et ses problèmes actuels de recherche', *Revue de la Conserve*, November 1951, pp. 30–34

Borgström, Georg. 'Que é a anchova da Scandinávia?', *Conservas de Peixe*, 6:68 (1951)

Borgström, Georg. *Jorden–vårt öde: Kan en permanent världshunger avvärjas?*, Stockholm, Forum, 1953

Borgström, Georg. 'Europa i historiens vågskål', Sveriges Radio, 29 June 1953

Borgström, Georg. 'European aspects of overpopulation: balance between resources and population', *Proceedings of the 5th International Conference of Planned Parenthood, Aug. 17–22, 1953*, Stockholm, 1954

Borgström, Georg. 'Naturskyddet och livsmedelsförsörjningen', *Sveriges Natur*, 3 (1954)

Borgström, Georg. 'Preservation of fruit juices by sterilization, filtration, chemical preservatives, etc.', in Donald K. Tressler and Maynard A Joslyn (eds), *The Chemistry and Technology of Fruit and Vegetable Juice Production*, New York, AVI Publishing Co., 1954

Borgström, Georg. 'Problemas de actualidad en la ciencia de conservación de alimentos', *Revista Tecnica Informacion Conservera*, 11:12 (1954), pp. 4–11

Borgström, Georg. 'Il rifornimento viveri dell'Europa', *Umana, Panorama di vita contemporanea*, 4:7–8 (1955), pp. 11–15

Borgström, Georg. 'Microbiological problems of frozen food products', in *Advances in Food Research*, Vol. VI, New York, Academic Press, 1955, pp. 163–230

Borgström, Georg (ed.). *Fish as Food*, 4 vols, New York, Academic Press, 1961–5

Borgström, Georg. *Mat för miljarder*, Stockholm, LTs Förlag, 1962

Borgström, Georg. 'Fish in world nutrition', in G. Borgström, (ed.): *Fish as Food*, Vol. II, New York and London, Academic Press, 1962, ch. 7

Borgström, Georg. *Gränser för vår tillvaro*, Stockholm, LTs Förlag, 1964

Borgström, Georg. *Japan's World Success in Fishing*, London, Fishing News, 1964

Borgström, Georg. 'The human biosphere and its biological and chemical limitations', in Mortimer P. Starr (ed.), *Global Impacts of Applied Microbiology*, New York, John Wiley & Sons, 1964

Borgström, Georg. *The Hungry Planet*, New York, Macmillan, 1965

Borgström, Georg. 'Back to reality', *Food Technology*, May 1965, pp. 71–3

Borgström, Georg. *Överflödets kris*, Stockholm, Stockholms FN-förening, 1966

Borgström, Georg. *Revolution i världsfisket*, Stockholm, LTs Förlag, 1966

Borgström, Georg. 'Hälsa och Hunger – livsmedelsförsörjningens globala dilemma', *Nordisk Medicin*, 51 (1966), pp. 1493–1524

Borgström, Georg. *Världens mat*, Stockholm, Lindblads, 1968

Borgström, Georg. *Flykt från verkligheten*, LTs Förlag, Stockholm, 1969

Borgström, Georg. *Too Many: A Study of Earth's Biological Limitations*, New York, Macmillan, 1969

Borgström, Georg. *Focal Points : A Global Food Strategy*, New York, Macmillan, 1971

Borgström, Georg. *Too Many: An Ecological Overview of Earth's Limitations*, New York, Collier Books, 1971

Borgström, Georg. *Brännpunkter*, Stockholm, Trevi, 1971

Borgström, Georg. *Glodujaca Planeta*, Warsaw, Panstwowe Wydawnictwo Rolnicze i Lesne, 1971

Borgström, Georg, and Greta Borgström (eds), *Malthus – Om befolkningsfrågan*, Stockholm, LTs Förlag, 1969

Borgström, Georg, and A. J. Heighway (eds). *Atlantic Ocean Fisheries*, London, Fishing News, 1962

Borgström, Georg, and R. Marcuse. 'Probleme des Fettverderbs: Zusammender Bericht über ein skandinavisches Symposium', *Fette und Seifen*, 55:8 (1953)

Borlaug, Norman. 'The Green Revolution: peace and humanity', in *The Nobel Prizes, Presentations Biography and Lectures*, Stockholm, Almqvist & Wiksell, 1970

Boserup, Ester. *The Conditions of Agricultural Growth: The Economics of Agrarian Change under Population Change*, London, Allen & Unwin, 1965

Bourdieu, Pierre, and Terry Eagleton. 'Doxa and common life: an interview', in Slavoj Zizek, *Mapping Ideology*, London, Verso, 1997 (1994), pp. 265–77

Bourdieu, Pierre. *Outline of a Theory of Practice*, Cambridge, Cambridge University Press, 1977

Bourne Jr, Joel K. *The End of Plenty: The Race to Feed A Crowded World*, London, Scribe, 2015

Bowler, Peter J. *The Environmental Sciences*, New York, Norton, 1993 (1992)

Bowles, Chester. 'Why Point Four is needed', in Walter M. Daniels (ed.), *The Point Four Program*, New York, Wilson, 1951

Boyer, Robert. *The Regulation School: A Critical Introduction*, New York, Columbia University Press, 1989

Brander, James A. 'Viewpoint: Sustainability: Malthus revisited?' *Canadian Journal of Economics*, 40:1 (2007), pp. 1–38

Braudel, Fernand. *Civilization and Capitalism: 15th–18th Century*, Vol. 2, *The Wheels of Commerce*, London, Collins, 1982 (1979)

Bretschger, Lucas. 'Malthus in the light of climate change'. *European Economic Review*, 127 (2020)

Broadley, Herbert. 'Critical shortage of food', in *Proceedings of the United Nations Scientific Conference on the Conservation and Utilization of Resources. 17 August–6 September 1949, Lake Success, New York*, Vol. I

Brower, David. 'Preface', in Paul R. Ehrlich, *The Population Bomb*, New York, Ballantine, 1968

Brown, Lester. *Seeds of Change: the Green Revolution and Development in the 1970's*, New York, Praeger, 1970.

Brown, Lester. 'The fuel that makes inflation soar: people – more people – cause scarcities the world over', *Los Angeles Times*, 28 March 1976

Brown, Lester R. *Who Will Feed China? Wake-up Call for a Small Planet*, New York, W.W. Norton, 1995

Brown, Lester. *The Interdepence of Nations*, New York, Foreign Policy Association, 1972

Caldwell, Lynton Keith. *International Environmental Policy: Emergence and Dimensions*, Durham, Duke University Press, 1984

Caldwell, Lynton Keith. *International Environmental Policy: From the Twentieth to the Twenty-first Century* (3rd edn), Durham, Duke University Press, 1996

Carlsson, Sten. *Den sociala omgrupperingen i Sverige efter 1866*, Uppsala, Samhälle och riksdag, 1966

Carson, Rachel. *The Sea around Us*, New York, Oxford University Press, 1951

Carson, Rachel. *Silent Spring*, Boston, Houghton Mifflin, 1962

Cassidy, Emily S., Paul C. West, James S. Gerber and Jonathan A. Foley. 'Redefining agricultural yields: From tonnes to people nourished per hectare'. *Environmental Research Letters*, 8: 034015 (2013)

Chancel, Lucas, Thomas Piketty, Emmanuel Saez, Gabriel Zucman et al. *World Inequality Report 2022*, World Inequality Lab wir2022.wid.world, 2021

Chandler, Alfred D. *The Visible Hand: The Managerial Revolution in American Business*, Cambridge, MA, Belknap, 1977

Charles, Daniel. *Lords of the Harvest: Biotech, Big Money, and the Future of Food*, Cambridge, MA, Perseus Publishing, 2001

Clapp, Jennifer. *Food* (3rd ed.), Cambridge, Polity Press, 2020

Clark, Colin. 'World resources and the world population', in *Proceedings of the United Nations Scientific Conference on the Conservation and Utilization of Resources. 17 August–6 September 1949, Lake Success, New York*, Vol. I

Clarke, I. F. *The Pattern of Expectation*, London, Jonathan Cape, 1979

Clément, Alain and Riccardo Soliani. 'The food weapon: Milestones in the history of a concept (17th–19th centuries)', in Yukihiro Ikeda and Annalisa Rosselli (eds). *War in the History of Economic Thought: Economists and the Question of War* (1st ed.), London, Routledge, 2017

Cohen, Joel E. 'How many people can the Earth support?', *Science*, November/December 1995

Cohen, Joel E. *How Many People Can the Earth Support?*, New York, W.W. Norton & Company, 1995

Cole, Sam. 'The global future debate 1965–1976', in Christopher Freeman and Marie Jahoda (eds), *World Futures: The Great Debate*, London, Robertson, 1978

Collins, Patrick. 'Population growth the scapegoat? Rethinking the Neo-Malthusian debate'. *Energy and Environment*, 13:3 (2002), pp. 401–422

Commoner, Barry. 'Survival in the environmental–population crisis', in S. Fred Singer (ed.), *Is There an Optimum Level of Population?*, New York, 1971, pp. 97–8

Commoner, Barry. *The Closing Circle: Nature, Man, and Technology*, New York, 1971

Conwentz, Hugo. *Über nationalen und internationalen Natursßutz: Rede bei der Internationalen Naturschutzkonferenz in Bern am 18. November 1913*, Lepzig, Verlag von Quelle & Meyer, 1914

Cooper, Richard N. *The Economics of Interdependence: Economic Policy in the Atlantic Community*, New York, McGraw-Hill, 1968

Cronon, William. 'Introduction: in search of nature', in *Uncommon Ground: Toward Reinventing Nature*, New York, W.W. Norton, 1995

Cronon, William (ed.). *Uncommon Ground: Toward Reinventing Nature*, New York, W.W. Norton, 1995

Cullather, Nick. *The Hungry World: America's Cold War Battle against Poverty in Asia*, Cambridge, MA, Harvard University Press, 2010

Dalton, Russell. J. *The Green Rainbow: Environmental Groups in Western Europe*, New Haven, Yale University Press, 1994

Daly, Herman E. 'Toward a stationary-state economy', in John Harte and Robert Socolow (eds), *The Patient Earth*, New York, Holt, Rinehart, and Winston, 1971

Daniels, Walter M. (ed.). *The Point Four Program*, New York, Wilson, 1951

Darlington, Cyril Dean. *The Evolution of Man and Society*, New York, 1969

Das, O. *The Journal of World Intellectual Property*, 3 (2000), pp. 577–88

Dillard, Dudley. *Economic Development of the North Atlantic Community: Historical Introduction to Modern Economics*, Swedish edn, *Västeuropas och Förenta staternas ekonomiska historia*, Malmö, Liber, 1985

Djurfeldt, Göran. *Mera mat: att brödföda en växande befolkning*, Lund, Arkiv, 2001

Dorsey, Kirkpatrick. *Dawn of Conservation Diplomacy: U.S.–Canadian Wildlife Protection Treaties in the Progressive Era*, Seattle, University of Washington Press, 1998

Dorward, Andrew, Shenggen Fan, Jonathan Kydd, Hans Lofgren, Jamie Morrison, Colin Poulton et al. 'Institutions and policies for pro-poor agricultural growth', *Development Policy Review*, 22:16, p. 613

Douglas, Mary. *Purity and Danger: An Analysis of the Concepts of Pollution and Taboo*, London, Routledge, 1966

Drangert, Jan-Olof. 'Asiens jordbruksproblem', *Svenska Dagbladet*, 10 August 1968

Dressel, Paul. *College to University: The Hannah Years at Michigan State, 1935–1969*, East Lansing, Michigan State University Publications, 1987

Drèze, Jean and Amartya Sen. *Hunger and Public Action*, Oxford, Oxford University Press, 1991

Dryzek, John. *The Politics of the Earth: Environmental Discourses* (3rd ed.), Oxford, Oxford University Press, 2013

Dublin, Louis I., Alfred J. Lotka, Mortimer Spiegelman. *Length of Life: A Study of the Life Table*, New York, Ronald Press, 1936

Eagleton, Terry. *Ideology: An Introduction*, London, Verso, 1991

Edberg: Rolf. *Spillran av ett moln: anteckningar i färdaboken*, Stockholm, Norstedt, 1966

Edberg, Rolf. *Vid trädets fot: lekmannafunderingar mot höstlig bakgrund*, Stockholm, Norstedt, 1971

Editors of *The Ecologist. A Blueprint for Survival*, Harmondsworth, 1972

Egan, Michael. 'The new Jeremiads: science, information, and environmentalism in the Commoner–Ehrlich debate', Paper presented at the American Society for Environmental History annual meeting, Denver, 2002

Egerton, Frank N. 'Changing Concepts of the Balance of Nature', *The Quarterly Review of Biology*, 48 (June 1973)

Ehrensvärd, Gösta. *Före – Efter: en diagnos*, Stockholm, Aldus/Bonnier, 1971

Ehrlich, Paul and L.C. Birch. 'The "balance of nature" and "population control"', *The American Naturalist*, 101:918 (1967), pp. 97–107

Ehrlich, Paul R. *The Population Bomb*, New York, Ballantine, 1968

Ehrlich, Paul. 'Population and panaceas: a technological perspective', *Bioscience*, 19 (1969)

Ehrlich, Paul. 'Eco-catastrophe', reprinted in Clem *et al.* (eds), *No Room for Man*, Totowa, NJ, Littlefield, Adams, & Co., 1970

Ehrlich, Paul and Anne Ehrlich. *Population, Resources, Environment: Issues in Human Ecology*, San Francisco, W.H. Freeman, 1970.

Ehrlich, Paul. 'Impact of population growth', *Science*, 171 (1971), pp. 1212–17

Ehrlich, Paul and John P. Holdren. 'Dispute', *Environment*, 14 (April 1972), pp. 23–52

Elgström, Ole. *En jämförelse mellan svensk och dansk parlamentarisk utrikesdebatt 1962–1978*, Lund, Studentlitteratur, 1982

Eliasson, Karin, Lotten Wiréhn, Tina-Simone Neset and Björn-Ola Linnér. 'Transformations towards sustainable food systems: Contrasting Swedish practitioner perspectives with the European Commission's Farm to Fork Strategy', *Sustainability Science*, 17 (2022), pp. 2411–2425

Ellis, Jeffrey C. 'On the search of a root cause: essentialist tendencies in environmental discourse', in W. Cronon (ed.), *Uncommon Ground: Toward Reinventing Nature*, New York, W.W. Norton, 1995

Ellis, Jeffrey C. 'When green was pink: environmental dissent in Cold War America' (Dissertation, University of California, Davis, 1995)

Elton, Charles. *Animal Ecology and Evolution*, Oxford, 1930

Elton, Charles. *Animal Ecology*, Methuen, London, 1967, (1927)

Erlander, Tage. *Tage Erlander, 1940–49*, Stockholm, Tidens Förlag, 1973

Es, I. 'Georg Borgström: jorden – vårt öde', *Medlemsblad för biologilärarnas förening*, 1 (1954)

Evenson, Robert E. and Douglas Gollin. 'Assessing the impact of the Green Revolution, 1960 to 2000', *Science* 300:5620 (2003), pp. 758–62

Evernden, Niel. *The Social Creation of Nature*, Baltimore, Johns Hopkins University Press, 1992

Eyerman, Ron, and Andrew Jamison. *Social Movements: A Cognitive Approach*, Cambridge, Polity Press, 1991

Eyerman, Ron. *Between Culture and Politics: Intellectuals in Modern Society*, Oxford, Polity Press, 1994

Fader, Marianela, Dieter Gerten, Michael Krause, Wolfgang Lucht and Wolfgang Cramer. 'Spatial decoupling of agricultural production and consumption: Quantifying dependences of countries on food imports due to domestic land and water constraints', *Environmental Research Letters*, 8:014046 (2013)

Fahlström, Jan Magnus. 'De oförenliga experterna', *Stockholms-Tidningen*, 18 December 1953

Fahlström, Jan Magnus. 'Överflödet geografi – eller hungerns', *Stockholms Tidningen*, 19 December 1953

Falcon, Walter P. 'The Green Revolution: Generations of problems', *American Journal of Agricultural Economics*, 52:5 (1970), p. 700

Fanon, Frantz. *The Wretched of the Earth*, Harmondsworth, Penguin, 1967

FAO. *World Food Survey*, Washington, DC, 1946

FAO. *Third World Food Survey*, Rome, FAO, 1963

FAO. *Rome Declaration on World Food Security and World Food Summit Plan of Action, World Food Summit, 13–17 November 1996*, Rome, 1996

FAO. *The State of Food Insecurity in the World 1999*, Rome, FAO, 1999

FAO. *The State of Food Insecurity in the World 2001*, Rome, FAO, 2001

FAO. *The State of Food Insecurity in the World 2003, Monitoring Progress Towards the World Food Summit and Millennium Development Goals*, Rome, FAO, 2003

FAO. *The State of Food and Agriculture 2019. Moving Forward on Food Loss and Waste Reduction*, Rome, FAO, 2019

FAO. *The State of the World's Biodiversity for Food and Agriculture*, J. Bélanger and D. Pilling (eds). Rome, FAO Commission on Genetic Resources for Food and Agriculture Assessments, 2019

FAO. *Food and Agriculture Statistics*, Rome, FAO, 2020 http://www.fao.org/food-agriculture-statistics/en/ (Accessed 29 June 2020)

FAO. *Strategic Framework 2022–2031*, Rome, FAO, 2021

FAO and WFP. Monitoring Food Security in Countries with Conflict Situations: A Joint FAO/WFP Update for the United Nations Security Council (FAO/WFP, 2018). (Accessed 15 December 2018)

Final Resolutions of the International Conference for the Protection of Nature, Brunnen, June 28th–July 3rd, 1947, Basel, Swiss League for the Protection of Nature, 1947

Fink, Hans. 'Humanøkologins naturbegrep', *Humanekologi*, 3/4 (1993), pp. 5–15

Finkbeiner, Elena M., Nathan J. Bennett, Timothy H. Frawley et al. 'Reconstructing overfishing: Moving beyond Malthus for effective and equitable solutions', *Fish and Fisheries*, 18 (2017), pp. 1180–1191

Flynn, Thomas. 'Foucault's mapping of history', in Gary Gutting (ed.), *The Cambridge Companion to Foucault*, Cambridge, Cambridge University Press, 1994

Food for Life, Food for Thought: The World Must Eat, New York, Study Guide Series, 1962

Forser, Tomas, and Per Arne Tjäder. *Tredje ståndpunkten: en debatt från det kalla krigets dagar*, Staffanstorp, Cavefors, 1972

Foucault, Michel. 'The discourse on language', appendix to *Archeology of Knowledge*, New York, Pantheon, 1972

Foucault, Michel. *Archeology of Knowledge*, New York, Pantheon, 1972

Foucault, Michel. 'Nietzsche, genealogy, history', in *Language, Counter-Memory, Practice: Selected Essays and Interviews*, Ithaca, NY, Cornell University Press, 1977

Fremlin, John H. 'How many people can the world support?', *New Scientist*, no. 415, 29 October 1964

Fremlin, John H. *Be Fruitful and Multiply: Life at the Limits of Population*, London, Rupert Hart-Davis, 1972

Frenander, Anders. 'Debattens vågor: om politisk-ideologiska frågor i efterkrigstidens svenska kulturdebatt' (Dissertation, Göteborg, 1998)

Fuller, R. Buckminster. *Utopia or Oblivion: The Prospects for Humanity*, Toronto, Bantam Books, 1969

Furon, Raymond. 'Protection of natural rresources: education and propaganda', in *Proceedings of the United Nations Scientific Conference on the Conservation and Utilization of Resources. 17 August–6 September 1949, Lake Success, New York*, Vol.1

Förslag till Naturskyddslag m. m.: Betänkande avgivet av Naturskyddsutredningen, SOU 1951: 5

Galbraith, John Kenneth. *The Affluent Society*, New York, Mentor, 1958

Garb, J.Y. 'The use and misuse of the Whole Earth image', *Whole Earth Review*, March 1985, pp. 18–25

Geertz, Clifford. *Agricultural Involution: The Process of Ecological Change in Indonesia*, Berkeley, University of California Press, 1963

Geertz, Clifford. *Interpretation of Cultures: Selected Essays*, New York, Basic Books, 1973

Gellner, Ernest. *Nations and Nationalism*, Oxford, Blackwell, 1983

George R. Lucas, Jr and Thomas W. Ogletree (eds). *Lifeboat Ethics: The Moral Dilemmas of World Hunger*, New York, Harper & Row, 1976

Gerholm, Tor-Ragnar. *Futurum Exaktum: The Technical Challenge*, Stockholm, Aldus/Bonnier, 1972

Gerholm, Tor-Ragnar. 'Domedagsporr för intellektuella', *Moderna Tider*, December 1999/January 2000, pp. 20–3

Giddens, Anthony. *The Consequences of Modernity*, Cambridge, Polity Press, 1990

Gillberg, Björn. *Mordet på framtiden: en uppgörelse med den politiska och ekonomiska kortsiktigheten*, Stockholm, Wahlström & Widstrand, 1973

Glacken, Clarence J. *Traces on the Rhodian Shore: Nature and Culture from Ancient Times to the End of the Eighteenth Century*, Berkeley, CA, University of California Press, 1990 (1967)

Global Nutrition Report. *Global Nutrition Report: Stronger Commitments for Greater Action*, Bristol, UK, Development Initiatives, 2022

Godfray, H. Charles J., John R. Beddington, Ian R. Crute, Lawrence Haddad et al. 'Food security: The challenge of feeding 9 billion people', *Science*, 327:5967 (2010), pp. 812–818

Goldblatt, David. *Social Theory and the Environment*, Cambridge, Polity Press, 1996

Goldstein, Joshua S. and David P. Rapkin. 'After insularity: hegemony and the future world order', *Futures*, 23 (1991), pp. 935–59

Golley, Frank B. *A History of the Ecosystem Concept in Ecology: More than the Sum of the Parts*, New Haven, Yale University Press, 1993

Golub R., and Townsend, J. 'Malthus, multinationals and the Club of Rome', *Social Studies of Science*, 7 (1977), pp. 202–22

Goodrich, Leland M. *The United Nations in a Changing World*, New York, Columbia University Press, 1974

Gottlieb, Robert. *Forcing the Spring*, Washington, DC, Island Press, 1993

Greer, Thomas. *A Brief History of Western Man*, New York, Harcourt Brace Jovanovich, 1977

Grenbäck, Erik. 'Världssvält – överproduktion', *RFL-tidningen* 1949: 1

Grigg, David. *The World Food Problem*, 2nd edn, Oxford, Blackwell, 1999 (1993)

Guha, Ramachandra, and Juan Martinez-Alier. *Varieties of Environmentalism: Essays North and South*, London, Earthscan, 1997

Gullander, Åke. 'Kan jorden föda oss?', *RLF-tidningen* 1953: 47

Handeln med Olja, SOU 1947:14

Hajer, Maarten. and Frank Fischer. 'Beyond global discourse: the rediscovery of culture in environmental politics', in M. Hajer and F. Fischer (eds), *Living With Nature: Environmental Politics as Cultural Discourse*, Oxford, Oxford University Press, 1999

Hansen, Roger (ed.). *The U.S. and the World Development: Agenda for Action*, New York, Praeger, 1976

Hanson, Earl Parker. 'Mankind need not starve', *Nation*, 169 (12 November 1949), p. 464. Reprinted in Walter M. Daniels (ed.), *The Point Four Program*, New York, Wilson, 1951

Haraldsson, Desirée. 'Skydda vår natur' (Dissertation, Lund, 1987)

Haraway, Donna J. *Primate Visions: Gender, Race and Nature in the World of Modern Science*, New York, Routledge, 1989

Haraway, Donna J. 'Universal donors in a vampire culture', in W. Cronon (ed.), *Uncommon Ground: Toward Reinventing Nature*, New York, W.W. Norton, 1995

Hardin, Garrett (ed.). *Population, Evolution and Birth Control: A Collage of Controversial Readings*, San Francisco, W.H. Freeman, 1964

Hardin, Garrett. 'The tragedy of the commons', *Science*, 162 (1968), pp. 1243–48

Hardin, Garrett. 'Living on a lifeboat', *Bioscience*, 24 (1974), pp. 561–8

Harrison, Harry. *Make Room, Make Room*, New York, Doubleday, 1966

Harvey, David. 'Population, resources and the ideology of science', *Economic Geography*, 50 (1974), pp. 256–77

Harvey, David. *Justice, Nature and the Geography of Difference*, Oxford, Blackwell, 1996

Harvey, David. *The Condition of Postmodernity*, Cambridge, MA, Blackwell, 1990

Hawley, Amos H. *Human Ecology: A Theory of Community Structure*, New York, The Ronald Press Company, 1950

Hays, Samuel P. 'From conservation to environment: environmental politics in the United States since World War II', in Kendall E. Bailes (ed.), *Environmental History*, Lanham MD, University Press of America, 1985

Hedlund, Johanna, Henrik Carlsen, Simon Croft, Chris West et al. 'Impacts of climate change on global food trade networks', *Environmental Research Letters*, 17: 124040 (2022)

Hedrén, Johan. *Miljöpolitikens natur*, Linköping, Linköping Studies in Art and Science, 1994 (Dissertation)

Herman, Arthur. *The Idea of Decline in Western History*, New York, The Free Press, 1996

Hickey, Leed T., Amber N. Hafeez, Hannah Robinson, Scott A. Jackson, Soraya C.M. Leal-Bertioli, Mark Tester, Caixia Gao et al. 'Breeding crops to feed 10 billion', *Nature Biotechnology*, 37:7 (2019), p. 744

Higbee, Edward. *The Squeeze: Cities Without Space*, New York, Morrow, 1960

Hillmo, Thomas, and Ulrik Lohm. 'Nature's ombudsmen: the evolution of environmental representation in Sweden', *Environment and History*, 3:1 (1997), pp. 19–29

Hinds, Lynn Boyd and Theodore Otto Windt, *The Cold War as Rhetoric: The Beginnings, 1945–1950*, New York, Praeger, 1991

Holmberg, Lars. 'Skall svälten segra', *Sydsvenska Dagbladet*, 24 October 1953

Homer-Dixon, Thomas F. *Environment, Scarcity, and Violence*, Princeton, Princeton University Press, 1999

Hubbert, M. King. *Resources and Man*, National Academy of Sciences and National Research Council, San Francisco, Freeman, 1969

Hubendick, Bengt. *Civilisation till döds?: kring människan som del av sin biologiska miljö*, Göteborg, Zinderman, 1970

Huldt, Bo. 'Svensk nedrustnings- och säkerhetspolitik från tjugotal till åtiotal', in Bo Hugemark (ed.), *Neutralitet och försvar: Perspektiv på svensk säkerhetspolitik 1809–1985*, Stockholm, Militärhistoriska förlaget, 1986

Hult, Jöran. 'Livsmedelsbrist och jordförstöring', *Samtid och Framtid*, no. 5, 1949

Huxley, Aldous. *Brave New World Revisited*, London, Chatto & Windus, 1958

Huxley, Julian. *Essays of a Humanist*, London, Chatto & Windus, 1964

International Technical Conference on the Protection of Nature. Proceedings and Papers, Paris, 1950

International Union for the Conservation of Nature and Natural Resources. *1973 IUCN Yearbook*, Morges, Switzerland, 1974

IPBES. *Global Assessment Report on Biodiversity and Ecosystem Services of The Intergovernmental Science-Policy Platform on Biodiversity and Ecosystem Services*, Eduardo S. Brondizio, Josef Settele, Sandra Díaz, and Hien T. Ngo (eds). Bonn, IPBES Secretariat, Germany, 2019

Isaksson, Ulla, and Erik Hjalmar Linder. *Elin Wägner 1922–1949: Dotter av moder jord*, Stockholm, Bonniers, 1980

Ise, John. *Our National Park Policy: A Critical History*, Baltimore, John Hopkins Press, 1962

Jacks, Graham V. and Robert O. Whyte. *The Rape of the Earth: A World Survey of Soil Erosion*, London, Faber & Faber, 1939

Jackson, L.A. *The Journal of World Intellectual Property*, 3 (2000), pp. 825–48

Jameson, Fredric. *The Political Unconscious: Narrative as a Socially Symbolic Act*, Ithaca, NY, Cornell University Press, 1981

Jameson, Fredric and Masao Miyoshi (eds), *The Cultures of Globalization*, Durham, NC, Duke University Press, 1998

Jarrick, Arne, and Johan Söderberg. *Praktisk historieteori*, Univeristy of Stockholm, 1993

Johansson, Alf W. 'Den svenska socialdemokratin och fascismen på trettiotalet: några reflexioner', in *Utrikespolitik och historia*, Stocholm, Militärhistoriska förlaget, 1987

Johansson, Alf W. *Herbert Tingsten och det kalla kriget: Antikommunism och liberalism i Dagens Nyheter, 1946–1952*, Stockholm, Tiden, 1995

Johansson, Alf W. 'Socialiseringen som kom av sig' (rew.), *Historisk Tidskrift*, 1996, 1, pp. 198–206

Johansson, Alf W. 'Varför gav socialdemokraterna upp planhushållningspolitiken', *Historisk Tidskrift*, 1997, 3, pp. 445–8

Johnson, D. Gale. *World Food Problems and Prospects*, Washington, DC, American Enterprise Institute for Public Policy Research, 1975

Jones, Joseph Marion. *The Fifteen Weeks*, New York, Harcourt Brace, 1955

References

Jonter, Thomas. *Socialiseringen som kom av sig: Sverige, oljan och USAs planer på en ny ekonomisk världsording 1945–1949*, Stockholm, Carlssons, 1994

Jonter, Thomas. 'Genmäle till Alf W. Johansson', *Historisk Tidskrift*, 1996, 1, pp. 150–58

Jonter, Thomas. 'Svar på Alf W. Johanssons genmäle', *Historisk Tidskrift*, 1997, 3, pp. 449–51

Jowett, A.J. 'China: the demographic disaster', in J.I. Clarke *et al.* (eds), *Population and Disaster*, Oxford, Basil Blackwell, 1989

Jörberg, Lennart. *Den svenska ekonomiska utvecklingen 1861–1983*, Lund, Ekonom-isk-historiska föreningen, 1984

Kahn, Herman, William Brown and Leon Martel. *The Next 200 Years: A Scenario for America and the World*, London, Associated Business Programmes, 1977

Keegan, John. *A History of Warfare*, New York, Alfred A. Knopf, 1993

Kellogg, Charles E. 'Modern soil science', *American Scientist*, 36, 4 (October 1948)

Keohane, Robert O. and Joseph S. Nye. *Power and Interdependence: World Politics in Transition*, Boston, Little, Brown, 1977

Kermode, Frank. *The Sense of an Ending: Studies in the Theory of Fiction*, New York, 1967

Keyzer, M.A., M.D. Merbis, I.F.P.W Pavel and C.F.A van Wesenbeeck. 'Diet shifts towards meat and the effects on cereal use: Can we feed the animals in 2030?' *Ecological Economics*, 55 (2005), pp.187–202

Koppes, Clayton R. 'Environmental policy and American liberalism: the Department of the Interior, 1933–1953', in Kendall E. Bailes (ed.), *Environmental History*, Lanham, MD, University Press of America, 1985

Kuznik, Peter. *Beyond the Laboratory: Scientists as Political Activists in the 1930s America*, Chicago, Chicago University Press, 1987

Kwa, Chunglin. 'Representations of nature mediating between ecology and science policy: the case of the International Biological Programme', *Social Studies of Science*, 17 (1987), pp. 413–42

Kylhammar, Martin. *Den okände Sten Selander: En borgerlig intellektuell*, Stockholm, Akademeja, 1990

Lacoste, Yves. *Contre les anti-tiers-mondistes: et contre certains tiers-mondistes*, Paris, Éditions la Découverte, 1986

Lagerberg, Torsten. 'Livsmedelsbrist och jordförstöring', *Samtid och Framtid*, no. 5, 1949

Lappé, Francis M. 'The politics of protein', *America's Biological Teachers*, 35 (1973), pp. 254–9

Lappé, Frances Moore. *Diet for a Small Planet*, revised edn., New York, Ballantine Books, 1975 (1971)

Lappé, Frances Moore and Joseph Collins. *Food First: Beyond the Myth of Scarcity*, Boston, Houghton-Mifflin, 1977

Larrain, Jorge. *The Concept of Ideology*, London, Hutchinson, 1979

Latour, Bruno. 'Guerre des mondes – offres de paix', in Bruno Latour, *Das Parlament der Dinge: Für eine politische Okologie*, Frankfurt, Suhrkamp, 2001

Laurence, William. 'Population outgrows food: scientists warn the World', *The New York Times*, 15 July 1948

Leander, Tom. 'U-hjälpens småsmulor', *Svenska Dagbladet*, 26 March 1969

Leffler, Melvyn P. *A Preponderance of Power: National Security, the Truman Administration and the Cold War*, Stanford, CA, Stanford University Press, 1992

Leopold, Aldo. 'The conservation ethic', *Journal of Forestry*, 31 (October 1933), pp. 634–43

Leopold, Aldo. *Game Management*, New York, 1933

Leopold, Aldo. 'The ecological consciousness', *Bulletin of the Garden Club of America*, 46 (1947)

Leopold, Aldo. *Sand County Almanack, and Sketches Here and There*, New York, Oxford University Press, 1949

Leopold, Starker A. 'Ecological aspects of deer production on forest land', in *Proceedings of the United Nations Scientific Conference on the Conservation and Utilization of Resources, 17 August–6 September 1949, Lake Success, New York*, Vol. VII

Lewin, Leif. *Planhushållningsdebatten*, Stockholm, Almqvist & Wiksell, 1967

Lewis, Christopher. 'Progress and apocalypse: science and the end of the modern world', (Dissertation, 2 vols, University of Minnesota, 1991)

Lewis, R. D. 'The influence of cropping systems on sustained production, soil management and conservation', in *Proceedings of the United Nations Scientific Conference on the Conservation and Utilization of Resources, 17 August–6 September 1949, Lake Success, New York*, Vol. V

Liang, Xin-Zhong, You Wu, Robert G. Chambers, Daniel L. Schmoldt et al. 'Determining climate effects on US total agricultural productivity', *Proceedings of the National Academy of Sciences of the United States of America*, 114:12 (2017) pp. 2285–2292

Liedman, Sven-Eric. 'Om ideologier', in Sven-Eric Liedman and Ingemar Nilsson, *Om ideologi och ideologianalys*, Göteborg, Arachne, 1989

Lima, Mauricio and Sebastián Abades. 'Malthusian factors as proximal drivers of human population crisis at Sub-Saharan Africa', *Frontiers in Ecology and Evolution*, 3 (2015)

Lindén, Jan-Ivar. 'Metaforen – en ricoeurisation', *Res Publica*, 9 (1987)

Linnér, Björn-Ola and Ulrik Lohm. 'Administering Nature Conservation in Sweden during a Century: From Conwentz and Back', *Jahrbüch für europäische Verwaltungsgeschichte*, 11 (Baden-Baden, Nomos, 1999), pp. 307–34

Linnér, Björn-Ola. 'Naturen som minnesmärke', in Annika Alzén and Johan Hedrén (eds), *Kulturarvets natur*, Stockholm, Symposion, 1998

Linnér, Björn-Ola and Jan Lundqvist. 'Ny strategi för världens vatten', *Göteborgs-Posten*, 22 January 2000

Linnér, Björn-Ola and Henrik Selin. 'Sustainable development and globalization: the Stockholm legacy', paper presented at the Nature and Culture Seminar, University of Kansas, 2 February 2002

Linnér, Björn-Ola and Henrik Selin. 'The quest for sustainability: the legacy of the Stockholm Conference 1972', paper presented at the International Studies Association, Portland, OR, 1 March 2003

Linnér, Björn-Ola and Henrik Selin. 'The United Nations Conference on Sustainable Development: Forty years in the making', *Environment and Planning. C: Government and Policy*, 31:6 (2013), pp. 971–987

Lipton, Michael. 'Reviving global poverty reduction: what role for genetically modified plants?', CGIAR Crawford Lectures, Washington DC, CGIAR, 1999

Lowe, Philip. 'Values and institutions in the history of British nature conservation', in A. Warren and F. Goldsmith (eds), *Conservation in Perspective*, Chichester, Wiley, 1983

Lowe, Philip, and Jane Goyder. *Environmental Groups in Politics*, London, Allen and Unwin, 1983

Lukács, Georg. *History and Class Consciousness: Studies in Marxist Dialectics*, London, 1983

Lundberg, Svante, Sven-Axel Månsson, Hans Welander. *Demonstranter: En sociologisk studie*, Stockholm, PAN/Nordstedts, 1970

Lundgren, Lars J. *Miljöpolitik på längden och tvären: Några synpunkter på svensk miljövård under 1900-talet*, Solna, Naturvårdsverket, 1989

Lundqvist, Lennart. 'Miljövårdförvaltning och politisk struktur', (Dissertation, Uppsala, 1971)

Löfgren, Orvar. 'Medierna i nationsbygget', in Ulf Hannerz (ed.), *Medier och kultur*, Stockholm, Carlssons, 1997

Maddison, Angus. *Phases of Capitalist Development*, Oxford, Oxford University Press, 1982

Magnusson, Torsten. 'Landsbygdens avfolkning sedd mot folkförsörjningens bakgrund', *Göteborgs Posten*, 21 February 1949

Maher, T. Michael. 'How and why journalists avoid the population–enviroment connection', *Population and Environment*, 18:4 (1997)

Malthus, Thomas Robert. *The Works of Thomas Robert Malthus. Vol. 1, An Essay on the Principle of Population*, London, Pickering and Chatto, 1986 (1798)

Mangus, Erik L. 'Besynnerlig Borgström utredning', *Göteborgs-Posten*, 1 March 1958

Marsh, George Perkins. *Man and Nature: Physical Geography as Modified by Human Action*, ed. David Lowenthal, Cambridge, MA, Belknap Press, 1965

Martinez-Alier, Juan. *Ecological Economics: Energy, Environment and Society*, Oxford, Blackwell, 1993 (1987)

Martinson, Harry. *Aniara: A Review of Man in Time and Space*, translated by Stephen Klass and Leif Sjöberg, Vekerum Förlag, 1991

de Martonne, Emmanuel. 'Interdependence of resources', in *Proceedings of the United Nations Scientific Conference on the Conservation and Utilization of Resources. 17 August–6 September 1949, Lake Success, New York*, Vol. I

Mbow, Cheik, Cynthia Rosenzweig, Luis G. Barioni , Tim G. Benton et al., '2019: Food security', in Priyadarshi R. Shukla, Jim Skea, Eduardo C. Buendia, Valérie Masson-Delmotte, et al. (eds), *Climate Change And Land: An IPCC Special Report On Climate Change, Desertification, Land Degradation, Sustainable Land Management, Food Security, And Greenhouse Gas Fluxes In Terrestrial Ecosystems*, Cambridge, UK, and New York, Cambridge University Press, 2021

McCormick, Thomas J. *America's Half-Century: United States Foreign Policy in the Cold War and After*, Baltimore, Johns Hopkins University Press, 1995 (1989)

McCoullough, David. *Truman*, New York, Simon and Schuster, 1992

McDougall, Walter A. *Promised Land, Crusader State: The American Encounter with the World Since 1776*, New York, Houghton Mifflin, 1997

McIntosh, Robert P. *The Background of Ecology: Concept and Theory*, Cambridge, Cambridge University Press, 1985

McNeill, John R. *Something New Under the Sun: An Environmental History of the Twentieth-century World*, New York, W.W. Norton & Company, 2000

Meadows, Donella H. et al. *The Limits to Growth: A Report for the Conservation Club of Rome's Project on the Predicament of Mankind*, New York, Universe books, 1972

Merchant, Carolyn. *The Death of Nature*, San Francisco, Harper & Row, 1989

Mészáros, István. *The Power of Ideology*, New York, New York University Press, 1989

Meyer, William B. *Human Impact on the Earth*, New York, Cambridge University Press, 1996

Miller, Char. *Gifford Pinchot and the Making of Modern Environmentalism*, Washington, DC, Island Press/Shearwater Books, 2001

Morse, Edward L. 'The politics of interdependence', *International Organization*, 23 (1969)

Myrdal, Gunnar. *Varning för fredsoptimism*, Stockholm, 1944

Myrdal, Janken. 'Miljökrisens roll i historien', *Historisk Tidskrift*, 2 (1997), pp. 268–9

Nash, Roderick. *Wilderness and the American Mind*, 3rd edn, New Haven, Yale University Press, 1982

Naso, Pedro, Bruno Lanz and Tim Swanson. 'The return of Malthus? Resource constraints in an era of declining population growth', *European Economic Review*, 128:103499 (2020)

National Academies of Sciences, Engineering, and Medicine. *Science Breakthroughs to Advance Food and Agricultural Research by 2030*, Washington, DC, NASEM, 2019

Nature. Editorial. 'License CRISPR patents for free to share gene editing globally'. *Nature*, 597:152 (2021)

Nelson, Gerald and C. Nelson. *Genetically Modified Organisms in Agriculture: Economics and Politics*, San Diego, Academic Press, 2001

Netzén, Gösta. 'Jorden – Vårt öde', *Arbetet*, 1953 October 20

New York Times Index. New York, 1948–50

Niehoff, Richard. *John A. Hannah: Versatile Administrator and Distinguished Public Servant*, Lanham, MD, University Press of America, 1989

Nilsson, Annika. *Genetically Modified Crops: Why? Why Not? Report from an International Conference in Stockholm, May 14–15, 2001*, Stockholm, Royal Swedish Academy of Agriculture and Forestry, 2002

Nilsson, Göran B. 'Om det fortfarande behovet av källkritik', *Historisk Tidskrift*, 2 (1973), pp.173–211

Nixon, Edgar B. (ed.). *Franklin D. Roosevelt and Conservation 1911–1945*, Vol. 2, Hyde Park, NY, Franklin D. Roosevelt Library, 1957

Noréen, Eric. *Brobygge eller blockbildning? De norska och svenska utrikesledningarnas säkerhetspolitiska föreställningar 1945–1948*, Stockholm, Carlssons, 1994

Norgaard, Richard B. *Development Betrayed: The End of Progress and a Coevolutionary Revisioning of the Future*, London, Routledge, 1994

Nwokoro, I.I.C. and Samuel O. Dekolo. 'Land use change and environmental sustainability: The case of Lagos metropolis', *WIT Transactions on Ecology and the Environment*, 155 (2012), pp. 157–167

O'Brien, Karen. 'Is the 1.5° C target possible? Exploring the three spheres of transformation', *Current Opinion in Environmental Sustainability*, 31 (2018), pp. 153–160

Ohlin, Bertil. 'Politisk propaganda och socialisering', *Tiden*, 1946

Opie, John. *Nature's Nation: An Environmental History of the United States*, Forth Worth, Harcourt Brace, 1998

Ordway, Samuel. *Resources and the American Dream, Including a Theory of the Limit of Growth*, New York, Ronald Press Co., 1953

d'Orico, Paolo, Joel A. Carr, Francesco Laio, Luca Ridolfi and Stefano Vandoni. 'Feeding humanity through global food trade', *Earth's Future* (2014), pp.458–469

Osborn, Fairfeld. *Our Plundered Planet*, Boston, Little, Brown and Company, 1948

Osborn, Fairfeld. 'World resource situation', in *Proceedings of the United Nations Scientific Conference on the Conservation and Utilization of Resources. 17 August–6 September 1949, Lake Success, New York*, Vol. I

Osborn Fairfeld (ed.). *Our Crowded Planet: Essays on the Pressures of Population*, London, Doubleday, 1962

Osvald, Hugo. 'Livsmedelsbrist och jordförstöring', *Samtid och Framtid*, no. 5, 1949

Our World in Data. *Future Population Growth*, https://ourworldindata.org/future-population-growth (Accessed 23 January 2020)

Paddock, Paul and William. *Famine – 1975! America's Decision: Who will Survive?*, Boston, Little, Brown and Company, 1967

Palme, Olof. 'Speech by the Prime Minister at the plenary session of the UN Conference on the Human Environment, 6th June', in *Documents on Swedish Foreign Policy 1972*, Royal Ministry for Foreign Affairs, New Series I: C:22, Stockholm, 1973

Palmstierna, Hans. *Plundring, svält, förgiftning*, Stockholm, Rabén & Sjögren, 1967

Palmstierna, Hans. *Besinning*, Stockholm, Rabén & Sjögren, 1972

Panos Institute. *Food for All: Can Hunger be Halved?*, London, Panos Institute, 2001

Pearl, Raymond. *The Natural History of Population*, New York, Oxford University Press, 1939

Pence, Gregory E. *Designer Food: Mutant Harvest or Breadbasket of the World?*, Lanham, MD, Rowman & Littlefield, 2002

Pepper, David. *The Roots of Modern Environmentalism*, London, Routledge, 1989

Perkins, John H. 'The Rockefeller Foundation and the Green Revolution, 1941–1956', *Agriculture and Human Values*, 7 (1990)

Perkins, John H. *Geopolitics and the Green Revolution: Wheat, Genes and the Cold War*, Oxford, Oxford University Press, 1997

Perkins, John H. 'The rhetoric of population and its consequences', Paper presented at the meeting of the American Society for Environmental History, Baltimore, 6–9 March 1997

Persley, G.J., and M.M. Lantin (eds). *Agricultural Biotechnology and the Poor*, Washington, DC, CGIAR, 2000

Petterson, Ivar. 'Kapplöpningen mot världssvälten', *Stockholms-Tidningen*, 14 October 1953

Pettersson, Knut. 'Den undernärda världen', *Göteborgs Handels- och sjöfartstidning*, 17 November 1953

Phogole, Bopaki and Kowiyou Yessoufou. 'Biodiversity and economy but not social factors predict human population dynamics in South Africa', *Sustainability*, 14 (2022)

Pielke, Roger and Björn-Ola Linnér. 'From Green Revolution to green evolution: A critique of the political myth of averted famine', *Minerva*, 57:3 (2019)

Pisani, Sallie. *The CIA and the Marshall Plan*, Lawrence, University Press of Kansas, 1991

Pixley, Kevin V., Jose B. Falck-Zepeda, Robert L. Paarlberg, Peter W. B. Phillips, Inez H. Slamet-Loedin, Kanwarpal S. Dhugga, Hugo Campos and Neal Gutterson. 'Genome-edited crops for improved food security of smallholder farmers', *Nature Genetics*, 54:4 (2022)

Pohl, Frederik and C.M. Kornbluth. *The Space Merchants*, New York, Walker & Co., 1953 (1952)

Poleman, Thomas. 'World food: a perspective', *Science*, 188 (May 1975), pp. 561–8

Poore, Joseph and Thomas Nemecek. 'Reducing food's environmental impacts through producers and consumers', *Science* (2018), pp. 987–92

Population Division of the Department of Economic and Social Affairs of the United Nations Secretariat. *World Population Prospects: The 2000 Revision*, ESA/P/WP.165, 2001

Population Division of the Department of Economic and Social Affairs of the United Nations Secretariat. *World Population Prospects: The 2000 Revision and World Urbanization Prospects: The 2001 Revision*, http://esa.un.org/unpp, 3 January 2003

Population Division of the Department of Economic and Social Affairs. *World Population Prospects: The 2022 Revision*, https://population.un.org/wpp/ (Accessed 28 November 2022).

van der Post, Laurens. *Venture to the Interior*, London, Hogarth Press, 1952

Postel, Sandra. *The Last Oasis: Facing Water Scarcity*, London, Earthscan, 1997 (1992)

Potts, Malcolm, Courtney Henderson and Martha Campbell. 'The Sahel: A Malthusian challenge?' *Environmental and Resource Economics*, 55 (2013), pp. 501–512

Proceedings of the United Nations Scientific Conference on the Conservation and Utilization of Resources. 17 August–6 September 1949, Lake Success, New York

Protocol of the Swedish Parliament. AK, 'Debatt vid remiss av statsverkspropositionen', no. 4, 1965

Protocol of the Swedish Parliament. AK, 'Internationellt utvecklingsbistånd', no. 21, 1967

Protocol of the Swedish Parliament. FK, 'Interpellation ang. professorn G. Borgströms avång från Institutet för konserveringsforskning', no. 25, 1958

Protocol of the Swedish Parliament, FK, 'Interpellation ang. vissa spörsmål i samband med professorn G. Borgströms avgång från Institutet för konserveringsforskning', no. 11, 1958

Protocol of the Swedish Parliament. FK, 'Remissdebatt angående Statsverkspropositionen', 19 January 1949

Public Papers of the Presidents of the United States. Harry S. Truman: Containing the Public Messages, Speeches, and Statements of the President, 1949, Washington, United States Printing Office, 1964

Public Papers of the Secretaries-General of the United Nations: Vol. 8, U Thant, 1968–1971; New York, Columbia University Press, 1977

Purcell, Warren, Thomas Neubauer and Kevin Mallinger. 'Digital twins in agriculture: challenges and opportunities for environmental sustainability', *Current Opinion in Environmental Sustainability*, 61 (2023)

Pursell, Carroll. 'Conservation, environmentalism, and the engineers: the progressive era and the recent past', in Kendall E. Bailes (ed.), *Environmental History*, Lanham, MD, University Press of America, 1985

Ramankutty, Navin Zia Mehrabi, Katharina Waha, Larissa Jarvis, Claire Kremen, Mario Herrero and Loren H. Rieseberg. 'Trends in global agricultural land use: Implications for environmental health and food security', *Annual Review of Plant Biology*, 69 (2018), pp. 789–815

Ray, Deepak K., Navin Ramankutty, Nathaniel D. Mueller, Paul C. West and Jonathan A. Foley. 'Recent patterns of crop yield growth and stagnation', *Nature Communications*, 3:1 (2012)

Ray, Deepak K., Nathaniel D. Mueller, Paul C. West and Jonathan A. Foley. 'Yield trends are insufficient to double global crop production by 2050', *PLOS ONE*, 8:6 (2013)

Readers' Guide to Periodical Literature, H. W. Wilson Co., New York, 1949, 1950

Report of the International Conference on Population and Development: Cairo, 5–13, September 1994, New York, 1994, A/CONF.171/13

Report of the United Nations Conference on the Human Environment: Stockholm, 5–16 June 1972, United Nations, A/CONF: 48/14/Rev.1

Ricoeur, Paul. *Interpretation Theory: Discourse and the Surplus of Meaning*, Fort Worth, Texas Christian University Press, 1976

Ricoeur, Paul. *The Rule of the Metaphor*, London, University of Toronto Press, 1978

Ricoeur, Paul. *Lectures on Ideology and Utopia*, edited by George H. Taylor, New York, Columbia University Press, 1986

Rodman, Peter W. *More Precious Than Peace: The Cold War and the Struggle for the Third World*, New York, Charles Scribner's Sons, 1994

Rome, Adam. *The Bulldozer in the Countryside: Suburban Sprawl and the Rise of American Environmentalism*, Cambridge, Cambridge University Press, 2001

Rosecrance, Richard and A. Stein. 'Interdependence: myth or reality?', *International Organization*, 35 (1973), pp. 553–60

Rothschild, Emma. 'Food Politics', *Foreign Affairs*, 54:2 (1976)

Rudebeck, Gustaf. 'Biologistuderande på 30-talet', in Gunvor Blomquist (ed.), *Under Lundagårds kronor*, 5, Lund University Press, 1991

Runte, Alfred. *National Parks: The American Experience*, Lincoln, University of Nebraska Press, 1979

Sachs, Wolfgang. 'Global ecology and the shadow of "development"', in Wolfgang Sachs (ed.) *Global Ecology: A New Arena of Political Conflict*, London, Zed Books, 1993, pp. 3–21

Sætra, Hartvig. *Den økopolitiske socialismen*, Oslo, Pax, 1973

Sanderson, Fred. *The Great Food Fumble*, Washington, DC, The Brookings Institution, 1975

Sauvy, Alfred. *Fertility and Survival: Population Problems from Malthus to Mao Tse-tung*, New York, Criterion, 1961

Sax, Karl. *Standing Room Only: The Challenge of Overpopulation*, Boston, 1955

Schipper, E. Lisa, F. Aromar Revi, Benjamin L. Preston, Edward. R. Carr, et al. 'Climate resilient development pathways', in Hans-Otto Pörtner, Debra C. Roberts, Melinda M.B. Tignor, Elvira S. Poloczanska et al., (eds). *Climate Change 2022: Impacts, Adaptation and Vulnerability. Contribution of Working Group II to the Sixth Assessment Report of the Intergovernmental Panel on Climate Change*, Cambridge, UK, and New York, Cambridge University Press, 2022

Schneider, William. *Food, Foreign Policy, and Raw Materials Cartels*, New York, Crane, Russak & Co., 1976

Schurmann, Franz. *The Logic of World Power: An Inquiry into the Origins, Currents, and Contradictions of World Politics*, New York, Pantheon, 1974

Science Citation Index: An International Disciplinary Index to Literature of Science, Philadelphia, Institute for Scientific Information, 1947–54, 1955–64, 1965–69, 1970–74

Scott, James C. *Against the Grain: A Deep History of the Earliest States*, New Haven, Yale University Press, 2017

Searchinger, Tim, Richard Waite, Craig Hanson, Janet Ranganathan, Patrice Dumas and Emily Matthews, *SYNTHESIS REPORT: Creating a Sustainable Food Future: A Menu of Solutions to Feed Nearly 10 Billion People by 2050*, World Resources Institute, 2018

Sears, Paul B. *Deserts on the March*, 2nd edn, Norman, University of Oklahoma Press, 1947 (1935)

Segrell, Björn. *Den attraktiva kusten: synsätt, konflikter och landskapsnyttjande*, Linköping, Linköping Studies in art and science, 1995 (Dissertation)

Selander, Sten. 'Modernt Naturskydd', *Svenska Dagbladet*, 30 May 1949

Selander, Sten. 'Mänsklighetens framtid', *Svenska Dagbladet*, 14 November 1953

Selander, Tom. 'Katastrofhotet', *Svenska Dagbladet*, 31 October 1971

Seliger, Martin. *Ideology and Politics*, London, Allen & Unwin, 1976

Selin, Henrik and Björn-Ola Linnér. 'The thirty-year quest for global sustainability: a historical look at the 1972 Stockholm conference and beyond', Harvard University, Belfer Center for Science and International Affairs, Discussion Paper, forthcoming 2003

Sen, Amartya. *Poverty and Famines: An Essay on Entitlement and Deprivation*, Oxford, Clarendon Press, 1981

Sen, Amartya. *Inequality Reexamined*, Oxford, Oxford University Press, 1992

Sevón, Cay. *Visionen om Europa: Svensk neutralitet och europeisk återuppbygnad 1945–1948*, Helsinki, Suomen historiallinen seura, 1995

Shah, Mahendra and Maurice Strong. *Food in the 21st Century: from Science to Sustainable Agriculture*, Washington, DC, CGIAR, 1999

Shapin, Steven. *A Social History of Truth: Civility and Science in Seventeenth-Century England*, Chicago, University of Chicago Press, 1994

Shapin, Steven. *The Scientific Revolution*, Chicago, University of Chicago Press, 1996

Shelestov, Dmitry. *Demography in the Mirror of History*, Moscow, Progress Publishers, 1987

Shiva, Vandana and Ingunn Moser (eds). *Biopolitics: A Feminist and Ecological Reader on Biotechnology*, London, Zed Books, 1995

Shiva, Vandana. 'A civil society perspective', in Birgitta Rydhagen and Carin Dackman (eds) *Proceedings of Dolly and the Bean: Understanding Biotechnology in Broader Contexts, International conference, Luleå, 19–21 January 1999*, Luleå, Sweden, Luleå Univ. of Technology, 2000

Singh, Garima, Anamika Singh and Gurjit Kaur. 'Chapter 16 – Role of artificial intelligence and the internet of things in agriculture', in Gurjit Kaur, Pradeep Tomar and Marcus Tanque (eds), *Artificial Intelligence to Solve Pervasive Internet of Things Issues* (Elsevier, 2021), pp. 317–330

Skovdal, Bernt. *Tingsten, Totalitarismen, och ideologierna*, Stockholm, Symposion, 1992

Skovdahl, Bernt. 'Idéhistoria och källkritik', in Lennart Olausson (ed.), *Idéhistoriens egenart: Teori- och metodfrågor inom idéhistorien*, Stockholm, Symposion, 1994

Smith, Harrison. 'What shall we do to be saved?', *The Saturday Review of Literature*, 35 (21 August 1948)

Snow, C.P. *The State of Siege*, New York, Scribners, 1971 (1969)

Social Sciences Citation Index: An International Multidisciplinary Index to the Literature of the Social, Behavioral and Related Sciences, Philadelphia, Institute for Scientific Information, PA, 1966–70, 1971–75

SOS. *Befolkningsrörelsen 1941–50*, Stockholm, SCB, 1955

Söderqvist, Thomas. *The Ecologists: From Merry Naturalists to Saviours of the Nation*, Stockholm, Almqvist & Wiksell International, 1986

Sörlin, Sverker. 'Hembygden mellan historia och framtid', *Västerbotten*, 1984, 1, pp 70–79

Sörlin, Sverker. *Naturkontraktet: Om naturumgängets idéhistoria*, Stockholm, Carlssons, 1991

Statsutskottets utlåtanden, 'Uttalande i anledning av finansiellt utvecklingsbistånd', no 54, 1967

Statsverkspropositionen, 1, bil. 9:E, 'Finansiellt utvecklingsbistånd', 1967

Stengers, Isabelle. *Cosmopolitiques,* 1–7, Paris, La Découverte, 1997

Stevenson, Adlai. 'Strengthening the international development institutions', *The Papers of Adlai E. Stevenson: Vol. 8, Ambassador to the United Nations, 1961–1965,* Boston, Little, Brown, 1979

Study of Critical Environmental Problems. *Man's Impact on the Global Environment: Assessment and Recommendations for Action,* Report of the Study of Critical Environmental Problems, Cambridge, MA, 1970

Suweis, Samir, Joel A. Carr, Amos Maritan, Andrea Rinaldoc and Paolo D'Odorico., 'Resilience and reactivity of global food security', *Proceedings of the National Academy of Sciences of the United States of America,* 112:22 (2015), pp. 6902–6907

Swedish Parliament. *1966 års revisionsberättelser,* 2 saml., 1967

Svensson, Waldemar. 'Brist eller överflöd?', *Expressen,* 26 October 1953

Svensson, Waldemar. 'En fråga om energi', *Stockholms-Tidningen,* 24 February 1954

Svärdson, Gunnar. 'Urvalet är vårt öde', *Expressen,* 29 October 1953

Taylor, Peter J., and Frederick H. Buttel. 'How do we know we have global environmental problems? Science and the globalization of environmental discourse', *Geoforum,* 23:3 (1992)

Teferra, Tadesse Fikre. 'Should we still worry about the safety of GMO foods? Why and why not? A review', *Food Science & Nutrition,* 9:9 (2021)

The Official Washington Post Index, Woodbridge, CT, Research Publications, 1949, 1950

The Oxford English Dictionary, 2nd edn, Oxford, Clarendon Press, 1989

Theisen, Heinz. 'Katastrophenstimmung und freiheitliche Demokratie', (Dissertation, Bonn, 1984)

Thurén, Torsten. *Medier i blåsväder: Den svenska radion och televisionen som samhällsbevarare och samhällskritiker,* Stockholm, Etermedierna i Sverige, 1997

Thörn, Håkan. *Modernitet, sociologi och social rörelser,* Göteborg, Kompendiet, 1997

Tingsten, Herbert. *Från idéer till idyll: den lyckliga demokratin,* Stockholm, Bonnier, 1966

Toffler, Alvin. *Future Shock,* New York, Random House, 1970

Tolba, Mostafa K. (ed.). *The World Environment, 1972–1992: Two Decades of Challenge,* London, UNEP/Chapman & Hall, 1992

Torbrink, Bengt. 'Min jord, din jord eller vår jord?', *Göteborgs-Posten,* 18 October 1971

Torstendahl, Rolf. *Introduktion till historieforskningen: Historia som vetenskap,* Stockholm, Natur och Kultur, 1978 (1971)

Truman, Harry S. *Memoirs of Harry S. Truman: The Years of Trial and Hope, 1946–52,* New York, Da Capo, 1956

United Nations Development Programme. *Human Development Report: Consumption for Human Development,* New York, 1998

United Nations Environment Programme. *Malmö Ministerial Decleration*, Nairobi, UNEP, 2000

United Nations Environment Programme. *Food Waste Index Report 2021*, Nairobi, UNEP, 2021

United Nations Food Conference. *Assessment of the World Food Situation Present and Future*, Rome, FAO, 1974

The United Nations Framework Convention on Climate Change. *Sharm El-Sheikh Climate Implementation Summit Declaration COP27 Presidency Summary Outcomes, The Sharm El-Sheikh Climate Implementation Summit, 6–20 November 2022*, Sharm El-Sheikh, Eygpt, 2022

United Nations Population Fund. *The State of World Population 1998*, E/31,000/1998, New York, 1998

United Nations. 'Assessment of the world food situation: present and future', E/Conf. 65/3, United Nations World Food Conference, November 1974, UNA

United Nations, ECAFE. *Econmic Survey of Asia and the Far East*, 1948

United Nations, ECE. *Economic Survey of Europe*, 1947

United Nations. *United Nations Millennium Declaration*, 55/2, New York, United Nations, 2000

United Nations. *Report of the United Nations Conference on Environment and Development: Rio de Janeiro, 3–14 June 1992*, (vol. 1–3) New York, 1993, A/CONF.151/26/Rev.1

United States Department of Agriculture. *The World Food Budget, 1963 and 1966*, USDA Economic Research Service, October 1961

United States House of Representatives, Committee on International Relations. *Use of U.S. Food Resources for Diplomatic Purposes – An Examination of the Issues*, Washington, DC, US Government Printing Office, 1977

Utredning om förhållanden vid konserveringsinstitutet, Reports of the Government Commissions, 'SOU series', SOU 1958:3

Viklund, Daniel. *Neutralitetsdebatten: Tro, vetande och illusioner*, Stockholm, Nordstedts, 1989

Vogt, William. *Road to Survival*, London, Victor Gollancz, 1949 (1948)

Vogt, William. *People! Challenge to Survival*, London, Victor Gollancz, 1961 (1960)

Vondung, Klaus. *Die Apocalypse in Deutchland*, Munich, DTV, 1988

Wackernagel, Mathis, and William E. Rees. *Our Ecological Footprint: Reducing Human Impact on the Earth*, Philadelphia, PA, New Society Publishers, 1996

Wadia, D. N. 'Metals in relation to living standards', *Proceedings of the United Nations Scientific Conference on the Conservation and Utilization of Resources. 17 August–6 September 1949, Lake Success, New York*, vol I

Wagar, Warren W. *Terminal Visions: The Literature of Last Things*, Bloomington, Indiana University Press, 1982

Wahlbäck, Krister. *The Roots of Swedish Neutrality*, Stockholm, The Swedish Institute, 1986

Wallerstein, Immanuel. 'The unintended consequences of Cold War area studies', in Noam Chomsky et al., *The Cold War and the University*, New York, The New Press, 1997, pp. 171–238

Waltz, Emily. 'Asexual crops whet industry appetite', *Nature Biotechnology*, 37:2 (2019), pp. 109–10

Warburg, James P. 'Four primary questions', in Walter M. Daniels (ed.), *The Point Four Program*, New York, Wilson, 1951

Water Committee of the Royal Academy of Engineering. *Vattnet i farozonen: vattenfrågans läge i Sverige*, Stockholm, 1956

Weart, Spencer R. *Nuclear Fear: A History of Images*, Cambridge, MA, Harvard University Press, 1988

Welsh, Caitlin, Joseph S. Bermudez Jr., Jennifer Jun and Emma Dodd. 'Spotlight on damage to Ukraine's agricultural infrastructure since Russia's invasion'. *Commentary* (Center for Strategic and International Studies, 15 June 2022.) https://www.csis.org/analysis/spotlight-damage-ukraines-agricultural-infrastructure-russias-invasion (Accessed 20 January 2023).

Wibeck, Victoria, Björn-Ola Linnér, Melisa Alves, Therese Asplund et al. 'Stories of transformation: A cross-country focus group study on sustainable development and societal change', *Sustainability*, 11 (2019)

Wijk, Johnny. *Svarta börsen: samhällslojalitet i kris: livsmedelsransoneringarna och den illegala handeln i Sverige 1940–1949*, Stockholm, Almqvist & Wiksell International, 1992

Williams, Raymond. *Problems in Materialism and Culture*, London, Verso, 1980

de Wit, Maywa Montenegro. 'Democratizing CRISPR? Stories, practices, and politics of science and governance on the agricultural gene editing frontier', *Elementa: Science of the Anthropocene*, 8:9 (2020)

Wittgenstein, Ludwig. *Philosophical Investigations*, Oxford, Blackwell, 1953

Woodbridge, George. *UNRRA: The History of the United Nations Relief and Rehabilitation Administration*, Vol. 1, New York, Columbia University Press, 1950

Woods, Randall B., and Howard Jones. *Dawning of the Cold War: The United States' Quest for Order*, Athens, GA, 1991

World Bank, *World Development Report 1999/2000: Entering the 21st century*, New York, Oxford University Press, 2001

World Bank, *Poverty and Shared Prosperity 2018: Piecing Together the Poverty Puzzle*, Washington, DC, World Bank, 2018.

World Bank. *Poverty and Shared Prosperity 2022: Correcting Course*, Washington, DC, World Bank, 2022

World Economic Forum, *The Global Risks Report 2019*, 14th edition, Geneva, WEF, 2019

World Food Council. *Assessment of the World Food Situation and Outlook*, WFC/17/Rev. 1, 7 June 1976

World Resources Institute. *World Resources 1998–99: A Guide to the Global Environment*, New York, Oxford University Press, 1998

World Resources Institute. *World Resources 2000–2001: People and Ecosystems*, New York, Oxford University Press, 2000

Worster, Donald. *The Dust Bowl: The Southern Plains in the 1930s*, New York, Oxford University Press, 1982

Worster, Donald (ed.). *The Ends of the Earth*, Cambridge, Cambridge University Press, 1988

Worster, Donald. *Nature's Economy: A History of Ecological Ideas*, 2nd edn, Cambridge, Cambridge University Press, 1994

Worthington, E.B. (ed.). *The Evolution of IBP*, Cambridge, Cambridge University Press, 1975

Yergin, Daniel. *Shattered Peace: The Origins of the Cold War and the Nation Security State*, Boston, Houghton Mifflin, 1977

Young, Oran R. 'Interdependencies in world politics', *International Journal*, 24 (1968–9), pp. 726–50

Zhou, Jisayi. *Producing Food, Security, and the Geopolitical Subject*. Dissertation, Linköping University, Faculty of Arts and Sciences, Linköping University Electronic Press, 2022

Index

Index

www.ingramcontent.com/pod-product-compliance
Lightning Source LLC
Chambersburg PA
CBHW020912210326
41598CB00018B/1838